AF842400

Regional Complementarity in International Criminal Law

Leiden Studies on the Frontiers of International Law

VOLUME 13

The titles published in this series are listed at *brill.com/lsfi*

Regional Complementarity in International Criminal Law

Making Sense of the Four-Tiered Justice Paradigm

By

Seun Solomon Bakare

BRILL | NIJHOFF

ISSN 2212-4195
ISBN 978-90-04-73679-5
ISBN 978-90-04-76180-3 (PDF)
DOI https://doi.org/10.1163/9789004761803

Library of Congress Control Number: 2026935196

© 2026 the author(s), published by Koninklijke Brill BV, Plantijnstraat 2, 2321 JC Leiden, The Netherlands.

All rights reserved. No part of this publication may be reproduced, translated, stored in a retrieval system, or transmitted in any form or by any means, electronic, mechanical, photocopying, recording or otherwise, without prior written permission from the publisher. Text and datamining for commercial purposes requires the publisher's permission.

Brill Nijhoff and Koninklijke Brill BV are part of De Gruyter Brill.
www.degruyterbrill.com

Questions about General Product Safety Regulation: productsafety@degruyterbrill.com.

Cover illustration: Image by the author.

Contents

Acknowledgements

This book is an adaptation of the Ph.D. thesis that I publicly defended at Leiden University on 6 November 2024. It would not have been possible without the unwavering support and encouragement of numerous colleagues, friends and family members. First, I extend my deepest gratitude to Professors Carsten Stahn and Sergey Vasiliev for their steadfast support and invaluable supervision throughout this research. I am also profoundly thankful to the esteemed members of the Doctorate Committee – Prof. Larissa van den Herik, Prof. Gerhard Kemp, Prof. Herman van der Wilt, Dr. Robert Heinsch and Dr. Giulia Pinzauti – for their willingness to serve on the committee, and their insightful contributions. I owe a special debt of gratitude to Prof. Kees Waaldijk for his regular advice during the Ph.D. studies. The extended Ph.D. community at the Grotius Centre and beyond has been a source of immense support.

Immense gratitude also to my mentor, friend and brother, H.E. Mohammed Bello Adoke (SAN) CFR, former Attorney General of the Federation and Minister of Justice of the Federal Republic of Nigeria, whose sponsorship and generosity made this research possible. Prof. Dire Tladi, Judge of the International Court of Justice, is a friend and mentor. He was instrumental to my sojourn in academics – I owe him my eternal thanks.

Family is everything. To Leo and Joy, who kept faith with me during the years of the research, I did this for you and generations yet unborn. To my father, who sadly passed on while I was completing this, something tells me you are smiling at me because I finished what I started. To NCB, in whose regime this came through, my love is boundless. To Dayo, Debo and Leke, my siblings in whom I am well pleased – thank you for the years of sacrifice and love in all ramifications. This research was a collective effort, and my heart is full of gratitude for each of you.

per adua ad astra

Introduction

In September 2023, the Office of the Prosecutor (OTP) of the International Criminal Court (ICC) published its latest policy on complementarity titled 'Draft Policy on Complementarity and Cooperation'.[1] In the policy, the OTP not only acknowledges the role of regional organizations in international criminal justice but also highlights 'the strong and new forms of relationships recently developed' between the ICC and regional organizations. There is a reason for this. The role that regional organizations play in international criminal justice has been hitherto understudied. Also, the regional dimensions of complementarity, which is the principle that governs the relationship between the ICC and other mechanisms in the field of international criminal justice, have equally received less attention. This book, therefore, seeks to make a novel contribution to scholarship by arguing in favour of a four-tiered approach to complementarity that includes international crimes prosecution by regional and regionally backed tribunals. This research sits in a line of studies on legal pluralism and the hybridization of international criminal justice. It is situated at the intersection of international criminal law, (institutional) international law, international relations and politics (including the regional political context of the African Union and its members), and the theory of international law. This book examines the question of the extent to which regionalism poses not only a challenge to the coherence of international criminal law, but also an opportunity for the field. It, therefore, engages with complementarity in a broad sense, i.e. as an organizing principle of institutional relations (or a 'big idea' as Sarah Nouwen put it),[2] and not solely as an admissibility device. This structural question is important because of certain developments relating to the resurgence of hybrid and regional/regionally backed tribunals as forums for international crimes prosecution. A few examples of this resurgence from Africa will suffice.

In May 2014, the UN Mission in South Sudan published a report where it recommended that 'a special or hybrid tribunal' should be established for South Sudan to prosecute perpetrators of international crimes.[3] Secondly, in June 2014, the African Union adopted a protocol to establish a criminal

---

1 ICC-OTP 'Draft Policy on Complementarity and Cooperation' at ICC-OTP 'Draft policy on Complementarity and Cooperation' September 2023.

2 S.M.H. Nouwen, *Complementarity in the Line of Fire: The Catalysing Effect of the International Criminal Court in Uganda and Sudan* (Cambridge University Press 2013) 8–33.

3 UNMISS 'Conflict in South Sudan: A Human Rights Report' 8 May 2014.

© 2026 THE AUTHOR(S) | HTTPS://DOI.ORG/10.1163/9789004761803-002

chamber within its human rights court. This chamber will have the jurisdiction to prosecute the crimes provided in the protocol establishing the court.[4] Thirdly, in August 2014, the UN and the government of the Central African Republic (CAR) entered into an agreement which required the latter to establish a Special Criminal Court.[5] Fourthly, in the same year, in the DRC, a call had gone out for the establishment of specialized mixed chambers in order to bring an end to continuous human rights violations occasioned by armed conflicts.[6] Lastly, the initiative to set up an Economic Community of West African States (ECOWAS)-backed court in the Gambia to try the Yahaya Jammeh regime crimes[7] has gained momentum with the ECOWAS Heads of States and Governments' approval in December 2024. In the conclusion of this book, I attempt a full discussion of regional complementarity and the Special Tribunal for the Gambia (STG).

The establishment of different criminal tribunals contributes to legal pluralism and the fragmentation of international law.[8] On the other hand, the emergence of criminal tribunals could be seen as a result or function of the existing legal pluralism, rather than a catalysing factor. As such, institutional pluralism does not always lead to fragmentation, but where it does, it requires some attention. In this book, I refer to the fragmentation of international criminal law using hybrid and regional tribunals in its enforcement. This is one of the overarching themes of this book. The fragmentation of ICL is not specific to hybrid/regional tribunals. It can also occur through the establishment and operation of international courts. This has been witnessed with the work of the ICTY, ICTR, MICT, and the ICC.[9] The idea of legal pluralism pervades the entire discourse in this book.

---

4 For the text of the protocol, see AU's 'Protocol on Amendments to the Protocol on the Statute of the African Court of Justice and Human Rights.'

5 For preliminary thoughts on this court, see P. Labuda, 'The Special Criminal Court in the Central African Republic' (2018) 22 *Insights on ASIL* 2.

6 H. Hobbs, 'Hybrid Tribunals and the Composition of the Court: In Search of Sociological Legitimacy' (2016) 16 *Chicago Journal of International Law* 2, 484.

7 O. Owiso & S. Nakandha, 'International Criminal Accountability for Yahya Jammeh's Administration: The Gambia-ECOWAS Court' *Just Security,* August 2023 [available at https://www.justsecurity.org/87511/international-criminal-accountability-for-yahya-jammehs-administration-the-gambia-ecowas-court/ – accessed 11 January 2024].

8 C. Stahn & L.J. van Den Herik (eds), *The Diversification and Fragmentation of International Criminal Law* (Martinus Nijhoff Publishers 2012), 21–89. See also E. van Sliedregt & S. Vasiliev (eds), *Pluralism in International Criminal Law* (Oxford University Press 2014).

9 R. Geib & N. Bulinckx, 'International and internationalised criminal tribunals: a synopsis' (2006) 88 *International Review of the Red Cross* 861, 49.

The second overarching theme of this book is the concept of regionalizing international criminal justice, or more concretely, the notion of regional complementarity and its application in theory and practice. This idea of regional complementarity, in my view, can be understood both as an admissibility idea (i.e. need for deference) and as a broader institutional principle involving division of labour, cooperation and other principles, to make sense of the four-tiered justice paradigm that this book focuses on. The four-tiered justice paradigm highlights that there are now four types of mechanisms that enforce international criminal justice: domestic courts, hybrid tribunals, regional tribunals, and the ICC. The OTP admitted the place and importance of these mechanisms when it stated in its September 2023 policy on complementarity and cooperation that 'there is no dichotomy in the character of the relevant accountability mechanisms in terms of whether it is purely national or regional, hybrid or internationalized.[10] In the following sections, I will introduce the fragmentation of international law and legal pluralism, the regionalization of international criminal justice, and the notion of regional complementarity as the three over-arching themes of this book.

1 Fragmentation of International Law and Legal Pluralism

In many ways, international law is fragmented. It has no homogenous system – only different norms, elements, institutions, procedures, systems, and subsystems.[11] Some authors have traced the increase of this fragmentation to the politics of the Cold War era.[12] In 2002, at its 54th Session, the International Law Commission (ILC) noted the risks associated with this fragmentation. It established a study group to examine the topic, 'Fragmentation of international law: difficulties arising from the diversification and expansion of international law'.[13] The fragmentation of international law accounts for the division of public international law into different categories like international

---

10 ICC-OTP Draft policy, (n. 1) para 80.

11 On fragmentation in international law, see UN Doc A/CN.4/L.702 (2006), 'Fragmentation of International Law: Difficulties Arising from the Diversification and Expansion of International Law' 1–25.

12 J. Delbruck, 'A More Effective International Law or a New "World Law?" – Some Aspects of the Changing Development of International Law in a Changing International System' (1993) 68 *Indiana Law Journal* 705; M.W. Reisman, 'International Law after the Cold War' (1990) 84 *American Journal of International Law* 859 at 864.

13 UN General Assembly, Report of the International Law Commission, 18 July 2006, A/CN.4/L.702.

humanitarian law (IHL), international human rights law (IHRL), and the latecomer: international criminal law (ICL). The multiplication of international courts and tribunals, as well as the multiplicity of treaties on various subjects of international criminal law, are some of the causes of this fragmentation in the field of ICL. Stahn and van den Herik have identified three aspects of fragmentation that include institutional, substantive law, and procedural fragmentation.[14] Institutional fragmentation relates to the 'lack of interaction between international institutions' and the roles that regional mechanisms may play in international law.[15] This is part of the problem that this study seeks to address. Fragmentation presents challenges as well as opportunities for the development of international law, especially as it provides an opportunity for membership of different international organizations, which states seize.

Moreover, the future of international law and order depends on the activities of international organizations (IOs).[16] States often scramble for membership of multiple international organizations,[17] and this is a testimony to their growing significance.[18] The result is that while states struggle to preserve their sovereignty,[19] they become interdependent on one another. Interdependence is not only because of membership of different international organizations; it is also the function of the interconnected world (trade, culture, food security, climate change, and global challenges). The emergence of multiple international organizations reflects the need for more intensive state cooperation and regulation of various spheres of activity.

14 C. Stahn & L. J. van Den Herik (eds), *The Diversification and Fragmentation of International Criminal Law* (Martinus Nijhoff Publishers 2012) 21–89.

15 *Ibid.*

16 H. Schermers & N. Blokker, *International Institutional Law* (Brill Nijhoff 2011), Preface.

17 J. Pevehouse, 'Democratisation, Credible Commitments, and Joining International Organizations' [available at http://www.press.umich.edu/pdf/0472112899-ch1.pdf – accessed 8 March 2023].

18 G. Sinclair, 'State formation, liberal reform and the growth of international organizations' (2015) 26 *European Journal of International* Law 2, 445–469; B.S. Chimni, 'International Institutions Today: An Imperial Global State in the Making' (2004) 15 *European Journal of International Law* 1. See also M. Ruffert & C. Walter, *Institutionalised International Law* (C.H. Beck, Hart, Nomos 2014) 3; J. Klabbers, *An Introduction to International Organizations Law* (Cambridge University Press 2022) 18.

19 The ability of States to participate in institutionalized international relations has also been described as an essential expression of their sovereignty (see Ruffert & Walter above, 55).

The states' interdependence and membership of different international organizations give rise to multiple obligations.[20] Multiple obligations often give birth to both normative and inter-institutional clashes.[21] The possibility of these clashes raises the need to address inter-institutional relationships in order to avoid anarchy or the 'general incoherence of the international legal system', which may be created by 'a surfeit of treaties that often overlap and, with increasing frequency, conflict with one another'.[22] According to Ebobrah, '[I]n the anarchic environment in which international courts operate, jurisdictions overlap…competition among international courts becomes a danger to the unity and legitimacy of the international legal system.'[23] Professor Charney, in his 1998 study titled 'Is international law threatened by multiple international tribunals?'[24] had also argued that there is a risk of general incoherence. In a 2006 keynote address, Justice Higgins of the ICJ had spoken of the implications of multiplying judicial institutions and how that contributes to the fragmentation of international law.[25]

Thus, when obligations owed to international institutions conflict,[26] as they often do,[27] states as well as treaty negotiators and drafters are left with a conundrum. In addressing this conundrum, different tools have been previously proposed. For example, the Vienna Convention on the Law of Treaties (VCLT) contains a set of (imperfect) rules for resolving treaty conflicts.[28] On their

20 UN Doc A/CN.4/120, Fourth report on the Law of Treaties by Mr. G.G. Fitzmaurice, Special Rapporteur, extracted from the Yearbook of the International Law Commission (1959) Vol II, 42, art 4(1).

21 T. Broude & Y. Shani (eds) *Fragmentation(s) of International Law: On Normative Integration as Authority Allocation* (Hart Publishing 2008).

22 C.J. Borgen, 'Resolving Treaty Conflicts' (2005) 37 *The Geo. Wash. Int'l L. Rev.* 574.

23 S. Ebobrah, 'Complementarity between the African Court and the judicial organs of Regional Economic Communities in Africa' in *PALU Guide to Complementarity within the African Human Rights System* (2014) 52.

24 J. Charney, 'Is international law threatened by multiple international tribunals' (1998) 271 *Collected Courses of the Hague Academy of International Law* 101.

25 R. Higgins, 'A Babel of Judicial Voices? Ruminations from the Bench' (2003) 55 *International and Comparative Law Quarterly* 4, 791–804.

26 G. Binder, 'The Dialectic of Duplicity: Treaty Conflict and Political Contradiction' (1985) 34 *Buffalo Law Review* 329–549; see also F. Londras and S. Kingston, 'Rights, Security and Conflicting International Obligations: Exploring Inter-Jurisdictional Judicial Dialogues in Europe' (2010) *American Journal of Comparative Law* 1; N. Bhuta, 'Conflicting International Obligations and the Risk of Torture and Unfair Trial: Critical Comments on *R (Al-Saadoon and Mufdhi) v Secretary of State for Defence; Al-Sadoon and Mufdhi v United Kingdom*' (2009) 5 *Journal of International Criminal Justice* 7, 1133.

27 J. Klabbers, Treaty Conflict and the European Union (2009), Book Review, 20 *European Journal of International Law* (2009) 7–10.

28 See C.J. Borgen, 'Resolving Treaty Conflicts' (2005) 37 *The Geo. Wash. Int'l L. Rev.* 578.

part, Du Plessis and Gevers argue that norm conflict 'can be resolved in one of two ways: with reference to hierarchy (such as a *jus cogens* norm or per article 103 of the UN Charter) or through "techniques of interpretation"'.[29]

In the African human rights system, as well as in the International Criminal Court (ICC), the concept of complementarity[30] was introduced to address normative or institutional conflicts. In that regard, complementarity has been described as 'usable in normative and descriptive dimensions', thus suggesting that it is a mechanism for describing, prescribing, as well as clarifying the relationship between institutions.[31] In the EU human rights system, it is the principle of subsidiarity that was introduced for a similar purpose.[32]

Complementarity and similar concepts exist for different purposes in regional human rights systems, primarily because of normative and structural expansion in these systems.[33] In the African human rights system, complementarity was conceived to manage the relationship between different institutions within the same system.[34] This is an intra-system coordination. In the ICC, complementarity was conceived to serve broader purposes of arranging intra- and inter-system relationships. Article 1 of the Statute provides that the

29 See M. Du Plessis and C. Gevers, 'Balancing competing obligations: The Rome Statute and AU decisions' (2011) *ISS Paper* 225.

30 C. Stahn, 'Complementarity: A Tale of Two Notions' (2008) 19 *Criminal Law Forum* 87–113.

31 S. Ebobrah, 'Towards a positive application of complementarity in the African human rights system: issues of functions and relations' (2011) 22 *European Journal of International Law* 3, 663–688; see also A. Clapham, 'On Complementarity: Human Rights in the European Legal Orders' (2000) 21 *Human Rights Law Journal* 313.

32 On subsidiarity as a principle of the EU human rights system, see P. Carozza, 'Subsidiarity as a Structural Principle of International Human Rights Law' (2003) 97 *American Journal of International Law* 1, 38–79.

33 M. Mutua, 'The African Human Rights System: A Critical Evaluation' (2000) *UNDP Human Development Report* 1. See also B. Gawanas, 'The African Union: Concepts and implementation mechanisms relating to human rights' [available at http://www.kas.de/upload/auslandshomepages/namibia/Human_Rights_in_Africa/6_Gawanas.pdf – accessed 11 February 2024]. Both authors discuss the normative and institutional expansions that have taken place in the African human rights system.

34 Article 2 of the Protocol to the African Charter on Human and Peoples' Rights on the Establishment of an African Court on Human and Peoples' Rights provides that 'the Court shall, bearing in mind the provisions of this Protocol, complement the protective mandate of the African Commission on Human and Peoples' Rights.' Article 8 of the same protocol requires the Court to bear in mind the principle of complementarity between the Commission and the Court when deciding cases brought before it. Additionally, rule 114 of the Rules of Procedure of the African Commission on Human and Peoples' Rights reiterates the notion of complementarity between the Court and the Commission.

Court shall be complementary to national criminal jurisdictions, while article 17 establishes the substantive rules that constitute the principle of complementarity. The Statute defines the question of complementarity as pertaining to the admissibility of a case rather than to the jurisdiction of the Court.[35] As such, the ICC cannot exercise the jurisdiction that it has if the case is inadmissible. The principle of complementarity does not affect the existence of jurisdiction of the Court; it regulates when the Court may exercise this jurisdiction.[36] Article 17 thus functions as a gatekeeper to the exercise of jurisdiction.[37] These provisions of the Rome Statute suggest that complementarity is one means through which domestic and international systems interact.

In the ICC's jurisprudence, several cases have brought increased attention to the principle of complementarity. Some of these cases involved sitting heads of states in Africa.[38] These cases also gave rise to the troubled relationship between the African Union (AU) and the ICC.[39] The strained relationship

---

35 M. Benzing, 'The Complementarity Regime of the International Criminal Court: International Criminal Justice between State Sovereignty and the Fight against Impunity' (2003) 7 *Max Planck UNYB* 591–632 at 594.

36 *Ibid.*

37 *Ibid.*

38 Examples of such cases include the ones that relate to Uhuru Kenyatta, President of the Republic of Kenya, and his Vice President, as well as the case against Omar Al-Bashir, the former President of Sudan.

39 See generally M. Du Plessis, 'The Obligation of African Union States to Implement ICC Arrest Warrants' (2011) *EJIL: Talk* [available at http://www.ejiltalk.org/the-obligation-of-african-union-states-to-implement-icc-arrest-warrants/ – accessed 23 January 2023], and D. Akande, 'The Genocide Convention and the Arrest Warrant Issued by the ICC' (2011) *EJIL: Talk* [available at http://www.ejiltalk.org/the-genocide-convention-and-the-arrest-warrants-issued-by-the-icc/ – accessed 7 March 2023]; S. Weldehaimanot, 'Arresting Al-Bashir: the African Union's opposition and the legalities' (2011) 19 *African Journal of International and Comparative* Law 2, 208–235; O. Imoedemhe, 'Unpacking the tension between the African Union and the International Criminal Court: the way forward' (2015) 23 *African Journal of International and Comparative Law* 1, 74–105; E. Keppler, 'Managing setbacks for the International Criminal Court in Africa' (2012) 56 *Journal of African Law* 1, 1–14; A. Abass, 'Prosecuting International Crimes in Africa: Rationales, Prospects and Challenges' (2013) 24 *European Journal of International Law* 933; and A. Mudukuti, 'South Africa abandoning the International Criminal Court? The build-up and potential consequences' (2016) 1 *European Human Rights Law Review* 1–10. See also O. Ba, States of Justice: The Politics of the International Criminal Court (Cambridge University Press 2020). See also P. Clark, Distant Justice: The Impact of the International Criminal Court on African Politics (Cambridge University Press 2018). Lastly, see K. Clarke, 'Distant Justice Symposium: How colonial inscriptions continue to matter in ICC and Africa dynamics' (2019) [available at https://opiniojuris.org/2019/10/01/distant-justice-symposium-how-colonial-inscriptions-continue-to-matter-in-icc-and-africa-dynamics/ – accessed 6 February 2024].

between the two entities has been extensively discussed in literature.[40] The reasons for this troubled relationship vary: allegations by the African Union that the ICC is a western tool designed to subjugate African leaders,[41] that the ICC has unfairly focused on African states in the first ten years of its operations[42] and that the court is a 'neo-imperialistic tool that illegitimately targets Africa'.[43] The AU conceived several retaliatory measures against the ICC, the most prominent ones being the AU's decision not to cooperate with the ICC in the execution of the arrest warrants issued against Omar Al Bashir; the AU's decision to confer international criminal jurisdiction on its African Court of Justice and Human Rights[44] and, lastly, the adoption of a 'proposal by President Uhuru Kenyatta for the AU to develop a road map for the withdrawal of African nations from the Rome Statute'.[45] Out of the three-pronged retaliatory

---

40 M. Du Plessis & C. Gevers, 'Balancing competing obligations: The Rome Statute and AU decisions' (2011) 225 *ISS Paper* 2; M. Kersten, 'The Africa-ICC Relationship – More and Less than Meets the Eye (Part 1)' [available at http://justiceinconflict.org/2015/07/17/the-africa-icc-relationship-more-and-less-than-meets-the-eye-part-1/ – accessed 9 December 2023]; C. Kreß, 'The Crime of Genocide and Contextual Elements: A Comment on the ICC Pre-Trial Chamber's Decision in the Al Bashir Case' (2009) 7 *Journal of International Criminal Justice* 297; A. Cayley, 'The Prosecutor's Strategy in Seeking the Arrest of Sudanese President Al Bashir on Charges of Genocide' (2008) 6 *JICJ* 829; R. Pati, 'The ICC and the Case of Sudan's Omar Al Bashir: Is Plea-Bargaining a Valid Option?' (2009) 15 *University of California at Davis Journal of International Law and Policy* 265; D. Akande, 'The Legal Nature of Security Council Referrals to the ICC and Its Impact on Al Bashir's Immunities' (2009) 7 *JICJ* 333; P. Gaeta, 'Does President Al Bashir Enjoy Immunity from Arrest?' (2009) 7 *JICJ* 312; T. Murithi, 'The African Union and the International Criminal Court: An embattled relationship' (2013) 8 *The Institute for Justice and Reconciliation Policy Brief* 1–12.

41 Coalition for the International Criminal Court, 'Africa and the ICC: Setting the facts straight' [available at https://coalitionfortheicc.org/explore-international-criminal-court-africa-icc – accessed 5 February 2024].

42 N. Waddell & P. Clark, 'Courting Conflict? Justice, Peace and the ICC in Africa' (2008) *Royal African Society,* 8.

43 O. Maunganidze & A. Du Plessis, 'The ICC and the AU' in C. Stahn (ed), *The Law and Practice of the International Criminal Court* (Oxford University Press 2014) 65.

44 F. Viljoen, 'AU Assembly should consider human rights implications before adopting the Amending Merged African Court Protocol' (2012) *AfricLaw*; M. Du Plessis, 'Implications of the AU decision to give the African Court jurisdiction over international crimes' (2012) 235 *Institute for Security Studies Paper* 1; D. Deya, 'Worth the Wait: Pushing for the African Court to exercise jurisdiction for international crimes' [available at http://www.osisa.org/sites/default/files/is_the_african_court_worth_the_wait_-don_deya.pdf – accessed 15 December 2023]. See generally A. Abass, 'The Proposed International Criminal Jurisdiction for the African Court: Some Problematic Aspects' (2013) *Netherlands International Law Review* 27–50.

45 'AU adopts Uhuru's proposal for withdrawal from the ICC' [available at https://citizentv.co.ke/news/au-adopts-uhurus-proposal-for-withdrawal-from-icc-113241/ – accessed 3

measures, the AU's decision to confer its human rights court with an international criminal jurisdiction and the implication that similar attempts by any region may have on complementarity with the ICC and domestic courts is the focus of this research.

2 The Regionalization of International Criminal Justice

The second major area of study in this book relates to the regionalization of international criminal justice. The proposed establishment of regional criminal courts is due in part to regionalism.[46] Regionalism has been variously defined.[47] In the context of this work, regionalism implies any arrangement that 'enables states within the same geographical region to deal with common transnational issues … and to establish the international machinery necessary for carrying out tasks of mutual interest, thereby establishing distinct centers of action that further common goals and have shared benefits.'[48] In this book, I restrict the meaning of regionalism to the use of regional bodies as mechanisms for enforcing international criminal law.[49] While there are different views on the legality and appropriateness of the prosecution of international crimes by regional criminal mechanisms, Professor Van der Wilt drew 'on Emile Durkheim's concept of the social function of criminal law and Antony Duff's idea of the requisite "political community" on whose behalf a penal institution speaks to argue that a region can constitute a political community

---

March 2023]. See also 'ICC: What next for Africa and the tribunal in quest for justice?' [available at http://www.dw.com/en/icc-what-next-for-africa-and-the-tribunal-in-quest-for-justice/a-19020659 – accessed 4 March 2023]. See also Library of Congress, 'African Union: Resolution Urges States to Leave ICC' [available at https://www.loc.gov/item/global-legal-monitor/2017-02-10/african-union-resolution-urges-states-to-leave-icc/ – accessed 5 February 2024].

46 M. Sirleaf, 'Regionalism, Regime Complexes, and the Crisis in International Criminal Justice' (2016) 54 *Columbia Journal of Transnational Law* 699–778. See also K.J. Alter & L. Hooghe, 'Regional Dispute Settlement' in T. Börzel and T. Risse (eds), *The Oxford Handbook of Comparative Regionalism* (Oxford University Press 2018) 1.

47 On regionalism, see L. Fawcett, 'Exploring Regional Domains: A Comparative History of Regionalism' (2004) 80 *Int'l Aff.* 429, 435; E.D. Mansfield and H.V. Milner, 'The New Wave of Regionalism' (1999) 53 *International Organization* 3, 589–627.

48 M. Swart, 'The Prospects for Regional and Sub-Regional Complementarity in Africa' in R. Slye (ed), *The Nuremberg Principles in Non-Western Societies: A Reflection on Their Universality, Legitimacy and Application* (International Nuremberg Principles Academy Press 2017) 217.

49 C. Landauer, 'Regionalism, Geography, and the International Legal Imagination' (2011) 11 *Chicago Journal of International Law* 2, 539.

capable of being protected by criminal law and represented by a regional criminal court'.[50] In his theory on foundations in political philosophy, he concludes that it is appropriate for a region to establish regional criminal mechanisms to counter crimes that are of particular concern to that region.[51]

States have been the primary subjects of international law. During the Industrial Revolution of the 19th century, regional arrangements to ensure international peace and security became commonplace.[52] The widening scope of regionalism has found its way into international criminal law, although it is not altogether new in international law at large. In other fields, particularly in human rights,[53] investment law,[54] and trade law,[55] regional judicial implementation of international norms is relatively common.[56]

Regionalism in international criminal law has been viewed as antagonistic to the universalism of international law and has therefore been criticized. Some say that universalism is preferable since regionalism may bring about fragmentation, incoherence, divergent jurisprudence and inconsistency in standards.[57] Many felt that a universal system that guarantees individual rights was a preferable option. However, others argue that a regional arrangement is needed to supplement the universal system.[58] To address these concerns, some have proposed a peculiar model of regionalization through the exercise of quasi-

50 H. van der Wilt, 'On Regional Criminal Courts as Representatives of Political Communities: The Special Case of the African Criminal Court' in K.J. Heller and others (eds), *The Oxford Handbook of International Criminal Law* (Oxford University Press 2020) 194–212.

51 *Ibid.*

52 J. Klučka & L. Elbert, *Regionalism and Its Contribution to General International Law* (Košice 2015) 13.

53 On regionalism in human rights law, see S.J. Powell & C. Pirez, 'Global Laws, Local Lives: Impact of the New Regionalism on Human Rights Compliance' (2011) 17 *Buffalo Human Rights Law Review* 117–154.

54 L. Trakman and N. Ranieri, *Regionalism in International Investment Law* (Oxford Scholarship Online 2013).

55 On regionalism in trade law, see A. Fabbricotti, 'Universalism and Regionalism in International Trade Law: Is the WTO a truly universal international organization?' in *Scritti in memoria di Maria Rita Saulle* (Editoriale Scientifica 2014), 559–574.

56 F.K. Tiba, 'Regional International Criminal Courts: An Idea Whose Time Has Come?' (2016) 17 *Cardozo Journal of Conflict Resolution* 52, 523.

57 R. Burchill, 'International Criminal Tribunals at the Regional Level: Lessons from International Human Rights Law' (2007) 4 *New Zealand Yearbook of International Law* 25. See also R. Rauxloh, 'Regionalisation of the International Criminal Court' (2007) 4 *New Zealand Yearbook of International Law* 67.

58 C. Jalloh, 'The Place of the African Criminal Court in the Prosecution of Serious Crimes in Africa' in C. Jalloh and Ors. (eds), *The African Court of Justice and Human and Peoples' Rights in Context: Developments and Challenges* (Cambridge University Press 2019) 295.

criminal jurisdiction by regional human rights courts.[59] Others have argued that a model that allows the ICC itself to develop more awareness of regional particularities and methods to adjust to regional needs is a better approach.[60] In international human rights law, since the adoption of the UN Charter, this tension has also been observed and addressed.[61] In the end, international human rights 'capitulated to the compromise of coexistence between international and regional arrangements',[62] even though the UN Charter gives preference to universal mechanism in matters regarding maintenance of international peace and security.[63] The universalism of international criminal justice is increasingly challenged by the involvement of regional mechanisms in its enforcement. For this reason, this book, while admitting that universalism might also benefit from regionalism if regional entities apply or reinforce universal norms, seeks to understand to what extent regionalism is a challenge to the coherence of international criminal law, and how such concerns can be accommodated. Considering that four levels of courts that could enforce international criminal law have emerged, how do we arrange the relationship and interaction between them? Moreover, the involvement of regional mechanisms in international criminal justice appears not to have been envisaged, given that the drafters of the Rome Statute did not appear to have contemplated any relationship between the ICC and regional criminal mechanisms. Additionally, there are those who have argued that international criminal prosecution before a regional mechanism will not be sufficient to act as a bar for an ICC prosecution because article 17(1) of the Rome Statute only refers to states. This book investigates this claim in light of the provisions of the VCLT in relation to the interpretation of statutes. Lastly, the problem of competing obligations owed by member states that belong to both the ICC and a regional criminal mechanism deserves attention and will thus be addressed in this book. Ultimately, my argument points towards a need for greater polycentricity – the idea that many decision-making centres can have limited and autonomous

59 See A.V. Huneeus, 'International Criminal Law by Other Means: The Quasi-Criminal Jurisdiction of the Human Rights Courts' (2013) 107 *American Journal of International law* 1.

60 See R. Rauxloh (n. 57 above).

61 C. Jalloh, 'The Place of the African Criminal Court in the Prosecution of Serious Crimes in Africa' in C. Jalloh and Ors. (eds), *The African Court of Justice and Human and Peoples' Rights in Context: Developments and Challenges* (Cambridge University Press 2019), 295. On this tension, see C. Schreuer, 'Regionalism v. Universalism' 6 *EJIL* (1995) 477–499.

62 *Ibid.*

63 Klučka (n. 52 above) 26.

prerogatives while operating under an overarching set of rules.[64] Some authors have previously presented 'legal polycentricity' as one of the consequences of pluralism in law.[65] I argue that while it is a consequence, it could also be a solution to friction between bodies dedicated to overlapping roles in ICL.

3 Introducing the Notion of Regional Complementarity

There is no scarcity of writings on the fragmentation of international law and legal pluralism.[66] Also, several authors have written on complementarity and its many notions.[67] This work, however, develops the emerging notion of

64 P.D. Aligica & V. Tarko, 'Polycentricity: From Polanyi to Ostrom, and Beyond' (2012) 25 *Governance* 167–361.

65 P. Hanne & Z. Henrik, *Legal polycentricity: consequences of pluralism in law* (Aldershot; Brookfield; Dartmouth 1995).

66 For example, see footnote 7 above.

67 C. Stahn & M. El Zeidy (eds), *The International Criminal Court and Complementarity: From Theory to Practice*, Vols. 1 &2 (Cambridge University Press 2011); M. El Zeidy, *The Principle of Complementarity in International Criminal Law: Origin, Development and Practice* (Martinus Nijhoff Publishers 2008); D. Tladi, 'Complementarity and cooperation in international criminal justice: Assessing initiatives to fill the impunity gap' (2014) *ISS Paper*; D. Kendal, 'The ICC and the Principle of Complementarity: How Denmark can help strike a balance between international and domestic justice mechanisms' *Policy Research Paper* (Kendal Human Rights Consulting 2013); C. Sriram & S. Brown, 'Kenya in the Shadow of the ICC: Complementarity, Gravity and Impact' (2012) 12 *International Criminal Law Review* 2, 219–244; ICC-OTP, Informal Expert Paper: The principle of complementarity in practice' (ICC-OTP 2003); AMICC, 'The principle of complementarity' (2005); M. Du Plessis, 'Complementarity and Africa: The promises and problems of international criminal justice' (2008) 17 *African Security Review* 4; C. Stahn, 'Complementarity: A Tale of Two Notions' (2008) 19 *Criminal Law Forum* 87–113; ICJ Kenya, International Criminal Justice: The ICC and Complementarity (ICJ 2014); J.T. Holmes, 'Complementarity: National Courts versus the ICC', in *The Rome Statute of the International Criminal Court: A Commentary*, Vol. I, 667–685 A. Cassese *et al.* (eds) (Oxford University Press 2002); W. Burke-White, 'Complementarity in Practice: The International Criminal Court as Part of a System of Multi-level Global Governance in the Democratic Republic of Congo' (2005) 18 *Leiden J. Int'l L.* 557; M. El Zeidy, 'The Principle of Complementarity: A New Machinery to Implement International Criminal Law' (2002) *Mich. J. Int'l L.*, 869; K.J. Heller, 'The Shadow Side of Complementarity: The Effect of Article 17 of the Rome Statute on National Due Process' (2006) 17 *Crim. L. Forum* 255; J. Kleffner, 'The Impact of Complementarity on National Implementation of Substantive International Criminal Law' (2003) 1 *JICJ*. 86; M. Benzing, 'The Complementarity Regime of the International Criminal Court: International Criminal Justice Between State Sovereignty and the Fight Against Impunity' (2003) 7 *Max Planck Yearbook of United Nations Law*, 591; J. Kleffner & G. Kor (eds), *Complementary Views on Complementarity – Proceedings of the International Roundtable on the Complementary Nature of the International Criminal Court*

regional complementarity. This is especially because the drafters of the Rome Statute did not appear to have contemplated a relationship between the ICC and regional criminal mechanisms. Again, some authors have written on the resurgence of interest in the prosecution of international crimes by hybrid and regional tribunals.[68] These regional and hybrid initiatives have both been

---

(TMC Asser 2006); F. Gioia, 'State Sovereignty, Jurisdiction and Modern International Law: The Principle of Complementarity in the International Criminal Court' (2006) 19 *Leiden J. Int'l L.* 1095; S.M.H. Nouwen, *Complementarity in the Line of Fire: The Catalysing Effect of the International Court in Uganda and Sudan* (Cambridge University Press 2013); K.J. Heller, 'A Sentenced-Based Theory of Complementarity' (2012) 53 *Harv. Int'l L.J.* 1; C. Stahn, 'One Step Forward, Two Steps Back? Second Thoughts on a "Sentence-Based" Theory of Complementarity' (2012) *Harv. Int'l L. J.* 85; D. Robinson, 'Three Theories of Complementarity: Charge, Sentence or Process?' (2012) 53 *Harvard International Law Journal Online*; B. Krings, 'The Principles of "Complementarity" and Universal Jurisdiction in International Criminal Law: Antagonists or Perfect Match?' (2012) 4 *Goettingen Journal of International Law,* 3 737–763; D. Robinson, 'The Mysterious Mysteriousness of Complementarity' (2010) 21 *Criminal Law Forum,* 1; W. Burke-White, 'Implementing a Policy of Positive Complementarity in the Rome System of Justice' (2008) 19 *Cr. L. Frm.* 59–85; S.T. Ebobrah, 'Towards a Positive Application of Complementarity in the African Human Rights System: Issues of Functions and Relations' (2011) 22 *European Journal of International Law* 3; W. Burke-White, 'Proactive Complementarity: The International Criminal Court and National Courts in the Rome System of International Justice' (2008) 49 *Harv. Int'l L.J.* 1; X. Philippe, 'The principles of universal jurisdiction and complementarity: How do the two principles intermesh?' (206) 88 *IRRC* 862; O. Solera, 'Complementary jurisdiction and international criminal justice' (2002) 84 *IRRC* 845; C. Stahn & G. Sluiter, The Emerging Practice of the International Criminal Court (Brill 2009); M.S. Ellis, *Sovereignty and Justice: Balancing the Principle of Complementarity between International and Domestic War Crimes Tribunals* (Cambridge Scholars Publishing 2014); J. Stigen, The Relationship between the International Court and National Jurisdictions: The Principle of Complementarity (Martinus Nijhoff 2008); M. El Zeidy, 'The Principle of Complementarity: A New Machinery to Implement International Criminal Law' (2002) 23 *Michigan Journal of International Law*; L. Clarke, 'Complementarity as Politics' (2016) 2 *Journal of International and Comparative Law* 2.

68 For example, see P.K. Mendez, 'The new wave of hybrid tribunals: A sophisticated approach to enforcing international humanitarian law or an idealistic solution with empty promises?' (2009) 20 *Criminal Law Forum* 53–95 at 95; see also C. Stahn, 'Tribunals Are Dead, Long Live Tribunals: MICT, the Kosovo Specialist Chambers and the Turn to New Hybridity' (23 September 2016) *EJIL: Talk Blog of the European Journal of International Law* [available at https://www.ejiltalk.org/tribunals-are-dead-long-live-tribunals-mict-the-kosovo-specialist-chambers-and-the-turn-to-new-hybridity/ – accessed 15 January 2023]; S. William, *Hybrid and Internationalised Criminal Tribunals: Selected Jurisdictional Issues* (Hart Publishing 2012); E.M. Bruch, 'Hybrid Courts: Examining hybridity through a post-colonial lens' (2010) 28 *Boston University International Law Journal* 1; S.M.H. Nouwen, 'Hybrid Courts: The hybrid category of a new type of international crimes courts (2010) *Utrecht Law Review.*

hailed[69] and criticized.[70] This work's contribution is, however, in establishing that the involvement of regional bodies in international crimes prosecution is an offshoot of globalization, regionalism, and an unavoidable milestone in the development of ICL. Several authors have written on the relationship between Africa and the ICC.[71] With few exceptions,[72] however, these writings concentrate on a general description of the rancorous nature of that relationship. Some of the available arguments are that the establishment of the ICL section of the African Court will violate the principle of *pacta sunt servanda* and represents an unnecessary duplication of the work of the ICC; the refusal to cooperate with the ICC on the arrest warrant against Sudan's President amounts to a violation of obligations under customary international law, the Rome Statute and article 4 of the AU's Constitutive Act; and lastly, the establishment of the ICL section will defeat the object and purpose of the Rome Statute and thereby impede the work of the ICC to punish individuals who commit international crimes in Africa.[73] Others have also argued that the creation of the ICL section in the African Court has no legal basis;[74] there is no possibility to accommodate

69 C.E. Carroll, 'Hybrid Tribunals are the Most Effective Structure for Adjudicating International Crimes Occurring Within a Domestic State' (2013), *Seton Hall University Law School Student Scholarship*, Paper 90, 1.

70 P. McAuliffe, 'Hybrid Tribunals at Ten: How International Criminal Justice's Golden Child Became an Orphan' (2011) 7 *Journal of International Law and International Relations* 1 at 1.

71 See for example, D. Tladi, 'The African Union and the International Criminal Court: The battle for the soul of international law' (2009) 34 *South African Yearbook of International Law*; M. Du Plessis (ed), *African Guide to International Criminal Justice* (Institute for Security Studies 2008); Human Rights Watch, 'Briefing Paper on Recent Setbacks in Africa Regarding the International Criminal Court' (Human Rights Watch 2010); N. Waddell & P. Clark (eds), *Courting Conflict? Justice, Peace and the ICC in Africa* (The Royal African Society 2008); Coalition for the International Criminal Court, 'Africa and the ICC: Setting the facts straight' [available at https://coalitionfortheicc.org/explore-international-criminal-court-africa-icc – accessed 5 February 2024]; M. Du Plessis, 'The International Criminal Court that Africa wants' (2010) *Institute for Security Studies*; M. Du Plessis, 'The International Criminal Court and its work in Africa; Confronting the myths' (2008) 173 *ISS Paper*; A. Abass, 'Prosecuting International Crimes in Africa: Rationale, Prospects and Challenges' (2013) 24 *The European Journal of International Law* 3; M. Du Plessis & ors '*Africa and the International Criminal Court*' (Chatham House 2013).

72 See for example, Jalloh and others (eds), *The African Court of Justice and Human and Peoples' Rights in Context: Development and Challenges* (Cambridge University Press 2019).

73 C.B. Murungu, 'Towards a Criminal Chamber in the African Court of Justice and Human Rights' (2011) 9 *Journal of International Criminal Justice* 5, 1.

74 In this regard, Du Plessis argued that the AU's power to expand the jurisdiction of its single court to accommodate international criminal jurisdiction is in article 4(h) of the AU Constitutive Act and only limits it to the three core crimes. Hence, the inclusion of

any prosecution by a regional tribunal under article 17 of the Rome Statute since the provision expressly mentions 'states';[75] the Malabo Protocol – the AU instrument that creates and confers international criminal jurisdiction on one of the chambers of the African Court – increases impunity, especially with its provision on immunity,[76] etc.

This book takes a different approach. While acknowledging counterarguments,[77] it proposes that the current understanding of complementarity should be expanded to accommodate genuine prosecutions before a regional or sub-regional mechanism, thus making a case relating to the same conducts and persons inadmissible before the ICC. While most writings have discussed regional complementarity from the angle of the interpretative disputes between the ICC and proposed regional courts, my approach takes a holistic look at the four-tiered model and principles governing the relationship between ICC and regional courts, on the one hand, regional courts and domestic courts, on the other hand. The relationship between the ICC and domestic courts has already been extensively discussed in literature. This book, therefore, brings together the relationship between these four levels of courts. I go beyond the partial study of regional complementarity that only looks into the relationship between regional mechanisms and the ICC to provide a more comprehensive account of the idea of regional complementarity that transcends the classical complementarity criteria, like inaction, unwillingness or inability test. I propose a more holistic framework in order to organize this relationship based on certain organizing principles. Conceptually, I argue in favour of regional complementarity. As will be shown, we need a broader theory than complementarity to organize relations between global international criminal mechanisms and regional counterparts. This is where I distinguish between complementarity in the technical/legal sense and elements of the theory that I propose. My holistic approach involves deference (which is grounded in prosecutorial discretion), cooperation, and

---

the other 11 transnational or novel crimes has no basis in law. See M. Du Plessis, 'Implications of the AU Decision to Give the African Court Jurisdiction Over International Crimes' (2012) 235 *Institute for Security Studies Paper* 1–14, 8.

75 *Ibid.*

76 Human Rights Watch, Coalition of African NGOs, 'Joint Civil Society Letter on the Draft Protocol on Amendments to the Statute of the African Court of Justice and Human Rights' 12 May 2014.

77 For instance, it could be argued that these relations should not be regulated through complementarity per se, but rather through mutual and transparent cooperation agreements. Complementarity is by no means the 'sole possible option' of contemplating relations. See M. Jackson, 'Regional Complementarity: The Rome Statute and Public International Law' (2016) 14 *Journal of International Criminal Justice* 1070.

other criteria that go beyond complementarity, such as the *forum non conveniens* theory, nexus to locality, etc. I admit that not all of this may be captured by complementarity in the strict sense and its traditional legal semantics, but will involve broader concepts, such as cooperation, new agreements, etc. Such elements are partly reflected in the new OTP policy paper on complementarity, where the OTP committed to 'creating a community of practice and bringing justice closer to communities'.[78] This is in alignment with the broader goals of international criminal justice that include accountability for crimes, deterrence, justice for victims and building international norms.

4 Structure of the Book

This book seeks to explore the macro-question: to what extent is regionalism a challenge to the universality or coherence of international criminal law and how such concerns can be accommodated?

Structurally, the book is divided into three parts. The first part focuses on the historical exclusion and neglect of regional complementarity in international criminal justice. It also focuses on the neglect of regional complementarity in the jurisprudence and practice of the ICC. The second part examines the turn to regionalism in practice. Through an analysis of different case studies of hybrid and regionally backed tribunals, I establish the strands of hybridity and regionalism that have emerged in practice. In this part, I focus on the assistance-driven strand of regional-hybridity, using the Extraordinary African Chambers in the Courts of Senegal (EAC) and the Kosovo Specialist Chambers and Specialist Prosecutor's Office (KSCSPO) as case studies. These two tribunals are important as examples of hybrids that are established and supported by regional organizations, as against the others that were supported and established by the UN. I examine how effective these two tribunals have been in practice. In the last chapter of this part, I analyse the Malabo Protocol as an example of the emerging fully independent strand of regionalism in ICL. In the third part of the book, I map the theoretical concept of regional complementarity and attempt to find solutions to the problems created by the application of the concept. I aim to show how different dimensions of complementarity that we have seen in the ICC are also relevant to the idea of regional complementarity. Also, I focus on the VCLT, article 17 of the Rome Statute, and an analysis of five relationship dimensions that the application of

78 ICC-OTP 'Draft Policy on Complementarity and Cooperation' at ICC-OTP 'Draft policy on Complementarity and Cooperation' September 2023, 9–17.

regional complementarity presents, to answer the question on interpretation. Lastly, I provide crosscutting analysis by synthesizing normative insights from previous chapters, especially with the information on specific institutions. The focus on the ICC and the proposed international criminal chamber of the African Court aims to provide general recommendations that are applicable between the ICC and any regional tribunal with an ICL mandate. In conclusion, recommendations for future research in this area are provided.

The book employs a doctrinal legal research methodology to examine the concept of regional complementarity in international criminal justice. This methodology focuses on the analysis and interpretation of legal texts, case law, and scholarly writings to establish relevant claims on specific legal issues. Doctrinal legal research methodology is best suited for a study of this nature, considering ICL's complexities and breadth, as it encompasses a vast body of treaties, conventions, soft laws, statutes, jurisprudence, opinions of scholars, and other academic writings. The book also employs a historical approach to analyse the place and origin of regional complementarity in the development of ICL.

The book makes use of primary and secondary materials sourced from electronic and physical libraries. It relies on academic articles, books, treaties, resolutions from international organizations including the UN and the AU, judicial decisions, press statements, and a plethora of reports and findings of previous studies on some of the areas covered in the research. Some of the primary sources include the Rome Statute, the Vienna Convention on the Law of Treaties, the Protocol on Amendments to the Protocol on the Statute of the African Court of Justice and Human Rights, otherwise known as the Malabo Protocol, and other relevant conventions and customary law principles. Secondary sources, including books and articles by leading scholars in the field of international law, will be consulted to provide further perspectives on the topics of the study.

The research process involves a scholarly review of primary and secondary sources in relation to the concept of complementarity in the practices and policy directions of relevant international, regional and national criminal mechanisms. A careful analysis of the *travaux préparatoires* of the Rome Statute and other treaties will also be done.

The book will conclude with specific recommendations on tackling legal and practical challenges associated with implementing regional complementarity, while providing suggestions for further research in this area of study.

CHAPTER 1

Historical Perspectives on the Neglect of Regional Complementarity

1 Introduction

This chapter focuses on history to answer the question: why was regionalism neglected in the history and development of ICL and complementarity? It seeks to establish that complementarity continuously reshaped itself and evolved in different models throughout its developmental stages, even though the central tenets remained the same. It also establishes that despite the continuous reshaping, complementarity did not consider the possible interaction between international and regional bodies in the realm of international criminal justice. It suggests three factors that may be responsible for ICL's neglect of regionalism and the ideas that underpin regional complementarity. It also shows why regionalism in ICL matters. It criticizes the failure of ICL to embrace regionalism earlier in its development. It concludes by arguing that, given the absence of any substantive discussion on regional complementarity, recent theory and practice, including certain developments in ICL, have necessitated a theory on regional complementarity. Structurally, the chapter begins with a discussion on certain significant attempts at complementarity after the two World Wars. These attempts did not, however, take regional prosecution of crimes into consideration. It also discusses the adoption of the Rome Statute in 1998. Thereafter, it provides a narrative on why the drafters of the Rome Statute ignored regionalism during the negotiations and discussions at the Rome Conference. It examines why regionalism (or regional efforts to prosecute international crimes) came so late in the history of international criminal justice. It notes that international law has witnessed the advent of many regional human rights institutions in the 1950s. It is, therefore, important to establish why there has been regionalism in the context of human rights and not in the context of international criminal justice until the early 2000s, after the establishment of the ICC. It explains that ICL's obsession with universality and cosmopolitanism; the liberal foundation of ICL; the understanding that ICL is an enemy of sovereignty; and the fact that ICL had developed more slowly and less dynamically are some of the factors responsible for the neglect of regionalism and regional complementarity in the history

© 2026 THE AUTHOR(S) | HTTPS://DOI.ORG/10.1163/9789004761803-003

of ICL. It concludes with a discussion on why there is a need for a theory on regional complementarity.

2 Origin of Complementarity

In international criminal law, the principle of complementarity is defined in the context of the relationship between two or more institutions that perform similar or overlapping roles.[1] However, the historical origin of the principle is closely tied to the historical origin of ICL itself. The Treaty of Sèvres (1920) contained provisions that mandated the Turkish government to hand over suspected war criminals of WWI to the Allied Powers.[2] This suggests that, from an early period in the history of ICL, concerns had arisen about cooperation between national and international institutions to avoid a clash of jurisdiction. In the Nuremberg, Tokyo and the *ad hoc* tribunals, there were also provisions that mandated states to surrender accused persons to these international tribunals.[3] The codification in the Rome Statute that 'the most serious crimes of concern to the international community as a whole must not go unpunished and that their effective prosecution must be ensured by taking measures at the *national* level and by enhancing *international* cooperation' firmly suggests the need to promote cooperation and avoid conflicts between national and international institutions. This provision of the Rome Statute also forms the core strand of the basic tenets of complementarity.[4]

However, in legal scholarship, El Zeidy is one of the first authors to argue that the origin of complementarity long predates the 1994 International Law Commission (ILC) Draft Statutes and the negotiations that took place before and during the Rome Conference of 1998.[5] He acknowledged a few authors who took the debate as far back as 1991, but not further.[6] Ellis argues that the

1 See footnote 67 in the Introduction.

2 See for example, Article 230 of the Treaty of Sèvres.

3 M. El Zeidy, *The Principle of Complementarity in International Criminal Law: Origin, Development and Practice* (Martinus Nijhoff Publishers 2008).

4 See M. Bergsmo, C.W. Ling and Y. Ping (eds) *Historical Origins of International Criminal Law*: Volume 1 (Torkel Opsahl Academic EPublisher 2014) 398.

5 See generally M. El Zeidy, *The Principle of Complementarity in International Criminal Law: Origin, Development and Practice* (Martinus Nijhoff Publishers 2008).

6 In this regard, El Zeidy acknowledged the works of I. Tallgren, 'Completing the "International Criminal Order": The Rhetoric of International Repression and the Notion of Complementarity in the Draft Statute for an International Criminal Court' (1998) 67 *Nordic Journal of International Law* 107, 120 and O. Solera, 'Complementary Jurisdiction and International Criminal Justice' (2002) 84 *International Review of the Red Cross* 145, 151.

United Nations War Crimes Commission (UNWCC) was the body that laid the grounds for the current design and interpretation of the principle of complementarity.[7] Kleffner noted that attempts to establish international judicial bodies for the enforcement of international criminal law could be traced back to the aftermath of WWI,[8] El Zeidy's main thesis was that 'the notion of complementarity is manifestly not the product of the 1994 International Law Commission's work. Nor is it the sole outcome of any recent work on the subject during the 21st century. It is an idea that developed over a long period of time until it was inserted into the 1998 Rome Statute.'[9] This work builds on El Zeidy's position as I argue that as long as there have been attempts at punishing individual violators who commit crimes at the supranational level, there have equally been discussions on how these prosecutions would fit in with existing national mechanisms and the notion of state sovereignty. Further, I establish that certain factors which are tied to the history of the development of ICL were responsible for the late engagement by ICL with regionalism.

2.1 Earliest Attempts at Enforcing 'International Criminal Law'

Long before the two world wars, there have been attempts at enforcing 'international criminal law', although these were actually attempts to prosecute certain wrongful acts from which present-day international crimes may have taken some roots.[10] These roots of contemporary international law/crimes were laws of war, which only attracted state responsibility as opposed to individual penalties.[11] Prohibitions against piracy, slavery and the slave trade in

7 M.S. Ellis, *Sovereignty and Justice: Balancing the Principle of Complementarity between International and Domestic War Crimes Tribunals* (Cambridge Scholars Publishing 2014) 13.

8 Jann K. Kleffner, *Complementarity in the Rome Statute and National Jurisdictions* (Oxford University Press 2008) 60, note 17. Here, he referenced the work of T.L.H. McCormack, 'From Sun Tzu to the Sixth Committee: The Evolution of an International Criminal Law Regime' in T.L.H. McCormack and G.J. Simpson (eds) *The Law of War Crimes: National and International approaches* (Kluwer Law International 1997) 31–63 at 37, where it was argued that the early beginnings of an attempt at establishing an international criminal body for the prosecution of international crimes dates back to the trial of Peter von Hagenbach in 1474 AD.

9 M.M. El Zeidy, *The Principle of Complementarity in International Criminal Law: Origin, Development and Practice* (Martinus Nijhoff 2008) at 6.

10 On this, see B.V. Schaack & R. Slye, 'A Concise History of International Criminal Law' (2007) *Santa Clara Law Digital Commons* 7.

11 On the law of war and state responsibility, where the author argued that 'punishment – at least in modern criminal law – constitutes individual responsibility, whereas the specific

the 19th century are other examples of strands of international law history upon which 'the norms, rules, instruments, and institutions that now make up the modern ICL machinery' are built.[12] This was at a time when slavery and colonialism were rife, and the independence and sovereignty of states were contested. This point is important, as I would later show that the fight against colonialism was a driving factor for some of the earlier regional and sub-regional arrangements in Africa and the Caribbean.[13]

Given this background, some of the earliest attempts at prosecuting individuals for violations of the laws of war were found in the trials of Conrandin, King of Jerusalem, in 1268,[14] Sir William Wallace in 1305,[15] Peter Von Hagenbach in 1474[16] and Henry Wirz in 1865.[17] These trials were conducted in respect of wrongful acts committed within the context of wars. They were like much of the acts that are now known as international crimes punishable by ICL. The trials also suggest that there have at least been attempts to punish acts that shock the conscience of humanity, especially when committed in the context of armed conflicts, through the use of special tribunals set up for those purposes: Conrandin was convicted by a panel of Knights;[18] Wallace by a military tribunal;[19] Von Hagenbach 'by a tribunal comprised of judges from several princedoms'[20] or, as stated by Gordon, 'ad hoc tribunal of twenty-eight judges

sanctions of international law constitute collective responsibility', see H. Kelsen, 'Collective and Individual Responsibility in International Law with Particular Regard to the Punishment of War Criminals' (1943) 31 *California Law Review* 5 at 533.

12 B.V. Schaack & R. Slye, 'A Concise History of International Criminal Law' (2007), *Santa Clara Law Digital Commons,* 7.

13 See R. Dadhich, 'Understanding SAARC: Regional Cooperation in Neo-Colonial Context' (2005) 18 *Indian Journal of Asian Affairs* 1, 49–64.

14 Conrandin was tried for crimes against peace, *to wit,* instigating an unjust war (due to papal opposition) to become the King of Sicily. See M. Cherif Bassiouni, *Introduction to International Criminal Law* (Martinus Nijhoff 2013), 1047.

15 Wallace was tried for 'sparing neither age nor sex, monk nor nun' in a brutal Scottish campaign against England. See Z. Bohrer, 'International Criminal Law's Millennium of Forgotten History' (2016) 34 *Law and History Review* 2, 393–485.

16 On this trial, see G.S. Gordon, 'The Trial of Peter Von Hagenbach: Reconciling History, Historiography, and International Criminal Law' in K. Heller & G. Simpson, *The Hidden Histories of War Crimes Trials* (Oxford Scholarship Online 2013).

17 On the trial of Henry Wirz, see Darrett B. Rutman, 'The War Crimes and Trial of Henry Wirz' (1960) 6 *Civil War History* 2, 117–133.

18 See Archibald Bower, *The History of the Popes: From the Foundation of the See of Rome, To the Present Time*, Vol. VI (Kessinger Publishing 2005) 14.

19 M. Keen, 'Treason Trials under the Law of Arms' (1962) 12 *Transactions of the Royal Historical Society* 85–103 at 98.

20 Z. Bohrer, 'International Criminal Law's Millennium of Forgotten History' (2016), 34 *Law & History Review* 1.

from various regional city-states',[21] and Henry Wirz by a military commission.[22] This then lends credence to the assertion that ICL's true history indeed spans across centuries and did not begin in or after Nuremberg.[23]

Additionally, the idea of 'regional city-states' participating in a joint effort at prosecuting crimes was seen in the case of Von Hagenbach, which has been described by some authors as 'the first international war crimes trial in history'.[24] The Von Hagenbach trial mirrors modern-day attempts at atrocity crimes prosecution by regional mechanisms. The idea that the trial was a regional arrangement was not without its contestations. Some argue that, since the judges 'were all subject of the Holy Roman Empire', the trial could not be said to have been of an international (or regional) nature.[25]

There are those who argue that modern international justice owes its earliest roots to the prosecution of pirates and the prohibition against piracy, as pirates were generally known as the universal enemies to whom universal jurisdiction first applied.[26] Piracy has even been described by others as the 'oldest international crime'.[27] In the trial of Henry Avery, one of Britain's most renowned pirates in the 17th century, an English central criminal court (the Old Bailey) had, in 1696, declared that 'the King of England hath not only an empire and sovereignty over the British seas, but also an undoubted jurisdiction and power, in concurrency with other princes and states, for the punishment of all piracies and robberies at sea, in the most remote parts of the world...'[28] Thus, some of the reasonings that underpinned the present-day international criminal law were also present since the 17th century, when some of the first trials for piracy were instituted. The idea of universal jurisdiction, as demonstrated in the old English central criminal court, was one.

---

21 G.S. Gordon, 'The Trial of Peter Von Hagenbach: Reconciling History, Historiography, and International Criminal Law' in K. Heller & G. Simpson, 'The Hidden Histories of War Crimes Trials' (Oxford Scholarship Online 2013), 1.

22 Darrett B. Rutman, 'The War Crimes and Trial of Henry Wirz' (1960) 6 *Civil War History* 2, 117–133.

23 Z. Bohrer, 'International Criminal Law's Millennium of Forgotten History' (2016) 34 *Law & History Review* 1.

24 G.S. Gordon, (n. 21) 1.

25 *Ibid.*

26 On this, see M. Chadwick, 'Piracy and the Origins of Universal Jurisdiction: On Stranger Tides?' (2018) 34 *Queen Mary Studies in International Law* 1.

27 M. Scharf & M. Taylor, 'A Contemporary Approach to the Oldest International Crime' (2017) 33 *Utrecht Journal of International and European Law* 84, 77–89.

28 Howell T.B and Howell T.J., *Cobbett's Complete Collection of State Trials and Proceedings for High Treason and Other Crimes and Misdemeanor from the Earliest Period to the Present Time* (R. Bagshaw 1809) Vol. 13, 455.

The idea, as expressed in the court's reasoning above, contemplates the concurrency of other princes' and states' 'jurisdiction', in the punishment of piracy. This is in tandem with universal jurisdiction on one hand, but also a reflection of the idea that states acting together in a regional arrangement can enforce ICL.

Lastly, the prohibition against slavery through the British Slave Trade Act of 1807,[29] the Slave Trade Felony Act of 1811,[30] and the Slavery Abolition Act of 1833[31] as well as the 'exploits'[32] of transatlantic admiralty courts[33] that tried crew members of captured slave ships across different jurisdictions, also lend credence to the argument that attempts to punish what were termed as 'crimes against humanity' pre-dated the two world wars.[34] Prohibition against slavery and slave trade has attained the status of *jus cogens* – for which no derogation is allowed under any guise or circumstance.[35] The history of their prosecutions offers interesting insights into how some modern crimes that are now often described as crimes against humanity took their name originally

---

29 The Slave Trade Act, which is better known by its longer title of 'An Act for the Abolition of the Slave Trade' was enacted on 25 March 1807 and it imposed fines which were not enough to deter entrepreneurs from engaging in such lucrative commercial activities of slave trade. See the text of the Act at http://www.esp.org/foundations/freedom/holdings/slave-trade-act-1807.pdf.

30 The 1811 Act made slave trading a felony/crime and imposed stiffer punishment as against the earlier 1807 Act, which only imposed fines. It was, however, the Slavery Abolition Act of 1833 that significantly expanded the jurisdiction of the slave trade acts of 1807 and 1811.

31 Its longer title was 'An Act for the Abolition of Slavery throughout the British Colonies; for promoting the industry of the manumitted Slaves; and for compensating the Persons hitherto entitled to the Services of such Slaves.' It received royal assent on 28 August 1833 and entered into force throughout most of the British Empire on 1 August 1834. It was repealed in 1998.

32 For an interesting account of proceedings before one of such courts, see Haslam E., Redemption, Colonialism and International Criminal Law: The Nineteenth Century Slave Trading Trials of Samo and Peters in Kirkby D. (ed.), *Past Law Present Histories* (ANU Press 2012). See also Haslam E., *The Slave Trade, Abolition and the Long History of International Criminal Law: The Recaptive and the Victim* (Routledge 2020).

33 These were often called the Courts of Mixed Commission for the Abolition of Slave Trade, and some have argued that they were the first international human rights court. See J. Martinez, 'Antislavery Courts and the Dawn of International Human Rights Law' (2008) 117 *Yale Law Journal* 4.

34 See generally J. Martinez, *The Slave Trade and the Origins of International Human Rights Law* (Oxford University Press 2011).

35 On *jus cogens*, see T. Kleinlein, 'Jus Cogens Re-examined: Value Formalism in International Law' (2017) 28 *The European Journal of International Law* 1.

from the prohibition of slavery and slave trade, while offering striking similarities to present-day prosecutions of international crimes.[36]

More importantly, there appeared to be some regional[37] and international initiatives at abolishing slavery and slave trade.[38] Added to this were the ideas of regional and international judicial arrangements which entertained prosecutions of slave owners and slave traders. Starting in 1817, Britain, for example, started to conclude treaties with different countries to establish international courts for the suppression of slave trades.[39] However, until recently, these initiatives have not inspired concrete efforts at international crimes prosecution by regional organizations.

2.2 Post-WWI Complementarity Attempts

When WWI ended, there were calls for the prosecution of those responsible for war crimes.[40] One such person was Kaiser Wilhelm II of Germany.[41] In answering these calls, the Allies, at the Paris Preliminary Peace Conference in 1919,[42] decided to establish a 'Commission on the Responsibility of the

---

36 A. Gross, 'Introduction: 'A Crime against Humanity': Slavery and The Boundaries of Legality, Past and Present' (2017) 35 *Law and History Review* 1, 1–8.

37 'Regional' in this context is used to distinguish slave trade within the Americas, as against the 'Trans-Atlantic' slave trade. See S. Westbury, 'Analysing a regional slave trade: The West Indies and Virginia, 1698–1775' (1986) 7 *Slavery and Abolition* 3, 241–256.

38 H. Suzuki, *The Suppression of the Transoceanic Slave Trade* (Oxford University Press 2022).

39 See E. Kontorovich, 'The Constitutionality of International Courts: The Forgotten Precedent of Slave Trade Tribunals' (2009) 158 *University of Pennsylvania Law Review* 1, 58–59. See also Jenny S. Martinez, 'Anti-slavery Courts and the Dawn of International Human Rights Law' (2008) 117 *Yale Law Journal* 550.

40 G. Hankel, *The Leipzig trials. German war crimes and their legal consequences after World War I* (Republic of Letters Publishing 2014); C Mullins 'The Leipzig trials. An account of the war criminals' trials and a study of German mentality' (1921) *H.F. & G. Witherb;* P. Betts, 'Germany, International Justice and the Twentieth Century' (2005) 17 *History & Memory* 1/2, 45–86.

41 For a full account of the events surrounding the never-to-be-held trial of the Kaiser, see W.A. Schabas, *The Trial of the Kaiser* (Oxford University Press 2018). See also J.B. Scott, 'The Trial of the Kaiser' in House and Seymour, *What Really Happened at Paris*, 231–258 and B. Kampmark, 'Sacred Sovereigns and Punishable War Crimes: The Ambivalence of the Wilson Administration towards a Trial of Kaiser Wilhelm II' (2007) 53 *Australian Journal of Politics and History* 4, 519–537.

42 For a general understanding of the Peace Conference and its achievements, see G.A. Finch, 'The Peace Conference of Paris, 1919' (1919) 13 *The American Journal of International Law* 2, 159–186.

Authors of the War and on Enforcement of Penalties'.[43] The Commission had a mandate to investigate and report on the facts and evidence necessary to determine who was responsible for the World War.[44] In executing its mandate, the Commission had to determine, among other things, the guilt of individuals and whether they could be tried, as well as what would amount to a suitable forum for prosecution. There were proposals for bringing accused persons of the Enemy States before a 'High Tribunal' composed of 22 judges from different countries. Given the novelty and the unprecedented nature of the idea of a criminal tribunal with an international composition, the United States and Japan objected, arguing that it was better to find recourse in an existing system. Despite the objections, the Allied National Military Tribunals were established under the Treaty of Versailles, with jurisdiction over perpetrators of crimes during the World War, including heads of states.[45] The objection by Japan and the USA is symptomatic of the present-day debate on whether the future of prosecutions of international crimes is domestic or remains international.[46]

Germany, as the 'vanquished' State, objected to certain provisions, particularly articles 228–230 of the treaty relating to turning over suspected war criminals to the Allies for trials and those provisions relating to penalties for the convicted. The Allies, however, insisted, resulting in an unconditional acceptance of the provisions by the German National Assembly.[47] By this acceptance, Germany agreed to turn over suspected war criminals to the Allies for trial. Where violations affected the nationals of more than one power, Germany agreed to turn suspects over to a Mixed (Inter-Allied) Military Tribunal composed of judges from the affected powers.[48]

---

43 For a general understanding of the Commission's work, see 'Commission on the Responsibility of the Authors of the War and on Enforcement of Penalties: Report presented to the Preliminary Peace Conference' (1920) 14 *The American Journal of International Law* No. 1/2, 95–154.

44 M. El Zeidy, *The Principle of Complementarity in International Criminal Law: Origin, Development and Practice* (Martinus Nijhoff Publishers 2008) 11.

45 *Ibid.*

46 On this debate, see M. du Plessis, 'The Future of International Criminal Justice is Domestic' [available at http://ilawyerblog.com/future-international-criminal-justice-domestic/ – accessed 23 January 2023]. See also A.M. Slaughter, 'The Future of International Law is Domestic' (2006) 47 *Harvard International Law Journal* 2.

47 On the unconditional acceptance of the Treaty of Versailles by the German Government, see A. Luckau, 'Unconditional Acceptance of the Treaty of Versailles by the German Government, June 22–28, 1919' (1945) 17 *Journal of Modern History* 3, 215–220.

48 M.M. El Zeidy, *The Principle of Complementarity in International Criminal Law: Origin, Development and Practice* (Martinus Nijhoff Publishers 2008) 14.

Germany, however, failed to comply with the treaty, arguing that it was unacceptable for the German government to surrender its citizens to be tried by foreign powers. The debate that followed led to a compromise between the Allies and Germany. The Allies accepted a German offer to prosecute some of the offenders before its Reichsgericht (Supreme Court), sitting at Leipzig, but with a proviso that the Allies retained the rights under article 228 of the Versailles Treaty to set aside any German verdict in case of unsatisfactory results.[49] Allies conceded some grounds to Germany through allowing prosecution of certain crimes before German domestic courts, while the Military Tribunals handled the other cases. This division-of-labour approach is consistent with the idea that this work promotes. Utilizing regional courts for international crimes prosecution could help maximize the advantages of the domestic system while minimizing the disadvantages of a purely international system.

Earlier attempts at complementarity can be gleaned from the Allies' commitment to step in if Germany failed to prosecute the offenders under its national laws. It is also an attempt to bridge the gap between domestic and international efforts at prosecuting crimes. Germany's efforts at protecting its sovereignty remind one of states' attitudes towards complementarity and sovereignty at every stage of the development of ICL. States had always preferred that their prerogative to prosecute is given primacy over any international arrangement, and it is the failure or absence of national efforts that ought to trigger international efforts. This is what El Zeidy refers to as the 'shift from the notion of primacy to the more restrained notion of complementarity'.[50] It is in this regard that 'article 228 of the Versailles Treaty could be regarded as the [first] precedent for the application of the principle of complementarity', irrespective of its limited scope in comparison to the current expanded notion of the concept.[51]

49 On Germany's protest and what has been called 'constant revisionism of the treaty', see S. Marks, 'Mistakes and Myths: The Allies, Germany, and the Versailles Treaty, 1918–1921' (2013) 85 *The Journal of Modern History* 3, 632–659.

50 M. El Zeidy, *The Principle of Complementarity in International Criminal Law: Origin, Development and Practice* (Martinus Nijhoff Publishers 2008) 15.

51 *Ibid.*

The Allies also concluded similar peace treaties with other 'enemy' governments, particularly Austria,[52] Bulgaria,[53] Hungary[54] and Turkey.[55] These treaties all had penalty provisions like that of the Treaty of Versailles.[56] The application of these penalty clauses in each of these cases followed the German experience that had been discussed earlier. In each of these cases, the national courts of these countries could prosecute a select number of perpetrators before their national courts. These experiences provided historical evidence that international crimes prosecution may have benefited from burden-sharing between national mechanisms and supranational tribunals, such as the ones established under these peace treaties. These ideas of division of labour and burden-sharing also underpin the notion of regional complementarity that I propose in this research.

One significant discussion at the 1919 preliminary Peace Conference, leading to the conclusion of the Treaty of Versailles, was the trial of the Kaiser. The Allies were clear about their intention to bring the Kaiser to trial. This was reflected in article 227 of the Treaty of Versailles.[57]

In hindsight, the attempt at prosecuting the Kaiser brought to the fore some of the issues that are still as relevant today as they were over 100 years ago: complementarity and the interaction between international and domestic mechanisms for crimes prosecution, extradition, command responsibility, prosecution of heads of state for international crimes and the push back against it, discussion on a proper forum to mete out international justice, among many others. Complementarity and the interaction between international and domestic mechanisms became obvious in the contestation by Germany that its nationals were going to be tried before its courts and not before any international criminal tribunal. As will be seen in the next sections of this

52 The Treaty of St. Germain was signed on 10 September 1919 between Austria and the Allies and took effect on 16 July 1920. The treaty dissolved the Austro-Hungarian monarchy.

53 The Treaty of Neuilly was the Allies' Peace Treaty with Bulgaria and was signed on 5 November 1919.

54 The Treaty of Trianon was the treaty between the Allies and Hungary. It was signed on 4 June 1920.

55 The Treaty of Sevres, the peace treaty with Turkey, was concluded on 10 August 1920.

56 Articles 173, 157, 118 and 226 of the Treaties of St. Germain, Trianon, Neuilly and Sevres, respectively.

57 It provides that 'The Allied and Associated Powers [will] publicly arraign William II of Hohenzollern, formerly German Emperor, for a supreme offence against international morality and the sanctity of treaties... The Allied and Associated Powers will address a request to the Government of the Netherlands for the surrender to them of the ex-Emperor in order that he may be put on trial.'

chapter, during the negotiations that led to the adoption of the Rome Statute, including the negotiations at the Rome Conference itself, many states rallied against relinquishing their prosecutorial powers to an international criminal tribunal. In the end, a compromise was reached, in a similar fashion to the compromise between the Allies and Germany. It reflects the central theme of complementarity, which is the working together of international and domestic criminal jurisdictions to achieve the aim of international crimes prosecution. At this point in history, though, thoughts about the regional arrangement and how it fits into international crimes prosecution had not emerged significantly. Complementarity and the interaction between international and domestic mechanisms became obvious in the contestation by Germany that its nationals were going to be tried before its courts and not before any international criminal tribunal.

2.3 Prosecution of International Crimes after WWII

The end of WWII again signalled not only the call for prosecutions of war criminals, but also the question of the appropriate forum for prosecution. This was because of the concerns about sovereignty and the roles of national courts in the prosecution of international crimes, which had overshadowed such discussions in the past. After the war, certain developments further increased the attention on creating an international criminal court. Such developments included the events at the 1941 London International Assembly (LIA), the activities of the 1943 UN War Crimes Commission (UNWCC), the Nuremberg International Military Tribunal (NIMT), the adoption of the 1948 Genocide Convention, as well as the activities of the 1951–1953 Committees on International Criminal Jurisdiction.

The London International Assembly (LIA) studied the question of war crimes and concluded that jurisdiction over such crimes should be vested in national courts, while certain categories of war crimes should be prosecuted by an international criminal court.[58] The LIA favoured the jurisdictional division of labour between international and national mechanisms. The body also adopted a 62-article convention for an international criminal court.[59]

The 1943 UN War Crimes Commission (UNWCC) was established to investigate crimes committed during WWII. It became immediately concerned

58 See UN, *Historical Survey of the Question of International Criminal Jurisdiction*, UN Doc A/CN.4/7/Rev.1, 18 (1949).

59 W. Schabas, 'The United Nations War Crimes Commission Proposal for an International Criminal Court' (2014) 25 *Criminal Law Forum* 171–189.

with establishing a war crimes court. It worked in committees, and Committee II on enforcement used the draft convention by the LIA as a basis for its discussions.[60] A draft prepared by the US for the Committee's consideration, first took the LIA's convention into account and then proposed that the court would exercise jurisdiction only where national courts lacked or preferred not to exercise jurisdiction.[61] After several amendments, the jurisdictional provisions of the UNWCC's draft conferred primary jurisdiction on national courts, while States had the liberty to either deal with a case or refer it to the proposed court.[62] Stahn argued that the UNWCC's focus on facts, evidence and interaction with domestic authorities represents both the past and the future of international crimes prosecution.[63] Attention, however, shifted away from the UNWCC, and its efforts were frustrated when it was opposed on several grounds by the UK government, while the allied powers decided to adopt the charter establishing the International Military Tribunal.

The Nuremberg International Military Tribunal (NIMT) reflected the guiding principle of the Moscow Declaration, wherein the Allies declared that German war criminals would be prosecuted in line with territorial jurisdiction, while 'major criminals whose offences have no particular geographical location will be punished by a joint decision of the Governments of the Allies'.[64] The NIMT only concentrated on major criminals while national mechanisms dealt with the bulk of cases. When contrasted with the position under the Treaty of Versailles and other peace treaties of the post-WWI era, this subsidiary approach reveals a different model of complementarity. Under the peace treaties, the Inter-Allied court would intervene where the German national courts failed in their duty to prosecute satisfactorily. Thus, the Inter-Allied court deferred jurisdiction to the German national courts, and this was generally seen as a victory for state sovereignty. On the contrary, however, under the NIMT, the complementarity model 'reflected the principle of primacy of international law over national law, regarding trying major war criminals for core crimes'.[65]

---

60 *Ibid.*

61 M. El Zeidy, *The Principle of Complementarity in International Criminal Law: Origin, Development and Practice* (Martinus Nijhoff Publishers 2008) at 71.

62 *Ibid.*

63 C. Stahn, 'Complementarity and cooperative justice ahead of their time? The United Nations War Crimes Commission, fact-finding and evidence' (2014) 25 *Criminal Law Forum* 1, 223–260 at 223.

64 M. El Zeidy, *The Principle of Complementarity in International Criminal Law: Origin, Development and Practice* (Martinus Nijhoff Publishers 2008) at 74.

65 *Ibid.*

Article VI of the 1948 Genocide Convention[66] clarified the anticipated relationship between national mechanisms and an international penal tribunal with jurisdiction in the following words: '[P]ersons charged with genocide or any of the other acts enumerated in article III shall be tried by a competent tribunal of the State in the territory of which the act was committed, or by such international penal tribunal as may have jurisdiction with respect to those Contracting Parties which shall have accepted its jurisdiction.'

The 1951–1953 Committees on International Criminal Jurisdiction drafted clauses that created a complementarity model like the one proposed by the LIA.[67] The International Law Commission (ILC), on the other hand, adopted the 1951 and 1954 Draft Codes of Offences against the Peace and Security of Mankind.[68] At the time, the ILC favoured the establishment of an international criminal court with exclusive competence over the crimes defined in the codes, and this idea of exclusivity of jurisdiction inspired the work of the ILC until as recently as the early 1980s.[69] It was only in the early 1990s that the ILC realized that the idea of exclusive jurisdiction was not viable; hence, the current approach of reconciling both international and national criminal jurisdictions.[70] From the day of its inception in 1946, the ILC continued to be the principal player in the project of creating a permanent international criminal court.[71]

2.4 Complementarity in the Draft Statutes and the Two Committees

The long history of the codification of complementarity began to yield results with its inclusion in the 1993 and 1994 ILC Draft Statutes and the

66 The Convention on the Prevention and Punishment of the Crime of Genocide was adopted by the General Assembly of The United Nations on 9 December 1948.

67 Established in 1950 by the General Assembly of the UN, the body was set up to prepare a concrete proposal for establishing an international judicial organ for the trial of persons charged with genocide or other crimes. See S.A. Williams, 'The Rome Statute on the International Criminal Court: From 1947–2000 and Beyond' (2000) 38 *Osgoode Hall Law Journal* 2 at 302.

68 See D.H.N. Johnson, 'The Draft Code of Offences against the Peace and Security of Mankind' (1945) 4 *International and Comparative Law Quarterly* 445.

69 *Ibid.*

70 See UN Doc A/CN.4/SER.A/1985/Add.l (Part 2) (1985) *Yearbook of the International Law Commission.*

71 B.E. Berg, 'The 1994 I.L.C. Draft Statute for an International Criminal Court: A Principled Appraisal of Jurisdictional Structure' (1996) 28 *Case Western Reserve Journal of International Law* 2, 223.

discussions that took place at the Ad Hoc (AHCom) and Preparatory Committees (PrepCom).

The 1993 Draft Statute touched on the question of complementarity in two provisions.[72] One was related to the commentary on article 1, where the purpose for the establishment of the Court was explained. The article explains that the Statute was meant to 'provide a venue for the fair trial of persons accused of crimes of an international character, in circumstances where other trial procedures may not be available or may be otherwise less preferable'.[73] The second was in respect of article 45 on *ne bis in idem*,[74] which provides as follows: 'a person who has been tried by another court for acts constituting crimes referred to in articles 22 or 26, may be subsequently tried under this Statute only if: (a) the act in question was characterized as an ordinary crime; or (b) the proceedings in the other court were not impartial or independent or were designed to shield the accused from international criminal responsibility or the case was not diligently prosecuted.'[75]

The 1994 Draft Statute contains the first express reference to the concept of complementarity. Its preamble stated that 'the Court is intended to be complementary to national criminal justice systems in cases where such trial procedures may not be available or may be ineffective.'[76] The ILC views the Court as one that should operate where there is no prospect that accused persons would be duly tried in national courts. It stressed that the Court is a body 'which will complement existing national jurisdictions and existing procedures for international judicial cooperation in criminal matters and which is not intended to exclude the existing jurisdiction of national courts, or to affect the right of States to seek extradition and other forms of international judicial assistance'.[77] Sub-paragraph 3 of the commentary to the preamble states that '[T]he purposes set out in the preamble are intended to assist in the interpretation and application of the Statute, and in particular in the exercise of the power conferred by article 35.'[78] The ILC explained that article 35 allows the Court to decide which case is admissible. The article relates to the *exercise,* as

72 J.K. Kleffner, *Complementarity in the Rome Statute and National Jurisdictions* (Oxford University Press 2008) at 72.

73 *Ibid.*

74 On the principle, see G. Conway, 'Ne Bis in Idem in International Law' (2003) 3 *International Criminal Law Review* 217–244.

75 J.K. Kleffner, *Complementarity in the Rome Statute and National Jurisdictions* (Oxford University Press 2008) at 72.

76 UN, Draft Statute for an International Criminal Court with Commentaries 1994 at 27.

77 UN Doc A/CN.4/SER.A/1994/Add.l (Part 2) 27*Yearbook of the International Law Commission* (1994).

78 *Ibid.*

opposed to the *existence,* of jurisdiction.[79] The provision is a response to suggestions from some States that the Court should only deal with cases in circumstances 'where it is really desirable to do so'.[80] This is not only a way of ensuring that the Court limited its focus to the most serious crimes, but also an important method by which the Court could manage its caseload according to available resources.[81] This implies that the original idea of the drafters of what would later become the Rome Statute was that the Court could not realistically take on every single case, even if it has jurisdiction to do so. In this regard, complementarity does not mean that the Court would be able to exercise jurisdiction in all circumstances where it can, but only in situations where it should, according to the presence of other enabling factors. To achieve this, the ILC streamlined the exercise of jurisdiction by summing up the grounds of inadmissibility as being '[t]hat the crime in question has been or is being duly investigated by any appropriate national authorities or is not of sufficient gravity to justify further action by the Court'.[82]

AHCom held two sessions.[83] The second session focused on complementarity, among other issues.[84] The AHCom detailed its discussions and understanding of the principle of complementarity under three headings, namely: a) the significance of the principle of complementarity; b) the implications of the principle of complementarity as regards the list of crimes which would fall under the jurisdiction of an international criminal court; and c) the role of national jurisdiction.[85] It remains surprising that in the discussions around the role of national jurisdictions, there was no consideration of the role that national jurisdictions, acting under the auspices of a regional arrangement, could play.

On the implications of complementarity for crimes under the jurisdiction of an international criminal court, there is a link between the scope of the proposed court's jurisdiction and complementarity.[86] While some delegations argued that the Draft Statute should provide for a single legal system for all crimes within the jurisdiction of the court, with a limited number of 'hard-

79 *Ibid.*
80 *Ibid.*
81 S. SáCouto & K. Cleary, 'The Gravity Threshold of the International Criminal Court' (2008) 23 *American Journal of International Law* 5, 807–854 at 820.
82 UN Doc A/CN.4/SER.A/1994/Add.1 (Part 2) (note 77) 52.
83 UN Doc A/50/22 *General Assembly Official Records, Fiftieth Session, Supplement No. 22,* para. 1.
84 Kleffner (n. 75) 76.
85 *Ibid* at 76; see also UN Doc A/50/22 (n. 83) 6–10.
86 Kleffner (n. 75) 76.

core crimes', others felt that a multiplicity of jurisdictional mechanisms was preferable.[87] On the role of national jurisdictions, the AHCom first noted the need to clarify the term 'national jurisdiction' in the context of complementarity. Some delegations observed that the term 'was not limited to territorial jurisdiction but also included States' competence to exercise jurisdiction in accordance with established principles and arrangements'.[88] The question was which State should be considered relevant in making the assessment on whether trial procedures were available and effective and which State(s) may be considered as an 'interested party', in an application for a decision of inadmissibility, within the ambit of article 35 of the Draft Statute.[89]

Cassese noted that the success of AHCom was that it helped to ensure that 'the primacy of national jurisdiction was to be respected, [and] the Court's prospective encroachment on national sovereignty was seen as less threatening'.[90]

While the AHCom had already emphasized the importance of complementarity, discussions at the Preparatory Committee (PrepCom) focused on the questions of what is to be understood by the principle, how the principle should be reflected in the Statute, and which articles of the Statute were of relevance in implementing the principle.[91] It was clear that a proper balance between the proposed court and national jurisdictions was crucial in order to make the Draft Statute acceptable to a large number of States.[92] While many states agreed on the desirability of the principle, the questions as to how, where, to what extent and with what emphasis complementarity should be reflected in the Statute required further deliberations.[93]

PrepCom began its work in 1996 and completed its Draft Statute in April 1998. Discussions were held in different sessions[94] and at the working group

87 Kleffner (n. 75) at 76–77. See also UN Doc A/50/22, (n. 83) para 38.

88 UN Doc A/50/22 (n 83) para 39.

89 Kleffner (n. 75) 77.

90 A. Cassese, Gaeta & Jones, The Path to Rome and Beyond, Drafting History and Further Developments in Cassese, Gaeta & Jones (eds) *The Rome Statute of the International Criminal Court: A Commentary* (Oxford University Press 2002) 15.

91 *Ibid.*

92 *Ibid.*

93 *Ibid.*

94 C.K. Hall, 'The First Two Sessions of the UN Preparatory Committee on the Establishment of an International Criminal Court' in 'Current Developments' (1997) 91 *American Journal of International Law* 177–181; C.K. Hall, 'The Third and Fourth Sessions of the UN Preparatory Committee on the Establishment of an International Criminal Court' in 'Current Developments' (1998) 92 *American Journal of International Law* 124; C.K. Hall, 'The Fifth Session of the UN Preparatory Committee on the Establishment of an Inter-

on complementarity and trigger mechanisms.[95] At the first session, various interpretations of the concept of complementarity were discussed, but two views were prominent. The first view underscored the primary rights of States to prosecute crimes within their territories, the need to incorporate complementarity in all aspects of State cooperation with the Court, as well as a more restrictive and limited role for the new Court.[96] The second view was that the preamble of the Draft Statute had to be amended so that the Court should act when States failed to carry out their duty to bring suspects to justice.[97] There was a third, but not so prominent, view that a very restrictive approach to complementarity may undermine the Court's authority and effectiveness. Proponents of this view suggest that the Statute should expressly provide exceptions to complementarity and that the Prosecutor should not be required to prove, in every case, that the Court's intervention is required.[98]

PrepCom only returned to the discussion on complementarity at its fourth session in August 1997. Prior to this, different delegations had submitted proposals and position papers as a fallout of the discussions on complementarity at the first session. Discussions resumed largely at informal debating and drafting in closed working groups.[99] The atmosphere was such that there seemed to be an understanding that the issues of complementarity and trigger mechanisms were so contentious that they may not be resolved until the diplomatic conference, considering their political nature.[100] Progress was, however, made in drafting consolidated texts, particularly in relation to the grounds for determining whether a case is admissible and the roles of the Security Council, States and the Prosecutor in initiating cases and prosecutions.[101] The drafting group, coordinated by the head of the Canadian delegation, Mr. John T. Holmes, mainly focused on Draft Article 35 and did not address other procedural aspects.[102] After a week of intense negotiations, the

national Criminal Court' in 'Current Developments' (1998) 92 *American Journal of International Law* 331; and C.K. Hall, 'The Sixth Session of the UN Preparatory Committee on the Establishment of an International Criminal Court' in 'Current Developments' (1998) 92 *American Journal of International Law* 548.

95 UN Doc A/AC.249/1997/L.8/Rev.1 (14 August 1997) *Decisions Taken by the Preparatory Committee at Its Session Held from 4 to 15 August 1997*, para. 1.

96 Cassese & ors (n. 90) 15.

97 *Ibid.*

98 Kleffner (n. 75), 80.

99 Hall, 'The Third and Fourth Sessions…', (n. 94) 130.

100 *Ibid.*

101 *Ibid.*

102 Kleffner (n. 75) 84.

Committee approved a new consolidated draft that was produced by Mr. Holmes.[103]

It was only at its last session in March 1998 that the PrepCom completed its work of preparing a consolidated text of a statute for a permanent international criminal court.[104] The text that was forwarded to the Rome Conference by the PrepCom greatly expanded the grounds on which the ICC can assume jurisdiction. It also helped to have a more focused debate on preconditions and trigger mechanisms by setting a better template for discussions and agreements at the Rome Conference.[105] With the Committee's work done, a consolidated Draft Statute was adopted. Further debates and final discussions about admissibility and complementarity then shifted to Rome.

2.5 Complementarity at the Rome Conference

Throughout the drafting process of the ICC Statute, the relationship between the proposed Court and national jurisdictions was a recurring theme.[106] The question of complementarity dominated the discussions.[107] It was clear that States did not want a replacement for national jurisdictions, but a Court that can work alongside existing national mechanisms.[108] The principal considerations at the time were the need to accommodate states' concerns about sovereignty and the necessity to ensure that the Court was strong enough to bring perpetrators of international crimes to justice. There was no doubt that any agreement on the Statute must strike a balance between these two considerations.[109]

The Conference's Committee of the Whole (CW) took up the discussions on complementarity during the second week of the Conference.[110] The substantive discussions centred around Draft Articles 15 to 19 on the criteria for

---

103 *Ibid.*

104 Hall, 'The Sixth Session...', (n. 94) 548.

105 O. Triffterer & K. Ambos, *The Rome Statute of the International Criminal Court: A Commentary* (CH. Beck, Hart & Nomos 2015) at 791.

106 Kleffner (n. 75) 72.

107 UN Doc A/CONF.183/C.1/SR.11, 'Summary Records of the 1998 Diplomatic Conference' (22 June 1998), para. 19, 213 in *The UN United Nations Diplomatic Conference of Plenipotentiaries on the Establishment of an International Criminal Court: Rome, 15 June–17 July 1998, Official Records Volume II.*

108 *Ibid.*

109 Kleffner (n. 75) 3.

110 J.T. Holmes, 'The Principle of Complementarity' in R.S. Lee (ed.), *The International Criminal Court: The Making of the Rome Statute, Issues, Negotiations, Results* (Kluwer Law International 1999) 52.

admissibility and procedure of complementarity.[111] Mr. Holmes, who had earlier coordinated the discussions at the PrepCom, introduced the subject. He explained the origin and substance of the provisions on admissibility and *ne bis in idem*. He went further to explain the long and difficult route to the compromises that produced these provisions and therefore urged the delegations not to reopen the discussions on these provisions.

This notwithstanding, certain states like China, Egypt, Mexico, Indonesia, India and Uruguay were not totally satisfied with the formulation of complementarity in Draft Article 15.[112] They called for the reopening of discussions on the issue, as the article did not fully meet their expectations. They argued that the article gave the Court too broad a discretion in determining 'unwillingness', as there are no objective criteria to guide the Court, and that the phrase 'undue delay' was a very low threshold for unwillingness. They equally submitted that the criterion 'partial collapse' of the national judicial system for the Court to determine inability was insufficient.[113] In an attempt to resolve these concerns, the phrase 'having regard to the principle of due process recognized by international law' was added to the yardstick for determining 'unwillingness' in paragraph 2.[114] Additionally, the term 'undue delay' was replaced with the term 'unjustified delay' as 'unjustified' was understood to establish a higher threshold than 'undue'[115] while the term 'substantial collapse' was used in the place of 'partial collapse' so as to narrow down the requirement.[116] Given the elaborative efforts on complementarity as contained in Draft Article 15 which became article 17 in the final text, States agreed not to include further elaboration on the subject in the Preamble, but to make a reference to it in article 1, considering its importance and for the purposes of clarity.[117]

On the relationship between complementarity and the principle of *ne bis in idem*, no significant discussion took place at the Conference.[118] But on *ne bis in idem* itself, some significant discussions took place. Accordingly, two amendments were proposed to the final text. One relates to the addition of the phrase 'with respect to the same conduct', which was included in the *chapeau*

111 Kleffner (n. 75), 90.
112 P.T.T. Huong, 'A Changing Notion of Complementarity under the Rome Statute of the International Criminal Court' (2002) [available at http://ir.nul.nagoya-u.ac.jp/jspui/bitstream/2237/16936/1/18-Pham%20Thi%20Thu%20Huong%E6%A7%98.pdf – accessed 12 May 2023] 616.
113 *Ibid*; see also Holmes at 52.
114 Holmes at 54.
115 Kleffner (n. 75) 90; see also Holmes (n. 110) 55.
116 Holmes (n. 110) 54–55.
117 *Ibid* 56.
118 Kleffner (n. 75) 90.

of paragraph 3. This was to underscore that the Court could still try a person even if the person had been tried at the domestic level, provided that different conduct was the subject of the new prosecution.[119] The second change related to the addition of the phrase 'in accordance with the norms of due process recognized by international law' to paragraph 3(b) of the *ne bis in idem* provision. This phrase was already included in the admissibility provision in Draft Article 15(2).[120]

The consolidated Draft Statute, as forwarded by PrepCom, remained largely unchanged at the Rome Conference except for three modifications, two of which had been discussed in the preceding paragraph. The third relates to the inclusion of articles 6 to 8, which set down the crimes within the jurisdiction of the Court.[121]

In terms of procedure, there was a debate on whether it was only State Parties to the Statute that could validly challenge the Court's jurisdiction, as there were States who argued that complementarity should apply irrespective of the fact that the State where national proceedings were taking place is a non-party to the Statute. To resolve this, it was agreed that any State, including non-State Parties, could make a challenge provided that it had jurisdiction over a case and was investigating or prosecuting or had done so already. This was to 'forestall situations where a State could challenge (and delay) the Court from proceedings with a case on the ground that it was investigating when in fact the investigation or prosecution was sure to fail because the State lacked jurisdiction'.[122] It was, however, further agreed that the Prosecutor may continue investigation pending the decisions on admissibility to avoid delays and loss of valuable evidence caused by the challenge of admissibility.[123]

The United States made certain proposals on 'preliminary rulings regarding admissibility' in respect of Draft Article 16.[124] While some States supported the proposal because they saw it as a necessary safeguard for sovereignty, others viewed it as unnecessarily setting up an obstacle to the Court's operation.[125] The US viewed the proposal as necessary to provide for a procedure that

---

119 Holmes at 59.

120 Holmes at 59; Kleffner at 91.

121 Kleffner at 91.

122 Holmes at 66; Huong at 615.

123 Huong at 615; Holmes at 66.

124 See Holmes 69–70; see also UN Doc A/CONF.183/C.1/L.25 (29 June 1998), in *United Nations Diplomatic Conference of Plenipotentiaries on the Establishment of an International Court (Rome, 15 June–17 July 1998), UN General Assembly Official Records, Volume III, Reports and Other Documents* (2002), *UN Doc A/CONF.183/13* (*Vol. III*) at 241–242.

125 UN Doc A/CONF. 183. C. 1/SR. *Summary Records of the 1998 Diplomatic Conference* at 11, 12, 29, 30, 31, 33.

would allow a State to investigate and prosecute the crimes concerned, even at the outset of or during a referral.[126] To resolve this and to modify the proposal, parties were mindful of the need to strike a balance between the need for the ICC to defer to genuine national efforts on one hand, and the danger of allowing provisions that can be used to frustrate investigations by the Prosecutor, thus undermining the essence of the Court.[127] In the end, though, compromises were reached, and Draft Article 16 became article 18 in the final text.[128] In the end, the Statute was made to contain 'a delicately balanced provision' that spells out rigorous criteria for the Court to assume jurisdiction. This is the present provision of article 17 of the Rome Statute.[129] Articles 18 and 19 of the Statute also spelt out rigorous procedures to ensure that the Court accords all due deference to the proceedings before national jurisdictions.[130]

The agreements reached at the Rome Conference arose out of the need for compromise from States who had divergent views of the purposes they want the Court to serve as well as its *modus operandi*. In this regard, it is observed 'the general idea of complementarity was agreed early in the negotiating process, it was the details of that principle in dealing with the appropriate relation between national courts and the ICC that proved controversial'.[131] This was also partly because the drafters had intended to develop a comprehensive complementarity regime.[132] This they seemed to have achieved, although other aspects of operationalizing the new Court had to be worked out. Hence, the Preparatory Commission[133] was established to elaborate a set of subsidiary instruments, including Rules of Evidence and the Elements of Crimes for the new Court.[134]

One surprising outcome of the discussions at Rome was the complete silence on the subject of regional organizations' participation in international crimes prosecution. This is also as there were several regional organisations with delegates at the conference. Examples include the Organization of Afri-

---

126 Kleffner at 93.

127 Holmes at 70; Huong at 614.

128 See Holmes at 71–73; Kleffner at 93.

129 A. Cassese and ors, *The Path to Rome and Beyond: Drafting History and Further Developments* (Oxford University Press 2002) 37.

130 *Ibid.*

131 Huong at 613.

132 Holmes at 75.

133 For a general understanding of its work and achievements, see P. Kirsch & V. Oosterveld, 'The Preparatory Commission for the International Criminal Court' (2001) 25 *Fordham International Law Journal* 3, 563–588.

134 Kleffner at 85.

can Unity (OAU), Organization of American States and the Council of Europe, among others.[135]

3 Contextualizing the Neglect of Regionalism in ICL History

From the historical analysis in the previous section of this chapter, it has emerged that in the development of ICL, and the discussions that attended the establishment of a permanent international criminal court, there has been little or no reference to the role those regional organizations can play in the enforcement of international criminal justice. Discussions at the Rome Conference revolved largely around creating a permanent court with jurisdiction over core crimes, without unnecessarily expanding it in a manner that overburdens the limited finance and personnel of the court.[136] Also, at the time, there appeared to be a general understanding that the Security Council may still be able to create tribunals that would address specific atrocity situations, like the ICTY and the ICTR; hence, there was no need for other mechanisms, including a regional criminal tribunal.

This is of interest because, prior to and at the Rome Conference, there were discussions that reflected specific concerns of practitioners and delegates in relation to crimes of specific regional concern. Some countries had identified regional challenges and sought to expand the remit of the proposed court to address some of those regional crimes. For instance, prior to the Rome Conference, Trinidad and Tobago had long sought the creation of an international criminal tribunal to deal with the crime of drug trafficking, which had become endemic in the Caribbean region. In fact, the renewed interest in the project of an international criminal court was traceable to the Trinidad and Tobago proposal.[137] Also, throughout the discussions at the PrepCom, there were delegates who supported the inclusion of drug trafficking as one of the crimes that the proposed court would have jurisdiction over. A 1997 Working Group of the PrepCom also 'discussed crimes involving illicit traffic in narcotic drugs

135 UN Doc A/CONR183/13 (Vol. II), United Nations Diplomatic Conference of Plenipotentiaries on the Establishment of an International Criminal Court Vol. II, Summary records of the plenary meetings and of the meetings of the Committee of the Whole, 40–42.

136 M. McConville, 'A global war on drugs: Why the United States should support the prosecution of drug traffickers in the International Criminal Court' (2000) 37 *American Criminal Law Review* 75, 92–93.

137 Philippe Kirsch & Valerie Oosterveld, 'Negotiating an Institution for the Twenty-First Century: Multilateral Diplomacy and the International Criminal Court' (2001) 46 *McGill Law Journal* 1141–1160.

and psychotropic substances without prejudice to a final decision on their inclusion in the Statute'.[138] At the start of the Rome Conference, drug trafficking was still included as one of the crimes to be prosecuted in the new court, but supporters of its inclusion could not garner sufficient support, leading to the expulsion of the crime from the final statute.[139] This suggests that prior to, and at the negotiations in Rome, there were voices that reflected regional concerns and that attempted to shift attention to crimes that were of particular concerns to certain regions. It is therefore surprising that there was no other discussion at the Rome Conference on how regional criminal mechanisms could address these crimes that were of concerns to specific regions, seeing that the proposed universal mechanism could not accommodate their prosecution.

In the light of this, there are at least three factors that may have accounted for the neglect of regionalism in ICL's development. This is in sharp contrast to development in the field of human rights, where regionalism has long been observed. Since at least the Cold War era, regional institutions have played some human rights protection roles in three regions – Europe, America and Africa.[140] What could be responsible, therefore, for the late interaction of ICL with regionalism?

3.1 ICL's Slow Pace of Development and Liberal Foundations

In comparison to human rights law and its institutions, international criminal law has developed more slowly and less dynamically.[141] As a product of the 20th century, it remains a body of law in the making.[142] It has not been stagnant, although its growth has been relatively slow. While many modern-day ICL norms developed well ahead of institutions that were subsequently created to enforce them, ICL had what has been termed 'conduct rules' and no

138 M. McConville, 'A global war on drugs: Why the United States should support the prosecution of drug traffickers in the International Criminal Court' (2000) 37 *American Criminal Law Review* 75, 92–93.

139 *Ibid*, 93.

140 On human rights protection roles played by regional institutions, see generally A. Huneeus & M.R. Madsen, 'Between universalism and regional law and politics: A comparative history of the American, European, and African human rights systems' (2018) 16 *International Journal of Constitutional Law* 1, 136–160.

141 See P. De Hert & ors (eds), 'Convergences and Divergences between International Human Rights, International Humanitarian and International Criminal Law' (Intersentia 2018).

142 C. Stahn, A Critical Introduction to International Criminal Law (Cambridge University Press 2019) 9.

corresponding 'enforcement rules'.[143] Other aspects and strands of public international law had developed and taken their place in legal science before WWII. The Tokyo and Nuremberg trials were the first actual international attempts at enforcing international criminal law. Since then, international criminal justice has continued to assert itself and acquire its identity. Some argue that it is neither completely international nor fully criminal.[144] It strives to exist as an independent body of criminal law rules, but 'its norms and its practitioners draw a deep intellectual inheritance from human rights and humanitarian law'.[145]

Not only was international criminal law slow in its development, but it could also be slow in dispensing justice.[146] The slow pace of development and justice dispensation has been attributed to the overall aims of international criminal justice, which are 'bringing perpetrators to justice and providing retribution for victims- or domestic-criminal-law-styled aims; creating a historical record of mass atrocities, and lastly, helping transitioning societies to achieve peace and reconciliation'.[147] These aims require different timelines for their achievement. The slow pace of ICL's development and current practice may, therefore, explain why it has taken a long time to embrace regionalism. It strives to construct a global order, with less attention on regional systems. Even when the Rome Statute was being negotiated and drafted, there was no experience of the *ad hoc* tribunals that the drafters could benefit from.

Additionally, ICL is based on a few liberal premises. Stahn identified 'juridification', 'criminalization' and 'individualization' as some of those premises that have been questioned.[148] ICL places the human person at its core and asserts that, irrespective of their criminal conducts, they possess basic procedural rights. It contends that international criminal justice ought to emphasize the fairness of the proceedings in any trial. ICL stresses rights to which a defendant is entitled. Article 67 of the Rome Statute consists of elaborate provisions concerning the rights of the accused. This is to prevent a harm of wrongly punishing an innocent person for a crime committed by another. It

---

143 B.V. Schaack & R. Slye, 'A Concise History of International Criminal Law' (2007) *Santa Clara Law Digital Commons*, 3.

144 C. Stephen, 'International Criminal Law: Wielding the Sword of International Criminal Justice' (2012) 61 *ICLQ* 55.

145 D. Robinson, 'Identity Crisis of International Criminal Law' (2008) *Leiden Journal of International Law* 21, 925–963 at 928.

146 J. Galbraith & ors, 'The Pace of International Criminal Justice' (2009) 31 *Michigan Journal of International Law* 1, 80.

147 *Ibid.*

148 C Stahn, 'A Critical Introduction to International Criminal Law' (Cambridge University Press 2019), 9.

holds its origin to the Blackstone formulation that 'it is better that ten guilty persons escape, than that the innocent suffers'.[149] While the purpose of international criminal law is to protect the society, it places restraints upon itself to achieve a just application of its rules to individuals.[150] The normative framework that underpins ICL is such that all its laudable objectives are 'constrained by basic procedural norms as well as consideration for the civil/human rights of the accused'.[151] This is distinguishable from a system which deals with individuals in any manner, so long as it achieves its aims.[152] An example of this in human rights law is situations where international human rights law is suspended for the greater good. International human rights treaties contain claw back clauses that allow suspension of its provisions under certain conditions that are provided by the same treaties. For example, in the African Charter on Human and Peoples' Rights, claw back clauses are built as restrictions to 'qualify rights and permit a state to restrict those rights to the maximum extent permitted by domestic law'.[153]

Given these differences in ICL and international human rights law, it is not surprising that ICL developed much more slowly and less dynamically than international human rights law. The late development also explains why international criminal justice embraced regionalism later than human rights law. The argument here does not detract from the counterview that some international criminal law systems, like the Nuremberg International Military Tribunal, preceded the advent of modern human rights law. It would appear, therefore, that ICL and IHRL developed according to their own distinct logic, given the rather different objectives and regulatory methods, particularly as they concern the challenges to state sovereignty.

3.2 Universality and Cosmopolitanism of International Criminal Law

International criminal law has long enjoyed a proclaimed universality. In this regard, it has tended to strive for universal systems, values, and institutions. Its

149 William Blackstone, *Commentaries on the Laws of England* (Clarendon Press 1765) 358. See also J. Keijser & ors, 'Wrongful convictions and the Blackstone ratio: An empirical analysis of public attitudes' (2014) 16 *Punishment and Society* 1, 32–49.

150 D. Robinson, 'Identity Crisis of International Criminal Law' *Leiden Journal of International Law*, 21 (2008), 928.

151 A Fichtelberg, 'Liberal Values in International Criminal Law: A Critique of Erdemović' (2008) 6 *Journal of International Criminal Justice* 1, p. 12.

152 D. Robinson, 'Identity Crisis of International Criminal Law' *Leiden Journal of International Law*, 21 (2008), 928.

153 S. Singh, 'The impact of claw back clauses on human and peoples' rights in Africa' (2009) 18 *African Security Studies* 4, 100.

obsession with universality can be seen from certain past events that are connected to its origin and continuous development. The Nuremberg and Tokyo Tribunals exemplified international justice's obsession with universality. The charges, proceedings and the enabling laws of these tribunals all espoused universality. The conception of 'crime against humanity', for example, reveals the tribunals' readiness to punish offences beyond territorial boundaries. Article 6(c) of the Nuremberg Charter defines 'crimes against humanity' as '...any crime within the jurisdiction of the Tribunal, whether or not in violation of the domestic law of the country where perpetrated'. That supranational posture has continued to underpin the values and direction of international law in general, and ICL in particular. This is reflective of Immanuel Kant's theory about universal law in the famous words: 'Act only according to that maxim by which you can at the same time will that it should become a universal law.'[154] For centuries, international law has been ambitiously concerned with universalism,[155] although critical approach to international law has attempted to refute that pretension.[156] There was a general sense that it was preferable to aim for universal institutions in order to avoid the fragmentation of international law.

In addition, cosmopolitanism has been one of the driving forces of international criminal justice.[157] It is the value that motivated rendering the crimes that the ICC would deal with as those 'that affect the international community as a whole' and 'are a threat to peace, to security and to the well-being of Humanity'. One piece of evidence of ICL's cosmopolitanism is its desire to apply 'universal principles of criminal law' and its pursuit of universal values.[158] According to McAuliffe, 'as an ideology, cosmopolitanism holds that all humans belong in the same, single, universal community based on a shared morality. The tenets of cosmopolitanism are individuality, universality, and generality. Individualism recognizes each human as an indispensable unit of concern. Universality holds that all humans have equal moral standing while

154 C.M. Korsgaard, 'Kant's formula of universal law' (1985) 66 *Pacific Philosophical Quarterly* 1–2 at p. 1.

155 See generally J. Klabbers, 'On Epistemic Universalism and the melancholy of International Law' (2019) 29 *European Journal of International Law* 4, 1057–1069.

156 *Ibid.*

157 On this, see generally F. Mégret, 'What Sort of Global Justice is International Criminal Justice?' (2015) 13 *JICJ* 77–96.

158 *Ibid*, 81.

generality presupposes that the fate of one individual should be a subject of concern for all.'[159]

McAuliffe states that there are two types of cosmopolitanism: moral and legal. Moral cosmopolitanism exemplifies the idea behind universality – the thinking that all humans operate under equal moral standards, irrespective of the national or ethnic divides. Legal cosmopolitanism on the other hand seeks 'to construct a global political order incorporating institutional schemes that will preserve and protect the rights of all human beings everywhere in the world'.[160]

Given ICL's obsession with universalism and cosmopolitanism, it is clear why the system continues to strive for institutions that advance universal ideals, without any thoughts towards regionalism. ICL's cosmopolitan posture may, therefore, have contributed to the delay in embracing regionalism. Regional systems are thought to further fragment the idea of a monolithic global structure that cosmopolitanism espouses.

Moreover, the Third World Approach to International Law (TWAIL) analytical method fundamentally opposes certain important questions of international law. By its tenets, TWAIL is 'anti-universalism', 'anti-hierarchical', 'counter-hegemonic' and 'suspicious of universal truths'.[161] For instance, TWAIL challenges the formal equality that embodies international law through its assumption that all states are equal before the law.[162] It counters the 'one size fits all' idea behind the enforcement of international law, contending that mainstream international law fails to take into cognizance the peculiarities of the history of colonialism and slavery, in its attempt to couch acceptable international law doctrines and standards that serve the purposes of all its adherents.[163]

Similar arguments can be made about the tension between regionalism and universalism. For one, concentrating all powers and options of pursuing international criminal justice in a universal entity like the ICC drives the narrative that such universal entities exist partly for the reason of subordinating weaker

159 P. McAuliffe, 'From Watchdog to Workhorse: Explaining the Emergence of the ICC's Burden-sharing Policy as an Example of Creeping Cosmopolitanism' (2014) 13 *Chinese Journal of International Law* 266–267. See also P. Hayden, 'Cosmopolitanism and the Need for Transnational Criminal Justice: The Case of the International Criminal Court' (2004) 104 *Theoria* 69–70.

160 *Ibid.*

161 M. Mutua, 'What is TWAIL?' (2000) 94 *Am Soc'y Int'l L Proc* 31.

162 J.D. Haskell, 'TRAIL-ing TWAIL: Arguments and Blind Spots in Third World Approaches to International Law' (2014) 27 *Canadian Journal of Law & Jurisprudence* 2, 389.

163 *Ibid.*

states and eroding such states' legitimacy.[164] As has been stressed, 'colonial practice pervades every aspect of the discipline of international law',[165] and the concentration of powers in a universal body undoubtedly perpetuates the narrative of Western powers dispensing justice to previously colonized territories.[166] These arguments are not without merits. The structural inequalities embedded in most weak, as well as third-world states, are often responsible for the conflicts that give rise to international crimes. International law and its universalism often prescribe uniform global standards that do not take into account national or regional peculiarities – such peculiarities that could make a regional body more fitting for responding to atrocity crimes within the region.[167] This is complicated by the understanding that the 'universal' doctrines of international law are not as universal and are clearly products of Western imperialism.[168] This is why Makau Mutua posited that international law 'is a predatory system that legitimises, reproduces, and sustains the plunder and subordination of the Third World by the West.'[169] As ICL therefore comes of age, it must wean itself off its universalist posture. More domestic and regional systems continue to engage with international law's structures, norms and institutions, and they deserve to be accommodated.

3.3 Perception of ICL as an Enemy of Sovereignty

International criminal justice has been viewed as an enemy of sovereignty.[170] This derives from the Westphalia model of international relations, to the effect that 'sovereign states acknowledge no equal at home, and no superior abroad'.[171] Sovereign states, therefore, expected to act within their spaces without interference from another sovereign – whether states or an external

164 O. Okafor, 'Is There a Legitimacy Deficit in International Legal Scholarship and Practice?' (1997) *International Insights* 13, 91–120; M. Mutua, 'What Is TWAIL?' (2004) *American Society of International Law Proceedings* 94, 31–40.

165 A. Anghie, 'The evolution of international law: colonial and postcolonial realities' (2006) 27 *Third World Quarterly* 5, 751.

166 J.D. Haskell, 'TRAIL-ing TWAIL: Arguments and Blind Spots in Third World Approaches to International Law' (2014) 27 *Canadian Journal of Law & Jurisprudence* 2, 389.

167 B. Chimni, 'Third World Approaches to International Law: A Manifesto' (2006) 8 *International Community Law Review* 3, 11.

168 Haskell (n. 166) 391.

169 M. Mutua, 'What is TWAIL' (2000) 94 *Am Soc'y Int'l L Proc* 31.

170 On this, see R. Cryer, 'International Criminal Law vs State Sovereignty: Another Round?' (2006) 16 *The European Journal of International Law* 5.

171 C. Brown, 'Sovereignty, Rights and Justice' (2002) *Polity Press*, 33.

tribunal.[172] The delay in the emergence of a single court is partly attributable to distrust from states who viewed a single international criminal court as one that undermines state sovereignty – the essence of disciplining and punishing power of state – and states were reluctant to give up this sovereignty. The idea of an international criminal court challenges states' monopoly to punish crimes committed within their territories.

Curiously, states did not view general regional court or regional human rights court with such scepticism. Studies have shown that states generally are more open to joining regional human rights institution, for different reasons.[173] This may explain why we have long had regional courts that dealt with human rights and economic subject-matters, and not international criminal law. For example, in the EU and the Americas, there were general regional courts, including one human rights court, but no regional criminal court.

The understanding that ICL is an enemy of sovereignty has, however, been challenged by other authors.[174] At the time states were pushing hard against ICL as a system that undermines sovereignty, dominant narratives on sovereignty 'became less absolutist and more human rights–friendly'.[175] This suggests that while ICL continued to be perceived as an enemy of sovereignty, the latter became less antagonistic to human rights. The result was that states concluded arrangements to establish regional human rights courts, while there was no agreement on regional criminal courts.

3.4 Regional *jus cogens*

Recent debates at the ILC signal some openness to the idea of regionalism in wider public international law – and the same reasoning may be applied to the concept in ICL. For example, the idea of regional peremptory norms of international law (regional *jus cogens*) has started gaining momentum.[176] While it

172 D. Partan & P. Rogic, 'Sovereignty and International Criminal Justice' (2003) *International Law: Revista Colombiana de Derecho Internacional* 1, 53–82.

173 For an example of such studies, see D. Hill, 'Why Governments Cede Sovereignty: Evidence from Regional Human Rights Courts' (2016) 14 *Foreign Policy Analysis* 3, 299–325.

174 See B. Broomhall, *International Justice and the International Criminal Court: Between Sovereignty and the Rule of Law* (Oxford University Press 2003).

175 J. Donnelly, 'State Sovereignty and International Human Rights' (2014) 28 *Ethics & International Affairs* 2, 225.

176 See generally R. Kolb, *Peremptory International Law (Jus Cogens): A General Inventory* (Oxford, Hart 2015); see also L. Carlos Lima & L. Marotti, 'An unlikely duo? Regionalism and jus cogens in international law' (2022) 12 *Goettingen Journal of International Law* 1, 219–239. A. Pellet, 'Comments in Response to Christine Chinkin and in Defense of Jus Cogens as the Best Bastion Against the Excesses of Fragmentation' in (2006) (XVII)

has been met with expected scepticism, it has not been totally discarded. It was recently amplified by the reports of the ILC Special rapporteur on *jus cogens*.[177]

On the face of it, an interaction between *jus cogens* and regionalism appears incompatible, as the basic definition of *jus cogens* is a norm that is 'widely accepted and recognised by the international community of States as a whole … from which no derogation is permitted'.[178] Given this definition that advances the universality of international law, it will appear that such peremptory norms do not accommodate regional perspectives. However, some scholars and delegates at the ILC hold a different view.

Professor Kolb argues that an agreement between two or more states that a rule is non-derogatory would qualify as peremptory norms between them.[179] One obvious implication of this is that the peremptory nature of *jus cogens* does not derive from the number of parties undertaking the agreement, but the non-derogatory nature of the agreement between them. While this interpretation appears inconsistent with the definition in article 53 of the VCLT, it suggests that a different approach could be adopted to interpret the concept of *jus cogens*. For example, many norms that are widely accepted by the generality of states do not necessarily constitute *jus cogens*, as an important part of the balance is the idea of non-derogation. As such, even if states generally accept a rule, without the other leg of non-derogation, it would still be acceptable to them – but will not be accepted as *jus cogens*. For instance, the diplomatic rule that allows states to establish embassies and consular representatives in other states is widely recognized and accepted, yet it is not considered non-derogatory, as states' ability to establish diplomatic premises in other states is hampered by several other factors, including economic and financial capacity. If, however, the states in a region, or indeed two or more states, elect to have an agreement on a norm that is acceptable to them and non-derogatory by them, this would possess all the qualities of *jus cogens*, albeit at a regional or bilateral level.

Professor Kolb's position had been earlier theorized by G. Gaja when he criticized the perceived restrictive provisions of the VCLT on peremptory norms.

Finnish Yearbook of International Law 89. See also M. Abdollahi and K. Behzadi, 'Regional Jus Cogens: Conceptual Difficulties and Practical Challenges' (2020) 3 *The Iranian Review for UN Studies (IRUNS)*, 33–74.

177 UN Doc A/CN.4/727. Fourth report on peremptory norms of general international law (jus cogens) by D. Tladi, Special Rapporteur and previous reports.

178 Article 53 of the VCLT.

179 R. Kolb, *Peremptory International Law – Jus Cogens: A General Inventory* (Oxford, Hart 2015), 97.

Accordingly, he submitted that 'no convincing reason has ever been given for ruling out the possibility of the existence of non-universal, or "regional" peremptory norms [particularly if those] values prevailing in regional groups do not necessarily conflict with values operating in a larger framework'.[180] An additional point is that regional necessities may have required the norms to attain a peremptory character in those specific regions.[181]

In the Inter-American system, the idea of a regional *jus cogens* has been met with a mixed and inconsistent reaction. As far back as 1987, the Inter-American Commission of Human Rights had held that 'in the member States (within the region), there is recognized a norm of *jus cogens* which prohibits the State execution of children'.[182] In a later case, the Commission submitted that this prohibition is a peremptory norm of general international law.[183] However, the ILC report, by the special rapporteur, concluded that 'the inter-American human rights system does not provide support for the notion of regional *jus cogens*'.[184] In the European regional system, authors like Prof. Erika De Wet have argued that obligations in the European Convention on Human Rights have arguably attained the status of regional *jus cogens*.[185]

The prohibition of genocide, crimes against humanity and war crimes, in addition to other elements and constituents of these crimes, are possible criminal norms to be covered under regional *jus cogens*. These norms are not only widely accepted but are also enshrined in regional treaties and declarations. For example, regional treaties from Africa and Latin America explicitly prohibit both genocide and crimes against humanity.

Whatever the merits or weaknesses of the debates on regional *jus cogens*, what is clear is that while majority of states seemed to have closed themselves to the idea, there is a growing number of scholars and practitioners who have started to tinker with the idea of regional *jus cogens*. While the analysis above suggests that there is a slow movement towards embracing the concept of regional *jus cogens*, there is a movement all the same, and it deserves some attention. It underscores the scepticism and limited openness to the idea of regionalism in public international law. The implication of this to the idea of regionalism in international criminal law is that while there has been limited

180 G. Gaja, 'Jus Cogens Beyond the Vienna Convention', 172 *Collected Courses of the Hague Academy of International Law* (1981), 284.

181 *Ibid.*

182 *Roach and Pinkerton v. United States*, IACHR Petition 12-439, No. 3/87.

183 *Michael Domingues v. United States,* Case No. 12.285.

184 ILC Fourth Report above, para. 40.

185 ILC Fourth Report above, para. 24.

interaction of regionalism in the realm of international criminal law, there appears to be some progress towards that trend.

4 Conclusion

In this historical account, I have explored the changing nature of states' approach to complementarity and have established that the concept of regional complementarity came late in the development of ICL. While complementarity continuously reshaped itself and evolved in different models, it has not interacted with regionalism until very recently. The first model, referred to as 'optional complementarity model', was based on states' agreement to voluntarily relinquish jurisdiction. The second model was the outcome of the Nuremberg Military Tribunal experience, which prioritizes division of labour between the national and international jurisdictions. The outcome of the last two models is the traditional idea of complementarity as seen in the Rome Statute. No significant discussions have taken place, nor have attempts been made to include regional institutions in the enforcement of international criminal law. This, in spite of the fact that, since the 1950s, regional institutions have been playing critical roles in the field of human rights. I explored the difference between human rights and ICL to explain ICL's late interaction with regionalism. I suggested three factors responsible for the neglect of regional complementarity in the history of ICL. I argue that international law's absolutist view of sovereignty, ICL's liberal foundation and slow development, as well as its obsession with universality and cosmopolitanism, are possible factors for ICL's late interaction with regionalism. My discussion on the concept of regional *jus cogens* also provided some context on international law's openness to the idea of regionalism in ICL. All these were to answer the question: why was regionalism neglected in the history and development of ICL and complementarity?

CHAPTER 2

Neglect of Regional Complementarity in the Jurisprudence and Practice of the ICC

1 Introduction

The establishment of the International Criminal Court (ICC) in 1998 represented a turning point in the development of international criminal law. It was conceived as the culmination of a century of efforts to institutionalize accountability for the most serious crimes under international law through a permanent and universal mechanism. At the heart of its framework lies the principle of complementarity, intended to preserve the primary responsibility of states to prosecute international crimes while ensuring that the Court intervenes only when national systems are unwilling or unable to act. Despite the centrality of this principle, the ICC's jurisprudence and institutional practice have revealed a striking neglect of one of its most significant dimensions: the potential role of regional institutions in complementing the Court's mandate.

This chapter explores how the ICC's approach to complementarity, both in its jurisprudence and in the policies of the Office of the Prosecutor (OTP), has remained heavily state-centred. The Court's interpretation of complementarity has focused almost exclusively on the relationship between the ICC and national jurisdictions, leaving little conceptual space for regional or hybrid institutions that could share in the administration of justice. Through an analysis of case law, procedural decisions, and policy documents, the discussion shows that the ICC's restrictive interpretation of complementarity has reinforced a centralized model of justice that fails to reflect the pluralist structure of international law. The Court's understanding of 'genuine proceedings' has been confined to national prosecutions and the work of the ICC itself, while overlooking the potential for regional or sub-regional judicial mechanisms to exercise legitimate criminal jurisdiction.

The absence of regional complementarity in ICC practice has broader implications for the international justice system. As regional institutions, such as the African Court of Justice and Human Rights and the Latin American initiatives, begin to assert jurisdiction over international crimes, the ICC's silence on regional cooperation risks perpetuating a hierarchical conception of justice rather than a collaborative one. By ignoring the contributions of regional systems, the Court limits the development of a decentralized and

© 2026 THE AUTHOR(S) | HTTPS://DOI.ORG/10.1163/9789004761803-004

cooperative framework that could make international criminal justice more responsive to localrealities and more legitimate in the eyes of affected communities. The neglect of regional mechanisms also reflects a deeper tension within the ICC's institutional identity, which often privileges universality and central authority over shared responsibility.

This chapter, therefore, situates the ICC's practice within a broader critique of institutional exclusivity. It considers how the Court's focus on national jurisdictions has constrained the emergence of a genuinely pluralist model of international criminal justice. The analysis proceeds in three parts. The first examines the Court's jurisprudence on complementarity and its evolution since the Rome Statute's entry into force. The second assesses the policy innovations of the Office of the Prosecutor, including burden sharing, positive complementarity, and self-referrals, and considers whether these innovations have expanded the meaning of complementarity beyond the national level. The final part explores the implications of the Court's approach for regional initiatives and argues that recognizing regional complementarity would not weaken but rather reinforce the integrity of the international justice system.

In essence, this chapter seeks to determine whether the ICC has advanced or constrained the ideals that underpin complementarity in its broader sense. It argues that the Court's current practice remains limited by a narrow understanding of the principle, which restricts cooperation to vertical relationships between the ICC and states rather than extending it horizontally to regional mechanisms. A recalibration of complementarity to include regional actors would strengthen both the legitimacy and the practical effectiveness of international criminal justice.

2 ICC Jurisprudence on Complementarity

From its earliest days, one of the biggest concerns of the ICC has been how it would manage the likely-contentious relationship between itself and national mechanisms that perform similar or overlapping roles of punishing international crimes. This much was revealed through the charged and contentious discussions at the Rome Conference, which led to the adoption of the Rome Statute. This concern was partly responsible for the detailed and long discussions on the complementarity provisions of the Rome Statute. At this early point in history, complementarity existed as a restrictive conception that exists to protect the sovereignty of states. This restrictive conception of complementarity has two sides to it: admissibility and the *ne bis in idem* principle. These two concepts jointly serve to implement the principle of complementarity. However, while the ICC has a developing jurisprudence on admissibility, it is yet to pronounce itself on *ne bis in idem*. I will therefore only focus on the ICC's developing jurisprudence on admissibility to trace how complementarity shifted from a restraining tool to a catalysing force.

Based on the language of article 17 of the Rome Statute, complementarity was meant to be a legal rule that organises the relationship between the ICC and national mechanisms. However, as practice began to evolve at the ICC, the need to clarify this, as well as other concepts, began to arise. This then gave rise to the notion of positive complementarity. What, however, led to this shift from complementarity as a restraining tool to a catalysing force? What roles did state, non-state actors and scholars play in the shift, and how have those roles heavily impacted our current understanding of the concept of complementarity? This section attempts to answer these questions. In so doing, it identifies the factors that have generally led to this shift, as well as the roles played by theorization and legal scholarship. I argue that the shift is evidence that ICL is alive, and it is a prototype and ground-breaking precedent for things to come: the notion of regional complementarity. I show that the latter understanding of complementarity as a catalysing force is more akin to the idea of regional complementarity that this work promotes.

2.1 Complementarity as a Restraining Tool in the Period before the Shift

The common understanding of the notion of positive complementarity as one that involves efforts to catalyse states to prosecute international crimes within their territories was not always so common, particularly in the early days after the coming into force of the Rome Statute.[1] This was a period when the new statute was experiencing its fair share of trials and errors in an attempt to put its provisions into practice. At this time, it was fairly expected that stakeholders would experience a measure of uncertainty in their efforts to operationalize the statute. These stakeholders consist of a fair blend of writers, theorists, activists, diplomats and civil society practitioners. They have played a lot of roles in the Court's work.[2] Their activities helped to shape the direction of the concept of complementarity during the early days of the Court. In drawing

1 C.M. De Vos, 'A Catalyst for Justice? The International Criminal Court in Uganda, Kenya, and the Democratic Republic of Congo' (2016) PhD Thesis, Leiden University, 33.

2 For the role that civil society has played in the Court's work generally, see, for example C. Bjork & J. Goebertus, 'Complementarity in Action: The Role of Civil Society and the ICC in Rule of Law Strengthening in Kenya' (2014) 14 *Yale Human Rights and Development Journal* 5.

attention to this period, Stahn observes that 'the "enabling" side of complementarity emerged only step-by-step'.[3] At this time, the traditional concept of complementarity was variously understood by states as useful for limiting the ICC's involvement in matters that should fall within the purview of states, and as a right to challenge the ICC's actions where the Court is perceived to have encroached on the sovereignty of states.[4] Thus, as far as states are concerned, the concept is a restraining tool, usable for limiting the powers of the ICC, with the resultant effect of preserving a state's sovereignty and powers to investigate and prosecute crimes within its jurisdiction. On its part, as noted by Stahn, the ICC viewed the concept as a tool to cover, mitigate or overcome its own weaknesses.[5] In this regard, it relied on states to enforce its decisions through promoting a regime of partnership and cooperation and promoted the idea as one to ensure that fewer cases proceed to the Court.[6]

Thus, whether as a restraining or a shielding tool, these traditional ideas of complementarity presented a limited understanding of the concept's inherent potential. This necessitated a need to strike a balance between the understanding that complementarity is both a restraining tool and a catalysing force. As it turned out, the balance was not sufficient to reflect the full potential of complementarity.

The drafting history of the Rome Statute reveals that this traditional understanding of complementarity informed all the discussions that led to the formal insertion of the concept into the Rome Statute. Discussions at the ILC, the UNGA through its Ad Hoc and Preparatory Committees, as well as discussions during the Rome Conference, sufficiently showed that the major concern was the need to limit the powers of the ICC to preserve state sovereignty.[7] It is therefore not surprising that, from its early days, many commentators referred to the Statute in a derogatory manner. For instance, a scholar had opined that the Statute is a document that 'pays too great a tribute to state sovereignty'.[8]

---

3 C. Stahn, 'Taking complementarity seriously: On the sense and sensibility of "classical", "positive" and "negative" complementarity' in C. Stahn & M. El Zeidy (eds) *The International Criminal Court and Complementarity: From Theory to Practice* (Cambridge University Press 2011) 234.

4 *Ibid.*

5 *Ibid.*

6 *Ibid.*

7 See Chapter 1 of this book.

8 F. Gioia, 'State Sovereignty, Jurisdiction, and "Modern" International Law: The Principle of Complementarity in the International Criminal Court', 19 *Leiden Journal of International Law* 4, 1096.

2.2 How the OTP Signals the Shift

Despite the balance and compromises reached at Rome, the adoption of the Rome Statute was heavily criticized.[9] In an attempt to mitigate this, the OTP began to articulate a more benign understanding of complementarity. As early as 2003, even when the work of the Court had yet to come into full gear, the OTP sensed the need to clarify many aspects of the Statute's complementarity provisions, which may pose a challenge to the work of the Court. Thus, it convened 'an expert consultation process on complementarity in practice for the benefit of the future Chief Prosecutor and the staff of his Office'.[10] The purpose was 'to prepare a reflection paper on the potential legal, policy and management challenges which are likely to confront the OTP as a consequence of the complementarity regime of the Statute'.[11] The outcome of this process was the 'Informal Expert Paper', which stressed that the success of the ICC would be seen from 'the establishment of an international order wherein national institutions respond effectively to international crimes, thereby obviating the need for trials before the ICC…'.[12] This approach to complementarity only served to expatiate the prosecutor's statement that 'as a consequence of complementarity, the number of cases that reach the Court should not be a measure of its efficiency. On the contrary, the absence of trials before this Court, because of the regular functioning of national institutions, would be a major success.'[13]

This approach to complementarity signified a shift from the earlier understanding that its purpose was to limit the powers of the ICC from descending into an arena meant for states. In the Informal Expert Paper, the need for cooperation and partnership between states and the ICC was stressed. The authors expressed hopes that the ICC's effectiveness can be seen through encouraging consistent and rigorous national proceedings. It hopes to achieve this not through prosecution by the Court, but instead, 'through encouragement and co-operation; the prospect of the ICC exercising jurisdiction; its own exemplary and standard-setting proceedings; and through ICC's moral

9 On the criticisms of the Rome Statute, see, for example, A. Teitelbaum, 'Statute of the International Criminal Court: A Critique' (1999) 26 *Social Justice* 107–114.

10 ICC-OTP, 'The principle of complementarity in practice' (2003).

11 *Ibid.*

12 ICC-OTP 'The principle of complementarity in practice' (2003) 3.

13 Statement by Mr. Luis Moreno-Ocampo at the Ceremony for the Solemn Undertaking of the Chief Prosecutor, 16 June 2003.

presence, which will shape perspectives and strengthen resolve on the need for accountability'.[14]

2.3 How the Chambers' Jurisprudence on Complementarity Restrains the Shift

While the OTP might have been the frontrunner in the race to signal a shift from restraint to cooperation, it was at the chambers that a firmer approach – which effectively balances the flexibility that the OTP's spearheaded-shift might have occasioned – was developed and communicated. In a few decisions, the earliest of which were between September 2008 and September 2009, the Court signalled the direction it wished to follow in relation to admissibility.

The early practice of the Court did not provide a deep understanding of the admissibility principle, nor did it give sufficient clarity for its application.[15] The Court's first opportunity to consider the issue of admissibility arose in 2005, where, as noted by Batros, the Court only stated that the case against the defendants 'appears to be admissible'.[16] In that case, admissibility was not addressed in detail by the Court.[17]

However, in the 2006 case of Thomas Lubanga Dyilo[18] and Bosco Ntaganda[19] in the *Situation in the Democratic Republic of the Congo (DRC)*, the Court delved into a greater analysis of the admissibility question. In this case, Pre-Trial Chamber I considered that the admissibility test was an integral prerequisite for an arrest warrant. The Court then ruled that the admissibility test has two parts. In its words, PTC I observed that:

> The Chamber considers that the admissibility test of a case arising from the investigation of a situation has two parts. The first part of the test relates to national investigations, prosecutions and trials concerning the case at hand insofar as such case would be admissible only if those States with jurisdiction

14 ICC-OTP, 'The principle of complementarity in practice' (2003), 4–5.

15 M. Konfort & M. Vajda, 'The Principle of Complementarity in the Jurisprudence of the ICC' (2014) 3 *ZPR* 1, 9–27, at 10.

16 *Prosecutor v. Kony et al.*, ICC-02/04-01/05-1-US-Exp, 12 July 2005, 2 (unsealed pursuant to ICC-02/04-01/05-52, 13 October 2005).

17 Ben Batros 'The evolution of the ICC jurisprudence on admissibility' in C. Stahn & M. El Zeidy (eds) *The International Criminal Court and Complementarity: From Theory to Practice* (Cambridge University Press 2011) at 560.

18 *Prosecutor v. Lubanga*, ICC-01/04-01/06-8-Corr (reclassified as public pursuant to ICC01/04-01/06-37), 9 March 2006, para. 33 ('Lubanga Arrest Warrant Decision').

19 *Prosecutor v. Ntaganda*, ICC-01/04-02/06-20-Anx2, 21 July 2008.

> over it have remained inactive in relation to that case, or are unwilling or unable, within the meaning of article 17(1)(a) to (c), 2 and 3 of the Statute. The second part of the test refers to the gravity threshold which any case must meet to be admissible before the Court. Accordingly, the Chamber will treat them separately.[20]

In the end, PTC I ruled that the case against both suspects is admissible under the first part, as the conducts the ICC sought to try are different from the conducts tried in the national proceedings (the same person/same conduct test).[21] On the second part of the test, while the Court found that the case against Lubanga was of sufficient gravity, it found otherwise for Ntaganda.[22] This 'two steps test' approach to admissibility has been the subject of multiple scholarly analyses[23] and was further solidified by the Appeals Chamber decision in the Gbagbo case.[24]

It was not until 2009, in the case of *Prosecutor v. Katanga and Ngudjolo,* that the ICC experienced its first admissibility challenge by an accused person.[25] Katanga argued against the application of the same conduct test to his case. He also contended that, even if the Court was to apply the same conduct test, the government of the DRC was already investigating him for the same conduct that the ICC was trying. In the end, both the Trial Chamber and the Appeals Chamber dismissed Katanga's challenge and held that the case against him was admissible.[26] The Katanga admissibility challenge was quickly and closely followed by the Bemba admissibility challenge, which was decided in the same

---

20 Situation in the Democratic Republic of the Congo, Decision on the Prosecutor's Application for Warrants of Arrest, Article 58. ICC-01/04-02/06-20-Anx2 21-07-2008 3/69 SL PT, at para. 29.

21 On this, see R. Rastan, 'What is "Substantially the Same Conduct"?: Unpacking the ICC's "First Limb" Complementarity Jurisprudence' (2017) 15 *Journal of International Criminal Justice* 1, 1–29, particularly at 2, where the author summarizes the bulk of existing literature as suggesting that 'the "same person/same conduct" test is too narrow, that it subverts the meaning of Article 17 ICC Statute, including its object and purpose, and that the "substantially the same conduct" variant has confused the test further.'

22 Batros (n. 17), 561.

23 See for example, T. Hamilton, 'Case Admissibility at the International Criminal Court' in (2015) 14 *The Law & Practice of International Courts and Tribunals* 2, 305–317.

24 Appeals Chamber, 27 May 2015, icc-02/11-01/12-75-Red ('*Simone Gbagbo* Judgment').

25 *Prosecutor v. Katanga and Ngudjolo*, ICC-01/04-01/07-949, of 11 March 2009 ('Katanga Admissibility Challenge').

26 See *Prosecutor v. Katanga and Ngudjolo*, ICC-01/04–01/07-T-67-ENG ET, 12 June 2009 and *Prosecutor v. Katanga and Ngudjolo,* ICC-01/04–01/07–1497, 25 September 2009.

manner as the Katanga admissibility challenge. The Chamber decided that the 'challenge is without foundation'.[27]

Several 'settled laws' have emerged from the Appeal Chamber's Katanga admissibility decision. For one, it is now clear that the Chambers entertaining an admissibility challenge must first consider the questions as to whether the national authorities are investigating or prosecuting, or, in the alternative, have investigated and decided not to prosecute the alleged crimes. The words employed by the Chambers were quite clear to this effect:

> Therefore, in considering whether a case is inadmissible under article 17(1) (a) and (b) of the Statute, the initial questions to ask are (1) whether there are ongoing investigations or prosecutions, or (2) whether there have been investigations in the past, and the State having jurisdiction has decided not to prosecute the person concerned. It is only when the answers to these questions are in the affirmative that one has to look to the second halves of sub-paragraphs (a) and (b) and to examine the question of unwillingness and inability. To do otherwise would be to put the cart before the horse. It follows that in case of inaction, the question of unwillingness or inability does not arise; inaction on the part of a State having jurisdiction (that is, the fact that a State is not investigating or prosecuting, or has not done so) renders a case admissible before the Court, subject to article 17(1)(d) of the Statute.[28]

In essence, it is now settled that the 'same conduct test' is what must be carried out first, before the test on unwillingness and inability, and the latter analysis is unnecessary where the previous test has failed. But, despite this settled aspect, other grey areas remain. For example, as expressed by Ben Batros,

> The Appeals Chamber in Katanga thus clarified one element of the test for admissibility under Article 17(1)(a) and (b) – the primary role of the activity, or inactivity, of the state. However, it expressly declined to rule or provide guidance on another critical aspect: inactivity with respect to what? Article 17 (1)(a) and (b) state that a case will be inadmissible where 'the case is being investigated or prosecuted', or 'the case has been investigated' (emphasis

27 Situation in the Central African Republic in the Case of *The Prosecutor V. Jean-Pierre Bemba Gombo*: Decision on the Admissibility and Abuse of Process Challenges.

28 ICC-01/04-01/07 OA 8. *Situation in The Democratic Republic of The Congo: The Prosecutor V. Germain Katanga and Mathieu Ngudjolo Chui.* Judgment on the Appeal of Mr. Germain Katanga against the Oral Decision of Trial Chamber II of 12 June 2009 on the Admissibility of the Case, para. 78.

> added). But what constitutes 'the case' for the purpose of admissibility under these provisions?[29]

Not only do these grey areas remain, but what was earlier thought to be settled was shown to be otherwise. In the *Gaddafi case*,[30] the same conduct test was not satisfied, and at that point, the Libyan challenge to admissibility ought to have failed. Yet, the PTC still turned to address inability, in a move that clearly departed from the Appeal Chamber's position.[31] Perhaps the PTC's intention was to give a stronger basis for its decision, but it unsettled an otherwise 'thought to be settled' position of the law. Additionally, the admissibility challenge against the second defendant, Abdullah al-Senussi, was allowed.[32] The Al-Senussi's case was hailed as pushing the Chambers' jurisprudence towards positive complementarity.[33] It was one case where the Chambers upheld a defendant's admissibility challenge. The Chambers, through the decisions earlier discussed, have always been cautious to entertain an expansive interpretation of the complementarity clause. In the present case, however, the PTC and the Appeal Chambers' decisions granted an expansive interpretation of the admissibility provisions of the Statute.[34]

In a 2011 decision, the ICC Appeals Chambers rejected Kenya's admissibility challenge, which was brought pursuant to Article 19(2)b of the Rome Statute. It was the first time that a state asserted that the ICC had no jurisdiction because the state was investigating the alleged crimes.[35] On an analysis that compares Kenya's argument with that of the Appeals Chambers, Jalloh submitted that:

29 Batros (n. 17) 571.

30 ICC-01/11-01/11 *The Prosecutor V. Saif Al-Islam Gaddafi and Abdullah Al-Senussi.* Decision on the admissibility of the case against Saif Al-Islam Gaddafi.

31 M. Tedeschini, 'Complementarity in Practice: the ICC's Inconsistent Approach in the Gaddafi and Al-Senussi Admissibility Decisions' (2015) 7 *Amsterdam Law Forum* 1.

32 ICC-01/11-01/11. *In The Case of The Prosecutor V. Saifal-Islam Gaddafi and Abdullah Al-Senussi.* Decision on the admissibility of the case against Abdullah Al-Senussi dated 11 October 2013.

33 Y. Rees, Towards Positive Complementarity', *PhD Studies in Human Rights Blogpost,* 26 July 2014 [available at https://humanrightsdoctorate.blogspot.com/2014/07/towards-positive-complementarity.html – accessed 6 February 2024].

34 See ICC-OI/II-OI/IIOA6. *In The Case of The Prosecutor V. Saif Al-Islam Gaddafi and Abdullah Al-Senussi.* Judgment on the appeal of Mr. Abdullah Al-Senussi against the decision of Pre-Trial Chamber I of 11 October 2013 entitled 'Decision on the Admissibility of the Case against Abdullah Al-Senussi' dated 24 July 2014.

35 C. Jalloh, 'Kenya vs. The ICC Prosecutor' (2009) 53 *Harvard International Law Journal Online* 270.

> The Kenya conception finds support in the Rome Statute and in the drafting history of the complementarity provision during the Rome Conference, as well as the preparatory committees, where the preservation of national sovereignty was a primary goal. The Court's conception appears to rest primarily on a broader, more interventionist and perhaps unrealistic vision of the ICC.[36]

The Chamber's strict interpretation appears to have turned complementarity into primacy.[37] The Court continues to interpret and apply the admissibility provisions of the Statute in a way that discourages states from prosecuting international crimes in their own territories.[38] An analysis of the information provided by the Kenyan government to support its position suggests that there was no investigatory inaction.[39] The dissenting opinion found that the Court 'did not give sufficient weight to the sovereign rights of Kenya in balancing the interests at stake'.[40]

The much-criticized admissibility jurisprudence of the Court[41] is propelled by cosmopolitanism. One of the strands of cosmopolitanism is the assumption that national mechanisms are incapable of carrying out investigation and prosecution that meets the standard provided by the Statute. This assumption goes against the fundamental intent of states when the Rome Statute was agreed upon by states. This also lends credence to my submission that it appears that the ICC, while holding itself out as a Court that wants states to prosecute international crimes occurring in their own territories, its jurisprudence suggests otherwise. This is also a pointer to the Court's likely approach towards the idea of regional complementarity.

The OTP articulates complementarity as a positive tool for the advancement of cooperation between states and the Court. The Chambers, however, have consistently interpreted it as a tool for restraining states in exercising their investigative or prosecutorial powers. The role of the Chambers in this regard has been tailored towards checking the tendency of states to interpret

36 *Ibid*, 277.

37 *Ibid*, 276.

38 See generally K. Jon Heller, 'A Sentence-Based Theory of Complementarity' (2012) 53 *Harvard International Law Journal* 1.

39 T. Obel Hansen, 'A Critical Review of the ICC's Recent Practice Concerning Admissibility Challenges and Complementarity' (2013) 13 *Melbourne Journal of International Law*, 16.

40 ICC Doc ICC-01/09-01/11 OA 'Judgment on the appeal of the Republic of Kenya against the decision of Pre-Trial Chamber II of 30 May 2011 entitled 'Decision on the Application by the Government of Kenya Challenging the Admissibility of the Case Pursuant to Article 19(2)(b) of the Statute' Dissenting Opinion of Judge Anita Ušacka, para. 28.

41 See, for example, P. Clark, *Distant Justice: The Impact of the International Criminal Court on African Politics* (Cambridge University Press 2018).

the positive complementarity notion from the OTP as a liberty to conduct non-genuine investigation or prosecution. The Chambers decisions on admissibility continue to cast the Court as one monolithic universal organization. What the Chambers pronounce, irrespective of the articulation by other organs of the Court, is the jurisprudence of the Court. According to Holmes, '[t]he prophecies of what the courts will do in fact, and nothing more pretentious, are what I mean by the law.'[42] It is therefore proposed that the Chambers need to align itself with the OTP's articulation of complementarity in order to be able to give more roles to states and regions in the investigation and prosecution of crimes.

3 ICC's Extension of Judicial Constructs and Jurisdictional Overreach

Its jurisprudence aside, the practice at the ICC, including its policy directions, may also suggest that the Court may be reserved towards the idea of regional complementarity. The way the Court has extended judicial constructs, its move towards interventionism and how it has translated itself to a workhorse from the initial conception of the Court as a watch dog,[43] all suggest that the Court may not be exactly open to the idea of giving states and regions more roles in the investigation and prosecution of international crimes in their territories.

Article 1 of the Rome Statute is clear that the ICC 'shall be complementary to national criminal jurisdictions'. The ICC was never intended to be the primary forum for the prosecution of international crimes. It is only in exceptional cases, where certain conditions are met, that the ICC ought to have jurisdiction over international crimes. The conditions were meant to guard against the ICC's arbitrary extension of its powers.[44] However, practices in the Court suggest that the ICC has been extending its powers by a mix of judicial activism and the extension of judicial constructs. It has gradually

42 O.W. Holmes, Jr., 'The Path of the Law', (1987) 10 *Harvard Law Review* 457, 460–461.

43 P. McAuliffe, 'From Watchdog to Workhorse: Explaining the Emergence of the ICC's Burden-sharing Policy as an Example of Creeping Cosmopolitanism' (2014) 13 *Chinese Journal of International Law* 294–295.

44 M. Newton, 'The Quest for Constructive Complementarity' in Stahn & El Zeidy (eds) *The International Criminal Court and Complementarity: From Theory to Practice* (Cambridge University Press 2011) 304.

become a Court that prioritizes interventionism to judicial restraint.[45] Two examples will suffice.

In the Lubanga case, the Chamber's decision as it relates to the commission of crime and command responsibility was criticized by scholars,[46] defence lawyers[47] as well as ICC judges who gave dissenting opinions.[48] The criticisms are to the effect that the Chamber was reluctant to apply the principle of command responsibility. Instead, the Court invented a new theory of individual responsibility by holding commanders and their subordinates as co-perpetrators.[49] The Appeals Chambers of the ICTY, in a different case, had declared that co-perpetratorship is alien to the settled jurisprudence of the Tribunal.[50] The Chamber declared that 'this mode of liability, as defined and applied by the Trial Chamber, does not have support in customary international law, or in the settled jurisprudence of this Tribunal, which is binding on the Trial Chambers'.[51] This example suggests that the Court's practice in this case, as in others, does not bode well for the idea of regional complementarity.

In another example, ICC's 'Decision Pursuant to Article 15 on the Authorization of an Investigation into the Situation in the Republic of Kenya'[52] has been criticized as lowering the threshold of crimes against humanity.[53] The decision appeared to have muddled up the distinction between 'crimes against

45 See generally Ignaz Stegmiller, 'Positive Complementarity and Legitimacy – Is the International Criminal Court Shifting from Judicial Restraint Towards Interventionism?' in N. Hayashi & C. Bailliet (eds) *The Legitimacy of International Criminal Tribunals* (Cambridge University Press 2017).

46 *Ibid*, 309–310. Newton calls the decision 'an erosion of the law of command responsibility'. See also A. Appazov, '"Judicial Activism" and the International Criminal Court' (2015) 17 *iCourts Working Paper Series*, 11–12.

47 Defence lawyers argued that the decision went 'beyond the clear terms of the Statute and was not supported by customary international law'. Lubanga (ICC-01/04-01/06-803-tEN), Decision on the Confirmation of Charges, 29 January 2007, para. 330.

48 Both Judges Adrian Fulford and Christine van den Wyngaert gave dissenting opinions, although Judge Van den Wyngaert's opinion was given in a different case before the Court. See Judge Van den Wyngaert's opinion in Ngudjolo Chui (ICC-01/04-02/12-4), Judgment Pursuant to Article 74 of the Statute, 18 December 2012.

49 Newton, (n. 44) 311.

50 Prosecutor v. Milomir Stakic, Case No. IT-97–24-A, Judgment, 22 March 2006, para. 62.

51 *Ibid.*

52 Situation in the Republic of Kenya, Case No. ICC-01/09, Decision Pursuant to Article 15 on the Authorization of an Investigation into the Situation in the Republic of Kenya (31 March 2010).

53 A. Appazov, '"Judicial Activism" and the International Criminal Court' (2015) 17 *iCourts Working Paper Series*, p. 15.

humanity, as a category of international crimes, and serious national crimes'.[54] The effect of the decision is that it expanded the scope of the crimes that the ICC could deal with to include those that states should prosecute. Judge Hans-Peter Kaul, in his dissenting opinion, stated that 'The qualitative requirement of "State or organizational policy" in article 7(2)(a) of the Statute distinguishes crimes against humanity from other common crimes which are to be prosecuted at the national level only.'[55] He goes further to warn against a broad interpretation of 'article 7(2)(a) of the Statute infinitely beyond its conceptual confines'.[56]

Surprisingly, in these two decisions, there was no lacuna or ambiguity in the law. The positions of the law on the two issues are supposedly clear. Yet, the Chambers found a need to 'artificially inject its own view of the law rather than sustain strict fidelity to the intent of state parties'[57] as expressed in the Rome Statute. Even if there were lacunae or ambiguity in the law, opinions are divided on whether international criminal judges should fill those lacunae in their interpretation and application of the law. There are those who argue that it is not judges' duty to fill those lacunae.[58] There are others who believe judges should do so.[59] I would support the view that judges should fill lacunae in the law, wherever it is appropriate. However, this should not be interpreted as freedom to introduce their own views into the law, especially where what they introduce goes against settled principles of law, as in the command responsibility case earlier discussed, or where it stands settled law on its head. In filling lacunae, judges should also refrain from an interpretation that goes against the intents of the drafters of the law. This is what is wrong with judicial activism and ICC judges' extension of judicial construct. This is also as judicial activism, in this case, portends the Court as a mechanism that is not open to the idea of regional complementarity.

There are arguments that support the introduction of judicial activism into international criminal justice. First, that ICL supports and complements

54 *Ibid.*

55 Situation in the Republic of Kenya, Case No. ICC-01/09, Decision Pursuant to Article 15 on the Authorization of an Investigation into the Situation in the Republic of Kenya, Dissenting Opinion of Judge Hans-Peter Kaul, para. 54 (31 March 2010).

56 *Ibid*, para. 55.

57 Newton (n. 44) 311.

58 See D. Jacobs, 'International Criminal Law', in J. Kammerhofer and J. D'Aspremont, *International Legal Positivism in a Post-Modern World* (Cambridge University Press 2014) 473.

59 See, for example, G. Maučec, 'The International Criminal Court and the Issue of Intersectionality – A Conceptual and Legal Framework for Analysis' (2021) *International Criminal Law Review*, p. 32.

national jurisdictions suggest that it may need to improvise in order to surmount different legal, practical and logistic hurdles, hence the need for activism or the progressive development of law.[60] Second, ICL is an emerging body of law – unclear and incomplete, thus necessitating 'judicial creativity'.[61] Third, ICL's interaction with various national mechanisms and systems sometimes requires broad interpretations that accommodate jettisoning judicial restraint. Fourth, certain provisions in the statute are left to the discretion and progressive interpretation of the judges. The Rome Statute has a few lacunas that were left by the drafters to be filled by the creative interpretation of the judges.[62] Lastly, some of the more regular subjects of ICL are senior political and military leaders, including leaders of armed groups, issues arising from trials are often complex and require activism to address them.[63]

My position is that judicial activism ought to be embraced, in principle. In fact, without activism, ICL may not have developed to the point it is today. The establishment and practice at the Nuremberg, Tokyo and the UN *ad hoc* Tribunals were steeped in activism.[64] However, the problem with judicial activism, as has been seen in the ICC context, is that it opens judges to the possibility of substituting the law with their personal opinions. It also increases the risk of suspending settled principles of law. Recent example of judicial activism by the Chambers has been described as 'an unreasonable encroachment on the OTP's discretion'.[65] Where judicial activism has had the effect of extending the Chambers' powers beyond the intent of states and the drafters of its statutes, it may reveal an institution that is more concerned with protecting and extending its powers without giving states sufficient room to function. This does not bode well for the idea of regional complementarity. The ICC must show itself as a Court of last resort that it was established to be. It must give room for states acting singly or jointly, where possible, to investigate and prosecute, without arrogating those powers to itself.

60 S. Zappalà, *Judicial Activism v. Judicial Restraint in International Criminal Justice* (The Oxford Companion to International Criminal Justice 2009) 4.

61 See generally S. Darcy & J. Powderly, *Judicial Creativity at the International Criminal Tribunals* (Oxford University Press 2009).

62 See M. Delmas-Marty, 'Ambiguities and Lacunae: The International Criminal Court Ten Years On' (2013) 11 *JICJ* 3, 553.

63 Zappalà, (n. 60) 5.

64 *Ibid.*

65 See L.P. Rossetti, 'The Pre-Trial Chamber's Afghanistan Decision: A Step Too Far in the Judicial Review of Prosecutorial Discretion?' (2019) 17 *JICJ*, 586.

4 Burden Sharing and Self-Referral as OTP Policies

Flowing from the idea that the ICC was never intended to be the primary Court for prosecuting international crimes is the understanding that states are expected to be monitored and supported by the ICC in the performance of this duty. However, it appears that the ICC has gradually rejected a monitoring role for active involvement in crimes investigation and prosecution. Two examples of this in the Court's policy direction are the adoption of 'burden-sharing' as a strategy and the commitment to the policy of 'self-referral'. In a 2003 report to the ASP, the Prosecutor introduced the ideas of burden-sharing and self-referral when he stated that his office's 'role could be facilitated by a referral or active support from [a state]. The Court and the territorial State may agree that a consensual division of labour could be an effective approach.'[66] I do not necessarily oppose self-referral and burden-sharing as international criminal law strategies. It is the idea that the ICC actively solicits cases by encouraging states to commit to these strategies that negates the intent underlying the Rome Statute. These policies suggest that the ICC may not be open to the idea of regional complementarity. It reveals a Court that wants to take on more roles while reserving lesser roles for states or a conglomeration of states acting under a regional arrangement.

Recent examples of collective referrals of situations to the ICC by groups of states appear to support the notion that states can collectively take an action that each of them, acting independently, can undertake – which is one of the strands of regional complementarity. For instance, 43 states had jointly referred the Ukrainian situation to the Chief Prosecutor of the ICC.[67] Also, in 2018, a group of states referred the Venezuelan situation to the ICC.[68] Suffice it to say that the idea that states can collectively refer a situation to the ICC mirrors the idea that such roles should be undertaken by states acting collectively, particularly when they act as a regional group, either to prosecute using their own mechanism or to 'outsource' that duty to another mechanism.

---

66 ICC Doc: ICC Second Assembly of States Parties to the Rome Statute of the International Criminal Court, Report of the Prosecutor of the ICC, Mr. Luis Moreno-Ocampo, 8 September 2003.

67 ICC 'Situation in Ukraine' [available at https://www.icc-cpi.int/situations/ukraine – accessed 7 February 2024].

68 ICC 'Situation in the Bolivarian Republic of Venezuela' [available at https://www.icc-cpi.int/venezuela-i – accessed 7 May 2022].

4.1 Burden-Sharing

The OTP summarizes its position on burden-sharing as follows:

> The Office will function with a two-tiered approach to combat impunity. On the one hand it will initiate prosecutions of the leaders who bear most responsibility for the crimes. On the other hand, it will encourage national prosecutions, where possible, for the lower-ranking perpetrators, or work with the international community to ensure that the offenders are brought to justice by some other means.[69]

Burden-sharing was not mentioned in the Rome Statute and was not considered at the Rome Conference. It was a creation of the OTP. It emerged partly because of early self-referrals by African states. The OTP consciously turned it to a policy to further the Court's cosmopolitan status. As a policy of the Court, the OTP concludes a Memorandum of Understanding on Burden-Sharing with states.[70] Aside from the need to remain relevant and busy, the OTP conceives of burden-sharing as a policy because of its belief that the ICC is a better forum for prosecuting serious international crimes.[71] The import of this for regional complementarity is that the Court continues to see itself as the primary avenue for international criminal trials. The ICC will not give sufficient room to states, even if they are acting jointly, under a regional arrangement. The Court will continue to contest the realm of international criminal justice with States whose primary function it is to prosecute international crimes. The burden-sharing policy, just like its subset policy of self-referral, continues to show the Court as a cosmopolitan project that consistently strives for cosmopolitan ideals. These ideals oppose the tenets of regional complementarity.

---

69 ICC-OTP 'Paper on some policy issues before the Office of the Prosecutor' (2003).

70 For example, see ICC Doc: ICC-01/11-01/11, Public Redacted Version of 'Request for Disclosure of Memorandum on Burden Sharing between the ICC Office of the Prosecutor and the Government of Libya'.

71 P. McAuliffe, 'From Watchdog to Workhorse: Explaining the Emergence of the ICC's Burden-sharing Policy as an Example of Creeping Cosmopolitanism' (2014) 13 *Chinese Journal of International Law* 294–295.

4.2 Self-Referral

The policy of self-referrals has been strongly promoted by the ICC and easily accepted by states.[72] In its 'Report on the activities performed during the first three years', the OTP stated that 'the Prosecutor adopted the policy of inviting and welcoming voluntary referrals by territorial states as a first step in triggering the jurisdiction of the Court.'[73] Article 14 of the Rome Statute stipulates self-referral. Scholars have argued that what was contemplated by the drafters of the Rome Statute is state-to-state referral, and not a situation where a state refers a situation in its own territory to the ICC.[74] The idea of state-by-state referral is what is currently playing out, where more than forty state parties have referred the situation in Ukraine to the ICC.[75] The validity of the argument on state-by-state referral is premised on the fact that the two other referral systems in the Rome Statute are that of the Security Council and the *proprio motu* referral by the Prosecutor. These two appear to have been put in place to fill the gap where states fail to refer other states to the Court.[76] It is also questionable if the drafters of the Rome Statute imagined a situation where a state would refer itself to the new Court. Not even with the strenuous debates that attended the thinking that the new court would compromise state sovereignty. Moreover, the Statute does not mention the possibility of the OTP or the Court fashioning self-referral as a proactive tool through a policy direction of the Court. Schabas had argued that self-referral was the creation of the OTP and not a result of any creative interpretation of the Statute.[77] He also contended that nowhere in the discussions leading to the adoption of the Statute at Rome was it contemplated as a strategy for the new Court.[78] There are other scholars who also question the idea of actively seek-

---

72 A. Mueller & I. Stegmiller, 'Self-Referrals on Trial: From Panacea to Patient' (2010) 8 *JICJ* 1293.

73 ICC-OTP 'Report on the activities performed during the first three years (June 2003 – June 2006)'.

74 See, for example, P. Kirsch & D. Robinson, 'Initiation of Proceedings by the Prosecutor' in A. Cassese, P. Gaeta and J.R.W.D. Jones (eds) *The Rome Statute of the International Criminal Court: A Commentary* Vol. 1 (Oxford University Press 2002) 622–623.

75 Situation in Ukraine (n. 67).

76 Cassese and others (n. 74).

77 W. Schabas, *The International Criminal Court: A Commentary on the Rome Statute* (Oxford University Press 2010) 309.

78 W. Schabas, 'Prosecutorial Discretion v. Judicial Activism at the International Criminal Court' (2009) 6 *JICJ*, 751.

ing self-referrals from states by the OTP.[79] For all of its merits, self-referral has its inherent demerits. One of them is the possibility of states employing it as a tool to abdicate responsibility and dump cases on the ICC.[80] Secondly, states have used this to refer cases of their political opponents, thus using the ICC to score political points against opponents.[81] How then, can national mechanisms develop if the ICC gives them a leeway to escape from their responsibility? It is even more worrisome that the OTP encourages self-referral as a policy, considering that it can be abused in a manner that fundamentally flaws the complementarity provisions of the Rome Statute. Self-referral and the ideas underpinning positive complementarity appear to be contradictory. It is irreconcilable to argue, on the one hand, that states be encouraged to take the duty of prosecuting international crimes seriously, while at the other end, encouraging the same states to refer cases to the ICC. A Court that preaches the gospel of self-referral appears as one that goes cap in hand to solicit and beg for cases from states, often catalysing them to self-refer, instead of seeking to help them develop their capacity for handling international crimes in their territories. This is a Court in search of relevance, and that relevance extends to erroneously contesting the space with states, whether acting singly, bilaterally or jointly in the prosecution of crimes within their territory.

The Chamber also appeared to have endorsed self-referral. For example, in its reaction to the challenge against self-referral in the Katanga Appeal, the Chamber ruled that it was not convinced by the Appellant's argument that states relinquishing their jurisdiction in favour of the ICC negates the Rome Statute.[82] The Chamber concluded that it 'may decide not to act upon a State's relinquishment of jurisdiction in favor of the Court'.[83] Here, the Chamber not only approved of such relinquishment, it also leaves the ICC with the sole choice of which cases to pick and those to discard, as if the ICC is the primary jurisdiction for international crimes prosecution.

Some of the earlier practical justifications for self-referral appear to be the need for the Court, as an emerging institution, to build its case load and justify

---

79 See, for example, K. Ambos, *Treatise on International Criminal Law – Volume III: International Criminal Procedure* (Oxford University Press 2016) 257.

80 D. Robinson, 'The Rome Statute and Its Impact on National Law' in A. Cassese & others (eds) *The Rome Statute of the International Criminal Court: A Commentary* (Oxford University Press 2002) 5.

81 S. Nouwen & W. Werner, 'Doing Justice to the Political: The International Criminal Court in Uganda and Sudan' (2011) 21 *European Journal of International Law* 4, 941–965.

82 *Prosecutor v. Katanga & Chui*, Case No. ICC-01/04-01/07OA 8, Judgment on the Appeal of Mr. Germain Katanga against the Oral Decision of Trial Chamber II of 12 June 2009 on the Admissibility of the Case, para. 85.

83 *Ibid.*

its existence;[84] the need to start an investigation promptly without a need for a PTC 1 authorization and the effectiveness of the OTP's work if its work in a particular state are supported by that state.[85] However, these justifications cannot continue to avail this practice as the Court continues to develop. The Court can no longer be referred to as a baby in the international legal space, having survived for more than two decades.

A preferable approach, therefore, is for the Court to reluctantly accept self-referral. Accepting self-referral must be based on strict conditions that do not leave room for states to deliberately dump cases on the Court. This can be done by avoiding open-ended referrals or as part of a completion strategy. This then poses the question: to what extent should the OTP have room to 'negotiate' the terms of referrals? The Court must realize that one of its key duties is to encourage states to fulfil their duty of international crimes investigation and prosecution. That duty was not imposed on states by the Rome Statute. States inherently possess the power to punish offenders in their own territories, in line with national and international standards. However, states have a duty to cooperate, imposed upon them by the Rome Statute. Without this cooperation, the ICC may not be able to function. For example, the ICC has no police of its own, and as such cannot effect the arrest of defendants without support from states. This is where it becomes necessary to contend that the goal of the ICC should relate more to encouraging and empowering states to prosecute crimes in their territory. Any effort to centralize this duty at the ICC still requires the support of states, including on arresting and surrendering defendants to the Court.[86]

This practice of encouraging states to self-refer suggests that the ICC wants more powers for itself. The practice reveals a Court that continues to encourage states to rely on it for international crimes investigation and prosecution. This approach shows a Court that is reluctant to yield grounds to states; rather, it is contesting grounds that are originally meant for states to function. This could mean that the ICC may be reluctant to open itself to the idea of regional complementarity. Its current practices and direction suggest a Court that is closed to the idea of allowing states (even if they choose to act under a regional arrangement) to take on more roles and responsibilities in international criminal justice. ICC's protectionism has also been observed in the

---

84 C. Stahn, 'Perspectives on Katanga: An Introduction' (2010) 23 *Leiden Journal of International Law* 2, 5.

85 P. Gaeta, 'Is the Practice of "Self-Referral" a Sound Start for the ICC?' (2004) 2 *JICJ* 950.

86 P. Hobbs, 'The Catalysing Effect of the Rome Statute in Africa: Positive Complementarity and Self-Referrals' (2020) 31 *Criminal Law Forum* 346.

debate over the Court's co-existence with the Special Tribunal for Ukraine.[87] In the conclusion of this book, I have discussed the establishment of the Special Tribunal for the Crime of Aggression against Ukraine and its relationship with the ICC in light of the Statute's provisions.

In a number of other situations before the Court, including the Ugandan situation, other authors have previously narrated the ICC's fierce resistance to attempts at amicable domestic resolution through a peace deal between the Ugandan government and the LRA rebels.[88] This is in addition to the idea that the ICC often elevates politics above the interests of justice.[89] This is why some TWAIL authors have argued that the ICC's application of international criminal law 'often appears to be more driven by the perpetuation of global power asymmetries and old patterns of subjugation'.[90] Surprisingly though, while these views about the ICC persist, it has also shown itself as a Court that consistently refers to and relies on human rights jurisprudence from regional human rights Courts across all the Court's judicial divisions, albeit in an inconsistent manner.[91] What is not in doubt, however, is that the ICC uses the jurisprudence of other Courts, including that of regional human rights tribunals, to build its own case law. Thus, it can be argued that the ICC has a selective engagement with regionalism. It chooses when and how it engages with regional institutions, often without 'a clear methodology for reference to regional human rights jurisprudence in the reasoning of the chambers'.[92] It has previously acknowledged the important role that regional courts may play in international criminal justice. In a judicial seminar organized and moderated by the judges of the Court, the ICC noted that

> The role of regional courts within the framework of the Rome Statute was discussed. The UN Charter, for example, contemplates and encourages regional arrangements to deal with international peace and security. This may encourage States to pool together sovereignties to solve problems which cannot be resolved individually. This is deemed to be a particularly important issue given

---

87 P. Butchard and N. Walker, *Potential Merits of a Special Tribunal on Ukraine* (House of Common's Library Debate Pack 2023), 4.

88 S. Nouwen & W. Werner, 'Doing Justice to the Political: The International Criminal Court in Uganda and Sudan' (2010) 21 *European Journal of International Law* 4, 941–961.

89 *Ibid.*

90 O. Okafor & U. Ngwaba, 'The International Criminal Court as a "Transitional Justice" Mechanism in Africa: Some Critical Reflections' (2014) 9 *International Journal of Transitional Justice*, 1–19.

91 A. Jones, 'Insights into an Emerging Relationship: Use of Human Rights Jurisprudence at the International Criminal Court' (2016) 16 *Human Rights Law Review* 4.

92 *Ibid*, 728.

> the Rome Statute's silence on regional jurisdictions. The ICC judges refer frequently to decisions of regional courts (notably human rights courts) in their decisions, fostering a positive relationship between the judicial bodies.[93]

This suggests that the Court ought to prepare itself for the inevitable: a more concrete role for regional courts in ICL. The ICC's comments also underscore that we have witnessed an increasing level of cooperation and contribution to international crimes prosecution from regional bodies, either as commitments to support through logistical and financial aid, or even outright attempts to prosecute at a regional level. This may not be surprising, given that some have contended that while international criminal law is universal in theory, its practice is regional.[94]

Given this background, there is no doubt that this engagement with regional mechanisms, which is based on power relations, requires a review. The analysis above suggests that the ICC has continually adopted an 'ICC-centric' interpretation of its relationship with other institutions, including national mechanisms that may choose to jointly operate under a regional arrangement. This excludes the virtue of regional complementarity and perpetuates the hierarchical notion of complementarity. If the current ICC-centric practice of complementarity was to be applied between ICC and any regional mechanism, that relationship will be criticized in the same manner that the current ICC and states relationship is being criticized. The thinking that the ICC should exist alone in the international justice firmament, as evidenced by the Court's application of complementarity, will not bode well for the practice of regional complementarity.

In the alternative, there are scholars who have posited that the ICC ought to embrace a polycentric vision of international criminal justice.[95] By this, I agree with the proposition that a justice system 'is not monocentric, but can have different centres that interplay'.[96] ICL's value is seen in the interplay between the different justice models and institutions that make up the ICL landscape.[97]

---

93 Judicial Seminar: Complementarity and Cooperation of Courts in an Interconnected Global Justice System. International Criminal Court (ICC), 18 January 2018, The Hague, Netherlands. Summary of seminar proceedings Welcoming remarks by Judge Silvia Fernández de Gurmendi, ICC President, 3.

94 W. Schabas, 'Regions, Regionalism and International Criminal Law' (2007), *New Zealand Yearbook of International Law,* 2.

95 C. Stahn, 'Re-imagining the ICC in a Multipolar World' in Stahn, C. (ed) *The International Criminal Court in its Third Decade: Reflecting on Law and Practices* (Brill Nijhoff 2024) 562.

96 *Ibid*, 570.

97 *Ibid.*

The implication of adopting greater polycentricity is that regional or national justice institutions do not necessarily need to model themselves after the ICC.[98] Secondly, it implies that complementarity should not be viewed only as a 'form of emancipatory interaction with the ICC as a model, but as a form of cooperative justice that respects the need for legitimate difference, contextual adjustment and greater regional input'.[99]

5 Conclusion

Complementarity has advanced from its previous status as a mere legal principle to a tool for encouraging state and non-state parties to the Rome Statute to take the business of accountability more seriously. While this is the OTP's articulation of positive complementarity, the Chamber seems to have applied the admissibility wing of complementarity as a tool to restrain states from being the primary forum for international criminal trials. As this chapter has shown, the ICC needs to open itself more in its complementarity jurisprudence and practice. As has been shown, the Court continues to close itself to the possibility of allowing states to take on more responsibility for international criminal trials. It has continued to conclude cooperation agreements with regions like the EU[100] and the Inter-American[101] regions. It continues to explore the possibility of cooperation agreements with others, like the Asia-Pacific region.[102] It sometimes holds high-level regional seminar on cooperation.[103] However, these agreements amount to nothing where the ICC continues to hold itself out as a cosmopolitan project that gives lesser roles to states. The Court's jurisprudence has shown that it prefers trials within its Chambers, rather than allow states whose primary duty it is to prosecute international crimes. Through its decisions, the Court has extended judicial constructs and applied the law in a manner that reveals an obsession with cosmopolitanism. The OTP has implemented policies that give it more responsibility to inter-

98 *Ibid.*

99 *Ibid*, 571.

100 ICC-PRES/01-01-06 Agreement between the International Criminal Court and the European Union on Cooperation and Assistance, 10 April 2006.

101 OAS, IACHR Signs Cooperation Agreement with International Criminal Court [available at https://www.oas.org/en/iachr/media_center/PReleases/2012/039.asp – accessed 21 May 2022].

102 ICC-ASP, Report of the Bureau on the Plan of Action of the Assembly of States Parties for achieving universality and full implementation of the Rome Statute of the International Criminal Court, ICC-ASP/18/24, 20 November 2019, para. 15.

103 ICC, 'High-Level ICC Regional Seminar on Cooperation Opens in Romania', 21 March 2016.

vene in areas where states should have primacy. The policy of burden-sharing and its sub-policy of self-referral negate the OTP's articulation of positive complementarity. The Court, therefore, continues to show itself as an institution that is closed to the idea of regional complementarity. The analysis in this chapter reveals a Court that wants more powers for itself. The Court's jurisprudence and practices need to return to the original intent of the drafters of the Rome Statute. The practice so far at the ICC seems to support the view that the Court is actively and deliberately dissuading states from taking the frontal stage in prosecuting international crimes. Primacy for international criminal trials lies with states, whether acting individually or under a regional arrangement. To that end, the question as to 'what implication does the jurisprudence and practice at the ICC have for the notion of regional complementarity' was aimed at ascertaining whether the ICC opens or closes itself to the idea of regional complementarity through its jurisprudence, practice and policy directions. The analysis in this chapter shows a Court that needs to do more to embrace the ideals underpinning regional complementarity. One such ideal is the concept of polycentricity which prescribes that different decision-making centres can exist in a whole, with substantial independence and autonomous prerogatives, while striving toward common goals.

CHAPTER 3

The Rise of Hybridity and Regionalism as New Accountability Models

1 Introduction

The evolution of international criminal law (ICL) has been marked by the search for effective and legitimate forums of accountability. In recent decades, a noticeable shift has occurred from the dominance of purely international tribunals to more diverse models of enforcement. Hybrid and regional institutions have emerged as important actors in this evolving landscape, reflecting both the practical limits of universal justice and the growing demand for context-sensitive responses to mass atrocity crimes. These developments illustrate the maturation of international criminal justice and its gradual adaptation to the realities of a fragmented yet interconnected world.

This chapter examines the typologies of regional and hybrid institutions that have appeared as new mechanisms for the enforcement of international criminal law. It traces the evolution of justice forums from national prosecutions and fully international tribunals to hybrid and regional arrangements. The analysis identifies hybridity and regionalism as complementary responses to the institutional and political challenges that have shaped international criminal accountability. Hybrid tribunals, created through cooperation between international or regional bodies and domestic authorities, represent a transitional model that bridges the gap between global norms and local realities. Regional institutions, by contrast, embody a more autonomous and sustainable form of justice that reflects the shared political and legal aspirations of specific regions.

The chapter argues that hybridity and regionalism should not be viewed as departures from international criminal justice but as natural extensions of it. Hybrid tribunals have laid the groundwork for regional mechanisms by demonstrating that shared responsibility can enhance both legitimacy and effectiveness. The establishment of the Extraordinary African Chambers in Senegal and the Kosovo Specialist Chambers in Europe, for instance, illustrates how regional and hybrid features can be combined to produce credible accountability processes. These experiences have inspired new regional initiatives, such as the proposed African Court of Justice and Human and Peoples'

© 2026 THE AUTHOR(S) | HTTPS://DOI.ORG/10.1163/9789004761803-005

Rights with an international criminal chamber, which aims to create a permanent, self-sustaining model of regional enforcement.

By analysing the progression from hybrid to regional mechanisms, this chapter situates both models within a broader continuum of institutional experimentation in international criminal law. It identifies two strands of regionalism that have emerged from these experiments. The first is the assistance-driven model, in which regional organizations collaborate with national systems to establish tribunals tailored to specific contexts. The second is the fully independent model, where regional institutions seek to exercise jurisdiction over international crimes without external dependence. Together, these models represent a new phase in the diversification of accountability, reflecting both the diffusion of international legal authority and the aspiration of regions to contribute meaningfully to global justice.

In exploring these developments, the chapter highlights the implications of hybridity and regionalism for the principle of complementarity and the future of international criminal justice. It argues that the move towards regionalization represents not a fragmentation of international law but a deepening of its cooperative fabric. The rise of these alternative models underscores the adaptability of international criminal justice and points toward a pluralistic order where international, regional, and national jurisdictions coexist within a shared framework of accountability.

2 Diverse Justice Enforcement Models

International criminal law, and the justice it portends to dispense,[1] are at intriguing crossroads.[2] At these crossroads, some say it has developed and has reached 'a remarkable benchmark of maturity'.[3] Yet, others say its advancement has been stifled by multiple challenges and a midlife crisis.[4] Call it what

1 On what justice means in ICL, and what ICL means for justice, see D. Robinson, 'International Criminal Law as Justice' (2013) 11 *JICJ* 3, 699–711.

2 On this, see K. Ambos, 'International Criminal Law at the Crossroads: From Ad Hoc Imposition to a Treaty Based Universal System' in C. Stahn & L. van den Herik (eds) *Future Perspectives on International Criminal Justice* (TMC Asser Press 2010) 161–177; M. Findlay, 'The Challenges for Asian Jurisdictions in the Development of International Criminal Justice' (2010) 32 *Sydney Law Review* 2, 205–219.

3 S. Vasiliev, 'International criminal trials: A normative theory' (2014) University of Amsterdam Ph.D. Thesis, Volume I, at 4.

4 On the challenges capable of stifling the growth of the ICC, see C. Gegout, 'The International Criminal Court: limits, potential and conditions for the promotion of justice and peace' (2013) 34 *Third World Quarterly* 5, 800–818. See also J.J. Vilmer, 'The African Union and

you may, the reality is that international criminal prosecution, with all its perceived flaws and weaknesses, is a present-day reality. Its practice has so far been somewhat impressive, yet grossly imperfect. The optimism of those who think it has come of age is understandable. It has been over 70 years since the first attempts at prosecutions through international criminal tribunals: the Nuremberg and Tokyo Tribunals. It has been more than 20 years since the ad hoc tribunals and the ICC were established. These have been years of learning and un-learning; years of making many mistakes and getting some things right. There is no doubt that lessons have emerged from these years. One of the most enduring legacies from these years of experimenting with international criminal justice is that hybrid and regional hybrid tribunals have become veritable mechanisms for securing accountability for international crimes.[5]

There is no universal agreement on the appropriate forums for enforcing international criminal law. Jalloh identified three pillars upon which the present enforcement of international criminal law rests: national Courts, international Courts and domestic Courts of third states.[6] On his part, Stahn identified four layers: 'domestic', 'international', 'hybrid' and 'regional',[7] with the last two being the most recent additions to the fold. Taking the two scholars' positions into account, I submit that there are currently five frameworks for the enforcement of international criminal law. These are national mechanisms, which are not only the primary enforcement frameworks but also enjoy primacy in relation to other frameworks; the second are prosecutions done in national Courts of third states through the application of universal jurisdiction; the third is the international framework, while the fourth and the fifth, which are the most recent additions, are hybrid and regional tribunals.

There are, however, scholars who argue that, in the formal sense, there are only domestic and international Courts. Accordingly, O'Keefe submits that what truly exists is 'national implementation of international crimes' and 'a state's international legal authority in relation to national laws'.[8]

---

the International Criminal Court: counteracting the crisis' (2016) 92 *International Affairs* 6, 1341.

5 See generally A. Fitchtelberg, *Hybrid Tribunals: A Comparative Examination of Their Origins, Structure, Legitimacy and Effectiveness* (Springer Press 2015).

6 C. Jalloh, 'The Place of the African Court of Justice and Human and Peoples' Rights in the Prosecution of Serious Crimes in Africa' in C. Jalloh and Ors., *The African Court of Justice and Human and Peoples' Rights in Context: Developments and Challenges* (Cambridge University Press 2019) 57.

7 C. Stahn, *Fair and Effective Investigation and Prosecution of International Crimes: Inventory and State-of-the-Art: Context, Cluster 1 and Cluster 2* (International Nuremberg Principles Academy Press 2018) 3–4.

8 R. O'Keefe, *International Criminal Law* (Oxford University Press, 2014).

Notwithstanding the contrary view above, the recent additions have brought with them significant challenges while expanding the institutional framework of international justice. I call this 'the four-tiered justice paradigm'. While there exists a distinction between prosecutions in national Courts of a state with jurisdiction over a crime and those done in national Courts of third states through the exercise of universal jurisdiction, I will adopt a four-tier paradigm for the purpose of this book, thus considering both forms of prosecution in a domestic Court as the same. I admit that it is quite fundamental whether a case is handled under universal jurisdiction or based on some other principles, particularly in terms of competition and/or coordination and cooperation between the two states concerned. The application of universal jurisdiction is one of the five principles upon which states' right to punish international crimes within their territory are founded. This chapter is concerned with the two recent additions and how one has led to the other. However, I will briefly discuss the previous forums for enforcing ICL.

2.1 ICL Enforcement before National and International Mechanisms

States have the primary responsibility of punishing international crimes in their territory. This is trite and undisputable in international law. The Rome Statute recalls 'that it is the duty of every State to exercise its criminal jurisdiction over those responsible for international crimes'.[9] This responsibility flows from a state's duty to maintain public order in their domain.[10] It is also a manifestation of a state's exercise of sovereignty.[11] Chapter 1 of this work demonstrates how states have historically sought to protect that sovereignty. This ensured that they only agreed to the creation of tribunals to address specific situations. According to Stahn, one early example is the states' agreement to establish the UN War Crimes Commission (UNWCC).[12] The Commission was created to facilitate domestic prosecutions of crimes committed in WWII.[13]

9 Para. 6 of the Preamble of the Rome Statute.

10 A. Sagalyn, 'Preservation of Law and Order: A Fundamental Function of Government' (1965) 40 *Notre Dame Law Review* 549–551.

11 A. Chehtman, 'The Extraterritorial Scope of the Right to Punish' (2010) 29 *Law and Philosophy* 127–157 at 130.

12 On the UNWCC, see C. Stahn, 'Complementarity and Cooperative Justice ahead of their time? The United Nations War Crimes Commission, Fact-Finding and Evidence' (2014) 25 *Criminal Law Forum* 223–260.

13 C. Stahn, *A Critical Introduction to International Criminal Law* (Cambridge University Press 2019) 161.

States' right to punish international crimes in their territories is founded on five principles. The principles of territoriality, active personality, passive personality, protective principle and, lastly, universal jurisdiction. Territoriality principle implies that a state has jurisdiction to punish international crimes that take place in their territory. It sees law enforcement as part of keeping peace in a territory.[14] Active personality is based on the nationality of the perpetrator of the crimes. It flows from the 'Roman Theory of Criminal Law'.[15] Passive personality relates to jurisdiction that is rooted in the victim's nationality. This is the 'Injured Forum Theory'.[16] The protective principle allows a state to claim jurisdiction over a crime if the conducts affect the interest of the state – even if the defendant is outside of the state's territory.[17] In universal jurisdiction, a state's power to prosecute is grounded in the idea that the crime being prosecuted harms humanity, and a state is acting on behalf of the international community. Jurisdiction here is exercised by a state even if it would lack jurisdiction based on the other four principles.[18] Accountability for international crimes within the domestic systems – own or third states' – has seen developments that warrant states adopting special laws and establishing special institutions within existing legal systems for the purposes of investigating and prosecuting international crimes.[19]

There are perceived advantages in prosecuting international crimes through national mechanisms. However, the heightened risk of an impartiality deficit and the intimidation of the judicial system by powerful perpetrators may drown out those advantages.[20] International crimes are often committed by powerful perpetrators. After the Nuremberg and Tokyo Tribunals, key trials for international crimes took place in domestic Courts. Prominent examples include the *Eichmann and Demjanjuk* cases in Israel, the *Menten* case in the

14 See R.M. Perkins, 'The Territorial Principle in Criminal Law' (1971) 22 *Hastings Law Journal* 5, 1115.

15 See W.D Aston, 'Problems of Roman Criminal Law' (1913) 2 *Journal of the Society of Comparative Legislation* 213–231.

16 See R.M. Perkins, 'The Territorial Principle in Criminal Law' (1971) 22 *Hastings Law Journal* 5, 1116.

17 M. Garrod, 'The Protective Principle of Jurisdiction over War Crimes and the Hollow Concept of Universality' (2012) 12 *International Criminal Law Review* 12, 763–826.

18 On Universal Jurisdiction, see X. Philppe, 'The principles of universal jurisdiction and complementarity: how do the two principles intermesh?' (2006) 88 *International Review of the* Red Cross 862, 375–398.

19 See J. Charney, 'International Criminal Law and the Role of Domestic Courts' (2001) 95 *The American Journal of International Law* 121–125.

20 J. Stigen, *The Relationship Between the International Criminal Court and National Jurisdictions: The Principle of Complementarity* (Brill Nijhoff 2008) 22.

Netherlands, the *Barbie and Touvier* cases in France, and the *Finta, Mugesera and Munyaneza* cases in Canada.[21] Some of these cases have contributed to the jurisprudence of more recent ICL institutions.[22]

Aside from the domestic systems, another commonly used forum for prosecuting international crimes, especially since the horrors of WWI and WWII have been international institutions created for that purpose. This is partly due to the understanding that international cooperation is often necessary in order to address impunity for atrocities. This was reiterated in paragraph 4 of the Preamble to the Rome Statute. The international nature of their enabling instruments is what confers international authority on them.[23] Stahn identifies two theories that justify international criminal jurisdiction. The first is the view that international tribunals only exercise international jurisdiction because of authorities that have been delegated to them by states. The second theory casts international tribunals as projects to protect humanity from crimes.[24] International criminal jurisdictions have been exercised through temporal and permanent platforms. The temporal platforms are those institutions that have been created, since at least the end of WWII, to punish perpetrators of crimes in respect of specific conflicts. Examples include the Nuremberg and Tokyo Tribunals. They are the predecessors of the hybrid tribunals that are discussed in this chapter. The second type of platform is the more permanent institution, like the International Criminal Court.

The emergence of hybrid and regional tribunals has added to the 'four-tiered justice paradigm' or 'the multi-layered accountability architecture of international justice'.[25] International criminal law has developed to an extent that the central issues are no longer about whether persons who commit international crimes should be prosecuted, but more about the appropriate forum and the proper prosecutorial strategies to adopt in prosecuting them. This is what Frédéric Mégret calls 'the normalization of international criminal justice'.[26] This

---

21 Sean D. Murphy, 'New Mechanisms for Punishing Atrocities in Non-International Armed Conflicts' (2015) 16 *Melbourne Journal of International Law* 299, 305.

22 See, for example, W. Schabas, 'The Contribution of the Eichmann Trial to International Law' (2013) 26 *Leiden Journal of International Law* 2, 667–699.

23 C. Stahn, *A Critical Introduction to International Criminal Law* (Cambridge University Press 2019) 191.

24 *Ibid.*

25 C. Stahn, *Fair and Effective Investigation and Prosecution of International Crimes: Inventory and State-of-the-Art: Context, Cluster 1 and Cluster 2* (International Nuremberg Principles Academy 2018) 3.

26 F. Megret, 'In Defense of Hybridity: Towards a Representational Theory of International Criminal Justice' (2005) 38 *Cornell International Law Journal* 3, 725.

normalization also accounts for the proliferation of international criminal adjudicatory bodies.[27] Now that there are more concerns relating to the finer points about forums and strategies, a discussion on the place of these alternative forums is necessary.

2.2 The New Wave of Hybridity

ICL has witnessed a new wave of hybridity[28] as 'hybrid criminal tribunals have returned as a viable option in international criminal justice'.[29] Since the 1990s, some of the more common forums for prosecuting international crimes have been tribunals and Courts created and/or supported by the UN, regional bodies and/or states.[30] It has been suggested that these tribunals became necessary as stop-gap measures during the period between the adoption of the Rome Statute in 1998 and its coming into force in 2002.[31] Some have described them as 'the most effective' mechanism for prosecution,[32] while others have called them 'the pre-eminent symbol of global justice'.[33] Beyond

27 See generally Tan, Alvin Poh Heng, 'Advancing international criminal justice in south-east Asia through the regionalisation of international criminal law' (2014) PhD Thesis, University of Nottingham.

28 On the new wave of hybridity in international criminal law, see P.K. Mendez, 'The new wave of hybrid tribunals: A sophisticated approach to enforcing international humanitarian law or an idealistic solution with empty promises?' (2009) 20 *Criminal Law Forum* 95; see also C. Stahn, 'Tribunals Are Dead, Long Live Tribunals: MICT, the Kosovo Specialist Chambers and the Turn to New Hybridity', 23 September 2016, *EJIL: Talk Blog of the European Journal of International Law* [available at https://www.ejiltalk.org/tribunals-are-dead-long-live-tribunals-mict-the-kosovo-specialist-chambers-and-the-turn-to-new-hybridity/ – accessed 6 February 2024]; E.M. Bruch, 'Hybrid Courts: Examining hybridity through a post-colonial lens' (2010) 28 *Boston University International Law Journal* 1; S. Nouwen, 'Hybrid Courts: The hybrid category of a new type of international crimes courts' (2010) 2 *Utrecht Law Review* 213.

29 H. Hobbs, 'Hybrid Tribunals and the Composition of the Court: In Search of Sociological Legitimacy' (2016) 16 *Chicago Journal of International Law* 2, 485.

30 See 'International and Hybrid Criminal Tribunals' [available at: https://www.un.org/ruleoflaw/thematic-areas/international-law-courts-tribunals/international-hybrid-criminal-courts-tribunals/ – accessed 15 June 2023].

31 M. Holvoet and P. de Hert, 'International Criminal Law as Global Law: An Assessment of the Hybrid Tribunals' (2012) 17 *Tilburg Law Review* 235.

32 C.E. Carroll, 'Hybrid Tribunals are the Most Effective Structure for Adjudicating International Crimes Occurring Within a Domestic State' (2013) 90 *Seton Hall University Law School Student Scholarship* 1.

33 D. Orentlicher, 'Striking a Balance: Mixed Law tribunals and Conflicts of Jurisdiction' in L. Mark & S. Philippe (eds) *Justice for Crimes Against Humanity* (Hart Publishing 2003) 212.

agreement about the reality of their emergence, scholars are divided on key questions around their usefulness and continuous relevance in ICL, with one scholar even suggesting that their popularity has declined dramatically.[34]

There is no agreement among academics on the definition of a hybrid tribunal,[35] but they tend to blend 'the international and the local as a judicial accountability sharing measure between states and the UN'.[36] They are composed of independent judges, working on the basis of predetermined rules of procedure and rendering binding decisions.[37] Moreover, their other common features are that they combine national and international components in their personnel and applicable laws; they are 'ad hoc institutions; created to address particular situations; for a limited amount of time and are the results of singular political and historical circumstances'.[38]

There have been two primary models of temporary criminal tribunals: the 'international' and the 'internationalized or hybrid' tribunals. The international tribunals refer to those institutions that enjoy an independent status, while the internationalized tribunals refer to those incorporated into a state's judiciary. Examples of the former are the UN *ad hoc* tribunals: the International Criminal Tribunal for the former Yugoslavia (ICTY) and the International Criminal Tribunal for Rwanda (ICTR). They applied international law *stricto sensu*. They, however, suffered from certain inherent disadvantages and fundamental drawbacks. Their operation was arguably costly.[39] They dispensed justice slowly and could only handle a relatively limited caseload,[40] although some scholars argued that, looking at the numbers, the two tribunals did well.[41] The ICTR's administration was alleged to have been corrupt.[42] Both

---

34 P. McAuliffe, 'Hybrid Tribunals at Ten: How International Criminal Justice's Golden Child Became an Orphan' (2011) 7 *Journal of International Law and International Relations* 1, 1.

35 C. Hicks, *The Trial of Hissène Habré: How the People of Chad Brought a Tyrant to Justice* (ZED Books 2018) 67.

36 E. Higonnet, 'Restructuring Hybrid Courts: Local Employment and National Criminal Justice Reforms' (2006) 23 *Arizona Journal of International and Comparative Law* 347.

37 The Graduate Institute Geneva, 'International tribunals: Hybrid Courts' [available at http://libguides.graduateinstitute.ch/icl/hybrid – accessed 5 February 2024].

38 *Ibid.*

39 P.K. Mendez, 'The new wave of hybrid tribunals: A sophisticated approach to enforcing international humanitarian law or an idealistic solution with empty promises?' (2009) 20 *Criminal Law Forum* 53, 61.

40 *Ibid.*

41 *Ibid.*

42 P.M. Wald, 'Accountability for War Crimes: What Role for National, International and Hybrid Tribunals?' (2004) *American Society of International Law: Proceeding of Annual Meeting* 192.

ICTY and ICTR were sited far away from the scenes of crimes, thus making them somewhat detached from the actual victims and local realities.[43] These distances make the trials less accessible and meaningful for victims.[44] In addition, evidence-gathering in faraway crime scenes proved difficult.[45] There were challenges with enforcement and non-cooperation from states.[46] The tribunals faced increasing political and financial constraints.[47] As a result of non-cooperation from states, the ICTR experienced a delay in apprehending its suspects. This is also probably because of overly ambitious prosecution strategies. In the ICTY, running costs were rising with indictments being overloaded with too many counts.[48]

2.3 The Rise of New Hybrid Tribunals

Given the shortcomings of the *ad hoc* tribunals, different hybrid tribunals began to emerge during the late 1990s and early 2000s. Their emergence was partly because of the criticisms against ICTY and ICTR.[49] These hybrids offered non-permanent solutions to specific situations.[50] Commenting on the factors responsible for their emergence, Kersten stated that

> [T]heir development owed much to a peculiar convergence of three factors: 1) wavering international commitment to the sprawling, costly, and lengthy ad hoc tribunals; 2) the absence of a permanent supranational criminal court; and 3) a growing appreciation that states should have primary responsibility to investigate and prosecute international crimes combined with a keen aware-

43 P. Clark, *Distant Justice: The Impact of the International Criminal Court on African Politics* (Cambridge University Press 2018) 45.

44 *Ibid.*

45 R. Dicker and E. Keppler, 'Beyond the Hague: The Challenges of International Justice' available at https://www.hrw.org/legacy/wr2k4/download/10.pdf.

46 G.K. McDonald, 'Problems, Obstacles and Achievements of the ICTY' (2004) 2 JICJ 558–571. See also L. Ljuboja, 'Justice in an uncooperative world: ICTY and ICTR foreshadow ICC ineffectiveness' (2010) 32 *Houston Journal of International Law* 780.

47 R. Dicker and E. Keppler Dicker R. and Keppler E., 'Beyond the Hague: The Challenges of International Justice' [available at https://www.hrw.org/legacy/wr2k4/download/10.pdf – accessed 12 January 2024].

48 M. Sterio & M. Scharf (eds) *The Legacy of Ad Hoc Tribunals in International Criminal Law: Assessing the ICTY's and the ICTR's Most Significant Legal Accomplishments* (Cambridge University Press 2019) 1–10.

49 Suzanne Katzenstein, 'Hybrid Tribunals: Searching for Justice in East Timor' (2003) 16 *Harvard Human Rights Journal* 245.

50 S. Williams, 'Hybrid Tribunals: A Time for Reflection' (2016) 10 *International Journal of Transitional Justice* 539.

ness that post-conflict states may not be able to try cases in accordance with international standards.[51]

Given these factors, it became obvious that hybrids were needed to address some of the shortcomings of the *ad hoc* tribunals. But what sorts of hybrids were expected and how are they defined? Like many terms in ICL, the term 'hybridity' does not lend itself to an ease of definition. For this reason, a description of its features seems to be more appropriate. In that regard, there are three ways in which tribunals display their hybridity. The first is through their origin, in which case they were created through domestic and international processes. The second is through their application of both domestic and international law, while the third is their composition, in that they combine domestic and 'international' members.[52] These descriptions explain hybridity better than an attempt at an all-encompassing definition.

On the other hand, there are those who argue that there are still no clear features through which hybrids can be recognized. According to Muharremi, 'the concept of hybrid Courts is unclear, and there are no clear criteria which would provide guidance for establishing if a judicial body is a hybrid Court or not. The idea of hybrid Courts is conceptually misleading because it creates the perception that hybrid Courts are a separate institutional category different from international and domestic criminal Courts.'[53] While there may remain some confusion on the actual features that a hybrid Court must possess, there is no doubt that some features have become well-known as displaying a Court's hybridity. Such features include that the tribunal performs a criminal judicial function; that the tribunal is temporary or transitional; that it has mixed composition;[54] and that it has a measure of international funding.[55] Existing examples, however, show that some hybrids, like the KSC, have

51 M. Kersten, 'International Criminal Justice Redux: A New Wave of Hybrid Courts' *Justice in Conflict,* 13 March 2018 [available at https://justiceinconflict.org/2018/03/13/international-criminal-justice-redux-a-new-wave-of-hybrid-courts/ – accessed 6 February 2024].

52 E.M. Bruch, 'Hybrid Courts: Examining hybridity through a post-colonial lens' (2010) 28 *Boston University International Law Journal* 1, 6.

53 R. Muharremi, 'The Concept of Hybrid Courts Revisited: The Case of the Kosovo Specialist Chambers' (2018) 18 *International Criminal Law Review* 4.

54 R. Muharremi, 'The Kosovo Specialist Chambers and Specialist Prosecutor's Office' (2016) *ASIL Online Post* [available at https://www.asil.org/insights/volume/20/issue/11/kosovo-specialist-chambers-and-specialist-prosecutors-office – accessed 6 February 2024].

55 On other features of hybrid Courts, see S. Williams, 'The Extraordinary African Chambers in the Senegalese Courts: An African Solution to an African Problem?' (2013) 11 *JICJ* 1139–1160.

a fully international bench, while some, like the SCSL and ECCC, often ignore domestic laws.

2.4 Typology of the New Hybrid Tribunals

There have been some academic writings on the typology of the new hybrid tribunals.[56] For example, Stahn identified two broad types of hybrids. The first are the 'hybrid Courts' properly so called. They have pure international legal basis and are generally independent and detached from the domestic jurisdiction. Examples are the Special Court for Sierra Leone (SCSL) and the Special Tribunal for Lebanon (STL). SCSL and STL were not incorporated into their respective states' judiciary. While STL applied domestic law alongside international law, the SCSL only applied international law. This implies that they shared attributes of both international and national tribunals. They are probably better referred to as 'internationalized' since there are doubts as to whether they are in a separate family of Courts. The second types are 'the mixed domestic–international Courts that form part of the domestic system, but with adjustments in relation to the composition of staff or the applicable law'.[57] These are the ones commonly referred to as the 'internationalized' or 'mixed-criminal' tribunals. Examples include the Special Panels for Serious Crimes in East Timor (SPSC), The Kosovo Specialist Chambers and Prosecutor's Office (KSCSPO), the Regulation 64 UNMIK Panels in Kosovo, the EULEX judicial panel,[58] the War Crimes Chamber in the State Court of Bosnia and Herzegovina (WCCSCBH), and the Extraordinary Chambers in the Courts of Cambodia (ECCC).[59]

What has emerged from these classifications is that the Courts that are referred to as 'hybrid tribunals' are diverse.[60] There have been at least ten of such 'hybrid tribunals', including the SCCCAR and the Hissène Habré Court.

---

56 For example, see S.M.H. Nouwen, 'Hybrid Courts: The hybrid category of a new type of international crimes Courts' (2006) 2 *Utrecht Law Review* 190.

57 C. Stahn, 'Tribunals are Dead, Long Live Tribunals: MICT, the Kosovo Specialist Chambers and the Turn to New Hybridity', 23 September 2016 *EJIL: Talk Blog of the European Journal of International Law,* [available at https://www.ejiltalk.org/tribunals-are-dead-long-live-tribunals-mict-the-kosovo-specialist-chambers-and-the-turn-to-new-hybridity/ – accessed 6 February 2024]; see also C. Stahn, *A Critical Introduction to International Criminal Law* (Cambridge University Press 2019) 198.

58 O. Dursun-Özkanca, 'The European Union Rule of Law Mission in Kosovo: An Analysis from the Local Perspective' (2018) 17 *Ethnopolitics* 1, 71–94.

59 Stahn (2016) 'Tribunals are Dead' (n. 57).

60 H. Hobbs, 'Hybrid Tribunals and the Composition of the Court: In Search of Sociological Legitimacy' (2016) 16 *Chicago Journal of International Law* 2, 489.

There are those who have contested that the Iraqi High Tribunal and the International Crimes Tribunal-1 Bangladesh[61] would not qualify as 'hybrid tribunals'.[62] The major argument is because they lacked international judges in their composition. The presence of international judges had been argued as the 'most defining feature' of such tribunals.[63] In the next sub-section, I will discuss five examples of hybrid tribunals. They are SCSL, STL, ECCC, SPSL and SCCCAR. The first two are international hybrid tribunals properly called, while the other three are mixed criminal tribunals.

2.4.1 The Special Court for Sierra Leone (SCSL)

Between 1991 and 2002, there was a civil war in Sierra Leone. In an effort to bring about peace and reconciliation, the government of Sierra Leone requested the United Nations to establish a special Court to try those suspected of having perpetrated atrocities during the war. In response, the Security Council, on 14 August 2000, adopted Resolution 1315, which requested the Secretary-General of the UN to negotiate the establishment of a special Court with the government of Sierra Leone. The Resolution specifically 'recommends that the subject matter jurisdiction of the special Court should include notably crimes against humanity, war crimes and other serious violations of international humanitarian law, as well as crimes under relevant Sierra Leonean law committed within the territory of Sierra Leone.'[64] The establishment of the Court was a product of direct request and engagement of the government with the UN.

In essence, this Court was a treaty-based entity that was jointly established by the government of Sierra Leone and the United Nations, as opposed to the ICTY and ICTR, which had been established by Security Council's resolutions under Chapter VII of the UN Charter. The import of this is that while ICTY and ICTR consisted of international judges, the SCSL benches and the OTP were a mix of international and domestic personnel.[65] Another difference is in its mode of establishment. While the SCSL had primacy over domestic Courts in Sierra Leone and could order surrender of accused persons, it lacked similar

---

61 See R. Mustakimur, 'Has the International Crimes Tribunal Bangladesh (ICT-BD) assisted to Reconcile Society?' (2023) 19 *AUDJ* 2, 115–149, for thoughts on this tribunal.

62 See S.M.H. Nouwen, 'Hybrid Courts: The hybrid category of a new type of international crimes Courts' (2010) 2 *Utrecht Law Review* 213.

63 S. Williams, *Hybrid and Internationalised Criminal Tribunals: Selected Jurisdictional Issues* (Hart Publishing 2012).

64 UN Doc S/RES/1315 (2000) Resolution 1315 (2000) adopted by the Security Council at its 4186th meeting on 14 August 2000.

65 M. Scharf, 'Special Court for Sierra Leone' (2000) 6 *Int'l Peacekeeping* 156.

powers of the ICTY/ICTR to compel cooperation from a third state. The SCSL did not have primacy over judicial mechanisms of any state outside Sierra Leone.[66] Lastly, while the subject-matter jurisdiction of the ICTY/ICTR related to customary international law, the SCSL had jurisdiction over these, alongside some other crimes under Sierra Leonean laws.[67]

While the African Union and its predecessor, the OAU, did not establish the SCSL, the regional body expressed political support and offered diplomatic assistance to the tribunal. It also facilitated regional cooperation for the Court.[68] These are the specific.

2.4.2 Special Tribunal for Lebanon (STL)

2005 was the decisive year for the establishment of a Special Tribunal for Lebanon. Many violent crises had taken place in Beirut, but none was as significant as the 14 February bombing of the motorcade of the then Prime Minister – Rafiq Hariri. His death, as well as the deaths of other 22 people in the bomb blast, were the triggers that led to the establishment of the STL. Its establishment was preceded by the establishment of the United Nations International Independent Investigation Commission (UNIIIC) through UNSC Resolution 1595.[69] The Commission started its work on 16 June 2005. As Harwood had noted, the UNIIIC is unique among international commissions of inquiry because, unlike others, it was established to make inquiries into domestic crimes and 'it is the only commission to have direct institutional links with an internationalized criminal tribunal'.[70]

In December 2005, the Lebanese Prime Minister sent a letter to the Secretary-General of the UN, requesting the latter 'to establish a tribunal of an international character to convene in or outside Lebanon, to try all those who are found responsible for the terrorist crime perpetrated against Hariri.'[71] Two days later, the UNSC responded by adopting Resolution 1644, which essentially extended the mandate of the UNIIIC, in accordance with the 5 Decem-

66 *Ibid.*

67 *Ibid.*

68 N. Novogrodsky, 'Speaking to Africa – The Early Success of the Special Court for Sierra Leone' (2006) 5 *Santa Clara Journal of International Law* 1, 194–216.

69 S/RES/1595 (2005) Resolution 1595 (2005) adopted by the Security Council at its 5160th meeting, on 7 April 2005.

70 C. Harwood, 'The UN International Independent Investigation Commission in Lebanon' in J. Meierhenrich (ed) *The Law and Practice of International Commissions of Inquiry* (Oxford University Press 2018).

71 S/2005/783, Letter dated 13 December 2005 from the *Chargé d'Affaires a.i.* of the Permanent Mission of Lebanon to the United Nations addressed to the Secretary-General.

ber 2005 letter from the Prime Minister.[72] After a series of political events in Lebanon, the UNSC invoked its powers under article IV of the UN Charter to pass Resolution 1757,[73] thus causing the agreement earlier signed between the government and the UN to come into force. STL was thus established. The model of establishment of STL is closely tied to the work of a commission of enquiry. But it shares similar feature with the SCSL in that its establishment was at the instance of the invitation by the Lebanese authorities to the UN.

There are divergent views on the place of the STL in ICL. For some, it was a triumph against impunity, while others argued that it was 'partial at best and illegal at worst'.[74] It has also been called 'an oddity'.[75] It was unique on many fronts: it was the first time a treaty-based tribunal came into existence through a UN Security Council resolution adopted under Chapter VII of the UN Charter. It was also an international tribunal that solely existed to prosecute and depended on 'domestic substantive crimes'.[76] At the time of its establishment, an international tribunal was used to resolve a domestic problem, albeit a problem with an international dimension. It was established to punish the perpetrators of the killing of Hariri. Other attacks may also be tried by the tribunal if certain criteria are fulfilled. This is different from other internationalized tribunals, which were set up to address 'mass atrocities'.

2.4.3 The Extraordinary Chambers in the Courts of Cambodia (ECCC)

The Khmer Rouge regime ruled Cambodia between 1975 and 1979.[77] During that period, the regime committed a catalogue of international crimes. The ECCC was established in 2003, exclusively under domestic law at that point, to try the most senior leaders in the regime. It was established pursuant to an agreement between the UNGA and the Cambodian government that suc-

---

72 UN Doc S/2005/762 'Letter dated 5 December 2005 from the Chargé d'Affaires of the Permanent Mission of Lebanon to the United Nations addressed to the Secretary-General'.

73 S/RES/1757 (2007), Resolution 1757 adopted by the Security Council at its 5685th meeting, on 30 May 2007.

74 See M.A. Bouhabib, 'Power and Perception: The Special Tribunal for Lebanon' (2010) 3 *Berkeley J. of Middle Eastern & Islamic Law* 1, 174.

75 M. Milanovic, 'The Oddity that is the Hariri Tribunal' [available at https://papers.ssrn.com/sol3/papers.cfm?abstract_id=1014906 – accessed 12 March 2023].

76 See N.N. Jurdi, 'The Subject-Matter Jurisdiction of the Special Tribunal for Lebanon' (2007) 5 *JICJ* 1125–1138.

77 See generally J.D. Ciorciari & A. Heindel, *Experiments in International Criminal Justice: Lessons from the Khmer Rouge Tribunal*, (2014) 35 *Michigan Journal of International Law* 369.

ceeded the Khmer Rouge.[78] It was the second hybrid tribunal to be established in Southeast Asia after the Special Panels for Serious Crimes (SPSC) in Dili, East Timor. The ECCC is a hybrid Court which was embedded into the domestic system of the Cambodian Courts. The UN wanted an international Court to guarantee 'independence, impartiality and objectivity' but the Cambodian government pushed to retain ownership. The compromise was, therefore, an internationalized Court in Cambodia's legal system.[79] The ECCC explained that its hybridity was chosen to ensure full national involvement and an adherence to international standards.[80] Article 3 of the Agreement provided for mixed bench composition consisting of Cambodian and international judges, with the latter being in minority. In terms of procedure, Vasiliev argues that adherence to the inquisitorial model distinguishes the ECCC from other international and hybrid tribunals.[81] The ECCC was equally dogged with criticisms that include corruption and political interference,[82] high costs and slow proceedings as well as insufficient outreach to the population.[83] There appeared to have been a 'power battle' between the international and national judges in the ECCC.[84] While the risk of political considerations and interferences are present in international tribunals, they are heightened in hybrids, regional or domestic criminal tribunals.[85] This is one potent argument against regional tribunals who may be subservient to few powerful states within a regional bloc.

---

78 Agreement between the United Nations and the Royal Government of Cambodia concerning the prosecution, under Cambodian law, of crimes committed during the period of Democratic Kampuchea, 6 June 2003.

79 C. Stahn, *A Critical Introduction to International Criminal Law* (Cambridge University Press 2019) 203.

80 Extraordinary Chambers in the Courts of Cambodia, 'Why was this model chosen for the ECCC?' [available at https://www.eccc.gov.kh/en/faq/why-was-model-chosen-eccc – accessed 7 February 2024].

81 S. Vasiliev, 'Trial Process at the ECCC: The Rise and Fall of the Inquisitorial Paradigm in International Criminal Law?' in S.M. Meisenberg and I. Stegmiller (eds), *The Extraordinary Chambers in the Courts of Cambodia: Assessing Their Contribution to International Criminal Law* (T.M.C. Asser Press 2016) 389.

82 T. Hamilton and M. Ramsden, 'The Politicisation of Hybrid Courts: Observations from the Extraordinary Chambers in the Courts of Cambodia' (2014) *International Criminal Law Review* 115–147.

83 C. Sperfeldt, 'From the Margins of Internationalized Criminal Justice: Lessons Learned at the Extraordinary Chambers in the Courts of Cambodia' (2013) 11 *JICJ*, p. 1113.

84 See M.J. Christensen & A. Kjeldgaard-Pedersen, 'Competing Perceptions of Hybrid Justice: International v. National in the Extraordinary Chambers of the Courts of Cambodia' (2018) 18 *International Criminal Law Review* 127.

85 E. Nielsen, 'Hybrid International Criminal Tribunals: Political Interference and Judicial Independence' (2010) 15 *UCLA J Int'l L Foreign Affair* 289.

2.4.4 Special Panels for Serious Crimes (SPSC) in East Timor

For decades, the people of East Timor had agitated for independence from Indonesia, which had unlawfully occupied East Timor since December 1975. Supporters of independence suffered many acts of systematic violence and crimes from Timorese militia groups sponsored and supported by the Indonesian Army. On 30 August 1999, under the supervision of the UN, a referendum conducted by the United Nations Mission to East Timor (UNAMET) voted overwhelmingly for independence, as against the option of remaining an autonomous entity within Indonesia. Shortly after the referendum in August 1999, through Resolution 1272, the Security Council, acting under Chapter VII of the Charter, established the UN Transitional Administrations for East Timor (UNTAET)[86] on 25 October 1999 to administer the territory during the transition period and, more importantly, to build capacity for self-governance for the new government.[87] The UN also set up an International Commission of Enquiry whose report was made public on 30 January 2000. The report recommended the establishment of a UN international tribunal.[88] In response, Indonesia promptly rejected the report of the Commission of Enquiry. Instead, it committed itself to investigate the violence and to prosecute those who are found culpable. Its argument was that the crimes were committed at a time when East Timor was a territory of Indonesia and as such, Indonesia could exercise jurisdiction over investigation and prosecution of the violations.

Faced with Indonesia's stiff opposition, the UN settled for a system that allowed the judicial systems in both Indonesia and East Timor to conduct investigations and trials into the alleged crimes and human rights violations. In Indonesia, the government established the National Commission of Inquiry on Human Rights Violations in East Timor (KPP-HAM)[89] and the Ad Hoc

---

86 In various contexts, the UN had proposed and used transitional administrations to restore peace in troubled or conflict areas. It has been previously used in Kosovo, East Timor and Cambodia. On this, see S. Chesterman, *You, The People: The United Nations, Transitional Administration, and State-Building* (Oxford Scholarship Online, 2004). See also M. Giffard-Lindsay, *Post-conflict peacebuilding: Lessons from transitional administrations in Cambodia and East Timor* (Lambert Academic Publishing 2012).

87 Paragraph 2(e) of Resolution 1272.

88 D. Cohen, 'Seeking Justice on the Cheap: Is the East Timor Tribunal Really a Model for the Future?' (2002) 61 *Analysis from the East-West Center 1*.

89 Human Rights Watch, 'Justice Denied for East Timor: Indonesia's Sham Prosecutions, the Need to Strengthen the Trial Process in East Timor, and the Imperative of U.N. Action' (2002) [available at https://www.hrw.org/legacy/backgrounder/asia/timor/etimor1202bg.htm – accessed 6 February 2024].

Human Rights Court.[90] On the other hand, there was a total lack of a functional judicial system in East Timor. The UNTAET had to build a judicial system for the country 'virtually from scratch'.[91] The UNTAET adopted some regulations, including Regulation 2000/11, which established a few district Courts.[92] Thus, the Special Panels for Serious Crimes in East Timor (SPSC) were created by the UNTAET for the purposes of prosecuting perpetrators of grave international and national crimes. Similar to the SCSL and STL, the mandate of the panels extended beyond international law to breaches of East Timorese national laws.[93]

The Special Panels and a Special Crimes Unit (SCU) were the two 'distinct institutions that made up what has now been called "the Serious Crimes Process" in Timor-Leste'.[94] The third organ was the Public Defender's Office, which functioned independently of the Special Panels.[95]

The normative framework for the Serious Crimes Process consisted of different regulations.[96] Some of the most referenced ones in literature are Regulation 2000/11 on the Organization of Courts in East Timor and Regulation 2000/15 on the Establishment of Panels with Exclusive Jurisdiction over Serious Criminal Offences. Aside from minor exceptions, this regulation mirrored the Rome Statute. Other regulations included Regulation 2000/16 on the Organization of the Public Prosecution Service in East Timor; Regulation 2000/30 on Transitional Rules of Criminal Procedure; and Regulation 2001/25 on the Amendment of UNTAET Regulation No. 2000/11 on the Organization of Courts in East Timor.

Section 7 of Regulation 2000/11 had provided that the district Courts shall have territorial jurisdictions in other cities apart from Dili. Section 10 however confers the district Courts in Dili with exclusive jurisdiction for serious crimes namely: genocide, war crimes, crimes against humanity, torture, murder and sexual offences. The same position was reiterated by section 2.3 of Regulation

---

90 See D. Cohen, 'Intended to Fail: The Trials Before the Ad Hoc Human Rights Court in Jakarta' (2003) *International Center for Transitional Justice Occasional Paper Series* 12.

91 D. Cohen, 'Seeking Justice on the Cheap: Is the East Timor Tribunal Really a Model for the Future?' (2002) 61 *Analysis from the East-West Center* 1.

92 Regulation No. 2000/11 on the Organization of Courts in East Timor.

93 UNTAET Regulation 2000/15.

94 Y. Beigbeder, 'Special Panels for Serious Crimes in East Timor-Now Timor-Leste' *International Criminal Tribunals: Justice and Politics* (Palgrave Macmillan 2011).

95 C. Reiger and M. Wierda, 'The Serious Crimes Process in Timor-Leste: In Retrospect' (2006) *ICTJ Prosecutions Case Studies Series*, 10.

96 See http://mj.gov.tl/jornal/lawsTL/UNTAET-Law/Regulations%20English/regenglish.htm for a comprehensive catalogue of all regulations relating to the UN Administration in East Timor.

2000/15, while restricting the District of Dili Panel's jurisdiction to offences committed between 1 January and 25 October 1999. The panels were localized, as they were established and operated in the location where the crimes took place. Unlike other hybrids considered in this chapter, the UN created judicial systems in Dili, where there was none previously existing.[97]

The SPSC shared judicial accountability and financial responsibility jointly between the state and the UN. It hoped to maximize the benefit of international support and resources with local prosecution. That hope appeared to have been dashed as the tribunal was failed by those who were meant to provide it with the necessary support and did not do so. Some suggested that instead of incorporating the best of both judicial systems, it only reflected their worst.[98] The panels sat from 2000 to 2006 and faced similar challenges as many of the other tribunals: lack of funding; lack of ownership by local community and thus affecting sociological legitimacy; non-cooperation from Indonesia, which ensured the prosecution of largely low-level defendants. The panels indicted a total of 391 people, but 339 could not be tried as they were outside of jurisdiction in Indonesia and other places. The high number of people indicted sometimes makes justice practitioners equate mere prosecutions with justice delivered, thus leading to a false sense of accomplishment.[99]

2.4.5 The Special Criminal Court in the Central African Republic (SCCCAR)

In August 2014, the UN and the government of the Central African Republic (CAR) entered into an agreement which required the latter to establish a 'Special Criminal Court'. Through the actions of the country's parliament, in 2015, the Special Criminal Court for the CAR (SCCCAR) was established. This was more than ten years after the ICC had opened an investigation into crimes committed in the CAR between 2002 and 2003. This investigation was succeeded by another September 2014 ICC investigation, making a total of two active investigations by the ICC in the CAR. This was the first time that the ICC would have two active situations in the same country. The SCCCAR has jurisdiction to try war crimes and crimes against humanity that were committed on the territory of CAR since 2003, matching the same timeline as the first ICC investigation. Its establishment is grounded in the Organic Law, which is

97 S. Katzenstein, 'Hybrid Tribunals: Searching for Justice in East Timor' (2004) 16 *Harvard Human Rights Journal* 252.

98 S. Katzenstein, 'Hybrid Tribunals: Searching for Justice in East Timor' (2004) 16 *Harvard Human Rights Journal* 252.

99 S. Linton, 'Rising from the ashes: The creation of a viable criminal justice system in East Timor' (2001) 25 *Melbourne University Law Review* 122, 178.

essentially a national law adopted by the CAR parliament, authenticated by the country's constitutional Court, and eventually promulgated by the President of the country.[100] As with all hybrid tribunals, its personnel is a mix of national and international staff, whose appointment is to be ratified by the CAR authorities.[101] The tribunal had its first trial in April 2022 and handed down its first judgement in October of the same year.[102]

In many ways, the SCCCAR, as a hybrid tribunal, represents an innovation that had hitherto not been seen in ICL. As noted by previous authors, it is the first tribunal to be established in an ICC situation country.[103] This underscores one of the macro-claims of this book: the understanding that ICC's involvement in any conflict situation should not automatically foreclose the involvement of other mechanisms, so long as the relationship can be arranged to avoid possible conflicts. In another criticized innovation, the tribunal enjoys primacy over national Courts while being subordinate to the jurisdiction of the ICC. This has been described as a 'three-tiered institutional hierarchy'.[104] It is one of the few mechanisms that have complementarity with the ICC and national mechanisms specified in its instrument and framework. Additionally, victims at the SCCCAR can be witnesses and/or civil parties, entitled to reparations.[105] This is more promising for reparative justice in comparison to previous internationalized tribunals like ICTR and SCSL, where victims were only witnesses. At the ICC, victims could only be parties (rather than mere participants) at the reparation stage alone, while the SCCCAR provides an opportunity for victims to be parties throughout all stages of the proceedings.[106]

While views about the tribunal's place in ICL vary, its existence has raised pertinent questions about complementarity.[107] Whereas the Organic Law gives primacy to the ICC over the SCCCAR, as per article 37, the provision appears to have reversed the settled understanding of complementarity in the Rome Statute.

---

100 See generally P. Labuda, 'The Special Criminal Court in the Central African Republic: Failure or Vindication of Complementarity?' (2017) 15 *Journal of International Criminal Justice* 175–206.

101 Article 60–61 of the Organic Law.

102 Amnesty International 'Amnesty International, 'Central African Republic: First-ever SCC trials ensures alleged war criminals face justice', 19 April 2022.

103 P. Labuda (n. 100), 175.

104 *Ibid.*

105 JP Perez Acevedo, 'Victims at the Central Africa's Republic Special Criminal Court' (2020) 39 *Nordic Journal of Human Rights* 1, 2.

106 *Ibid.*

107 P. Labuda (n. 100), 175.

2.5 Hybrid's Legal Basis, Legitimacy and Justification

In terms of the background to their establishment, STL, ECCC and SCSL, with relatively active governments, requested the UN to help in prosecuting the perpetrators of atrocities in their respective countries. That was slightly different from the situation in East Timor and the CAR, where, though the UN was involved, the internationally backed transitional authorities were the active governments in place. In Sierra Leone, the UN Security Council took a decision while the issue was still on the agenda of the Security Council, and there were UN troops on ground.[108] While the UN Security Council did not invoke Chapter VII of the Charter in Sierra Leone, in order to request the Secretary-General to enter an agreement with the government to establish a special Court, it did so in the case of East Timor.[109] Chapter VII was invoked to establish interim administration for East Timor. In Sierra Leone and Lebanon, the UN was requested to assist in prosecuting perpetrators of crimes, while in East Timor, the UN or at least, the interim administration was responsible for all facets of governance, including the administration of criminal justice. For the CAR, the origin of the tribunal is traceable to the activities of the UNSC-authorized multi-dimensional peacekeeping mission and the internationally backed transitional government.

The founding documents of these hybrids varied from one to another. In the case of Sierra Leone, it was the bilateral treaty or agreement between the country and the UN that established the SCSL. The Statute of the SCSL was only annexed to the agreement. The bilateral treaty was also incorporated as domestic legislation through the Special Court Agreement Ratification Act. The legal basis of the SCSL was thus a combination of domestic and international instruments that interacted jointly. This was true also for SCSL and the ECCC. For East Timor, there was no government to negotiate with; hence, the UN established an interim administration, which promulgated regulations to establish and operationalize the tribunal. The UN Security Council derived that authority from Chapter VII resolutions that were passed to establish the interim administration.[110] In the CAR, the Organic Law establishing the tribu-

108 Sarah M.H. Nouwen, 'Hybrid Courts: The Hybrid Category of a New Type of International Crimes Courts', (2006) 2 *Utrecht L. Rev.* 195.

109 *Ibid.*

110 On Chapter VII actions of the UN SC, see N. Krisch, 'Ch. VII Action with Respect to Threats to the Peace, Breaches of the Peace, and Acts of Aggression, Introduction to Chapter VII: The General Framework' in B. Simma & Ors (eds) *The Charter of the United Nations: A Commentary,* Volume II (Oxford University Press 2012).

nal was a result of the combined efforts of the country's parliament, judiciary and the executive.

One of the hottest contested issues on hybrid tribunals and, indeed, many systems of international and domestic governance,[111] is their legitimacy.[112] They are said to be suffering from 'a crisis of legitimacy'.[113] Without legitimacy, a tribunal's ability to discharge its core functions is called into question. The validity of a tribunal's judgements and decisions, and the subsequent acceptability of the decision by parties to a case, the witnesses or the society are significantly eroded if the tribunal lacks legitimacy.[114] In the next chapter, I discuss the Extraordinary African Chambers that tried former Chadian President Hissène Habré and the impact that the challenge to its legitimacy had on the trials. Suffice it to say that one of the justifications for hybrid tribunals, as earlier noted, is that they advance the need to make justice more visible to the affected people, thus improving the chances of acceptability by the local communities. This is a result of the proximity of the justice-dispensing institutions to the affected communities. Generally, other factors that have improved hybrid tribunal's legitimacy included: the presence of local judges;[115] availability of victim participation;[116] the presence of international judges, in addition to local judges, as this may infuse some balance into the judicial process; proximity to the scenes of crimes; application of domestic legal system alongside international order, among others.

---

111 Bodansky argued that 'the legitimacy of domestic government has been a central focus of political theory since at least the time of Hobbes and Locke'. In the same vein, he wondered why legitimacy of international governance systems has been undertheorized until recently. See D.M. Bodansky, 'The Legitimacy of International Governance: A Coming Challenge for International Environmental Law?' (1999) 93 *American Journal of International Law*, 596.

112 For discussions on legitimacy of hybrid tribunals, see S. Williams, 'Hybrid and Internationalized Criminal Tribunals: Jurisdictional Issues' (2009) PhD Thesis at Durham University. See also M. Wierda & ors, 'Early Reflections on Local Perceptions, Legitimacy and Legacy of the Special Tribunal for Lebanon' (2007) 5 *Journal of International Criminal Justice* 1065. See also H. Hobbs, 'Hybrid Tribunals and the Composition of the Court: In Search of Sociological Legitimacy' (2016) 16 *Chicago Journal of International Law* 2.

113 See D. Luban, 'After the Honeymoon: Reflections on the Current State of International Criminal Justice' (2013) 11 *JICJ* 505 at 509.

114 See generally Yvonne McDermott, *Fairness in International Criminal Trials* (OUP 2016).

115 H. Hobbs, 'Hybrid Tribunals and the Composition of the Court: In Search of Sociological Legitimacy' (2016) 16 *Chicago Journal of International Law* 2.

116 H. Hobbs, 'Victim Participation in International Criminal Proceedings: Problems and Potential Solutions in Implementing an Effective and Vital Component of Justice' (2014) 49 *Texas International Law Journal* 9–12.

Many justifications have been adduced for hybrids' existence. Mendez classified the justifications into legal, ethical and consequentialist categories.[117] One legal justification could be the idea that 'hybrid Courts may be alternatives to the ICC where national Courts are unwilling or unable to render justice'.[118] The ethical justification centres around making victims and affected communities the focus of international criminal justice and accountability measures. Prioritizing the victims' interests appears to be a better ethical approach towards holding perpetrators accountable.[119] The consequentialist justification puts into context 'the impact of [such] tribunals on the victims and affected communities in the short and long terms'.[120] The short-term and long-term consequences of prosecutions before hybrid tribunals could be rebuilding the affected community's legal system and, consequently, overall nation-building. This practical approach envisages interaction between foreign and local professionals, which may lead to the transfer of skills and knowledge about ICL and international law generally.[121]

Other motivations for establishing hybrid tribunals are that they offer the benefits of both domestic and international prosecutions;[122] they are developed as pragmatic solution to the international community's failure to bridge the impunity gap;[123] they help to resolve the tension between maintaining state sovereignty and ending impunity for atrocity crimes;[124] they collapse the artificial distinction between domestic and international crimes prosecution;[125] they remedy the ICC's limited jurisdictional reach and resources;[126] they advance the ambition to make justice more visible to populations affected;[127] and they fulfill the ultimate goal of increasing capacity within the national judicial system.[128] Moreover, hybrids have been established and useful in circumstances where the international tribunal with jurisdiction would

117 Mendez (n. 39) 71.
118 *Ibid.*
119 *Ibid* at 73.
120 *Ibid.*
121 *Ibid.*
122 Williams (n. 63) 5.
123 *Ibid.*
124 Williams (n. 63) 58.
125 F. Mégret, 'In Defense of Hybridity: Towards a Representational Theory of International Criminal Justice' (2005) 38 *Cornell International Law Journal* 3, 747.
126 William (n. 63) 58.
127 Stahn (n. 57).
128 For this and many other benefits of hybrid tribunals, see T. Moghadam, 'Revitalizing Universal Jurisdiction: Lessons from Hybrid Tribunals Applied to the Case of Hissene Habre' (2008) 39 *Columbia Human Rights Law Review* 471.

have been overwhelmed with caseloads. A fitting example is the Kosovo hybrid Courts. As explained by Professor Dickinson, 'the U.N. established hybrid Courts in Kosovo precisely because the ICTY could not handle the volume of atrocities cases from the region. The ICTY prosecutor made it clear that the ICTY would be reserved for only the highest profile cases from Kosovo, leaving many suspects without a forum for trial.'[129]

Whether hybrid tribunals have lived up to their expectations is an ongoing debate. Authors like McAuliffe have argued that they have failed to live up to their lofty goals.[130] Schabas submits that their enormous productivity has contributed in no small measure to ICL through building 'an impressive body of case law'.[131] Ciorciari and Heindel argue that 'hybrid Courts have downsides [which include being] susceptible to confusion and inefficiency as they merge multiple legal systems and personnel with disparate backgrounds, training, and approaches to justice'.[132] Holvoet and de Hert opine that while an analysis on whether hybrids have achieved their aims may be premature, 'these institutions have not entirely lived up to their promises'.[133] They have had some successes, but clearly, there is a lot of room for improvement. For instance, while trying to avoid costly trials like those at the *ad hoc* tribunals, many tribunals have had their jurisdictions so narrowed down that, in the end, much money was spent to achieve too little. There were criticisms that the EAC gulped a lot of money, yet only Hissène Habré was tried and convicted by it.[134] Again, experiences have shown that many tribunals struggle to secure cooperation and needed assistance from states, thus limiting their effectiveness. Despite UN backing, ICTY also struggled to get coopera-

129 L.A. Dickinson, 'The Relationship Between Hybrid Courts and International Courts: The Case of Kosovo' (2003) *New England Law Review* at 1071.

130 P. McAuliffe, 'Hybrid Tribunals at Ten: How International Criminal Justice's Golden Child Became an Orphan' (2011) 7 *Journal of International Law and International Relations* 1, 1–65.

131 W. Schabas, 'International Criminal Courts' in Cesare P.R. Romano, K.J. Alter, and Y. Shany (eds) *The Oxford Handbook of International Adjudication* (Oxford University Press 2013).

132 J.D. Ciorciari and A. Heindel, 'Experiments in International Criminal Justice: Lessons from the Khmer Rouge Tribunal' (2013) *Michigan Journal of International Law*, 369–442.

133 M. Holvoet and P. de Hert, 'International Criminal Law as Global Law: An Assessment of the Hybrid Tribunals' (2012) 17 *Tilburg Law Review* 233.

134 L.E. Carter, M.S. Ellis, C. Jalloh, *The International Criminal Court in an Effective Global Justice System* (Edward Elgar Publishing 2016) 39–40.

tion from states.[135] The situation is graver for other tribunals who do not have such resources and backing from the UN.

Tribunals are 'no longer viewed as an alternative to the ICC, but as a possible complement'.[136] In future practice, they may even be considered useful in situations where the ICC is not likely to be able to exercise jurisdiction.[137] In that regard, there are at least three circumstances in which the ICC may have no jurisdiction over a crime: where it lacks jurisdiction *ratione temporis*;[138] where the ICC lacks jurisdiction *ratione loci*;[139] and where it lacks jurisdiction *ratione materiae*.[140]

In conclusion, there have been different models of hybridity, which suggest that there are now wide varieties of international criminal law adjudicatory models. Secondly, that a lot of 'trial and error' had gone into establishing these

135 UN 'War Crimes Denial, Failure to Cooperate with National Authorities Hampering Progress of Former Yugoslavia Tribunal, Security Council Told' [available at https://www.un.org/press/en/2017/sc12858.doc.htm – accessed 23 May 2023].

136 S. William (n. 63) 61; Mendez (n. 39) 71.

137 S. William (n. 63) 61.

138 The ICC lacks jurisdiction *ratione temporis* over crimes that were committed before the coming into force of the Rome Statute. Article 11(1) of the Rome Statute provides that, 'The Court has jurisdiction only with respect to crimes committed after the entry into force of this Statute.' Hybrid tribunals could be useful in situations where the crimes to be prosecuted occurred before the Rome Statute entered into force, since the ICC would not have jurisdiction in that circumstance. The Extraordinary Chambers in the Courts of Senegal, which were employed to prosecute crimes that took place between 1982 and 1990, offers a good example.

139 Article 13(b) of the Rome Statute provides that the ICC may exercise its territorial jurisdiction if '[A] situation in which... crimes appear to have been committed is referred to the Prosecutor by the Security Council acting under Chapter VII of the Charter of the United Nations.' This provision operates to grant the ICC territorial jurisdiction throughout the world, since the Security Council can potentially refer any situation to the Court. However, this possibility is often hampered by political interests. For instance, members of the Security Council have used veto powers to defeat a draft resolution seeking to refer the situation in Syria to the ICC. Thus, where the ICC has no jurisdiction *ratione loci*, perhaps as a result of political considerations or other factors, a hybrid tribunal may become an attractive alternative.

140 The ICC lacks jurisdiction *ratione materiae* in situations where the conducts to be prosecuted fall outside of the crimes that are codified in the Rome Statute. In that circumstance, a hybrid tribunal could be an alternative for the prosecution of such crimes. A good example is the Malabo protocol which codifies several transnational crimes for which the ICC lacks jurisdiction. For general thoughts on the different dimensions of the ICC's jurisdictions, see F. Eboibi, 'Jurisdiction of the International Criminal Court: Analysis, Loopholes and Challenges' (2012) *Nnamdi Azikiwe University Journal of International Law and Jurisprudenc* 28–46.

tribunals, which suggests that different approaches had evolved to address the specific circumstances that surrounded the establishment of different tribunals. That there is no-one-size-fits-all approach has allowed for 'individualized attention and specificity'.[141] Thirdly, in spite of the trial and error, a number of common features have been observed: they were all established as a result of agreement between the UN and the states affected or by a UN transitional authority, mostly in post-conflict situations; they all comprise international and local personnel as judges and staff; their subject matter jurisdiction consisted of international and national crimes. They were all developed in instances where the domestic judicial mechanisms were grossly inadequate or totally non-existent. In this regard, judicial infrastructures were either destroyed during the conflict, as in East Timor and Kosovo, or local judges and lawyers were scarce or incompetent where available.

2.6 Strands of Regionalism and Models of Hybridity

The typology of hybrid tribunals has shown that there are different models of hybridity. I conceive hybridity itself as a strand of regionalism. The first model of hybridity I considered are STL, SCSL, SPSC, SCCAR and the ECCC, which were established because of the actions of various UN organs, specifically the UNSC for the first four, and the UNGA in the case of the latter tribunal. In the next chapter, I will discuss and analyse KSCSPO and EAC, whose establishment is linked to the actions and support of regional organizations. This first mode of classification considers the organization that established the tribunal as a basis for comparison. In that regard, we see two classes of tribunals. First are those whose establishment were midwifed through the joint efforts of states and a UN organ. The second class of tribunals are those whose establishment proceeded from the joint effort of a regional organization and a state within the region. This second class has provided a foundation for the current attempts to set up full-blown ICL regional Courts. I view the involvement of regional organization in ICL through setting up of hybrid tribunals in their regions as some of the building blocks that have contributed to the attempt to set up regional supranational tribunals. This assistance-driven strand of regionalism is one that seeks to strengthen and support the domestic jurisdic-

141 C. Carroll, 'Hybrid Tribunals are the Most Effective Structure for Adjudicating International Crimes Occurring Within a Domestic State' (2013) *Law School Student Scholarship* 90 at 18.

tion to deal with a specific crisis situation. It is the model that 'internationalizes' the domestic systems. One way through which the support for the domestic system happens is the embedment of the tribunal into the domestic system. The ECCC is one example of a hybrid that is embedded into the domestic judicial system. A similarity in the five examples discussed earlier is that the tribunals were established to address crimes that arose out of a conflict which had taken place. They were all established because of agreements between the UN, or a regional organization, and the states affected, mostly in post-conflict situations.

In the next chapter, I will discuss regional hybridity, using the KSCSPO and the EAC in the Courts of Senegal as examples of the first strand of regionalism that I present. This can be distinguished from the second strand that attempts to construct a supranational regional institution to deal with future crimes in a specific region. As has been seen in the African continent, this kind is not established to deal with a singular past crisis. Instead, it is created to address crimes that may occur, usually after its establishment. As opposed to the first strand, which does not seek to replace the domestic system, but rather strengthens it, this strand constructs a regional tribunal as a replacement for domestic systems, especially in a situation where the domestic system is unable to deal with a specific crime. Like the ICC, this will require the cooperation of states to discharge its responsibilities. Their activities will influence inter-state relations, as their subject matters are individuals of several states within the region. Their power and influence extend beyond the state where they are sited. Their actions are not attributable to one state. In this regard, they are only comparable to the ICC, ICTY and ICTR, and not any of the mixed criminal tribunals. Member states are compelled as a matter of obligation to cooperate with such regional tribunals.

While the African continent is the first to establish such a supranational entity, it is not unlikely that other regions may attempt the same. The EU and the CoE's efforts at establishing the KSCSPO may suggest that the European continent is open to the idea of taking more regional initiatives at international crimes prosecution. Also, it is my contention that Africa did not suddenly arrive at a place where it sought to establish a regional criminal Court. One of the preceding developments in ICL is the AU's establishment of the EAC that tried late Hissène Habré. This progression from establishing a single tribunal to try a former leader, to an attempt to establish a fully functional regional tribunal is consistent with AU's approach to international law. It will appear that the establishment of a regional tribunal is a natural progression from the previous ICL efforts in the region. Also, it is to be recalled that regional systems' adoption of human rights regional instruments was motivated by the need to fill the gaps in international human rights instruments.[142] Consistent with that pattern is the idea that a regional criminal Court is a necessity that flows from the gap that the current ICC system evinces. Such gaps include ICC's lack of jurisdiction to try transnational crimes that are of importance to the respective regions. In the next chapter, I will consider other past and current regional practices and initiatives that suggest that more regions are interacting with ICL through different approaches.

3 Conclusion

The future of international criminal justice appears to be in its past. By this, I mean that in the early days, international criminal tribunals were initially created to address specific problems. Recall my reference to the UN War Crimes Commission (UNWCC) that was created to facilitate domestic prosecutions of crimes committed in WWII. Before and after the establishment of the ICC, regional and hybrid tribunals are being created to address specific problems and situations. The turn to regionalism is grounded in the development of these hybrid tribunals. Hybrid tribunals have evolved in different models: some through the cooperation between the UN and affected states and others through the cooperation between regional organizations and the affected states. Their development has now led to the possibility of the existence of a full-fledged regional criminal tribunal. The analysis has shown that regionalism is just one of the necessary strands of alternative forums for prosecutions that have been developed. Regional hybridity, or the assistance-driven model, and the establishment of full regional criminal Courts are the two strands of regionalism. They share similar goals, part of which is to develop tailor-made responses to atrocities, outside the traditional realm of domestic jurisdiction. The development of hybrid tribunals has served as a roadmap that led ICL towards full-fledged regionalism. Development in different regions also suggests that there is a progressive move towards the second strand of regionalism: the establishment of regional Courts to deal with transnational and international crimes. Other regions might be encouraged by the steps taken by the African Union in the adoption of the Malabo Protocol. As states continue to face common transnational crimes in their region, their joint responses may continue to deepen regional interaction with international criminal justice.

142 M. Sirleaf, 'Not Your Dumping Ground: Criminalization of Trafficking in Hazardous Waste in Africa' (2018) 35 *Wisconsin Journal of International Law* 348.

The chapter sets out to investigate the typologies of regional and hybrid institutions that have been emerging in ICL. While there is perhaps no linear trajectory towards a regional approach, I have now established that the development and practice of hybrid tribunals were necessary building blocks for regionalism in ICL.

CHAPTER 4

Regional Hybridity: The EAC and the KSCSPO

1 Introduction

The evolution of international criminal law has not been a linear progression but a process shaped by experimentation and adaptation. Among the most innovative developments in this evolution is the emergence of hybrid and regionally anchored mechanisms that combine international and domestic elements to address accountability for mass atrocities. These institutions have filled crucial gaps between purely national prosecutions and fully international tribunals. Their hybrid character and regional embeddedness demonstrate how justice can be both locally grounded and internationally legitimate.

This chapter focuses on the first strand of regional complementarity: the assistance-driven model. It examines two case studies that illustrate how regional collaboration has shaped hybrid accountability mechanisms – the Extraordinary African Chambers (EAC) within the Courts of Senegal, and the Kosovo Specialist Chambers and Specialist Prosecutor's Office (KSCSPO). Both institutions were established through partnerships between regional or sub-regional bodies and national governments to prosecute international crimes committed within their respective regions. These examples reflect an evolving understanding that regional institutions can play a vital role in bridging global and local justice initiatives while enhancing ownership, legitimacy, and accessibility.

The analysis begins by situating regional hybridity within the broader historical context of international criminal justice. It then explores the legal foundations, jurisdictional structure, and institutional design of the EAC and the KSCSPO, assessing their significance as practical expressions of regional complementarity. The discussion highlights how these tribunals navigate the complex relationship between regional political will, national sovereignty, and international legal standards. It also considers the ways in which these courts contribute to a pluralistic system of accountability that complements, rather than competing with, universal mechanisms such as the International Criminal Court.

The EAC and KSCSPO represent distinct yet related trajectories of regional hybridity. The EAC, created through cooperation between the African Union and Senegal to prosecute the former Chadian president Hissène Habré, dem-

© 2026 THE AUTHOR(S) | HTTPS://DOI.ORG/10.1163/9789004761803-006

onstrates how regional organizations can empower domestic jurisdictions to deliver justice for international crimes. The KSCSPO, established through an agreement between Kosovo and the European Union, represents a different configuration of regional influence, where external oversight and regional legitimacy coexist to address crimes arising from regional conflict. Both examples underscore that regional hybridity can operate as a dynamic mechanism for accountability that balances proximity with impartiality, and regional ownership with adherence to international norms.

By examining these case studies, this chapter seeks to draw broader lessons about the promise and limits of regional hybridity. It argues that these mechanisms represent more than transitional solutions; they form part of a durable and evolving architecture of international criminal justice. The experiences of the EAC and KSCSPO illustrate how regional cooperation can advance accountability where global mechanisms face political or jurisdictional constraints. They also demonstrate that regional initiatives, when properly structured, can enhance the legitimacy and sustainability of justice processes while deepening the cooperative fabric of international criminal law.

In sum, the chapter situates the EAC and KSCSPO as pioneering examples of how regional hybridity contributes to the maturation of international criminal law. Their achievements and shortcomings provide valuable insights into how future regional or hybrid mechanisms might be designed to promote both justice and complementarity in an increasingly interconnected legal order.

2 Historical Background on Regional Enforcement of ICL

The trend towards the enforcement of international criminal law through regional means has its roots in common regional efforts against transnational crimes. It has been previously utilized or proposed in the maintenance of international peace and security, in line with Article 52(1) of the UN Charter.[1] It provides that '[n]othing in the present Charter precludes the existence of regional arrangements or agencies for dealing with such matters relating to the maintenance of international peace and security…'. There are multiple instances where regional organizations have taken steps, including military actions, to enforce compliance with international norms under this Charter

1 W. Burke-White 'Regionalization of International Criminal Law Enforcement: A Preliminary Exploration (2003) 38 *Texas International Law Journal* 732.

provision. NATO in Kosovo[2] and the ECOWAS in Liberia[3] are classic examples.[4] Regional attempts at criminalizing and prosecuting money laundering are another example of enforcement of transnational crimes through regional means. The Council of Europe,[5] the Organization of American States[6] as well as the African Union[7] all have legal and/or institutional frameworks for the crime of money laundering.[8] A third example is piracy on the high seas, which has been described as the 'oldest international crime'.[9] There are existing regional arrangements for maritime security.[10] International fisheries law, media and intellectual piracy as well as international environmental law are other examples of enforcement of international law through regional mechanisms.[11] Also, there has been regional cooperation in relation to the crime of terrorism. These developments often reflect regional priorities as Europe,[12] Africa,[13] Central

---

2 For an analysis of NATO's involvement in Kosovo, see M.E. O'Connell 'The UN, NATO, and International Law after Kosovo' (2000) 22 *Human Rights Quarterly* 1, 57–89.

3 For the roles played by ECOWAS in Liberia, see generally C.E. Adibe 'The Liberian Conflict and the ECOWAS-UN Partnership' in Weiss T.G. (eds) Beyond UN Subcontracting *International Political Economy Series* (Palgrave Macmillan 1998).

4 *Ibid.*

5 The Convention on Laundering, Search, Seizure and Confiscation of the Proceeds from Crime (1990). Article 6 of the Convention specifically deals with laundering offences.

6 'The Organization of American States (OAS), through the Inter-American Drug Abuse Control Commission (CICAD) ... devotes efforts to strengthen the capacities of law enforcement agencies, bank regulators, financial intelligence units (FIUs), specialized public prosecutors, the judiciary, and other agencies involved in money laundering control and terrorism financing detection, investigation, and prosecution throughout the Americas'. See https://www.state.gov/j/inl/rls/nrcrpt/2015/vol2/239468.htm.

7 Article 28I Bis of the Malabo Protocol makes money laundering a crime.

8 W. Burke-White (n. 1).

9 See M. Scharf and M. Taylor 'A Contemporary Approach to the Oldest International Crime' (2017) 38 *Utrecht Journal of International and European Law* 84. It is noteworthy that the Malabo Protocol criminalizes piracy in Article 28F.

10 See for example D. Fantaye *Regional Approaches to Maritime Security in the Horn of Africa* (Friedrich-Ebert-Stiftung 2014).

11 Burke-White (n. 1) 733.

12 'In 2005, the European Council adopted the EU counter-terrorism strategy to fight terrorism globally and make Europe safer. The strategy's four pillars are to prevent, protect, pursue and respond.' See [https://www.consilium.europa.eu/en/policies/fight-against-terrorism/eu-strategy/ – accessed on 20 May 2023].

13 The AU specifically notes that its regional efforts to prevent and combat terrorism have a long history. The continental legislative framework in this regard is the 1999 OAU Convention on the Prevention and Combating of Terrorism adopted by the 35th Ordinary Session of the OAU Summit, held in Algiers, Algeria, in July 1999.

Asia,[14] the League of Arab States, comprising member states from the Middle East, Gulf and North Africa states[15] as well as Southeast Asia[16] all have mechanisms and frameworks for dealing with terrorism.[17] These examples all share two important elements. The first is that the legal problems they intend to solve are of regional concern and, secondly, regional mechanisms are better suited to enforce compliance and punish violations.[18] The significance of this is that, in a comparative sense, regional enforcement was put forward as a better response for addressing these categories of crime. The next sub-section therefore briefly examines ICL developments in specific regions, namely Europe, the Latin American and the Caribbean, Southeast Asia, and concludes with a more robust discussion on specific tribunals in Africa and Europe.

3 ICL Development in Specific Regions

Bodies that have hitherto been remotely concerned with international criminal law are beginning to get increasingly concerned about it and consequently involved with its work. Support for its expansion has come from unlikely quarters. For example, regional bodies have taken a special interest in the growth of ICL, and in some ways, they have helped to chart a course for it. Regional human rights courts have also performed quasi-criminal functions.[19]

---

14 The UN is spearheading 'an initiative to assist Central Asian States to devise a regional Plan of Action to implement the UN Global Counter-Terrorism Strategy'. See 'Implementing the United Nations Global Counter-Terrorism Strategy in Central Asia Concept Paper [available at The UN Global Counter-Terrorism Strategy (unmissions.org) – accessed on 21 March 2024].

15 In 1998, the LAS adopted the Arab Convention for the Suppression of Terrorism.

16 The ASEAN has adopted a Convention on Counter-terrorism whose objective is to 'provide for the framework for regional cooperation to counter, prevent and suppress terrorism in all its forms and manifestations and to deepen cooperation among law enforcement agencies and relevant authorities of the Parties in countering terrorism'. See ASEAN Convention on Counter Terrorism, April 1998.

17 See generally A. Du Plessis 'A snapshot of international criminal justice cooperation against terrorism since 9/11' in L. van den Herik & N. Schrijver (eds) *Counter-Terrorism Strategies in a Fragmented International Legal Order: Meeting the Challenges* (Cambridge University Press 2013) 29–67.

18 C. Jalloh 'The Place of the African Criminal Court in the Prosecution of Serious Crimes in Africa' in Jalloh C and Ors (eds) *The African Court of Justice and Human and Peoples' Rights in Context: Developments and Challenges* (Cambridge University Press 2019) 295.

19 A.V. Huneeus 'International Criminal Law by Other Means: The Quasi-Criminal Jurisdiction of the Human Rights Courts' (2013) 107 *American Journal of International law* 1.

The European Union has especially been involved in the project of international criminal justice, through its commitments and the continuous support it offers.[20] For example, all the 27 EU member states are state parties to the ICC Statute. It was also the first regional organization to sign an agreement on cooperation and assistance with the ICC, as far back as 2006.[21] Additionally, more than any other region, it funds the activities of the ICC and other criminal justice initiatives around the globe. Some of the biggest financial contributors to the ICC have been France, Germany and the United Kingdom.[22] The European Council has enacted several legal instruments to strengthen cooperation and assistance initiatives at the national level. This is in addition to the Council of Europe's decision on assistance to the ICC in 2011.[23] The EU established a European Public Prosecutor's Office (EPPO) in relation to financial crimes. Crimes within the jurisdiction of the EPPO include cross border VAT and other types of fraud, corruption that affects EU's financial interests, money laundering and organized crimes, as well as misappropriation of EU funds.[24] The EPPO functions as a supranational entity, under the jurisdiction of national courts of member states.[25] The establishment of the EPPO has contributed to efforts aimed at moving the EU from cooperation to integration.[26] It also foreshadows the idea behind states within a region, cooperating on issues that concern them as a bloc of states. The European Arrest Warrant (EAW) is another development in the regional criminal justice system. It pushes European integration into realms that were once unthinkable.[27] It allows a country within the EU to issue a warrant of arrest which is binding and executable in all member states. An author has argued that the EAW

20 On the EU and ICL, see J. Wouters & S. Basu 'The Creation of a Global Criminal Justice System: The European Union and the International Criminal Court' in C. Ryngaert (ed) The Effectiveness of International Criminal Justice (Intersentia 2009) 117–140.

21 ICC-PRES/01-01-06 Agreement between the International Criminal Court and the European Union on Cooperation and Assistance, 10 April 2006.

22 See, for example, status of contributions as at 31 December 2018 in ICC-ASP, 'Financial statements of the International Criminal Court for the year ended 31 December 2018' ICC-ASP/18/12, 42.

23 Council Decision 2011/168/CFSP of 21 March 2011 on the International Criminal Court and repealing Common Position 2003/444/CFSP.

24 EPPO 'Mission and Tasks' [available at https://www.eppo.europa.eu/en/mission-and-tasks – accessed on 12 May 2022].

25 V. Mitsilegas 'European prosecution between cooperation and integration: The European Public Prosecutor's Office and the rule of law' (2021) 22 *Maastricht Journal of European and Comparative Law* 2, 263.

26 *Ibid*, 262.

27 C. Kaunert '"Without the Power of Purse or Sword": The European Arrest Warrant and the Role of the Commission' (2007) 29 *European Integration* 4, 388.

could serve as an additional tool for prosecuting ICC crimes.[28] The earlier adoption of the Framework Decision on the European Evidence Warrant for the purpose of obtaining objects, documents and data for use in proceedings in criminal matters also adds to a growing list of regional initiatives towards strengthening criminal justice within the EU.[29] The EEW was replaced with the European Investigation Order.[30] There is a high degree of economic, social, political and industrial integration among EU member states. This may explain why there seem to be some real movements towards judicial and legal cooperation in the realm of regional criminal law.[31]

In terms of actual attempts at prosecuting international crimes through regional efforts, the EU agreed with the Kosovo authorities to establish the Kosovo Specialist Chambers and Specialist Prosecutors Office (KSC-SPO) after a 2011 report of the Council of Europe Parliamentary Assembly.[32] Cimiotta concludes that the establishment of the KSC-SPO 'represents a regional variation of mixed criminal tribunals'.[33] The developments in the EU could suggest that the region is opened to the idea of establishing mechanisms that could address international and transnational crimes.

In Africa, through the Malabo Protocol, the AU has proposed to add international criminal jurisdiction to the African Court of Justice and Human Rights (ACJHR).[34] This remains the clearest indication that regional mechanisms may embrace international crimes prosecution. At a sub-regional level, state parties to the East African Court of Justice have also discussed the possibility of extending the jurisdiction of the court to try crimes against human-

---

28 L Vierucci 'The European Arrest Warrant: An Additional Tool for Prosecuting ICC Crimes' (2004) 2 JICJ 275–285.

29 On the Evidence Warrant, see P. De Hert, K. Weis and N. Cloosen 'The Framework Decision of 18 December 2008 – A Critical Assessment' (2009) 1 *New Journal of European Criminal Law* 55–78.

30 See Directive 2014/41/EU of The European Parliament and of The Council of 3 April 2014 regarding the European Investigation Order in criminal matters.

31 Relevant provision from the Treaty on Functioning of the EU (TFEU) includes Article 82 (1).

32 See generally R. Muharremi 'The Concept of Hybrid Courts Revisited: The Case of the Kosovo Specialist Chambers' (2018) 18 *International Criminal Law Review* 4.

33 E. Cimiotta 'The Specialist Chambers and the Specialist Prosecutor's Office in Kosovo: The 'Regionalization' of International Criminal Justice in Context' (2016) 14 *Journal of International Criminal Justice* 1, 53–72.

34 M. Du Plessis 'Implications of the AU decision to give the African Court jurisdiction over international crimes' (2012) *ISS Paper* 235. See also L. van den Herik and E. van Sliedregt 'International Criminal Law and the Malabo Protocol About Scholarly Reception, Rebellion and Role Models' (2017) *Grotius Center Working Paper Series* 2017/066-ICL.

ity.[35] We have seen a readiness to use domestic courts to prosecute international crimes. Many African countries already have international crimes provisions in their domestic laws. This suggests that non-ratification of the Rome Statute is not equal to a reluctance to prosecute conducts amounting to international crimes.[36] Out of 55 African countries surveyed in a report, only 19 do not have international crimes provisions within their domestic laws, with as many as 22 having laws that criminalized the three Rome Statute crimes of genocide, war crimes and crimes against humanity. Others have provisions that criminalized one or more of the three Rome Statute crimes, and this is irrespective of whether they have ratified the Rome Statute.[37]

There are strong but scattered moves towards regional integration in Africa. Currently, the AU recognizes eight regional economic communities.[38] While the continent has prioritized the project of economic integration for several decades now, cooperation in respect of international and transnational crimes has been slower. One primary motivation for these moves towards economic integration appears to be Africa's past economic situation. These economic communities were established to engender cooperation to address the economic challenges on the continent. It is therefore unsurprising that the earlier focus within the African region was to address the pressing need for economic prosperity. In my view, this, in addition to other factors that I have discussed in Chapter 1, may have accounted for the slow development of integration in international criminal justice. There appeared to have been an urgent need to first address the economic challenges that were common to most countries on the continent. With the existence of several economic communities and the development in human rights law, the continent appears to be ready to construct a regional criminal mechanism. One noticeable trend on the continent is the desire to collaborate on issues that generally affect many of the member states. It is therefore understandable that a problem of transnational crimes has begun to make the project of a regional criminal tribunal a necessity.

The Caribbean region has a Caribbean Court of Justice which was established in 2001. According to the agreement establishing the court, 'an appeal shall lie to the Court with the special leave of the Court from any decision of

35 Chimp Reports, 'East African Courts to Hear Crimes Against Humanity' 29 April 2013 [available at https://chimpreports.com/9681-east-african-court-to-hear-crimes-against-humanity/ – accessed on 6 February 2024].

36 C. Meinicke 'Domestic prosecution of International Crimes – Africa', 15 May 2019.

37 *Ibid.*

38 African Union 'Regional Economic Communities (RECs) [available at https://au.int/en/organs/recs – accessed on 9 February 2024].

the Court of Appeal of a Contracting Party in any civil or criminal matter'.[39] This appellate criminal jurisdiction appears to be the first in a regional court. The criminal jurisdiction has been less used, compared to the civil jurisdiction.[40] In 2016, the Inter-American Commission signed a Memorandum of Understanding with the ICC to engender a new regime of cooperation and support between the two institutions.[41] The Commission consists of member states from Latin America and the Caribbean countries.

Beyond cooperation between the Inter-American Court on Human Rights (IACtHR) and the ICC, there have also been calls for the creation of a regional criminal court – the Latin American Court Against Organized Crime (the COPLA Initiative).[42] These calls have largely been made by coalition of civil societies and political organizations in Latin America, chief of which are the South American Coalition for the International Criminal Court and *Democracia Global*.[43] A number of reasons have been given for this campaign. One is the need to advance regional integration which is facing a stalemate and backward trend.[44] Secondly, the activities of violent criminal organizations engaging in drugs, arms and human trafficking across borders in the region have necessitated the need to devise approaches that take regional peculiarities into account.[45] The region continues to witness proliferations of extremely

39 Article XXV (4) of the Agreement Establishing the Caribbean Court of Justice, 14 February 2001.

40 A.N. Maharajh 'The Caribbean Court of Justice: A Horizontally and Vertically Comparative Study of the Caribbean's First Independent and Interdependent Court' (2014) 47 *Cornell International Law Journal* 747.

41 ICC Press Release: ICC and Inter American Court Sign MOU at https://www.icc-cpi.int/Pages/item.aspx?name=pr1191.

42 COPLA is the Spanish acronym for the Latin American and Caribbean Criminal Court Against Transnational Organized Crime. See 'The "Cienfuegos Affair" and the Proposal for a New Regional Transnational Criminal Court in Latin America (COPLA)', *Opinio Juris*, 16 July 2021 [available at http://opiniojuris.org/2021/07/16/the-cienfuegos-affair-and-the-proposal-for-a-new-regional-transnational-criminal-court-in-latin-america-copla/ – accessed on 7 February 2024]. See also WFM, 'COPLA Campaign', [available at https://www.wfm-igp.org/campaign/copla-campaign/ – accessed on 7 February 2024].

43 COPLA [available at https://www.coalicioncopla.org/ – accessed on 7 February 2024].

44 The Federalist Debate, F.A. Iglesias 'A Regional Criminal Court Against Transnational Organized Crime' (2014) 1 [available at https://www.federalist-debate.org/archive/year-xxxiv-number-3-november-2021/borderless-debate/the-latin-american-criminal-court-an-approach-for-regional-integration-against-transnational-organized-crime – accessed on 8 February 2024].

45 For thoughts on the effects of drug trafficking and the attendant violence in Latin America, see Corporación Andina de Fomento CAF, Development Bank of Latin America 'Towards a safer Latin America: A new perspective to prevent and control crime' (2014) 137–165.

violent criminal gangs. It is also one of the most violent regions in the world.[46] Thirdly, the inability of governments in the region to effectively deal with transnational crimes makes a regional court a viable alternative. National security mechanisms are increasingly becoming inadequate to address the challenges posed by these organized groups.[47] The governments and people of Latin America share a common problem of insecurity that continuously defy national efforts. The pervasiveness of the security challenges has assumed a regional dimension. As observed,

> The problem of organized transnational crime is not national, but regional. Therefore, regional problems require regional policies. And regional policies require regional institutions in order to overcome succumbing to the inefficiency and arbitrariness of power imbalances between states, or at the mercy of inability of local powers.[48]

The proposed court will operate as a 'transnational criminal court'.[49] It may draw membership from all Latin American and Caribbean countries. It will apply among other instruments, the United Nations Convention against Transnational Organized Crime (Palermo Convention) and its three supplementary Protocols. It is also proposed to complement domestic laws and have jurisdiction over seven transnational crimes, including drugs and human trafficking, money laundering and transnational bribery.[50] While the campaign for its establishment continues, what is of importance is that the prevalence of organized transnational crimes, over which the ICC may not have jurisdiction, is one of the reasons that have necessitated the call for a regional criminal court in the Latin American region. Government Ministers of MERCOSUR – an economic and political bloc consisting of some countries in Latin America, have adopted a declaration that commits their governments to formally study

---

46 COPLA, 'Latin American Criminal Court Against Transnational Organised Crime' [available at http://www.europarl.europa.eu/meetdocs/2014_2019/documents/dlat/dv/07_copla_abstractnov2016/07_copla_abstractnov2016en.pdf – accessed on 8 February 2024].

47 *Ibid.*

48 *Ibid*, 2.

49 R. Currie & J. Leon 'Copla: A Transnational Criminal Court for Latin America and the Caribbean' (2019) 88 *Nordic Journal of International Law* 592.

50 WFM Canada 'The proposal for a Latin American and Caribbean Criminal Court against Transnational Organized Crime reaches the United Nations General Assembly (December 2017)' [available at http://www.wfmcanada.org/2018/01/proposal-latin-american-caribbean-criminal-court-transnational-organized-crime-reaches-united-nations-general-assembly-december-2017/ – accessed on 8 February 2024].

the feasibility of establishing such a regional court.[51] It is yet to be seen how the court, if it is ever established, will operate in practical terms. However, regionalism will continue to be an attractive alternative where regions are confronted with common transnational challenges that have defied national efforts, as is the case in Latin America. The inter-American region has faced similar transnational crimes issues across member states. It is also the region with the most developed transitional justice jurisprudence by its regional human rights court.[52] It is not therefore surprising that earlier cooperation efforts have centred around addressing joint problems of organized crimes.[53] As with the African region, the Latin American region also confronted pressing challenges which required a common front.

It has been argued that the Southeast Asian region is generally reluctant towards embracing the ICC.[54] Certain facts may support this assertion. As of today, only two states in the region – Cambodia and Bangladesh, are parties to the ICC Statute. Philippines pulled out of the ICC in 2018.[55] In 2019, Malaysia backtracked on its earlier accession to the Rome Statute.[56] Three hybrid criminal tribunals have been established in the region.[57] None of the three was established through the actions or support of the regional body: the Association of Southeast Asian Nations (ASEAN). The three tribunals are the Special Panels for Serious Crimes (SPSC) in Timor-Leste, which concluded its assign-

51 WFM Canada 'COPLA Update Regional governments agree to study proposed criminal court' [available at http://www.wfmcanada.org/2018/07/copla-update-regional-governments-agree-study-proposed-criminal-court/ – accessed on 8 February 2024].

52 See generally E. M. Ceia 'The Contributions of the Inter-American Court of Human Rights to the Development of Transitional Justice' (2015) 14 *The Law and Practice of International Courts and Tribunals* 3, 457–475.

53 R. van Ellis '*Transnational Organized Crime in Latin America and the Caribbean: From Evolving Threats and Responses to Integrated, Adaptive Solutions* (Lexington Books 2018) 6.

54 On this reluctance and possible reasons for it, see S. Freeland 'International Criminal Justice in the Asia-Pacific Region: The Role of the International Criminal Court Treaty Regime' (2013) 11 *Journal of International Criminal Justice* 5. See also Takemura H 'The Asian Region and the International Criminal Court' in Nakanishi Y. (ed) *Contemporary Issues in Human Rights Law* (Springer 2018) 107–125.

55 ICC 'Situation in the Republic of Philippines' [available at, https://www.icc-cpi.int/philippines – accessed on 7 February 2024].

56 Coalition for the International Criminal Court, 'Malaysia backtracks on accession to the Rome Statute' 12 April 2019.

57 L. Schuldt 'Southeast Asian Hesitation: ASEAN Countries and the International Criminal Court' (2015) 16 *German Law Journal* 1, 77.

ment in 2006,[58] and the Extraordinary Chambers in the Courts of Cambodia (ECCC) and the International Crimes Tribunal-1, Bangladesh.[59]

From the foregoing, it appears that there has not been significant development in relation to regionalization of international criminal justice within the Southeast Asian region. However, like most regions, the ASEAN also recognized the need for a common front to address transnational crimes that are peculiar to that region. For this reason, the regional body adopted the 1997 ASEAN Declaration on Transnational Crimes.[60] The Declaration significantly notes that 'the continuity of existing global framework against transnational crime rests on consolidated regional action in the institutional and operational spheres'.[61] The Declaration identified six transnational crimes as capable of disrupting regional stability and development. The six crimes are 'terrorism, illicit drug trafficking, arms smuggling, money laundering, traffic in persons and piracy'.[62] The African region has already proposed the creation of a regional court to prosecute these same crimes. The ASEAN region may set up a regional court for the purposes of prosecuting these crimes. In any case, paragraph 1 of the Declaration already states that the regional body has resolved to 'strengthen the commitment of Member Countries to cooperate at the regional level in combating the transnational crime'.[63]

In essence, the development in every region is driven by the challenges that are peculiar to those regions. This is partly the idea that regional complementarity champions – the need to develop context-specific solutions to impunity. States acting under the auspices of regional organizations may continue to embrace and actively participate in the project of international criminal justice as seen from ongoing efforts across different regions.

Historically, since the days of the International Military Tribunal after the WWII, international crimes prosecutions have largely occurred at a supranational level.[64] More recently, states have utilized their domestic jurisdictions –

---

58 On the Special Panels, see S. Katzenstein 'Hybrid Tribunals: Searching for Justice in East Timor' (2003) 16 *Harvard Human Rights Journal* 245–278.

59 S. Linton 'Completing the Circle: Accountability for the Crimes of the 1971 Bangladesh War of Liberation' (2010) 21 *Criminal Law Forum* 2, 191–311.

60 The 1997 ASEAN Declaration on Transnational Crimes, 20 December 1997.

61 Preamble to the Declaration.

62 *Ibid.*

63 *Ibid.*

64 See also J.N. Maogoto 'The 1919 Paris Peace Conference and the Allied Commission: Challenging Sovereignty Through Supranational Criminal Jurisdiction' in M. Bergsmo & Ors (eds) *Historical Origins of International Criminal Law* (Torkel Opsahl Academic E-Publisher 2014) 171–193.

through activating universal and extra-territorial jurisdiction[65] and establishing mixed tribunals – for the same purposes.[66] These two enforcement mechanisms have inherent benefits and drawbacks.[67] To remedy the drawbacks, Burke-White has argued that 'regional enforcement would be situated at a unique midpoint … balancing the benefits and dangers of both…'.[68] Bruch calls it the 'best of both worlds' approach.[69] In this chapter, I approach the regional system, not only as one that sits in-between the two worlds, but as an independent and integral part of a global architecture of justice. This is what has begun to emerge, first in the AU's support for the creation of a tribunal to try the former President of Chad, and subsequently, in the establishment of the Criminal Chamber in the African Court.

4 The Extraordinary African Chambers (EAC)

The EAC was created in Senegal, through an agreement with the AU, to try international crimes committed in Chad between 7 June 1982 and 1 December 1990. Many reports from NGOs already contain exhaustive details of crimes committed by the government of Hissène Habré in that period.[70] The relevance of the EAC derives from the idea that many have described its establishment and perceived 'success' as an example of 'an African solution to an African problem'.[71] As a transitional justice mechanism, it was 'simultaneously

65 For an understanding of the principle of universal jurisdiction, see R. O'Keefe 'Universal Jurisdiction: Clarifying the Basic Concept' (2004) 2 *Journal of International Criminal Justice* 3, 735–760.

66 W. Burke-White 'Regionalization of International Criminal Law Enforcement: A Preliminary Exploration' (2003) 38 *Texas International Law Journal* 732.

67 *Ibid.*

68 *Ibid.*

69 E.M. Bruch 'Hybrid Courts: Examining hybridity through a post-colonial lens' (2010) 28 *Boston University International Law Journal* 1 at 38.

70 For examples of such reports, see Human Rights Watch, 'Chad: The Victims of Hissène Habré Still Awaiting Justice', 12 July 2005. See also Amnesty International 'Chad: The Habre Legacy', 15 October 2001. Human Rights Data Analysis Group, R. Silva, J. Klingner, and S Weikart, 'State Coordinated Violence in Chad under Hissène Habré: A Statistical Analysis of Reported Prison Mortality in Chad's DDS Prisons and Command Responsibility of Hissène Habré, 1982–1990, 3 February 2010.

71 For example, see S. Williams 'The Extraordinary African Chambers in the Senegalese Courts an African Solution to an African Problem?' (2013) 11 *JICJ* 1139–1160. See also African Union 'Report of the Committee of Eminent African Jurists on the Case of Hissène Habré' at https://www.peacepalacelibrary.nl/ebooks/files/habreCEJA_Repor 0506.pdf where the Committee stated in paragraph 22 that '[I]t considered the estab-

international, regional and local'[72] in nature. It also stands as a unique example of attempts at regionalizing international criminal justice. The trials and the Chambers that conducted them signalled many 'firsts' in African and wider international criminal justice system. It was the first time that the African Union (AU) had established a criminal tribunal to try international crimes. It was also the first time a former African head of state had been tried before a court in another African country. Thirdly, it was the first time that a universal jurisdiction case had proceeded to trial in Africa.[73] Lastly, it was the first time that an African war criminal had been convicted on African soil.[74] It may be too early to write about the far-reaching impact and the legacy of the trials, but even at this early stage, there are already scholars who hold pessimistic views about the importance of the trial.[75] Irrespective of what anyone thinks, the trials marked an important milestone in the development of ICL in Africa,[76] and it was a precursor to Africa's decision to establish an international criminal chamber in its regional court.

4.1 Background to the Establishment of the EAC

The events leading to the prosecution and eventual conviction of Habré in 2016 started in 1992. Habré had been deposed in 1990, and his successor had taken power in Chad. The latter established the Chadian National Commission of Inquiry. The mandate of the Commission was to 'investigate illegal detentions, assassinations, disappearances, torture, mistreatment, other attacks on the physical and mental integrity of persons; all violations of human rights, illicit narcotics trafficking and embezzlement of state funds between 1982 and

lishment of an ad hoc tribunal as another good opportunity for an African solution to be found.'

72 T. Bouwknegt "Beyond 'African Solutions to African Problems' at the Extraordinary African Chambers and 'Distant Justice' at the International Criminal Court" (2019) 0 *JICJ* 1.

73 M. Kersten 'The Trial of Hissène Habré and What it Could Mean for Justice in Africa' [available at https://justiceinconflict.org/2018/03/27/the-trial-of-hissene-habre-and-what-it-could-mean-for-justice-in-africa/ – accessed on 4 March 2023].

74 C. Hicks, *The Trial of Hissène Habré: How the People of Chad Brought a Tyrant to Justice* (ZED Books 2018).

75 See, for example, Konstantinos D. Magliveras 'Fighting Impunity Unsuccessfully in Africa: A Critique of the African Union's Handling of the Hissène Habré Affair' (2014) 22 *Afr. J. Int'l & Comp. L.* 420–447.

76 See generally S. Weill and others (eds) *The President on Trial: Prosecuting* Hissène Habré (Oxford University Press 2020).

1990'.[77] Similar to the 'future' Malabo Protocol, 'the crime jurisdiction' of the Commission contained a wide range of 'core' and 'transnational crimes'. The Commission issued a report dated 7 May 1992.[78] In it, the Commission found that Habré's government was responsible for an estimated 40,000 deaths. The Commission also recommended the establishment of an independent judiciary, a reform of the security forces, timely creation of a National Human Rights Commission and prosecutions as well as symbolic reparations.[79] It was only in January 2000, that some Chadian nationals, through the support of a coalition named the International Committee for the Fair Trial of Hissène Habré, filed criminal charges against Hissène Habré at a Dakar court. In February, a Senegalese judge indicted Habré for crimes against humanity and torture. He was subsequently placed under house arrest.[80] The Senegalese Appellate Court, however, quashed the indictment and dismissed the case. The Court of Appeal held that although the state of Senegal had ratified the UN Convention Against Torture, the state had yet to domesticate it and as such, could not try crimes committed abroad.[81] In essence, the court held that Habré could not stand trials in Senegal for crimes committed elsewhere. In March 2001, the Court of Cassation also upheld the position of the Appellate Court. Prior to this time, Habré had been released from detention, but his respite was short-lived, as a Belgian court had been approached by Chadians and Belgians of Chadian origin.[82] The Belgian court indicted Habré on the same charges as those filed before the Senegalese court. The court issued an international warrant of arrest against Habré.[83] The state of Belgium followed up with an extradition request to Senegal in November 2005. There were other extradition requests from Belgium to Senegal.[84]

It is significant that the Senegalese Appeals Court refused to grant the extradition request from Belgium, but instead, upheld the argument that Habré should enjoy immunity for acts committed in the discharge of his duty, in his

---

77 United States Institute of Peace, Chad: Report of the Commission of Inquiry into the Crimes and Misappropriations Committed by Ex-President Habré, his Accomplices and/or Accessories: Investigation of Crimes Against the Physical and Mental Integrity of Persons and their Possessions, 7 May 1992.

78 *Ibid.*

79 *Ibid.*

80 R. Brody 'Bringing a Dictator to Justice: The Case of Hissène Habré' (2015) 13 *JICJ* 209–217.

81 For a fuller understanding of the case, see R. Brody, 'The Prosecution of Hissène Habré: An "African Pinochet"', (2001) 35 *New England Law Review* 321–345.

82 Human Rights Watch 'Ex-Chad Dictator Indicted in Belgium: Hissène Habré to Face Extradition to Belgium for Human Rights Atrocities' 29 September 2005.

83 *Ibid.*

84 *Ibid.*

capacity as head of state. The Appeal Court purported to have upheld jurisdictional immunity of a head of state, pursuant to customary international law.[85] Another significant development on the extradition request was the decision of the UN Committee Against Torture, in respect of a communication filed before it in 2001. The decision was made on 17 May 2006. The Committee held *inter alia* that 'by refusing to comply with the extradition request from Belgium, the State party has again failed to perform its obligations under article 7 of the Convention Against Torture'.[86]

In summary, Senegal refused to accede to the demands from Belgium, but instead, approached the AU for assistance. The AU in response to Senegal adopted a decision mandating its chairperson to constitute a committee of eminent African jurists to study and present options on what to do.[87] The committee reported that it took the following benchmarks into consideration while carrying out its assignment: (a) adherence to the principles of total rejection of impunity; (b) adherence to international fair trial standards including the independence of the judiciary and impartiality of proceedings; (c) jurisdiction over the alleged crimes for which Mr. Habré should be tried; (d) efficiency in terms of cost and time trial; (e) accessibility to the trial by alleged victims as well as witnesses; (f) priority of an African mechanism.[88]

The benchmarks considered by the Committee and the proposals made suggested that the AU was beginning to take seriously the issue of impunity and the need to address it on the continent. This was to fulfil the first benchmark: total rejection of impunity. The second benchmark became necessary, considering that Habré had alleged that he would not get a fair trial in Chad if he was extradited. The AU was interested in allaying those fears, while showing to the international community that it has the capacity to put one of its own on trial. On the third benchmark, Habré had also argued that the Senegalese courts had no jurisdiction over the crimes that he was alleged to have

---

85 See extracts of the decision at 'L'avis de la Cour d'appel de Dakar sur la demande d'extradition de Hissène Habré (extraits)'[available at http://www.asser.nl/upload/documents/20120419T034141-Habr%C3%A9_Cour_Appel_Avis_Extradition_25-11-2005(Extraits).pdf – accessed on 9 February 2024]. On immunities of heads of state and its place in the Hissene Habré case, see P. Gaeta '*Ratione Materiae* Immunities of Former Heads of State and International Crimes: The Hissène Habré Case' (2003) 1 *Journal of International Criminal Justice* 1 186–196.

86 See UN Doc CAT/C/36/D/181/2001, decision on Communication No. 181/2001 Suleymane Guengueng *et al.* (represented by counsel) v Senegal.

87 See African Union 'Report of the Committee of Eminent African Jurists on the Case of Hissene Habré' at https://www.peacepalacelibrary.nl/ebooks/files/habreCEJA_Repor0506.pdf.

88 *Ibid* at 1.

committed. Of course, the Senegalese courts had earlier agreed with him and had quashed his indictment. The AU was willing to balance these concerns with the need to mete out justice for international crimes. On the fourth benchmark, Senegal, and indeed the government of Abdoulaye Wade, had reportedly found the proposal to try Habré at a cost of 66 million Euro too exorbitant.[89] There was a need to explore the possibility of circumventing these difficulties in order not to derail the trial. Moreover, it had become clear that there are inherent challenges in securing witnesses to testify to crimes which occurred in a different country from which the trials are taking place. The fifth benchmark was aimed at addressing this challenge. Lastly, the AU saw a Habre trial as an opportunity to show the international community that it could indeed provide African solutions to African problems, hence the last benchmark.

The committee eventually made three proposals as to the appropriate court before which Hissène Habré could be validly tried. The first option was to try him before the domestic court in Senegal, given the country's obligation under the Convention against Torture. The second option was a trial by any African country that is a party to the Convention against Torture, employing the principle of universal jurisdiction. The last option was to establish an *ad hoc* tribunal sitting in any African country for the trial.[90] It was also in relation to these discussions that the committee then suggested that Africa could establish an independent mechanism to bridge the impunity gap.[91]

After receiving the report of the jurists, the AU decided that Senegal could try Habré, acting in the interest of the AU and on behalf of Africa.[92] To demonstrate its willingness to leave no stone unturned in the trial, the AU leadership urged Senegal to put in place all fair trials guarantee.[93] It requested cooperation from all African countries[94] while committing itself to the effective

89 Human Rights Watch 'Hissène Habré and the Senegalese Courts A Memo for International Donors' at https://www.hrw.org/legacy/backgrounder/africa/habre1207/habre1207web.pdf at 5.

90 *Ibid*, paragraphs 27–33.

91 *Ibid*, paragraphs 34–35.

92 This point is important as it was obvious from the beginning that the AU was striving to show the world that it is capable of proffering solutions to the problems that confront the continent. See generally AU Doc Assembly/AU/Dec.111(VII) Decisions and Declarations at Decision on the Hissène Habré Case and the African Union: Doc Assembly/AU/3 (VII), paragraph 5(ii).

93 *Ibid*.

94 *Ibid*, paragraph 5(iv).

conduct of the trial.[95] Additionally, it enjoined the international community to help with resources.[96]

The AU decision and the subsequent agreement between the AU and Senegal for the establishment of the EAC took into consideration the report of the eminent jurists, the UN Convention Against Torture which Senegal had ratified in 1986, as well as the decisions from ECOWAS[97] and the ICJ,[98] as parts of the motivation and basis for establishing the EAC. As noted elsewhere, the creation of the EAC resulted from Senegal's efforts at reconciling rules, agreements and decisions emanating from diverse international law sources.[99]

In response to the AU decision, and to give effect to complementarity under the Rome Statute,[100] Senegal implemented some reforms to be able to legally prosecute Hissène Habré. Some of the reforms included the addition of genocide, crimes against humanity, war crimes and torture to its penal code. It also amended the country's code of criminal procedure,[101] which the Chambers

95 *Ibid*, paragraph 5(iii).

96 *Ibid*, paragraph 5(v).

97 In *Habre v Senegal*, case ECW/CCJ/JUD/06/10 before the Court of Justice of the Economic Community of States of West Africa (ECOWAS), the court ruled that Senegal could not try Hissène Habré before its courts, on the basis of non-retroactivity of criminal law. It, however, enjoins Senegal to establish an ad hoc tribunal for this purpose, since the acts in question already constitute crimes which are prohibited by international law at the time of commission. See generally Hissène Habré v. Republic of Senegal at http://www.internationalcrimesdatabase.org/Case/220.

98 In *Questions relating to the Obligation to Prosecute or Extradite* (*Belgium v. Senegal*), Belgium had argued before the ICJ that Senegal's failure to prosecute or extradite Mr Habre for crimes committed during his time as head of state violated Article 7 of the Convention against Torture and Other Cruel, Inhuman or Degrading Treatment or Punishment and customary international law. (See Memorial of the Kingdom of Belgium, 1 July 2010). On the other hand, Senegal argued that it is not in violation of the CAT as its actions show that it is fulfilling its obligations under the CAT. (See Senegal's Counter-Memorial at https://www.icj-cij.org/files/case-related/144/16931.pdf). In its decision, the ICJ finds that 'the Republic of Senegal, by failing to submit the case of Mr. Hissène Habré to its competent authorities for the purpose of prosecution, has breached its obligation under Article 7, paragraph 1, of the United Nations Convention against Torture and Other Cruel, Inhuman or Degrading Treatment or Punishment of 10 December 1984'. (See International Court Of Justice 'Reports of Judgments, Advisory Opinions and Orders Questions Relating to the Obligation to Prosecute or Extradite (Belgium V. Senegal) Judgment of 20 July 2012.)

99 E. Cimiotta 'The First Steps of the Extraordinary African Chambers: A New Mixed Criminal Tribunal?' (2015) 13 *JICJ* 185.

100 M. Niang 'The Senegalese Legal Framework for the Prosecution of International Crimes' (2009) 7 *Journal of International Criminal Justice* 5, 1047–1062 at 1047.

101 See V. Spiga 'Non-retroactivity of Criminal Law: A New Chapter in the Hissene Habre Saga' (2011) 9 *JICJ* 5-23 at 17.

relied upon, alongside its application of substantive international criminal law. According to Brody, this was a compromise that was born out of necessity.[102] Senegal also concluded and signed a cooperation agreement with Chad.[103] The cooperation agreement underscored the importance of innovation in international criminal justice. Additionally, this instance also reveals the catalytic roles that regional efforts may play in helping countries to fulfil their obligations under the Rome Statute. The trial eventually commenced in 2015, and conviction was entered in 2016. The appeals judgement was rendered in 2017.[104] Overall, the Hissène Habré affair reveals one thing: Africa and its leaders have been involved in the project of regionalizing international criminal justice.

4.2 Establishment, Structure, Jurisdiction and Crimes

The EAC was established because of a bilateral agreement between a regional organization and a member state. The EAC, however, differs from other existing hybrid tribunals. Its establishment marked the first time that such a tribunal would be established under the auspices of a regional organization. The previous tribunals had been established under the auspices of the UN. It is also the first time such a tribunal would be established in one country for the purpose of prosecuting the ex-leader of another country, for the host country's failure to prosecute or extradite. But these are perhaps the only points of divergence. Like other tribunals, its lifespan was already determined from its establishment. It was, like all others before it, established to be a temporal tribunal with limited function. This was also reiterated in Article 37 of the statute where it provides that 'the EAC shall be dissolved automatically once all judgments have been pronounced'.

On structure, Article 2 of the Statute of the EAC provides that 'Extraordinary African Chambers are hereby established within the judicial system of the Republic of Senegal, as follows: a) a Pre-Trial Chamber within the Dakar Special Regional Court; b) an Indictment Chamber at the Dakar Court of Appeals; c) a Trial Chamber at the Dakar Court of Appeals; and d) an Appeals

---

102 R. Brody Updated Edition after the Final April 2017 Verdict, *Victims Bring a Dictator to Justice: The Case of Hissène Habré* (Bread for the World 2017) 33.

103 'Accord de coopération judiciaire entre la République du Senegal et la République du Tchad pour la poursuite des crimes internationaux commis au Tchad durant la période du 7 juin 1982 au 1 décembre 1990', 3 May 2013 at http://forumchambresafricaines.org/docs/AccordCooperationJudiciaireSenegalTchad.pdf.

104 Amnesty International 'Chad: Hissène Habré Appeal Ruling Closes Dark Chapter for Victims', 27 April 2017.

Chamber at the Dakar Court of Appeals'. An Indictment Chamber was one of the four chambers in the EAC. This is due to the inquisitorial procedural model of the civil law systems of Senegal.[105] As noted by the ICTY's Trial Chamber, '[I]n many civil law systems, indictments are subject to judicial scrutiny by the investigating judge before the trial.'[106] This is the reason why its duties, according to Article 31(1) (b) of the EAC Statute is to '...examine and rule on any appeals [from the Pre-Trial chamber] lodged pursuant to the Senegalese Code of Criminal Procedure'. As an 'appellate court' for the Pre-Trial chamber, it performs similar functions as the Trials Chambers of the ICTY. Article 19 of the ICTY Statute provides that it is the duty of the judge of the Trial Chamber to either confirm or dismiss indictment. Its role is also somewhat like the roles performed by the Appeals Chamber of the ICC. It, however, appears that there are some significant differences between the roles performed by the Appeal Chambers in both institutions. The Appeals Chamber in line with Article 25 of the EAC Statute 'shall hear appeals from persons convicted by the Trial Chamber'. This implies that the EAC's Appeal Chamber will only entertain appeals from substantive decision from the Trial Chamber, while preliminary appeals from the decision of the Pre-Trial Chamber would have been dealt with by the Indictment Chamber. The situation is slightly different in the ICC because it does not have an Indictment Chamber and all appeals, including those on preliminary issues, are heard at the Appeals Chamber. The decisions of both the Indictment Chamber and the Appeal Chambers of the EAC are therefore final and not subject to appeal. Highlighting these procedural differences is necessary to establish that diverse procedural policies may be adopted by different tribunals, if the overall goal is the dissemination of justice. It also fits into the proposition of this work: the idea that different routes can be taken to promote the overarching goals of the Rome Statute, and one of such routes is the prosecution of crimes through a regional tribunal.

On jurisdiction, Article 3(1) & (2) of the Statute of the EAC provides as follows:

1) The Extraordinary African Chambers shall prosecute and try the person(s) most responsible for crimes and serious violations of international law, customary international law and international conventions

105 On the inquisitorial procedural model, see S. Vasiliev 'Trial Process at the ECCC: The Rise and fall of the Inquisitorial Paradigm in International Criminal Law' in S. Meisenberg & I. Stegmiller (eds) *The Extraordinary Chambers in the Courts of Cambodia: Assessing their Contribution to International Criminal Law* (Springer 2016) 390–432.

106 *Prosecutor V. Milan Kovacevic*, Decision on Prosecutor's Request to File an Amended Indictment, Decision Dated 5 March 1998, para. 10.

ratified by Chad, committed on the territory of Chad during the period from 7 June 1982 to 1 December 1990.

2) The Extraordinary African Chambers may choose to prosecute the most serious crimes within their jurisdiction.

This provision has a number of implications. First, the Statute reveals an intention to prosecute *the person or persons* most responsible for crimes during Habré's regime, but ultimately, only Habré was prosecuted. In 2013, the chief prosecutor had sought the indictment of five other suspects who were officials in Habré's government. For various reasons, this did not happen, and thus, only Habré was tried and convicted.[107] This 'politics of a singular focus on individualized criminal accountability'[108] is connected with ICL's desire to punish suspects who are most responsible for crimes. It is also an admission of the limit of international criminal law to punish all perpetrators of crimes, owing to many supervening factors. Secondly, it was obvious that the overwhelming desire of the victims of Habré's crimes was to see the head of the government punished for the crimes perpetrated by his agents. All the activities leading to the eventual setting up of the EAC were centred upon and spurred on by the desire to bring a former head of state to justice. It was believed that this may have a greater deterrent effect on would-be-perpetrators, even if they are heads of state. The important thing is that the trials were meant to establish that crimes that have attained the status of *jus cogens* should not go unpunished, irrespective of who the perpetrators are, or even their location.

Article 4 of the Statute gives the EAC power to try the crimes of genocide, crimes against humanity, war crimes and torture. Articles 5 to 8 outline the elements of each crime. One observation is that the crime of torture appears as a separate crime in Article 8, but also as part of war crimes in Article 7(2) and crimes against humanity in Article 6(g). There is no explanation for this repetition, but it is probable that the drafters of the statute were willing to underscore the *jus cogens* nature of torture,[109] given the overwhelming evidence that Hissène Habré had employed torture as a weapon against his vic-

107 Human Rights Watch, 'Q&A: The Case of Hissène Habré before the Extraordinary African Chambers in Senegal', 3 May 2016.

108 See K.J. Bluen 'Justice, But Only for Some: The trial of Hissene Habre' *Justice in Conflict*, 30 July 2015 [available at https://justiceinconflict.org/2015/07/30/justice-but-only-for-some-the-trial-of-hissene-habre/ – accessed on 9 February 2024].

109 On the *jus cogens* nature of the crime of torture, see Erika de Wet 'The Prohibition of Torture as an International Norm of *jus cogens* and Its Implications for National and Customary Law' (2004) 15 *EJIL* 97–121. See also the Report of the International Law Commission, Sixty-sixth session, (5 May–6 June and 7 July–8 August 2014).

tims. This was also echoed in the ICJ decision on Habre, where the court submitted that 'the prohibition of torture is part of customary international law and it has become a peremptory norm (*jus cogens*)'.[110] Unlike other international crimes which largely depend on goodwill of interested states for them to be prosecuted, torture is one crime where states have established an obligation to either prosecute or extradite suspects who are located within their territories, as per Article 7 of the Convention against Torture (CAT).[111]

It is also observed that the crimes in the statute are similar to the crimes in the Rome Statute, except for a few differences relating to definition and elements of crime.[112] As such, unlike other hybrid tribunals, the EAC does not have jurisdiction over 'domestic crimes', but over purely international crimes. However, unlike the ICC, the jurisdiction of the EAC, according to Article 9, is not subject to any statutory limitations. Additionally, Article 10(3) provides that '[T]he official position of an accused, whether as Head of State or Government, or as a responsible government official, shall not relieve him or her of criminal responsibility under this Statute, nor shall it, in and of itself, constitute a ground for reduction of sentence.' The inclusion of this provision appears to have marked a radical departure from the well-known AU's stance on immunity for heads of states and governments, in line with customary international law. The AU's position was again, recently re-emphasized, in its 'Amicus Brief Submission in the Hashemite Kingdom of Jordan's Appeal Against the Decision under Article 87(7) of the Rome Statute on the Non-Compliance by Jordan with the Request by the Court for the Arrest and Surrender of Omar Al-Bashir', dated 13 July 2018. In its submission, the AU argued that 'the rule that, under international law, heads of State enjoy immunity *ratione personae* from foreign criminal jurisdiction, is virtually uncontested'.[113] Thus, that it temporarily departed from its widely known position could not have been unconnected to the overwhelming pressure that had been exerted on Senegal and the wider continent, on the need to see Habré

---

110 *Questions Relating to the Obligation to Prosecute or Extradite (Belgium v Senegal)*, Judgment of 20 July 2012, ICJ Reports 2012, para. 99.

111 K. Neldjingaye, The Trial of Hissène Habré in Senegal and its Contribution to International Criminal Law' in C. Murungu and J. Biegon (eds) *Prosecuting International Crimes in Africa* (Pretoria University Law Report 2011) 193.

112 For thoughts on the differences, see M. Niang 'The Senegalese Legal Framework for the Prosecution of International Crimes' (2009) 7 *Journal of International Criminal Justice* 5, 1047–1062.

113 See ICC Doc: ICC-02/05-01/09 OA2 The African Union's Submission in the 'Hashemite Kingdom of Jordan's Appeal Against the Decision under Article 87(7) of the Rome Statute on the Non-Compliance by Jordan with the Request by the Court for the Arrest and Surrender of Omar Al-Bashir', para. 11.

brought to justice. In essence, this one-off approach to the implementation of international criminal justice, albeit defective, had served, in certain respects, the goal of closing the impunity gap. Also, the drafters of the EAC statute were aware that this specific instrument was targeted at a former head of state who does not enjoy immunity after office. This is consistent with the AU's formulation of the immunity clause in the Malabo Protocol. As will be shown in the next chapter, the AU position in this statute is therefore consistent with what was reflected in the Malabo Protocol. It maintains immunity for sitting head of state and government, while they are in office.

4.3 Legal Status of the EAC

There have been some debates on the actual legal status of the EAC.[114] It has been fondly called 'a "local" international criminal tribunal',[115] and 'a "minimalist" internationalized criminal court'.[116] Sarah Williams acknowledges the EAC's description as a hybrid or internationalized court. She notes that the original idea behind hybrid tribunals is to evolve 'a mechanism that avoids the weaknesses of "purely" international and domestic prosecutions'. [117] She further notes that the perceived benefits of the hybrid model include capacity building and increased penetration of international norms into the domestic system, while enhancing independence, impartiality and legitimacy, as a result of the participation of the UN (or other international organizations) in such tribunals.[118] Some of the defining features of this type of tribunals are: performance of a criminal judicial function; temporal or transitional nature of the tribunal; the possibility or actual participation of international judges working alongside national judges, added to the possibility or actual international involvement in other organs of the tribunal; full or partial international financing of the tribunal; mixture of international and national elements in the mate-

114 For example, see E. Cimiotta 'The First Steps of the Extraordinary African Chambers: A New Mixed Criminal Tribunal?' (2015) 13 *JICJ* 1. See also S. Williams 'The Extraordinary African Chambers in the Senegalese Courts: An African Solution to an African Problem?' (2013) 11 *JICJ* 1139–1160.

115 K.B. Carlson 'Trying Hissène Habré 'On Behalf of Africa: Remaking Hybrid International Criminal Justice at the Chambres Africaines Exraordinaires' in J. Nicholson (ed) *Strengthening the Validity of International Criminal Tribunals* (BRILL 2018) 345.

116 S.A. E. Høgestøl (2016) The Habré Judgment at the Extraordinary African Chambers: A Singular Victory in the Fight Against Impunity (2016) 34 *Nordic Journal of Human Rights* 3, 147–156.

117 S. Williams 'The Extraordinary African Chambers in the Senegalese Courts: An African Solution to an African Problem?' (2013) 11 *JICJ* 1144.

118 *Ibid.*

rial jurisdiction of the tribunal; and lastly, the involvement of another party apart from the affected state.[119] The EAC meets five of these features. It is therefore 'best characterized as an *internationalized criminal tribunal,* which are "essentially domestic institutions but with significant participation from other states or from international organisations"'.[120]

Schabas agrees with the classification of the EAC as an internationalized tribunal. He submits that '[T]he Chambers are international not only by virtue of the crimes that they prosecute but also because of the involvement of the President of the Commission of the African Union in the appointment of judges and at least one of the judges is to be a national of another African State.'[121] Emanuele Cimiotta, however, disagrees with Schabas and Williams. He argues that the view that the EAC is an international tribunal is not persuasive.[122] He explains that it is necessary to examine the legal nature of the EAC to be able to properly classify it. He criticized the view that the EAC is an internationalized tribunal because the view fails to consider where the legal consequences of the activity of the EAC take place, and for not considering the relationship between the EAC and the persons subject to its jurisdiction.[123] He submits that the EAC is a Senegalese organ, and its activity belongs to Senegal. He supports this position with the reasoning that where the Statute of the EAC evinces a lacuna, Senegalese laws are resorted to as per Articles 12, 15, 16, 18 and 26 of the Statute, which generally emphasize the Senegalese character of the EAC. He concludes that the points he raised 'reflect the national rather than the international character of the EAC'.[124]

From the foregoing, it seems that the consensus is that the EAC possesses some features distinguishing it from other internationalized tribunals. In this regard, it is a court whose background is fully regional and unrelated to the United Nations' (UN) post-conflict peace building activities.[125] The tribunals forming part of the UN post-conflict peace-building architecture share certain features which are absent from the EAC. Some examples of this kind of tribunals include the Extraordinary Chambers in the Court of Cambodia, the Spe-

119 *Ibid;* see also C. Stahn 'The Geometry of Transitional Justice: Choices of Institutional Design' (2005) 18 *Leiden Journal of International Law* 425–466.

120 S. Williams (n. 114) 1144.

121 W. Schabas 'Senegal's Chambres africaines extraordinaires to judge Habré', *PhD Studies in Human Rights Blogpost,* 5 February 2013 [available at https://humanrightsdoctorate.blogspot.com/2013/02/senegals-chambres-africaines.html - accessed on 12 May 2023].

122 E. Cimiotta 'The First Steps of the Extraordinary African Chambers: A New Mixed Criminal Tribunal?' (2015) 13 *JICJ* 1, 189.

123 *Ibid.*

124 *Ibid,* 191.

125 *Ibid.*

cial Panels of the Dili District Court and the Special Criminal Court in Central African Republic. All these tribunals are located in the countries where the crimes they seek to prosecute are committed. They were created by collaboration between the UN and national governments, in response to specific internal armed conflict.[126] But the EAC is an AU initiative. It is not strictly in response to particular internal armed conflict, although its jurisdiction is limited to crimes committed within a specific period in the political history of Chad. The EAC is also not a pure international tribunal like the ICTY or the ICTR. Those were created as independent tribunals and were fully separated from the domestic systems of the countries in whose territories the crimes were committed. They also only applied international law. The EAC on the other hand was created to be 'embedded within the current Senegalese judicial system' and applied the Senegalese penal code, alongside international law.

These differences notwithstanding, the EAC shares certain similar features with other 'internationalized' criminal tribunals under the auspices of the UN. These features include the composition of national and international judges, as well as application of both domestic and international law. The EAC had no other international staff in the prosecution or other organs.[127] It had minimal content of international elements and was more of a court that received financial and technical assistance form international bodies.[128] The international elements were limited to its application of international law, its governance by a special statute and the presence of international judges appointed by the AU.[129] The EAC had jurisdiction to try international crimes, although, those had been grafted and included in the Senegalese penal code. The statute granted primacy to the EAC and provided in Article 16 that 'for those cases not provided for in this statute, the Chambers shall apply Senegalese law'. The presidents of the EAC's Trial and Appeal Chambers were non-Senegalese from other AU member states.[130]

Thus, the limited international content of the EAC puts the tribunal in a different class from other chambers. This unique status has proved to be a necessary innovation to finally arrive at the goal of serving justice for breach of international crimes, albeit by the domestic legal system of a member state, spurred on by decisions and agreements from regional and sub-regional bodies *to wit*, the ECOWAS decision and the AU decision/agreement.

---

126 *Ibid*, 179.

127 See generally Article 12 of the EAC Statute on the office of the prosecutor.

128 See S. Williams (n. 114) 1147.

129 Høgestøl (n. 116) 152.

130 See generally Article 11 of the EAC Statute on composition of the EAC and appointment of judges.

4.4 Legitimacy of the EAC Tribunal

During the lifespan of the EAC, there were debates on the legitimacy of the tribunal, especially because the only defendant – Hissène Habré – had refused to accept the tribunal's jurisdiction over him and consequently refused to appear before it.[131] The private counsel retained by the defendant also refused to participate in the pre-trial stage of the proceedings. The case then went into full trial, solely on the evidence adduced by the prosecution. At the beginning of the trial stage of the proceedings, Mr Habre who has refused to appear was forcefully brought to court, prompting protests from Senegalese lawyers who argued that his rights had been breached by the tribunal's order to forcefully produce him in court.[132] The tribunal also appointed lawyers for the defendant. Mr Habre's refusal to accept the tribunal's legitimacy and the subsequent appointment of lawyers by the tribunal led to a 45-day delay in the commencement of the proceedings. The newly appointed lawyers needed time to study the bulky case files. The delays had varying impacts on the different actors in the proceeding. For the lawyers to the defendants, 45 days were too short to study and understand the case; for the victims who had waited for many years for Habre to be brought to justice, justice delayed was justice denied and for the tribunal itself, that was existing on a limited time and budget, the delays could have adverse effects on its ability to complete its assignment within the allotted time.[133]

4.5 Complementarity and the EAC

The EAC Statute and Agreement had no complementarity provisions similar Article 17 (1) of the ICC Statute. However, there is a provision on *ne bis in idem* (the rule against double jeopardy). *Ne bis in idem* functions to aid complementarity in many ways. As noted by the OTP of the ICC in its submissions to the Appeals Chamber, *ne bis in idem* and the concepts of admissibility jointly serve to implement the principle of complementarity.[134] Article 19 of the EAC Statute replicates almost completely, the exact provisions of Article 20 of the Rome Statute. The purpose of that provision is to avoid duplicity and

131 International Bar Association 'Legal Representation, Fairness and Access to Justice in Hybrid Tribunals and Specialised Chambers' (2018), 59–60.

132 *Ibid.*

133 *Ibid.*

134 ICC-OTP, Doc: ICC-01/11-01/11 'Corrigendum to Prosecution Response to the "Document in Support of the Government of Libya's Appeal against the Decision on the admissibility of the case against Saif Al-Islam Gaddafi"' dated 23 July 2013, page 26 at para. 55.

ensure that no defendant is tried twice for the same conduct. It helps to smoothen relationships between different courts or tribunals that are given to similar or overlapping roles. It was important to have included this provision, considering that in 2007, a working group led by Malick Sow, had submitted a report to the effect that *ne bis in idem* would not bar Habré from trials.[135] This was a reaction to concerns that Mr. Habré could raise such defence, given, for example, that at the time the report was being submitted, there was an ongoing trial in Chad, for which he was eventually sentenced to death in absentia.

During the trial itself, the judges of the EAC did not have an opportunity to make pronouncements on *ne bis in idem*, in relation to Mr. Habré. But if a situation arose where there was a need to pronounce on it, how would the Chamber have resolved this legal question?

As has been shown, the EAC is a Chamber within the Senegalese court system, however with limited international elements. The agreement establishing the EAC remained binding on Senegal and the AU, who are the two parties to the agreement. On the other hand, the statute operates to 'implement the decision of the AU concerning the Republic of Senegal's prosecution of international crimes committed in Chad between 7 June 1982 and 1 December 1990, in accordance with Senegal's international commitments'.[136] Thus, while the agreement governs activities between these two parties, the Statute applies to implement the decision in the agreement, for the purposes of prosecuting person(s) whose conducts fall within the jurisdiction of the statute, irrespective of location, status or nationality, on the basis of universal jurisdiction.

Flowing from this, the appropriate interpretation of Article 19(2) of the EAC Statute, which provides that '[N]o person shall be tried by another court…', is that another court would legally refer to another Senegalese court, considering that the Statute and the Agreement basically operate as Senegalese instruments and are thus binding on Senegal. It is inconceivable that Senegal or any other state would make a law that would bar other states from actions that would not be illegal for them to take, under international law. Therefore, Chad or any other state cannot be precluded from bringing charges again Habre based on *ne bis in idem* provisions of the EAC statute.

---

135 See Rapport du Groupe de Travail sur l'Affaire Hissène Habré, Ministère de la Justice (March 2007), referenced in Human Rights Watch 'Hissène Habré and the Senegalese Courts: A Memo for International Donors' December 2007.

136 See Article 1 of the EAC Statute.

To find further support for this interpretation of the *ne bis in idem* provisions of the EAC, I draw inspiration from similar provisions in the statute of similar tribunals: The Special Tribunal for Lebanon (STL) and the Special Court for Sierra Leone (SCSL). Article 5(1) of the STL statute and Article 9(1) of the SCSL statute similarly provide that '[N]o person shall be tried before a national court of Lebanon/Sierra Leone for acts for which he or she has already been tried by the Special Tribunal/Court.' While it is clear that Article 4 of the STL statute and Article 8 of the SCSL statute have expressly provided that the tribunal/court shall have concurrent jurisdiction with the national courts in the two countries, and the EAC statute does not contain similar provision, the other similarities between the STL and SCSL on the one hand, and the EAC on the other hand, strongly support the argument that their provisions on *ne bis in idem* may be interpreted in the same way. The ambiguity in the EAC statute might have been a product of ambiguous drafting that resulted from careless replication of the provisions of the Rome Statute.

The EAC statute lacked an admissibility provision like Article 17(1) of the Rome Statute. There may be many reasons for this, chief of which could be because, unlike the Rome Statute which shares jurisdiction over crimes with national mechanisms, the EAC statute served as an *ad hoc* instrument that shares no jurisdiction with any other mechanism outside Senegalese judicial system. As such, it was not envisaged that there would be a clash of jurisdiction, which was the reason for an admissibility provision in the Rome Statute. Overall, the EAC statute only contained one leg of the complementarity provisions in the Rome Statute: the issue of *ne bis in idem*. The other part was absent for the reasons suggested above.

4.6 The Habré Trial and the Lessons Learned

Tribunals start their work long before their first trials commence. In the same way, the legacy of a tribunal will continue to be seen and felt, long after its closure. While the concept of legacy could mean different things to different people, as it could lend itself to a broad range of interpretations,[137] the idea of legacy that is conceptualized here refers to the general contributions that the EAC has made or may yet make to ICL. It may be too early to speak of its legacies and contributions to ICL in definite and conclusive terms. For deca-

137 S. Vasiliev 'Trial Process at the ECCC: The Rise and fall of the Inquisitorial Paradigm in International Criminal Law' in S. Meisenberg & I. Stegmiller (eds) *The Extraordinary Chambers in the Courts of Cambodia: Assessing their Contribution to International Criminal Law* (Springer 2016) 391.

des to come, efforts to quantify the EAC's legacies will continue, in the same manner that the Nuremberg and Tokyo trials still offer lessons for the present, and perhaps, the future. This work does not pre-empt what the future analysis will be, but it offers some preliminary thoughts on what the trials have contributed to ICL and the potentials for instruction and guidance that are inherent in some of its practices.

First, the EAC is a court based in Senegal but dealing with crimes committed in Chad. For this reason, its success was heavily reliant on the cooperation it could get from Chad, being the domicile of most of the witnesses.[138] To operationalize this, the two countries needed to conclude a cooperation agreement, which they did in May 2013. The lesson here is the need for cooperation between stakeholders for the success of crimes prosecution. A criminal tribunal is as strong and effective as the support it gets from states, especially states connected to the trials.

Secondly, there are instances where a universal institution like the ICC does not have jurisdiction to try certain conducts. One example is where the crimes to be tried happened before 2002, when the Rome Statute came into force. The statute does not have retroactive capacity. Hence, in instances where the ICC cannot or does not have jurisdiction, employing a similar model as the Habré chambers will further help to fulfil the goals of the Rome Statute. Recall that Article 9 of the EAC Statute specifically provides that '[T]he crimes within the jurisdiction of the EAC shall not be subject to any statutory limitations.'

Thirdly, the minimalist nature of international elements and involvement may yet make the EAC or similar model an attractive model for international crimes prosecution in Africa. The EAC model has the capacity to stretch backwards, farther than the reach of even the ICC or a similar court created within the African court.

Fourthly, the establishment of the EAC became a necessity because of the inability of the domestic systems to prosecute Habré. The failure of the domestic system in Chad to prosecute Habré was partly because of his absence in the country. The failure in Senegal was because of the legal impossibilities that the decisions from the Senegalese courts had placed on the efforts to prosecute him. Thus, the EAC model became an attractive alternative where the domestic systems are unable to prosecute.

---

138 C. Sperfeldt 'The trial against Hissène Habré: networked justice and reparations at the Extraordinary African Chambers' (2017) 21 *The International Journal of Human Rights* 9, 1247.

Fifthly, as noted by Kersten and Ainley, one of the most enduring legacies of the EAC is the success of its outreach program.[139] This is important because justice must not only be done but must also be seen to have been done. The EAC externalized its outreach program to a consortium of NGOs from Chad, Senegal and Belgium.[140] This partly accounted for its effectiveness. One of the biggest challenges with the ICC and indeed many international criminal tribunals, especially those sited outside of the location of crimes, is the idea that the justice it metes out is foreign to the affected communities. This aspect can be effectively handled where a robust program of outreach has been put in place by the tribunal itself. What the EAC taught us in this regard is that outsourcing outreach to local or community-based networks, wholly or in a consortium, may improve visibility of the tribunal while conferring a measure of acceptance on it from victims and affected communities. As posited by Kersten and Ainley, and I agree, the success of the outreach program of the EAC was a major determinant in the overall perception of the success of the work of the EAC.[141]

Sixthly, the roles played by civil societies to ensure that the trial took place are significant. When civil societies collaborate with victim-networks, it increases the likelihood of getting justice for victims. Civils societies and victims-networks that were involved in the advocacy to bring Habré to justice included the Chadian Association of Victims of Crimes and Political Repression (AVCRP), International Federation for Human Rights (FIDH), the Chadian Association for the Promotion and Defence of Human Rights (ATPDH), Human Rights Watch (HRW), the Dakar-based based African Assembly for the Defence of Human Rights (RADDHO), among others. The pressures mounted by these organizations helped to ensure accountability.

Furthermore, the role that the sub-regional human rights court played in bringing Habré to justice is significant. As shown above, it was the ECOWAS court that first pronounced that Habré could only be tried by 'an *ad hoc* special tribunal of an international character'. Human rights bodies have always played some roles in the application of international criminal law.[142] Again, one of the outcomes of the involvement of CSOs was in reducing the impact

139 M. Kersten and K. Ainley, 'Hybridization – A Spectrum of Creative Possibilities' in S. Weill and ors. *The Habré Trial and Beyond: New Models of Prosecuting International Crime?* (Oxford University Press 2020), 267–281.

140 Brody (n. 102) 18.

141 *Ibid* at 6.

142 M. Pinto, 'Awakening the Leviathan through Human Rights Law – How Human Rights Bodies Trigger the Application of Criminal Law' (2018) 34 *Utrecht Journal of International and European Law* 2, 161–184.

that hosting the trials in a country far removed from the scenes of crimes could have had on the perception of legitimacy of the trial. These CSOs launched many initiatives and creatively used new technologies to bring the trials home to Chadians. Twitter, YouTube and other Websites were creatively engaged as all the sessions of the trials were posted on these platforms. The CSOs and the EAC also ensured that there were debates, public screening of the trial and other outreach activities with locals across the country.[143]

Lastly, the impact of the Habré trials has continued to reflect itself in the Senegalese and the Chadian judiciaries and legal systems. Representatives of the victims had opportunities to not only appear at an international stage, but also to learn from experienced international criminal lawyers.[144] In the words of the Chadian Justice Minister, the trial 'has had a significant impact on our understanding of the role of justice. It's made us realize that courts can be independent, and no one is above the law.'[145] In Senegal, the impact was much more direct and visible. As noted earlier, Senegal amended its laws to be able to carry out the trials. Part of the amendment was to accommodate retroactive application of criminal law and universal jurisdiction.[146] The next section of this chapter now turns to an analysis of how the Habre trials promoted the ideas behind the notion of regional complementarity that this work promotes.

4.7 Promoting Regional Complementarity

There are at least four different ways in which the establishment of the EAC supports the notion of regional complementarity that this work promotes.

One of the motivations for regional complementarity is the understanding that the ICC cannot realistically be available and capable of prosecuting all cases of international crimes that this vast globe may experience, especially with its limited budget. The EAC model may be an attractive alternative. There is no doubt that the Habré trials have set a precedent and may continue to encourage prosecution of international crimes at the regional level. The trials may spur regions to look inwards and create tailor-made approaches to

143 South African Institute of International Affairs, 'The Hissène Habré trial: a triumph for victims and civil society' [available at https://saiia.org.za/research/the-hissene-habre-trial-triumph-over-opposition-oblivion-and-distance-for-the-victims-and-civil-society/ – accessed on 12 February 2024].

144 C. Hicks *The Trial of Hissene Habre: How the People of Chad Brought a Tyrant to Justice* (ZED Books 2018) at 140.

145 *Ibid*, 141.

146 *Ibid* at 142.

crimes prosecution at a regional level. This is more so because the EAC model may afford states the channel to prosecute crimes that the ICC may not have the jurisdiction to try. Examples include crimes that have been committed prior to 2002 when the ICC statute entered into force.[147] Many regions, including the African and the South American regions, are crying for justice for egregious human rights violation and international crimes. To address these concerns, the EAC model presents an alternative for justice. Secondly, this notion of regional complementarity implies that all efforts – including regional efforts – must be channelled towards closing the impunity gap, thereby fulfilling the overall goal of the ICC. The EAC model may encourage states, as it did to Senegal, to put in place measures to ensure that they live up to their commitments under the Rome Statute. A case in point was the legal measures by Senegal to facilitate the trials. It was rightly observed that '[T]he EAC were a last-minute creature of necessity.'[148] This suggests that a creative world of opportunities is available for regions in their bid to regionalize international criminal justice. The EAC may have moved the world closer to less impunity. Thirdly, this idea promotes regional and local ownership of initiatives geared towards international crimes prosecution. One of the major arguments against the ICC is the idea that the justice it portends to dispense is western-styled and too removed from the people that it purports to serve. At least, this is one of the arguments from African leaders and their apologists. An EAC model has the potential to reverse this argument. In a sense, when a state adopts the EAC approach, perhaps through the support of a region, there is a greater tendency for an increased perception, which contributes to the credibility of the tribunal. In addition to this, this approach helps a region to claim ownership of the process and outcome of the tribunal. Lastly, the thought that regional courts can complement the ICC in a regime of robust collaboration and cooperation is no longer strange. In January 2018, the ICC itself convened a judicial seminar titled 'Complementarity and Cooperation of Courts in an Interconnected Global Justice System'.[149] This was primarily because the ICC itself has begun to envisage that a more effective court would require the cooperation and collaboration of national as well as regional

147 P. Fabricius Now to make this extraordinary court, ordinary' *Institute for Security Studies Today*, 11 February 2016 [available at https://issafrica.org/iss-today/now-to-make-this-extraordinary-court-ordinary – accessed on 11 February 2024].

148 Brody (n. 102) 32.

149 ICC, Judicial Seminar: Complementarity and Cooperation of Courts in an Interconnected Global Justice System, International Criminal Court (ICC), 18 January 2018, The Hague, Netherlands. Welcoming remarks by Judge Silvia Fernández de Gurmendi, ICC President.

courts. In relation to the themes of this book, the seminar touched on many interesting topics including the role of regional courts as well as the relationship/convergence of criminal courts and human rights courts. The topics addressed at this seminar reveals that the ICC is now more concerned about the inevitable roles that regional courts will begin to play in the subject of international criminal justice, particularly using regional human rights courts. What remains to be seen is how these relationships will be operationalized and arranged in a manner that reduces friction and jurisdictional clashes.

5 The Kosovo Specialist Chambers and Specialist Prosecutor's Office (KSCSPO)

5.1 Background and Establishment

This tribunal started operation in 2017. It was set up in 2015 to prosecute crimes against humanity, war crimes and other crimes under Kosovo national law, in respect of allegations contained in a Council of Europe (CoE) report.[150] While it was set up by Kosovo, it is a tribunal with a strong link to regional international organizations – the CoE and the EU. The tribunal was set up by a law adopted by the Assembly of the Republic of Kosovo.[151] The allegations were that serious international crimes were committed in Kosovo between 1 January 1998 and 31 December 2000. The Assembly also amended the Kosovo National Constitution to accommodate the establishment of the KSCSPO as part of the Kosovo domestic judicial system.[152] The CoE had urged Kosovo to start serious investigation to find the truth about specific allegations,[153] and to cooperate with the EU Rule of Law Mission in Kosovo (EULEX).[154] It was thus the CoE that kick-started the process of establishing the KSCSPO by requesting all CoE members to judicially cooperate on ongoing and future war crimes investigation.[155] The EU also played a role in the establishment of the KSCSPO.

---

150 Council of Europe Document 12462 of 7 January 2011, 'Council of Europe Parliamentary Assembly Report on Inhuman treatment of people and illicit trafficking in human organs in Kosovo.

151 'Law on Specialist Chambers and Specialist Prosecutors Office'. Law No.05/L-053, 31 August 2015.

152 'Amendment of the Constitution of the Republic of Kosovo' No.05-D-139, 3 August 2015.

153 CoE Report, para. 19.5.3.

154 CoE Report, para 19.5.1.

155 CoE Report, 1.

The Kosovo authorities had exchanged letters with the EU. An international agreement then arose out of the exchange of letters.[156]

5.2 Legal Status, Structure and Composition

Stahn had argued that the legal nature of the KSCSPO is disputed. One view is that the tribunal was created by the international act of exchanging letters between the EU and the Kosovo authorities. The other is the view taken by Kosovo's Constitutional Court that the KSCSPO are part of the legal order of Kosovo but internationalized.[157] Cimiotta had referred to it as a 'regional mixed criminal tribunal'.[158] Williams calls the KSCSPO 'clearly internationalized institutions'.[159] Stahn refers to it as 'mixed domestic regional Chambers'.[160] Whatever the view, one undeniable fact is that the KSCSPO was established as a result of the actions of regional organizations, just like the Extraordinary African Chambers. Their establishment further extends the regionalization of international criminal justice, which has become inevitable. The KSCSPO consists of three distinct organs – the Chambers, the Registry and an independent Prosecutor's Office.[161] The composition presents a new category of hybrids as it is only staffed with foreign judges and personnel.[162] It has shown that it may not always be essential to include local staff in a hybrid tribunal before it can be called such.[163]

5.3 Jurisdiction, Crimes and Applicable Laws

Articles 6–10 of Law No.05/L-053 stipulate the subject-matter, temporal, territorial, personal and concurrent jurisdictions of the KSCSPO. The law contains similar extensive provisions as the Rome Statute, on war crimes and crimes against humanity. It, however, does not contain genocide and the crime of aggression. The Tribunal applies customary international law and Kosovo

156 E. Cimiotta 'The Specialist Chambers and the Specialist Prosecutor's Office in Kosovo: The 'Regionalization' of International Criminal Justice in Context' (2016) 14 *JICJ* pg. 56.

157 C. Stahn *A Critical Introduction to International Criminal Law* (Cambridge University Press 2019) 206–207.

158 Cimiotta (n. 156) 60.

159 S. Williams 'The Specialist Chambers of Kosovo: The Limits of Internationalization?' (2016) 14 *JICJ* 27.

160 Stahn (n. 157) 207.

161 (n. 151).

162 R. Muharremi 'The Kosovo Specialist Chambers and Specialist Prosecutor's Office' (2016) 76 *ZaöRV* 967.

163 Williams (n. 159) 35.

national criminal law, where the latter complies with the former. Article 15 also contains reference to specific and general national criminal laws in Kosovo. Thus, while the KSCSPO is like other hybrids in the application of national and international laws, it differs from others in the strict composition of international judges. One obvious challenge raised by this is the suitability of international judges to apply local laws that they are not familiar with. Also, some have described the jurisdiction of the KSCSPO as a 'contested jurisdiction' in that it only focuses on allegations of crimes by former Kosovo Liberation Army (KLA) members.[164] Others described the justice it dispenses as 'mono ethnic justice for victors'.[165]

5.4 Perception of Legitimacy

Among ethnic Albanians, the KSCSPO's mandate to only prosecute crimes allegedly committed by the KLA appears unfair.[166] Unlike the Nuremberg trials, for example, this is novel in that it concentrates on accountability of the 'victors' in the conflict, as against the 'vanquished'.[167] The fact that the Kosovar authorities only caved in to international pressures has also not enhanced local legitimacy of the tribunal.[168] Other reason is that the tribunal is sited far away in the Hague and is also officiated by foreign judges and officials who are appointed by the EU. This presents a difference from other hybrids that have been considered in Chapter 3 of this work. The Tribunal has just started its assignment, and it has only confirmed indictments in a few cases. The Tribunal has also recently issued two judgements. The trial judgement for the Salih Mustafa case was issued on 16 December 2022, while the appeal judgement was issued on 14 December 2023. In the Pjetër Shala case, the trial judgement was pronounced on 16 July 2024.[169]

One of the key lessons that has already come out of the KSCSPO is the need for a tribunal to focus on all sides on the conflict, and not on one side. Also, the KSCSPO could learn from the EAC's outreach efforts to bridge the physical

164 A. Mucaj 'The Kosovo Specialist Chambers and Specialist Prosecutor's Office Paradox' (2021) 21 *International Criminal Law Review* 380.

165 M. Holvoet 'Introducing the Special Issue 'Critical Perspectives on the Law and Politics of the Kosovo Specialist Chambers and the Specialist Prosecutor's Office' (2020) 20 *International Criminal Law Review* 3.

166 G. Visoka 'Assessing the potential impact of the Kosovo Specialist Court' (PAX 2017) 1–48.

167 Stahn (n. 157) 207.

168 A. Trigoso 'The Kosovo Specialist Chambers: In Need of Local Legitimacy', *Opinio Juris,* 8 July 2020 [available at https://opiniojuris.org/2020/06/08/the-kosovo-specialist-chambers-in-need-of-local-legitimacy/ – accessed on 12 February 2024)].

169 See 'Cases' at https://www.scp-ks.org/en/cases. (Accessed on 20 September 2021).

distance between the location of crimes and the venue of the tribunals. These efforts may help to enhance its acceptance by the locals.

5.5 How KSCSPO Promotes Regional Complementarity

As explained, regional complementarity could imply efforts geared towards the prosecution of international crimes by a region. This is irrespective of the unwillingness on the part of the national authorities to cooperate with the region. In relation to KSCSPO, the Kosovar authorities had limited political will and were initially unwilling to cooperate with the EU on the establishment of the Tribunal. However, regional and international pressures were mounted, and the national authorities eventually accepted the establishment of the Tribunal.[170] This is a victory for regional efforts to prosecute international crimes. Although KSCSPO is not a regional tribunal, it is to some extent a regional organization's project. The cost of the court is borne by the EU as part of its Common Foreign and Security Policy.[171] There are different levels of cooperative relations between the KSCSPO and the EU. For example, there is a 'Working Arrangement establishing cooperative relations between the KSCSPO and the European Union Agency for law Enforcement Cooperation (EUROPOL)'.[172] This is one example of the support that the EU as a regional organization gives to the KSCSPO, among others.

6 Conclusion

In this chapter, I have considered the practice of regional complementarity in the contexts of the EAC and the KSCSPO. I show that regionalism in ICL is inevitable. One reason for this is that the turn to regionalism in ICL is not novel. It is rooted in the UN Charter's provisions on states' responsibility to take joint actions within a regional arrangement to ensure global peace and security. I establish that complementarity between the Habré tribunal and the ICC is not a discussion that is worth entertaining, considering that the tribunal has concluded its assignment. The Law on the establishment of KSCSPO did

170 Muharremi (n. 162) 968.

171 European Commission, Helping international justice to thrive: support to Kosovo Specialist Chambers and EUAM Ukraine, 17 July 2023.

172 'Working Arrangement establishing cooperative relations between the KSCSPO and the European Union Agency for law Enforcement Cooperation (EUROPOL)' (2020).

not consider any possible relationship between the tribunal and the ICC. This is probably because there is no overlap of temporal jurisdiction between the two courts. I also examine the place of precedent in inspiring developments in ICL. Evidence shows that the Pinochet case, in which a Spanish court exercised universal jurisdiction to try the former Chilean dictator, was a major inspiration for the agitations that finally led to the prosecution of Habré.[173] The Habré case has been called 'the first successful application of the Pinochet precedent'.[174] In the same manner, the 'success' of the Habré case may yet inspire the prosecution of perpetrators of international crimes, in the same way that the Pinochet case trans-regionally influenced the Habré trial. The place of precedent in law cannot be underestimated. As noted by a commentator, when the Appeal Chambers of the ICC overturned the conviction of Jean-Pierre Bemba for crimes against humanity and war crimes by the Trial Chamber in June 2018, it stood in stark contrast to the Hissène Habré conviction which was confirmed on appeal, thus showing that 'Africa can indeed successfully prosecute the most serious of international crimes.'[175] In the KSCSPO, we have already seen the indictment of Kosovo's former president, who had to step down in 2020, in order to face charges.[176] The EAC and KSCSPO have thus shown the capacity and potential of regionally backed criminal tribunals in bringing the most senior political officers to trial for crimes committed by them or under their watch. In the EAC, we see how advocacy mounted by victims-network groups and civil society organizations within the continent contributed to the establishment of the tribunal and the success of the trial. In the KSCSPO, I have shown how the regional organization mounted pressure on the Kosovar authorities, despite the latter's initial reluctance. All these underscore the importance of a multi-faceted approach in bringing justice to victims of international crimes. For the EAC, I have shown the role that the sub-regional human rights court played. It was the ECOWAS court that first ruled that Senegal could try Habré in an *ad hoc* tribunal established for that purpose. This shows that regional and sub-regional human rights mechanisms may be able to play more role in the regionalization of ICL. I have also shown that in the context of the assistance driven

173 Høgestøl (n. 116).

174 I. Sansani, 'The Pinochet Precedence in Africa: Prosecution of Hissène Habré' (2001) 8 Human *Rights Brief* 1.

175 M. Nel 'Can a regional court be a viable alternative to the ICC in Africa?' *The Conversation* (6 August 2018), [available at https://theconversation.com/can-a-regional-court-be-a-viable-alternative-to-the-icc-in-africa-100788 – accessed on 12 February 2024].

176 Mucaj (n. 164) 387.

strand of regionalism, regional organizations are active in supporting ICL through the establishment of tribunals in the domestic system of member-states. This is to be distinguished from the other strand where regional organization moves towards full regionalism. The next chapter will consider this second strand of regionalism.

CHAPTER 5

Practice of Regional Complementarity in the Fully Independent Strand of Regionalism: The Malabo Protocol

1 Introduction

This is the second of the two chapters where this book investigates the existing practice of regional complementarity. In the previous chapter, it examined how effective the assistance-driven strand of complementarity has been in practice. Secondly, it identified some of the lessons that can be drawn from these newly emerging practices. In this chapter, the author investigates the same questions, however, in relation to the full and independent strand of regionalism. The chapter uses the Malabo Protocol as a case study. It provides some analysis on the historical evolution of Africa's judicial landscape to contextualize how regional courts have evolved within the continent. After the historical discussion, it proceeds by discussing the establishment, jurisdiction and crimes covered by the protocol establishing the ICL section of the ACJHPR. It concludes with a discussion on complementarity through the lens of the ACJHPR.

2 Africa's International Justice Project and the Roadmap to the Malabo Protocol

Africa's interaction with international justice project has been enmeshed in complexities.[1] In May 2014, the AU adopted an instrument in Malabo, Equatorial Guinea to create the first ever regional criminal tribunal. The Protocol was adopted by the Assembly of the AU on 30 June 2014 at its Twenty-Third Ordinary Session. The Protocol extends the jurisdiction of the yet to be established ACJHR to international and transnational crimes. The initial plan was for the ACJHR to have two sections: a general affairs section and a human rights section. With the adoption of the Malabo Protocol, the world's first regional crim-

1 For a discussion on these complexities, see K. M. Clarke 'New frontiers in international human rights: Actionable non-actionables and the (non)performance of perpetual becoming' (2021) *Journal of Human Rights* 2, 152.

© 2026 THE AUTHOR(S) | HTTPS://DOI.ORG/10.1163/9789004761803-007

inal tribunal has now been established, awaiting the required number of ratifications from states for the protocol to come into force and for the court to become fully operational. Accordingly, the Protocol shall only 'enter into force thirty (30) days after the deposit of instruments of ratification by fifteen (15) Member States'.[2] At the time of writing, only fifteen states have signed, but no state has ratified.[3] It is yet to be seen whether the Malabo Protocol (the 2014 protocol) would garner enough ratifications to enter into force, as the Protocol on the Statute of the African Court of Justice and Human Rights (the 2008 merger protocol) that it amends has also not entered into force. As of the date of writing, the 2008 merger protocol has garnered 32 signatures but only seven states have ratified and deposited their instruments of ratification.[4] The ACJHPR was established to serve as Africa's single court, and in accordance with Article 4, it shall complement the protective mandate of the African Commission on Human and Peoples' Rights. The intention of the AU is to reduce inter-institutional rivalry which may occur because of multiple continental institutions with overlapping jurisdictions. Some of such rivalries have already been witnessed between the African Commission and the currently functional African court. The ICL section is therefore created and added to the court by virtue of Article 3(1) of the Malabo Protocol. The proposed single court with its ICL section will be housed in Arusha, the United Republic of Tanzania. The protocol was adopted on 27 June 2014. Historical analysis, however, suggests that the continent had been on a long journey of international justice, before it arrived at this point, and that the proposal to establish an international criminal chamber may have been borne out of a need to protest non-accountability for historical crimes.

Moreover, the African Union (AU), and its predecessor, the Organisation of African Unity (OAU) had always worked through judicial or quasi-judicial mechanisms, among other approaches, in their attempt to entrench international justice. So far, Africa has had four regional courts, which were all at different stages of evolution. The African Court on Human and Peoples' Rights (ACtHPR) came into being because of a Protocol adopted by the Organisation of African Unity (OAU) in 1998.[5] The Protocol came into effect

---

2 Protocol on the Statute of the African Court of Justice and Human Rights' (undated) [available at https://www.african-court.org/pt/images/Basic%20Documents/ACJHR_Protocol.pdf – accessed on 1 January 2023].

3 'OAU/AU Treaties, Conventions, Protocols & Charters' at https://au.int/en/treaties/protocol-amendments-protocol-statute-african-court-justice-and-human-rights.

4 Protocol on the Statute of the African Court of Justice and Human Rights' (n. 2).

5 F. Viljoen 'AU Assembly should consider human rights implications before adopting the Amending Merged African Court Protocol', *AfricLaw*, 23 May 2012 [available at https://afri

in 2004.[6] The court came into being before the AU Constitutive Act was adopted. Upon coming into force, the AU Constitutive Act created the African Court of Justice (ACJ), which was established in 2003.[7] In 2008, ACtHPR became functional when its judges were elected.[8] The Protocol establishing the ACJ came into effect in 2009 but the ACJ could not function because as at this time, the AU Assembly had already started discussing the possibility of merging the ACtHPR and the ACJ into one single court. On 1 July 2008, the AU adopted the Protocol on the Statute of the African Court of Justice and Human Rights to merge the ACJ and the ACtHPR. The merged court, which is the third court, is called the African Court of Justice and Human Rights (ACJHR). In essence, this merger protocol simply created one court out of the two initial courts. This one court was meant to combine the jurisdictions of the two previous courts.[9]

However, before the coming into force of this merger protocol, the AU proposed granting jurisdiction over international crimes to this new single court, and by virtue of the Protocol on the Amendments of the Statute of the African Court of Justice and Human Rights, a new court, which is the fourth court, has been created with three jurisdictions, namely human rights, general affairs and international crimes jurisdiction. This court is the African Court on Justice and Human and Peoples' Rights (ACJHPR). Thus, this court was created by amending a protocol, which had not entered into force.[10] Essentially, in one fell swoop, Africa created for itself its own International Court of Justice (ICJ) and its own International Criminal Court (ICC) as the totality of the mandates of the three different sections of the single court rightly mirrors the combined jurisdictions of the ICJ and the ICC. The Malabo Protocol, if it comes into force, will replace and supersede the 2008 merger protocol.

Given this broad mandate, there are already divergent views on the motivation for the establishment of the International Criminal Law Section within

---

claw.com/2012/05/23/au-assembly-should-consider-human-rights-implications-before-adopting-the-amending-merged-african-court-protocol/ – accessed on 6 February 2024].

6 *Ibid.*

7 *Ibid.*

8 *Ibid.*

9 *Ibid.*

10 A. Abass 'Prosecuting International Crimes in Africa: Rationales, Prospects and Challenges' (2013a) 24 *European Journal of International Law* 933; also A. Abass 'The Proposed International Criminal Jurisdiction for the African Court: Some problematic aspects' (2013b) *Netherlands International Law Review* 27–50; F. Viljoen (n. 5); D. Deya 'Worth the Wait: Pushing for the African Court to exercise jurisdiction for international crimes' [available at http://www.osisa.org/sites/default/files/is_the_african_court_worth_the_wait_-don_deya.pdf – accessed on 24 January 2023].

the African Court of Justice and Human and Peoples' Rights. While some say the AU is trying to secure 'regional exceptionalism'[11] because of ICC's investigation and prosecution in Africa, others argue that it is part of the regional body's broader commitment to accountability and justice.[12] Those in opposition argue that the establishment of the Criminal Chamber will defeat the object and purpose of the Rome Statute, thereby impeding the work of the ICC to punish individuals who commit international crimes in Africa.[13] Kamari Clarke expresses this controversy aptly when she submits that there is a 'curious paradox between the aspirational aspects of the Malabo Protocol' and the vehement debate about the integrity of the judicial innovations that the international criminal chamber represents.[14]

Whatever the view is, the AU-ICC relationship only served as one of the catalysts for establishing regional frameworks to prosecute international crimes in Africa.[15] The adoption of the Malabo Protocol in 2014 was a continuation of the journey that began decades earlier. In fact, it is Abass' contention that 'Africa first expressed a desire to prosecute international crimes in the 1970s during the discussion on the African Charter on Human and Peoples' Rights'.[16] There are long-term and short-term factors[17] and some fundamental reasons that necessitated the prosecution of international crimes by an African regional court.[18]

African countries owe a legal duty to strengthen regional cooperation for the purposes of enhancing human security, including through the prosecution of international crimes. This was exemplified by the transformation of the

---

11 M. Du Plessis 'A Case of Negative Regional Complementarity? Giving the African Court of Justice and Human Rights Jurisdiction over International Crimes' (2012) [*EJILTalk* available at http://www.ejiltalk.org/a-case-of-negative-regionalcomplementarity-giving-the-african-court-of-justice-and-human-rights-jurisdiction-overinternational-crimes/ – accessed on 24 January 2023].

12 K.M. Clarke *et al* 'Africa and the ICC: An Introduction' in K.M Clarke and ors (eds) *Africa and the ICC: perceptions of justice* (Cambridge University Press 2016) 21.

13 C.B. Murungu 'Towards a Criminal Chamber in the African Court of Justice and Human Rights' (2011) 9 *Journal of International Criminal Justice* 5, 1.

14 K. M. Clarke 'New frontiers in international human rights: Actionable non-actionables and the (non)performance of perpetual becoming' (2021) *Journal of Human Rights* 2, 152.

15 C. Jalloh 'The Place of the African Criminal Court in the Prosecution of Serious Crimes in Africa' in C. Jalloh & I. Bantekas (eds) *The International Criminal Court and Africa* (Oxford University Press 2017) 304.

16 A. Abass 'Historical and Political Background to the Malabo Protocol' in G. Werle & M, Vormbaum (eds) *The African Criminal Court: A Commentary on the Malabo Protocol* (Asser Press 2017) at 15.

17 Murungu (n. 13).

18 Abass (n. 16) 11.

Organisation of African Unity (OAU) to the African Union (AU) just after the Cold War.[19] The transformation was motivated by several factors, chief of which was the desire to shift from the OAU's policy of non-intervention in the domestic affairs of member states.[20] The non-intervention policy showed respect for member states' sovereignty. Consequently, the OAU had been unable to intervene in conflicts that had broken out in many member states. This inability ensured that gross rights violations and other abuses went unattended through regional efforts, especially in states that lacked the proper structure to address these violations.[21] The Rwandan Genocide and the conflicts in Sierra Leone and Liberia were sore reminders that Africa needed to do more. It was therefore in a bid to address this and other failings of the OAU that the Constitutive Act established the AU as an organization with objectives to 'encourage international cooperation' and 'promote peace, security, and stability on the continent'.[22] The AU was meant to be more proactive in addressing conflicts and the attendant gross human rights violations as well as serious crimes. This was in furtherance of discussions from as far back as the 1970s on the establishment of an African human rights system through the adoption of an African Charter on Human and Peoples' Rights. This charter was eventually adopted in 1998, and it created the African Commission on Human and Peoples' Rights as its enforcement mechanism.[23] However, because the African Commission cannot make binding decisions,[24] it was conceded that a court that should complement the Commission ought to be created.[25] This court was established by virtue of Article 1 of the Protocol to the African Charter on Human and Peoples' Rights on the Establishment of an African Court on Human and Peoples' Rights.[26] The Protocol was adopted in 1998 and came into force in 2004.[27] Discussions on the possibility of establishing an African criminal court resurfaced in July 2004 when the question of election of judges

---

19 O. Abegunrin 'From Organization of African Unity to African Union' in *Africa in Global Politics in the Twenty First Century* (Palmgrave Macmillan 2009) 141–172.

20 *Ibid.*

21 Jalloh (n. 15) 305.

22 Article 3 (e) & (f) of the Constitutive Act of the AU.

23 Jalloh (n. 15) 304.

24 *Ibid.*

25 *Ibid.*

26 Protocol to the African Charter on Human and Peoples' Rights on the Establishment of an African Court on Human and Peoples' Rights [available at https://www.african-court\.org/wpafc/wp-content/uploads/2020/04/Protocol-of-the-Establishment-of-the-African-Charter-on-Human-and-Peoples-Rights-.pdf – accessed on 12 February 2023].

27 *Ibid.*

to the African Court on Human and Peoples' Rights came before the AU Assembly.[28]

The Committee of Legal Experts saddled with the responsibility of drafting the African Charter in the early 1980s, briefly considered a proposal by the Republic of Guinea. This proposal was for the establishment of a court with jurisdiction over crimes against humanity. The proposal was, however, defeated due to two reasons. The first reason was African nations' preference for an international penal court which was already been anticipated as an enforcement mechanism for the International Convention on the Suppression and Punishment of the Crime of Apartheid. Secondly, the UN was already considering the establishment of an international court to repress crimes against humanity, and as such, there was no need to duplicate efforts.[29] The foregoing shows that there was already a 'growing regional sensitivity to impunity' in Africa, considering that several provisions of the AU Constitutive Act reveal a willingness to close the impunity gap by 'intervening in a Member State… in respect of grave circumstances, namely war crimes, genocide and crimes against humanity'.[30]

Thus, various legal instruments adopted from the OAU through the AU years do not only show commitment towards closing impunity gap, but there is also no incompatibility between these instruments and the AU's attempt at prosecuting crimes in the region. If anything, the adoption of these instruments exemplifies the point that the adoption of the Malabo Protocol in 2014 was not the first time that Africa had attempted or discussed the idea of establishing a court with jurisdiction over international crimes. As Abass noted, 'it cannot be the case that the AU legislates on crimes it does not intend its own court to prosecute'.[31]

Also, the 'abuse' and 'misuse' of the principle of universal jurisdiction[32] 're-stimulated' the AU's interest in creating its own regional criminal court.[33] African leaders and state officials were at different times indicted in the domestic courts of certain European countries. French and Spanish judges had issued warrants of arrest for some military and political leaders of Rwanda. French

28 Amnesty International 'Malabo Protocol: Legal and Institutional Implications of the Merged and Expanded African Court', 22 January 2016.

29 Jalloh (n. 15) 306.

30 Article 4(h) of the Constitutive Act of the AU; Jalloh (n. 15) 308.

31 Abass (n. 16) 17.

32 For a general understanding of the principle, see X Philippe 'The principles of universal jurisdiction and complementarity: how do the two principles intermesh?' (2006) 88 *IRRC* 862, 375–398.

33 Jalloh (n. 15) 311.

Magistrate Bruguière indicted nine Rwandan officials, while Spanish Magistrate Merelles indicted forty Rwandese military and political leaders.[34] In Belgium, an indictment was issued against the Congolese Minister for Foreign Affairs. The government of the DRC opposed this and requested the ICJ to pronounce that the action of the Belgian authorities was against customary international law. The ICJ ruled that

> [G]iven the nature and purpose of the warrant, its mere issuance constituted a violation of an obligation of Belgium towards the DRC, in that it had failed to respect the immunity which Mr. Yerodia enjoyed as incumbent Minister for Foreign Affairs. The Court also declared that the international circulation of the disputed arrest warrant from June 2000 by the Belgian authorities constituted a violation of an obligation of Belgium towards the DRC, in that it had failed to respect the immunity of the incumbent Minister for Foreign Affairs.[35]

Accordingly, the legal issue that these indictments raised was their 'alleged incompatibility' with the well-settled customary international law principles on immunities for heads of states and governments. This same issue prompted the AU, at its 30th Session of the Summit of Heads of State and Governments in January 2018, to among other things,

> Request the African Group in New York to immediately place on the Agenda of the UN General Assembly a request to seek an advisory opinion from the International Court of Justice on the question of immunities of a Head of State and Government and other Senior Officials as it relates to the relationship between Articles 27 and 98 and the obligations of States Parties under International Law.[36]

While further actions on the AU's decision to seek an ICJ's advisory opinion appeared to have been dropped, it suffices to state here that the issue of indictments against African leaders based on universal jurisdiction also played a prominent role in accelerating Africa's call for its own international criminal

34 C. Jalloh 'Universal Jurisdiction, Universal Prescription? A Preliminary Assessment of the African Union Perspective on Universal Jurisdiction' (2010) 21 *Criminal Law Forum* 1–65, 29.

35 See *The Case Concerning Arrest Warrant of 11 April 2000 (Democratic Republic of the Congo v. Belgium)*.

36 Decision at the 30th Ordinary Session of the Assembly, 28–29 January 2018, Addis Ababa Ethiopia. AU Doc: Assembly/AU/Draft/Doc.8(XXX) Draft Decision on the International Criminal Court Doc EX.CL/1008(XXXII).

mechanism. Van der Wilt observed that the creation of the Criminal Chamber was an attempt to pre-empt both the universal jurisdiction of European states and the ICC. In his words, 'it is telling that the Preamble of the Malabo Protocol explicitly refers to the African Union Assembly's Decision on the Abuse of the Principle of Universal Jurisdiction'.[37]

One other factor that has been identified as Africa's motivation for seeking its own distinct regional international criminal mechanism is the willingness to prosecute crimes that are peculiar to Africa but over which the ICC has no jurisdiction.[38] In this regard, mention has been made of the AU's adoption of the African Charter on Democracy Election and Governance. The charter criminalizes the peculiar act of unconstitutional change of government and explicitly provides for regional prosecution.[39] This certainly is because of the high number of conflicts in Africa that originated from *coup d'etat* and unconstitutional takeover of governments.[40]

Lastly, the pervasive narrative that African leaders are generally afraid of being held accountable and this may have prompted them to establish the Criminal Chamber of the African Court to evade prosecution, deserves some attention here. While not holding brief for African leaders, a closer look reveals a different narrative and suggests the need for a more balanced approach which has been described as 'African states *falling out* with the ICC and the ICC *falling in* to patterns of behavior that African states raised legitimate concerns about, and thus sought to guard against, at Rome in 1998'.[41] These legitimate concerns were raised by different African groups in Rome, during the conclusion of the ICC statute.[42] Such concerns included the call for an independent prosecutor; equal treatments of states; respect for complementarity between the court and national mechanisms; and lastly, the need for the court to further the ends of peace and justice in the world.[43] Several events since

37 See H.G. Van der Wilt 'Complementary Jurisdiction (Article 46H)' in G. Werle and M. Vormbaum (eds.) *The African Criminal Court: A Commentary on the Malabo Protocol* (Asser Press 2017) 190.

38 Abass (n. 16) 18.

39 A. S. Knottnerus and E. de Volder 'International Criminal Justice and the Early Formation of an African Criminal Court' in K.M. Clarke and ors (eds) *Africa and the ICC: perceptions of justice* (Cambridge University Press 2016) 380.

40 *Ibid.*

41 See M. Du Plessis & C. Gevers 'The Sum of Four Fears: African States and the International Criminal Court in Retrospect–Part I' *Opinio Juris*, 8 July 2019 [available at https://opiniojuris.org/2019/07/08/the-sum-of-four-fears-african-states-and-the-international-criminal-court-in-retrospect-part-i/ – accessed on 23 May 2021].

42 *Ibid.*

43 *Ibid.*

1998, including the recent inability of the court to hold either Russia or the USA accountable in relation to the Georgia[44] and Afghanistan[45] situations, respectively, have strengthened doubts that the Court and its prosecutor are independent. Other examples include the ICC's 'failure' to take any concrete actions on Ukraine prior to 2022; the court's failure to hold the UK accountable for alleged war crimes in Iraq and the failure to investigate Israel for alleged war crimes in Palestine.

The ICC-AU relationship was the final straw that broke the camel's back in relation to the AU's effort of establishing its regional mechanism for the purposes of international crimes prosecution and African efforts to establish frameworks for prosecuting international crimes predate the recent ICC-AU debacle. In fact, authors like Kamari Clarke argued that some of the factors that shaped the AU's desire to establish a criminal chamber within its court are traceable to 'historic and contemporary struggle for African state autonomy and Pan-African solidarity'.[46] She concludes that lack of accountability for historic crimes relating to slavery, apartheid, imperialism, colonialism and economic plunder, while there is much focus on other crimes 'within spheres of structural inequality' accounted for the protest court.[47]

3 Jurisdiction, Structure and Crimes in the Malabo Protocol

3.1 Jurisdiction

Article 3(1) of the Malabo Protocol provides that 'the Court is vested with an original and appellate jurisdiction, including international criminal jurisdiction, which it shall exercise in accordance with the provisions of the Statute annexed hereto'. Article 3(2) also provides that 'the Court has jurisdiction to

44 In its first case outside Africa, the ICC has continued to fail victims as it has been unable to make any progress since the Chamber granted an authorization to the prosecutor to open investigation. For more thoughts on how the ICC is failing victims in the Georgian situation, see N. Jeiranashvili 'The Georgian Experience: A Story of How the ICC is Failing Victims in its First Case Outside Africa', International Justice Monitor, 10 May 2018.

45 In a decision that has been heavily criticized, the judges of the pre-trial chambers declined to open an investigation stating that it would not be in the interest of justice to do so. See ICC 'ICC judges reject opening of an investigation regarding Afghanistan situation', 12 April 2019. The OTP, however, appealed the chamber's decision. See OTP 'Prosecution Appeal Brief' in The Situation in the Islamic Republic of Afghanistan, 30 September 2019.

46 Clarke (n. 14).

47 *Ibid.*

hear matters referred to it in any other agreements that the Member States or the Regional Economic Communities or other international organizations recognized by the African Union may conclude among themselves or with the Union'. These provisions suggest that the single court will have and exercise jurisdiction in accordance with the jurisdictional provisions of the three instruments, namely the Protocol to the African Charter on the Establishment of the African Court on Human and Peoples' Rights (which established the ACtHPR), the Protocol on the Statute of the African Court of Justice and Human Rights (the merger protocol), and the Malabo Protocol (which seeks to add an ICL section to the single court). These three instruments also contain provisions on who can access the court. Accordingly, Article 15 of the Malabo Protocol adds the Peace and Security Council and the Office of the Prosecutor as the other entities that can access the single court. These are in addition to the entities mentioned in Articles 29 and 30 of the 2008 merger protocol. In essence, the following are the entities that can access the three sections of the single court in order to trigger its jurisdiction: AU member states; the AU Assembly; the AU parliament and other organs of the AU authorized by the AU Assembly; a staff member of the AU on appeal in a dispute and within the limits and under the terms and conditions laid down in the Staff Rules and Regulations of the Union; the African Commission on Human and Peoples' Rights; the African Committee of Experts on the Rights and Welfare of the Child; African Intergovernmental Organizations accredited to the AU or its organs; African National Human Rights Institutions as well as individuals or relevant NGOs accredited to the African Union or its organs.

Given the large array of the entities that can access the court, as well as its wide jurisdictional mandate, it has been suggested that the single court has 'an ambitious jurisdictional reach' whose scope is 'breathtaking'.[48] Others called it 'an overloaded court'[49] and concerns have been raised over its structure, manpower, budget and relationship.[50] It is exceedingly worrying that the single court will only have a total of 16 judges manning the entire three sections with all the arrays of possible issues that can be brought before the court. While it is understandable that this is a regional court with a limited focus on the continent, it is worrisome that the ICC, which only hears ICL cases for four core crimes, has a larger number of judges compared to the entire single African court. In the same vein, the ICL section with extensive jurisdiction *ratione*

48 Du Plessis 'Implications of the AU Decision to Give the African Court Jurisdiction Over International Crimes' (2012) 235 *Institute for Security Studies Paper* 5–6.

49 Amnesty International (n. 28) 24.

50 Du Plessis (n. 48).

materiae may indeed be overloaded since it will only have one judge in its PTC, three judges in its Trial Chamber and five judges in its Appeal Chamber, as per Article 10 of the Malabo Protocol. In essence, the long-term effectiveness and efficiency of the court are already in doubt,[51] but since it is yet to become functional, it is difficult to see whether it would, in actual terms, be overloaded.

3.2 Structure of the Proposed Court

Article 6 of the Malabo Protocol replaces Article 16 of the merger protocol and provides that 'the Court shall have three sections: a General Affairs Section; a Human and Peoples' Rights Section; and an International Criminal Law (ICL) Section'. It also provides that the ICL Section of the Court shall have three Chambers: a Pre-Trial Chamber, a Trial Chamber and an Appellate Chamber,[52] thus mirroring the current ICC model.

The General Affairs Section shall have competence to hear cases submitted under Article 28 of the merger protocol, except for the cases assigned to the two other sections. For the Human and Peoples' Rights Section, Article 7 of the Malabo Protocol simply states that 'it shall be competent to hear all cases relating to human and peoples' rights' without defining in clear terms what amounts to human and peoples' rights cases. However, guidance can be sought from the merger protocol which states in Article 28C that the court shall have jurisdiction over cases which relate to 'the interpretation and the application of the African Charter, the Charter on the Rights and Welfare of the Child, the Protocol to the African Charter on Human and Peoples' Rights on the Rights of Women in Africa, or any other legal instrument relating to human rights, ratified by the State Parties concerned'. This then implies that the General Affairs Section will exercise jurisdiction on general issues of a legal nature except those relating to the human rights instruments earlier mentioned. Again, these issues are outlined in Article 28 of the merger protocol. On its part, the ICL section will have competence to hear cases relating to the crimes specified in the Malabo Protocol. While the other two sections are not divided into different chambers, only the ICL section has three chambers, including an appellate chamber. There is, however, room for the review of the decisions of the other sections. Article 8 of the Malabo Protocol provides that in the case of the two sections, a revision of the judgement from them can be

51 *Ibid.*

52 Article 6 of the Malabo Protocol. See also M. Sirleaf 'The African Justice Cascade and the Malabo Protocol' (2017) 11 *International Journal of Transitional Justice* 1. See also K. Magliveras 'Substituting International Criminal Justice for an African Criminal Justice?' (2017) 14 *International Organizations Law Review* 291–320.

made in terms of Article 48 of the merger protocol. Such revisions may be necessitated by the discovery of new facts. On the other hand, in the case of the ICL section, according to Article 8 of the Malabo Protocol, an appeal may be lodged by the accused or the prosecutor if there is a procedural error, an error of law or an error of fact.

Given the above, the main difference between the revision and appeal processes is that the decisions of the first two sections may only be revised if there is discovery of a new fact which may substantially affect the decision of the court, while the decision of the ICL section can be appealed on the three grounds of procedure, fact and law. The revision process does not anticipate an error of law.

3.3 Crimes Covered in the Protocol

Article 14 of the Malabo Protocol provides for the insertion of Article 28A-N and outlines fourteen crimes over which the ICL Section of the court would exercise jurisdiction. Adopting Bassouni's penal characteristics,[53] Jalloh classified this 'mixed basket of crimes into four categories, namely 'international crimes', 'transnational crimes', 'partly international crimes' and 'partly transnational crimes'.[54] The core international crimes of genocide,[55] aggression,[56] war crimes[57] and crimes against humanity[58] are classified as 'international crimes'. These are generally known as core crimes, which are sometimes distinguished from treaty crimes, albeit with much ambiguity.[59] Secondly, piracy,[60] mercenarism,[61] money laundering,[62] trafficking in persons,[63] trafficking

---

53 Bassiouni developed guidelines for classifying crimes under different headings and set out characteristics that conducts constituting international crimes must possess. For a description of the five guidelines and ten characteristics, see generally M. C. Bassiouni *Introduction to International Criminal Law* (Martinus Nijhoff 2013).

54 C. Jalloh 'The Nature of the Crimes in the African Criminal Court' (2017) 15 *JICJ* 799–826.

55 Art. 28B.

56 Art. 28M.

57 Art. 28D.

58 Art. 28C.

59 On the distinction between core crimes and treaty crimes, see C. Schwöbel-Patel 'The Core Crimes of International Criminal Law' in K. J. Heller & ors (eds) *The Oxford Handbook of International Criminal Law* (Oxford University Press 2020).

60 Art. 28F.

61 Art. 28H.

62 Art. 28Ibis.

63 Art. 28J.

in drugs,[64] trafficking in hazardous wastes[65] as well as illicit exploitation of natural resources[66] were classified as 'transnational crimes'. Examples of 'partly international crimes' are terrorism[67] and unconstitutional change of government.[68] Lastly, corruption[69] was cited as an example of 'partly transnational crimes'.[70] From the foregoing, the protocol creates jurisdiction over crimes that are not yet fixed in 'international criminal law firmament'[71] and caters for future developments in international law. It expressly provides that 'the AU Assembly may extend .... the jurisdiction of the court to incorporate additional crimes to reflect development in international law'. There is no similar provision in the Rome Statute. Articles 121 and 123 of the Rome Statute jointly deal with amendment and review and they are both silent about the likely motivation for a review. They do not exactly provide for an amendment to cater for future developments in international law as was expressly done in the Malabo Protocol. This is another example of the progressive and forward-looking nature of the Malabo Protocol.

In analysing the nature of the crimes in the Protocol, it must first be recalled that international crimes are 'breaches of international rules entailing the personal criminal liability of the individuals concerned', while transnational crimes are 'certain criminal phenomena transcending international borders, transgressing the laws of several states or having an impact on another country'.[72] Article 3(2) of the UN Convention Against Transnational Organized Crime also defines transnational crimes as those committed in more than one state; committed in one state but a substantial part of its preparation, planning, direction or control takes place in another state; committed in one state but involves an organized criminal group that engages in criminal activities in more than one state or committed in one state but has substantial effects in another state.

Given the definition in Article 3(2) of the UNTOC, the drafters of the Malabo Protocol gave little or no regard to the different classifications and nature of the crimes included in the protocol. In international law, these classifications are still muddled up in confusion primarily because states generally have lim-

64 Art. 28K.
65 Art. 28L.
66 Art. 28Lbis.
67 Art. 28G.
68 Art. 28E.
69 Art. 28I.
70 C. Jalloh 'The Nature of the Crimes in the African Criminal Court' (2017) 15 *JICJ* 799–826.
71 Du Plessis (n. 48).
72 *Ibid.*

ited guidance on the appropriate criteria for including crimes in international instruments.[73] Different attempts have therefore been made by scholars to bridge this gap and find a doctrinal basis for transnational crimes. For example, Boister argues that re-labelling treaty crimes – which are different from the core international crimes – as 'Transnational Criminal Law' may help to find a doctrinal match for transnational crimes, seeing that the core crimes already enjoy a doctrinal labelling as international criminal law.[74] Thus, in the absence of a firm doctrinal framework for transnational crimes like its counterparts, the core crimes, the Malabo Protocol may have presented opportunities to consider a doctrinal categorization of international and transnational crimes.

Another consideration is whether transnational crimes are better prosecuted by domestic courts rather than regional or international ones. Some have argued that national criminal mechanisms remain the best suited forum for prosecuting transnational crimes.[75] Boister asserts that a state's inability or unwillingness to prosecute are not sufficient grounds to elevate transnational crimes to the same status of core crimes requiring international response.[76] Others, however, argue that domestic mechanisms are limited and thus, international or regional response may be more appropriate.[77] According to Parrish, unilateral domestic responses are often problematic and can undermine comprehensive and meaningful multilateral efforts.[78] While analysing the challenge with prosecuting ordinary crimes instead of more serious crimes, Kemp and Nortje suggest that 'a prima facie case of apartheid as a crime under customary international law' may exist and certain persons whose actions contributed to apartheid [the bigger crime] could be prosecuted, even when they were not in leadership positions.[79]

Given these divergent views, it will appear that while transnational crimes have been included in the Malabo Protocol, there is nothing to suggest that states have been disempowered from prosecuting those crimes if they are

---

73 Jalloh (n. 70).

74 N. Boister 'Transnational Criminal Law?' 14 (2003) *EJIL* 953–976.

75 N Boister 'Responding to transnational crime: the distinguishing features of transnational criminal law' in H. Van der Wilt & C. Paulussen (eds) *Legal Responses to Transnational and International Crimes: Towards an Integrative Approach* (EE Publishing 2017) 48.

76 *Ibid*, 47.

77 A. Parrish 'Domestic Responses to Transnational Crime: The Limits of National Law' (2012) 23 *Criminal Law Forum* 4, 275–293.

78 *Ibid.*

79 G. Kemp & W. Nortje 'Prosecuting the Crime against Humanity of Apartheid: The Historic First Indictment in South Africa and the Application of Customary International Law' (2023) 21 *Journal of International Criminal Justice* 430.

criminalized within the domestic system, and where there exists a functional and effective domestic system for such investigation and prosecution. In any case, this is the essence of the principle of complementarity which exists in both the ICC and the emerging system under the Malabo Protocol. While the debate on the appropriateness or otherwise of including transnational crimes in the Malabo Protocol continues, it does not detract from the ability of the domestic system to address these crimes since primacy already inheres in them. In any case, the idea that a single court should prosecute international and transnational crimes is not entirely novel. In the post–WWI era, Baron Descamps and Vespasian Pella had argued for the establishment of a single court that could prosecute 'crimes against the international order and transnational offences'.[80]

Most of the crimes in the Protocol relate to the common security threats that African countries face.[81] These security challenges may be too politically complex for national mechanisms to handle. Yet, they are not adjudged to be serious enough for an international court like the ICC, hence the need for a mid-level mechanism like the regional court.[82] This reinforces the argument that creating its own criminal court was Africa's way of providing specific African solutions to African problems. This is what has been missing in the ICC context. There is a clear delinking of international crimes from transnational crimes. There are, however, some benefits in having transnational and international crimes as part of a common system, as they have a lot of synergy.[83] This is one of the good features of the protocol.

Like the last point raised, the protocol extends the jurisdiction of the court to corporate criminal liability. In Article 46C, the Protocol provides that 'for the purpose of this Statute, the Court shall have jurisdiction over legal persons, apart from states'. This also reflects a specific African reality: the unwholesome impact of the activities of foreign and multinational companies on the human rights landscape as well as the economies of African states. Illegal mining, deforestation, illicit financial outflows, money laundering and corrup-

80 M. Lewis, *The Birth of the New Justice: The Internationalization of Crime and Punishment, 1919–1950* (Oxford University Press 2014) 79.

81 M. Sirleaf 'The African Justice Cascade and the Malabo Protocol' (2017) 11 *International Journal of Transitional Justice* 75.

82 Kenyans for Peace With Truth and Justice, 'Seeking Justice or Shielding Suspects: An Analysis of the Malabo Protocol' [available at http://kptj.africog.org/wp-content/uploads/2016/11/Malabo-Report.pdf – accessed on 12 February 2024].

83 R. Smith 'Book Reviews: Legal Responses to Transnational and International Crimes: Toward an Integrative Approach' (2018) 46 *International Journal of Legal Information* 3, 200–201.

tion are some of the activities that have become major sources of concern in Africa. Thus, the Protocol's extension of the court's jurisdiction is an attempt at curbing these African realities.[84] There is currently no international criminal tribunal with jurisdiction over corporate entities and the Malabo Protocol advances ICL in this regard.[85]

The inclusion of novel crimes in the Malabo Protocol is grounded in certain structural critiques of ICL. The idea that international criminal justice is limited in scope and does not often address the root causes of international crimes appears to be one of the motivations for the creation of the African criminal chamber, and indeed the inclusion of novel crimes in the protocol.[86]

3.4 Innovative Crimes Jurisdiction of the Court

For the first time, an ICL mechanism will assume jurisdiction over environmental, political as well as economic and financial crimes. As previously argued, the reason for the inclusion of environmental and other crimes in the Malabo Protocol is that the new court responds to specific problems that African countries have had to grapple with, which may not have been wholly or partly addressed by the Rome Statute. I will now discuss one example each of political crime: unconstitutional change of government, economic crime: corruption and financial crime: money laundering.

3.4.1 Unconstitutional Change of Government (Article 28E)

The Protocol's inclusion of the political crime of unconstitutional change of government was inspired by decades of coups and counter coups that have been experienced by many African states. Since the 1960s, Africa has witnessed countless successful and failed coup attempts in at least forty countries.[87] These incidences have also led to many instances of civil wars and

84 See generally J. Kyriakakis 'Article 46C: Corporate Criminal Liability at the African Criminal Court' in K. Clarke & C. Jalloh (eds) The *African Court of Justice and Human and Peoples' Rights* (Cambridge University Press 2019).

85 Sirleaf (n. 81) 76–77.

86 On the narrow scope of international criminal justice, see M. Renzo 'Crimes against humanity and the limits of international criminal law' (2012) 31 *Law and Philosophy* 4, 443–476.

87 P. Roessler 'The enemy within: Personal rule, coups and civil war in Africa' in 63 *World Politics* 2, 300–346.

attendant war crimes in Africa.[88] The protocol therefore prohibits the crime of unconstitutional change of government which it defines in Article 28E to include such acts as:

> a coup d'état against a democratically elected government; intervention by mercenaries, armed dissidents or rebels to replace a democratically elected government; political assassination to replace a democratically elected government; any refusal by an incumbent government to relinquish power to the winning party or candidate after free, fair and regular elections; any amendment or revision of the Constitution or legal instruments, which is an infringement on the principles of democratic change of government or is inconsistent with the Constitution; and any substantial modification to the electoral laws in the last six months before the elections without the consent of the majority of the political actors.

This description, except for the last part on modifying electoral laws, was sourced from Article 23 of the AU's African Charter on Democracy, Elections and Governance. This approach of sourcing provisions from other AU instruments, in line with practices at the international level, reflects AU's intention to ensure that its single court sufficiently relies on, and interprets different AU instruments in the discharge of its functions. Also, the wide variety of acts that have been criminalized under this provision suggest that the Malabo Protocol considers the problem of unconstitutional change of government, and its impact on the political terrain as an issue that requires the full weight of the continent's response using its ICL mechanism. Its importance is also reflected in its place in the protocol. It is the first of the new crimes to be included in the protocol, immediately after the three core crimes. As I mentioned earlier, the commission of the acts that make up the crime of unconstitutional change of government, as is the case with most transnational crimes, is capable of leading to the commission of any of the three core crimes. Africa is particularly replete with examples of instances where political violence has led to the commission of core crimes. An example is the Nigerian Biafra war of 1967–1970 where hundreds of thousands of people from the Igbo ethnic groups were killed. The conflict arose because of coup and counter coups.[89] Thus, one way

88 See generally H. van der Wilt 'Unconstitutional Change of Government: A New Crime Within the Jurisdiction of the African Criminal Court' (2017b) 30 *Leiden Journal of International Law* 4.

89 See L. Heerten and A. Dirk Moses 'The Nigeria–Biafra war: postcolonial conflict and the question of genocide' (2014) 16 *Journal of Genocide Research* 169–203. See also C. Korieh *The Nigeria-Biafra War: Genocide and the Politics of Memory* (Cambria Press 2012).

of understanding the inclusion of transnational crimes is the direct link that their commission has with core crimes, and as such, if they are not criminalized, they could lead to the perpetration of other core crimes. This thinking is, however, not entirely novel, and the Malabo Protocol was not the first time that the AU had linked unconstitutional change of government with serious conflict. In the African Charter on Democracy, Election and Governance, which the AU adopted in 2007, it had noted in paragraph eight of the preamble that the AU was 'concerned about the unconstitutional changes of governments that are one of the essential causes of insecurity, instability and violent conflict in Africa'.[90] The AU recognizes the need to not only punish perpetrators of international crimes, but also put in place measures to ensure that predicate conducts are criminalized.

The last point is exceedingly important and may further explain why the criminalization of unconstitutional change of government – and such other 'new crimes' – in the Malabo Protocol ought to be encouraged and applauded. As argued by van der Wilt, 'causal connections between unconstitutional change of government and subsequent core crimes have emerged in the context of inquiries by the ICC Pre-Trial Chambers into the admissibility of cases before the ICC'.[91] On this note, many of the African cases before the ICC emanated as a result of crimes committed over political occurrences, particularly in the context of post-election violence and the struggle to hold on to power. The Kenyan, Libyan and the Ivorian situations are classic examples. At the ICC, states have argued that there is a strong nexus between the crimes that they investigate and/or prosecute and the ones that the ICC seeks to prosecute.[92] These have largely occurred during admissibility challenge. States have always argued that the ICC should find the cases inadmissible because the domestic mechanisms are already investigating or prosecuting them. The ICC, or more specifically the OTP, on the other hand, has always insisted that the acts being investigated do not meet the two-pronged admissibility test. However, in the Ivorian situation, the ICC ruling against the admissibility challenge reveals that the court at least acknowledges that certain acts or conducts – which are not international crimes themselves may occur preparatory to the commission of international crimes. The ICC only ruled against Ivory Coast for its failure to 'explain, how, in its view, the preparatory nature of

90 Paragraph 8, Preamble to the African Charter on Democracy, Election and Governance.

91 H.G. Van der Wilt 'Complementary Jurisdiction (Article 46H)' in G. Werle and M. Vormbaum (eds.) *The African Criminal Court: A Commentary on the Malabo Protocol* (TMC Asser Press 2017) 626.

92 *Ibid.*

the conduct underlying those crimes shows that it is substantially the same conduct as that alleged in the proceedings before the Court…'.[93] Conversely, in the Al-Senussi case, both the PTC 1 and the Appeal Chambers agreed with Libya that Al-Senussi's prosecution in Libya was based on the same facts as those for which he was convicted by the Court.[94] In writing about this, van der Wilt submits that '[T]he Chamber acknowledged thus that in both the international and domestic proceedings the core crimes had been inspired by the political motive to repel popular insurrections in the quest to remain in power.'[95] Thus, what the ICC jurisprudence continuously shows is that while the ICC may lack the jurisdictional capacity to entertain many of the crimes against the state that are capable of leading to international crimes, regional courts like the criminal chamber of the African court, if established, may be able to fill in the gap while ensuring that the more serious crimes are left for the ICC. The resultant effect is that impunity for atrocity crimes is discouraged, and the overall goal of the Rome Statute and indeed international criminal justice is achieved.

In what ways will the regionalization of the prosecution of the crime of unconstitutional change of government – which may possibly be sufficiently dealt with at a domestic level – qualify as a crime of concern to the international community? This question is valid considering that the wider goal of ICL is to punish crimes which are of concern to the international community.[96] In answering this, I choose to first assess what factors may be considered to arrive at the conclusion that a particular conduct will qualify as being of concern to the international community. One of the factors is the impact that the commission of those conducts can have on the states on whose territories the conducts are taking place, and their impact on neighbouring countries. Secondly, I am interested in state practices and whether there is a consensus from states as regards suppressing these acts. This could be gleaned from the attention that states, acting under a regional or global organization,

93 In the case of *The Prosecutor v. Simone Gbagbo*: Judgment on the appeal of Côte d'Ivoire against the decision of Pre-Trial Chamber I of 11 December 2014 entitled 'Decision on Côte d'Ivoire's challenge to the admissibility of the case against Simone Gbagbo' Para. 101.

94 See ICC PTC 1 Decision on the admissibility of the case against Abdullah Al-Senussi and Abdullah Al-Senussi 11 October 2013 and ICC Appeals Chambers in Judgment on the appeal of Mr. Abdullah Al-Senussi against the decision of Pre-Trial Chamber I of 11 October 2013, 24 July 2014.

95 Van der Wilt (n. 91) 628.

96 Para. 4 of the Preamble to the Rome Statute.

have given to these conducts through treaties and agreements that have been concluded.

As regards whether a conduct is of concern to the international community, examples abound to show that many of the conducts that are outlined in Article 28E have led to upheaval, not only in the countries where they were committed, but also in neighbouring countries. The international dimension of their impact is no longer in doubt. For instance, *coup d'etat* in many West African countries in the 1990s have led to displacements of hundreds of thousands, if not millions, thus creating problems of refugees and internally displaced persons within the sub-region.[97] When unchecked, these could lead to instability in many more countries than the country where the conflict originated. An entire region or sub-region could experience a deluge of migrants and refugees where any of the acts outlined in Article 28E takes place in one country. Secondly, as argued by Abass, even before the adoption of the Malabo Protocol, African countries have adopted treaties and instruments to outlaw acts described in Article 28E. In his words,

> The acts constituting unconstitutional changes of government, listed under Article 23 of the ACDEG (military coup d'états, the rigging of elections, and so on) have, for a long time, been practices which have been consistently rejected by the majority of African states, as evidenced by myriad treaties and declarations adopted over several decades to outlaw them. The ACDEG is therefore merely a codification of what had become a quintessential custom in Africa: the rejection of UCG.[98]

Having said that, it could be argued that African countries' commitment to outlawing these conducts predates the Malabo Protocol and may have attained the status of 'particular customary international law' within the region. This term has variously been described as 'regional customary international law', 'local customary international law' and 'special customary international law', albeit with slight difference in meaning. The ILC defines the term as 'a rule of customary international law that applies only among a limited number of States'.[99] The ILC further states that 'to determine the existence and content of a rule of particular customary international law, it is necessary to ascertain

97 P. McGowan 'Coups and Conflict in West Africa, 1955–2004 Part I, Theoretical Perspectives' (2005) 32 *Armed Forces and Society* 1, 5–23.

98 A. Abass, 'The Proposed International Criminal Jurisdiction for the African Court: Some Problematic Aspects' (2013) 60 *Netherlands International Law Review* at 34.

99 ILC 'Draft conclusions on identification of customary international law, with commentaries' (2018).

whether there is a general practice among the States concerned that is accepted by them as law (opinio juris) among themselves'.[100] Thus, the AU's codification of unconstitutional change of government and the acts that constitute it in the Malabo Protocol and other previous treaties may have attained the status of regional customary international law and the prosecution of such conducts through the regional court is the logical next step.

One counter view is that unconstitutional change of government is not capable of triggering individual criminal responsibility and should only be viewed as a violation of international law. The argument is that there is no state practice demonstrating criminality, and some argue that it is simply one of the cases of over-criminalization in the Malabo Protocol.[101] Accordingly, this conduct could at best be a treaty-based crime – if the protocol comes into force. With recent coup d'états in a number of West African countries, including Mali, Niger, Guinea and Burkina Faso, and the threats of military intervention by ECOWAS, there appears to be a renewed interest in unconstitutional change of government as a crime in international criminal law.[102]

3.4.2 The Crimes of Money Laundering and Corruption (Articles 28Ibis and 28I)

The protocol's inclusion of the financial/economic crime of money laundering and its predicate crime of corruption in Articles 28Ibis and 28I, respectively, is also novel in that it is again, one of the first instances, where a protocol brings international and transnational crimes under the jurisdictional umbrella of one court. I will discuss the two provisions jointly in this sub-section. The Protocol restricted the crime of money laundering as only capable of emanating from the crime of corruption. As such, in its description of what constitutes money laundering, Article 28Ibis employs the phrase '…such property is the proceeds of corruption' or similar expression on three occasions. Descriptions of the acts that constitute money laundering were sourced from the AU Convention on Preventing and Combating Corruption. However, as noted by Fernandez, the difference between the provisions in the protocol and the convention is that the former only criminalizes corruption if it is serious enough

100 *Ibid.*

101 M. Garcia-Casas 'The Crime of Unconstitutional Change of Government: Concept and Main Hurdles in Its Implementation' (2021) 19 *JICJ* 3, 565–581.

102 P. Melly 'Niger coup underlies challenge to democracy across West Africa' (2023) [available at https://www.chathamhouse.org/2023/08/niger-coup-underlines-challenge-democracy-across-west-africa – accessed on 12 January 2024].

to affect 'the stability of a state, region or the Union'.[103] The protocol is therefore concerned with the most serious types of corruption, in accordance with the goal of ICL to prosecute only the most serious crimes of concern to humanity. This has been described as 'grand corruption'[104] – the type often perpetrated by high level government officials and private sector leaders.[105] There is therefore no doubt that the AU places a certain premium on economic crimes. This is also seen in the fact that five out of the fourteen crimes in the Malabo protocol are economic crimes. These are the crimes of piracy, corruption, money laundering, trafficking in person and trafficking in drugs. This subsection will therefore explore the AU's real and perceived rationale for aspiring to prosecute money laundering and corruption. It will also attempt to analyse the challenges that may need to be navigated in that quest. Lastly, I will offer certain thoughts on how prosecution of money laundering and corruption can facilitate the prosecution of other core crimes; support the idea behind regional complementarity and contribute to the overall goal of ICL.

3.4.2.1 Rationale for Including Money Laundering and Corruption in the Malabo Protocol

The Malabo Protocol was not the first AU treaty that dealt with the subject of money laundering and corruption. Since 2006, the African Union Convention on Preventing and Combating Corruption had entered into force with over forty ratifications from African states.[106] The convention deals with both crimes of corruption and money laundering. Also, a few sub-regions in Africa have also put in place mechanisms to combat these crimes. For example, in the West African sub-region, the ECOWAS had established the Inter-Governmental Action Group against Money Laundering and Terrorism Financing in West Africa (GIABA). Its stated mandate is to enhance the capacity of member states to prevent and control money laundering and terrorism financing.[107] In Southern Africa too, the Eastern and Southern Africa Anti-Money Laundering Group of countries (ESAAMLG) have committed themselves to

103 L.D. Fernandez 'Corruption (Article 28I) and Money Laundering (Article 28Ibis)' in G. Werle & M. Vorbaum (eds) *The African Criminal Court International Criminal Justice Series* (TMC Asser 2017) 92, citing article 28I (1) of the Malabo Protocol.

104 *Ibid.*

105 Paraphrasing Transparency International's definition of the term 'grand corruption'.

106 AU Convention on preventing and combatting corruption 2003.

107 GIABA 'About GIABA' [available at https://www.giaba.org/about-giaba/index_656.html – accessed on 12 June 2023].

put in place effective measures against money laundering.[108] There is therefore no doubt that African countries viewed these crimes as requiring international cooperation for their control and prosecution. According to the preamble of the UN Convention, 'corruption is no longer a local matter but a transnational phenomenon…, making international cooperation to prevent and control it essential'.[109] Recent events in Africa point to this. One of the root causes of the Arab spring is the impact of grand corruption on the living standards of the people.[110] Also, after President Al-Bashir was ousted from power in Sudan, large sums of money running into over 130 million USD were found in his home.[111] The sums are believed to have been corruptly procured and stashed away. The event places in focus the question of corruption by sitting heads of state and government officials. It is a sad reminder of how leaders sometimes corruptly enrich themselves to the detriment of the people they serve; hence a concerted effort at the regional level to address these crimes. Despite being accused of different human rights violations, including allegations of war crimes and crimes against humanity by the ICC; the ex-leader has only been put on trial on corruption charges and was recently sentenced to two years in prison for same.[112]

Anderson had identified the international dimension of the problems that money laundering could create.[113] The effects on both the financial institutions and the economies of countries are not in doubt. African countries have specifically suffered from the effect of money laundering and corruption, up to the point that they have led to serious conflicts. In the African context, there are already studies that show the link between corruption and money laundering on the one hand, and serious conflicts on the other hand.[114] Gen-

108 C. Goredema 'Money laundering in Southern Africa Incidence, magnitude and prospects for its control' (2004) 92 *ISS Paper* 1–12.

109 Preamble to the UN Convention on Corruption, para 4.

110 A. Mnawar 'Corruption and the "Arab spring" As one of the main elements leading to revolutions' (2015) 1 *Polish Journal of Political Science* 3 36–49. See also S. Cook & ors. 'Corruption and the Arab Spring' (2012) 18 *The Brown Journal of World Affairs* 2, 21–28.

111 BBC News, 'Sudan crisis: Cash hoard found at al-Bashir's home' 20 April 2019 [available at https://www.bbc.com/news/world-africa-47997729 – accessed on 13 February 2024].

112 The Guardian 'Ex-Sudan leader Omar al-Bashir sentenced to two years for corruption' 14 December 2019 [available at https://www.theguardian.com/world/2019/dec/14/sudanese-court-sentences-omar-al-bashir-to-2-years-in-prison – accessed on 13 February 2024].

113 M. Anderson 'International Money Laundering: The Need for ICC Investigative and Adjudicative Jurisdiction' (2013) 53 *Virginia Journal of International Law* 1.

114 See, for example, J. C. Andvig 'Corruption and Armed Conflicts: Some Stirring Around in the Governance Soup' (2007) *Norwegian Institute of International Affairs Working Paper*

erally, the studies find that corruption and money laundering may contribute to or perpetuate violent conflicts, especially if the crimes have an international dimension. Again, the preamble to the UN Convention on Corruption stresses that corruption threatens stability and security of societies.[115]

While I have acknowledged the novelty of AU's inclusion of corruption and money laundering provisions in its protocol, Cecily Rose had pointed out that the yet to be functional AU criminal chamber will not be the first ICL mechanism to 'undertake financial investigations in connection with criminal prosecutions'.[116] Accordingly, reference was made to the OTP's investigation of money laundering by armed groups in one of the earliest DRC situations before the court.[117] This shows that there is a strong link between money laundering and/or corruption and core international crimes.[118] At the ICC, the prosecutor had investigated money laundering as predicate crimes to international crimes committed in Ituri. However, in the African court, it will be possible to charge perpetrators wholly on the strength of their commission of money laundering, and not just as a supporting fact to a core crime. The advantages are manifold, with the most obvious being that money laundering can be prosecuted as a stand-alone offence. This then requires that efforts are not scattered to hinge the evidence that is procured from such investigations on other crimes that the prosecutor may be pushing to establish.

3.4.2.2 Challenges to Prosecuting Money Laundering and Corruption

There are several jurisdictional and evidentiary challenges that may be thrown up to prosecute money laundering and corruption at the African Court. In the first place, money laundering and corruption, especially 'grand corruption' as contemplated by the protocol, may prove difficult to establish and often involve senior government officials who perpetuate such crimes in secret, away from the prying eyes of the public; sometimes by just pushing pens or computer keyboards. There are often no witnesses, collaborators and conspirators are often senior government and banking officials who have closed ranks and evidence can be easily destroyed or hidden. In fact, exposing corruption or

720; see also S. Asongu & O. Kodila-Tedika 'Crime and Conflicts in Africa: Consequences of Corruption?' (2013) 2 *European Economic Letters* 2, 50–55.

115 Para. 1, UN Convention on Corruption.

116 C. Rose 'Money Laundering and the African Court of Justice and Human and Peoples' Rights' in C. Jalloh and Ors., (eds) *The African Court of Justice and Human and Peoples' Rights in Context: Development and Challenges* (Cambridge University Press 2019) 505.

117 *Ibid.*

118 See J.D Serio 'Fueling global crime: the mechanics of money laundering' (2007) 18 *International Review of Law, Computers and Technology* 3, 435–444.

money laundering 'was regarded as futile and even harmful'.[119] It is capable of being 'hidden in plain sight', 'hard to pin down' and it 'thrives in the dark'.[120] The modern use of internet and machines to perpetuate these crimes has made it even more difficult to establish. Not only does it thrive in the dark, 'there are few darker places than the black-box algorithms and embedded artificial intelligence that now control so much of our daily lives'.[121] In essence, any attempt to prosecute corruption and money laundering must be properly thought out to navigate these difficulties.

I have earlier noted that the protocol predicates money laundering on corruption alone. This means that the crime of money laundering can only be committed out of the crime of corruption. However, this restricted view of the crime of money laundering is slightly problematic. It is a known fact that money laundering can emanate from other acts or crimes including some of the ones listed in the protocol like terrorism, piracy, mercenarism, trafficking in drugs, persons and hazardous wastes as well as illicit exploitation of natural resources. In relation to terrorism, laundered monies have been a major financing source for terrorism. When the other crimes from which money laundering can emanate are excluded from the ambit of Article 28Ibis, it betrays the principle of coherence which should underpin a treaty like the Malabo protocol. The import of this is that many crimes of money laundering which ought to be prosecuted will remain inadmissible so long as the proceeds are from other conducts that are not necessarily linked to corruption. Linked to this is the transnational nature of money laundering presents challenges relating to procuring defendants and witnesses for trials. For instance, imagine where a proceed of corruption moves from several countries in Africa to be domiciled in a bank in Switzerland, having crisscrossed many jurisdictions and involved many corporate actors. This challenge is exhaustively dealt with in the section on corporate criminal responsibility further in this chapter.

Also, money laundering and corruption are not international crimes under customary international law. There are limited instances where corruption can take the form of crimes against humanity.[122] GOPAC has suggested that grand corruption be established as a crime under international criminal law.[123] Anderson argued that the ICC should adopt frameworks for prosecuting

119 Transparency International, '25 Corruption Scandals that Shook the World' 5 July 2019.

120 UK Fraud Advisory Panel, Hidden in plain sight: domestic corruption, fraud and the integrity deficit, 27 October 2023.

121 *Ibid.*

122 I. Bantekas 'Corruption as an International Crime and Crime against Humanity: An Outline of Supplementary Criminal Justice Policies' (2006) 4 *JICJ* 3, 466–484.

123 GOPAC 'Prosecuting Grand Corruption as an International Crime' (2013) at http://gopacnetwork.org/Docs/DiscussionPaper_ProsecutingGrandCorruption_EN.pdf.

money laundering.[124] In all, the preponderance of opinion is that money laundering and corruption have not attained the status of international crimes. With this view, a likely challenge to the prosecution of these crimes in the African court, is the defence that a person cannot be prosecuted before an international tribunal, for acts that do not constitute international crimes. It is a variant of the principle of *nullum crimen sine lege* which literally translates as 'no crime without law'. The principle has many strands that include the idea that no one can be punished for a crime that is not clearly stated in a statute; and also that laws must not have retroactive effects.[125] It also implies that 'criminal statutes be drafted with precision, to be strictly construed without extension by analogy, and to have ambiguities resolved in favor of the accused'.[126] These strands all undergird the modern day principle of legality, which is used interchangeably with *nullum crimen sine lege*. The principle protects the rule of law and ensures its application in domestic and international criminal proceedings.

A defendant will therefore not be able to claim a defence to corruption or money laundering under the principle of legality or *nullum crimen sine lege* for a number of reasons: that the Malabo protocol criminalizes the conducts and lays down appropriate punishment; that such conducts are already criminalized in many of the domestic systems of the parties to the protocol thus attaining a status of regional customary international law; that their commission could be directly and indirectly linked to the commission of some of the most serious crimes and lastly, that their prosecution advances the wider goals of ICL. These conclusions are premised on the assumption that the provisions of the protocol are already transposed to domestic penal legislation, where such conducts have not previously been criminalized in domestic law.

4 Certain Problematic Aspects of the Malabo Protocol

4.1 Immunity Provisions in the Protocol

There are two main provisions dealing with immunity for government officials in the Malabo protocol. They are Articles 46Abis and 46B (2). Whereas the first

124 M. Anderson 'International Money Laundering: The Need for ICC Investigative and Adjudicative Jurisdiction' (2013) 53 *Virginia Journal of International Law*.

125 Jerome Hall 'Nulla Poena Sine Lege' (1937) 47 *The Yale Law Journal* 2, p. 165.

126 B. Van Schaack 'Crimen Sine Lege: Judicial Lawmaking at the Intersection of Law and Morals' (2008) 97 *The Georgetown Law Journal* p. 121.

confers immunity on sitting heads of states and governments and on other officials, the latter strips immunity from officials in relation to all crimes in the protocol. The first provision has been heavily criticized.[127]

As a matter of background, Article 46Abis entitled 'Immunities' generally protects three categories of persons: 'serving AU Head of State or Government, anybody acting or entitled to act in such capacity and other senior state officials based on their functions during their tenure of office'. The provision emphasizes that these officials only enjoy immunity during their tenure of office. As simple as it sounds, it becomes worrisome when the phenomenon of sit-tight leaders in Africa is taken into cognizance. Recent events in Africa, including the AU's stance against Yahya Jammeh, have pointed to the fact that the AU is progressively against the idea of a sit-tight leader.[128] Also, the protocol does not explain the exact persons who may be entitled to benefit from this provision, seeing that it refers to 'anybody acting or entitled to act' and 'other senior state officials'. It therefore opens a floodgate for all sorts of state officials to claim immunity under this provision. This immunity that has come to be known as 'immunity ratione personae'[129] only attaches to a person's office while serving in that position. It is some kind of 'status immunity' which protects external representation and exercise of functions that are crucial for state – and not all types of governmental function.

Akande and Shah identify two types of status immunities: the first is absolute and limited to foreign heads of states and governments, including shielding them from prosecution for international crimes, even when they are not

127 There is a belief that the inclusion of the immunity provision in the protocol was for the purposes of shielding African leaders from prosecution and was thus criticized. See, for example, a letter titled 'Joint Civil Society Letter on the Draft Protocol on Amendments to the Protocol on the Statute of the African Court on Justice and Human Rights' which was co-signed by more than 50 CSOs operating in over 20 countries in Africa [available at https://www.hrw.org/news/2014/05/12/joint-civil-society-letter-draft-protocol-amendments-protocol-statute-african-court – accessed on 12 February 2024]. In denouncing what they call 'presidential absolutism and 'the attempts to limit impunity through immunity provisions', C.M Fombad and E. Nwauche reviewed many constitutional reforms in Africa and concluded that immunity provisions in African constitutions must be balanced with the need for accountability. See C.M Fombad & E. Nwauche 'Africa's Imperial Presidents: Immunity, Impunity and Accountability' (2012) 5 *African Journal of Legal Studies* 91–118.

128 AU press release 'AU expresses grave concern over State of Emergency, insists President Yahya Jammeh must hand-over power to President-elect Adama Barrow' [available at https://au.int/en/pressreleases/20170118 – accessed on 10 February 2024].

129 S.D. Murphy 'Immunity Ratione Personae of Foreign Government Officials and other Topics: The Sixty-Fifth Session of the International Law Commission' (2014) 108 *American Journal of International Law* 1–30.

on official duties. The second applies to those abroad on special mission and is for the duration of the mission.[130] Akande has also previously argued that this kind of immunity dates back hundreds of years and has taken roots in international law.[131] It traditionally applies to three persons: head of state, head of government and minister of foreign affairs.[132] The inclusion of foreign affairs minister has been open to debate; however, the ICJ had re-affirmed the immunity of foreign affairs ministers in the *Arrest Warrant Case*.[133] These three officials have special status under international law as supported by Article 7 (2)(a) of the VCLT. They do not even need to present full powers before they can take actions that bind their states, including entering treaties on their state's behalf. This immunity allows them to carry out such duties without undue and unnecessary interference from other states, including their host states. In contrast, 'immunity ratione materiae'[134] or functional immunity attaches to official acts and functions of state representatives. It continues to shield such officials (for acts performed while in office) even after they have left office. Their acts are deemed to be acts of their states and as such, they cannot be held liable for those acts. This immunity, however, does not cover international crimes.[135] Akande provides two reasons for this: first, that acts amounting to international crimes cannot be deemed as acts of states and, secondly, international crimes constitute a violation of *jus cogens* which are higher in status to the rules of immunity.[136] While this makes sense as a nor-

---

130 See D. Akande and S. Shah 'Immunities of State Officials, International Crimes and Foreign Domestic Courts: A Rejoinder to Alexander Orakhelashvili' (2011) 22 *EJIL* 3, 857–858.

131 D. Akande 'International Law Immunities and the International Criminal Court' (2004) 98 *American Journal of International Law* 3, 407–433 at 410.

132 'Opinion by Legal Advisory Committee to the Minister of Foreign Affairs of the Republic of Poland on immunities of State officials from foreign criminal jurisdiction' 27 April 2015, 5.

133 See M. Ubeda-Saillard 'Foreign Officials Entitled to (Absolute) Personal Immunity during Their Time in Office' in T. Ruys & Ors (eds) *The Cambridge Handbook of Immunities and International Law* (Cambridge University Press 2019) 481–495. In the Arrest warrant Case, the ICJ had submitted 'that the functions exercised by a Minister for Foreign Affairs were such that, throughout the duration of his or her office, a Minister for Foreign Affairs when abroad enjoyed full immunity from criminal jurisdiction and inviolability'. Arrest Warrant of 11 April 2000 (Democratic Republic of the Congo v. Belgium).

134 For thoughts on this, see R. O'Keefe 'Immunity Ratione Materiae from Foreign Criminal Jurisdiction and the Concept of "Acts Performed in an Official Capacity"' [available at https://rm.coe.int/1680097836 – accessed on 12 January 2023].

135 See also D. Akande 'International Law Immunities and the International Criminal Court' (2004) 98 *American Journal of International Law* 3, 413.

136 *Ibid*, 414.

mative argument, I submit that there is no uniform or consistent state practice on this. There are just a few isolated examples of prosecution of former foreign senior state officials, but they are not enough to undermine the customary international law on *ratione materiae* immunity. Most domestic prosecutions that have taken place were based on charges flowing from the respective states' treaty obligations (e.g. UNCAT), not custom. An example is the Pinochet prosecution that was undertaken based on treaty-derived obligations.[137]

Where does this leave Article 46Abis of the Malabo protocol and is it fair to conclude that the provision gives room for impunity? Kamari Clarke and others argued that Article 46Abis only contemplates immunity *ratione personae* and not functional immunity.[138] But I disagree. The plain reading of the provision reveals that both types of immunity (*ratione personae* and *ratione materiae*) are contemplated in Article 46Abis. The first part of the provision references sitting head of state or government or anyone acting in that capacity. Without doubt, this refers to *immunity ratione* personae. The other part provides that 'other senior officials, based on their functions' shall have immunity. This part clearly refers to functional immunity, although, quite innovatively, it restricts it to 'during their tenure of office'. This should not be surprising, seeing that the Malabo protocol innovatively combines transnational and international crimes. Thus, while functional immunity covers an official, even after leaving office, the plain reading of Article 46Aarticle of the protocol restricts it to the tenure of office. This lends credence to the argument that rather than encouraging impunity, the Malabo protocol advances ICL by discouraging impunity in ways hitherto unknown to international law. The converse argument is that this provision may incentivize sit-tight leaders to remain in office, long after their constitutional term of office might have elapsed.[139]

Additionally, Article 46B (2), which relates to the substantive issue of criminal responsibility, reaffirms that 'subject to article 46Abis, the official position of any accused person' does not matter. The Malabo Protocol had to re-emphasize that irrespective of a person's official position while the act was committed, it should not relieve criminal responsibility or mitigate punishment. The drafters saw a need to re-emphasize this to drive home the point that under the protocol, immunity will not be a reason for impunity, save for the immunities which are already recognized under customary international law and, therefore, settled in law.

---

137 A. Bianchi 'Immunity vs Human Rights: The Pinochet Case' (1999) 10 *EJIL* 2, 237–277.

138 K. Clarke and Ors. 'Introduction' in C. Jalloh and Ors., (eds) *The African Court of Justice and Human and Peoples' Rights in Context: Development and Challenges* (CUP 2019) 33.

139 *Ibid*

The second point is my earlier assertion that the provisions relating to immunity for heads of state in the Malabo protocol better reflect customary international law (CIL), while Article 27 of the Rome Statute remains at best, a treaty provision. In fact, over the last decade, the ICC itself has made conflicting decisions on this issue. For instance, Malawi and Chad decisions of 2011 differ from the position the Court took in the 2014 DRC decision. Orina concludes that 'this hardly makes for convincing jurisprudence and has resulted in a great deal of legal uncertainty'.[140] It is therefore my view that Article 27 does not reflect customary international law. If this was even in doubt, many states, including leading members of the UNSC have not ratified the Rome Statute. That a rule is contained in treaties, does not qualify that rule as customary international law; it is perhaps the strongest reason why that rule may not qualify as such, seeing that CIL often arises from general, consistent and established international practices. Authors like Bodansky have argued that 'the law of diplomatic immunities remains customary international law because they emerged through a customary law-making process'.[141]

My position above differs from the ICC Appeal Chamber's finding in *The Prosecutor v Al Bashir*. The Chamber maintained that 'there is neither State practice nor an impelled sense of such a practice as law, which would support the existence of Head of State immunity under customary international law, in relation to an international criminal court in the exercise of its proper jurisdiction'.[142] This is consistent also with the later decision in the Jordanian Appeal where the question arose as to whether the ICC jurisprudence recognizing an 'international tribunal exception' in relation to individuals from non-ICC parties reflects customary law. The Appeals Chamber said no customary law protecting immunity exists in this relation.[143] Further, it will appear that non-applicability of immunities before international courts (i.e. once the accused ends up in their jurisdiction) is hardly contested. The bone of contention appeared to be how those individuals end up before those courts. It is almost uncontestable that immunity continues to apply in inter-

140 N. Orina 'Should the ICJ render an advisory opinion on the immunity question re Articles 27 & 98 of the Rome Statute?' *ICJ Africa Blog* (2018) [available at https://www.academia.edu/44290443/Should_the_ICJ_render_an_advisory_opinion_on_the_immunity_question_re_Articles_27_and_98_of_the_Rome_Statute – accessed on 21 March 2024].

141 D.M Bodansky 'The Concept of Customary International Law' (1995) 16 *Michigan Journal of International Law* 3, 667. See also P. Dupuy 'Formation of Customary International Law and General Principles' in D. Bodansky and ors., (eds) *The Oxford Handbook of International Environmental Law* (Oxford University Press 2008).

142 Summary Judgment of the Appeals Chamber in *The Prosecutor v Al-Bashir*, para. 38.

143 *Ibid.*

state relations, making the arrest of the head of state and government, as well as foreign minister highly controversial and unlikely. This is therefore a distinction that can be made between Article 27 and the issue of state enforcement of ICC arrest warrants, particularly against officials of non-ICC state parties. A look at charters and statutes of international criminal tribunals and how they functioned since Nuremberg, will suggest that Article 27 reflects their uniform but admittedly limited practice. State practices also appear to support the provisions of Article 27.[144]

4.2 Corporate Criminal Responsibility in the Malabo Protocol

Corporate criminal responsibility (CCR) is codified in Article 46C of the Malabo protocol. While this is innovative, it is not the first time that an international organization or states (acting jointly or singly) will contemplate codifying it in an international criminal treaty. It is also not the first time that an international criminal tribunal will attempt to pronounce on it. The *Al Akhbar* case at the Special Tribunal for Lebanon (STL) presents an example of prior adjudication on this theme. It was one of the first cases before an international criminal tribunal in which corporate criminal responsibility was imputed to a corporation and eventually led to its sentencing.[145]

Efforts at codifying and imputing corporate criminal responsibility have been largely contemplated and rejected in different settings. During the Rome Conference leading to the adoption of the Rome Statute, France made a proposal for corporate criminal responsibility to be included in the Statute. The proposal failed owing to lack of support from other states.[146] The lack of support is understandable as many states that participated in the Rome Conference did not have such forms of liability in their domestic systems. Support for it is, however, growing. The ILC, which had discussed and rejected the idea previously, has included corporate criminal responsibility in its draft Conven-

144 However, a survey carried out by the ICRC found that about half of the states surveyed (from Europe and the Americas) had constitutional provisions that are compatible with Article 27 of the Rome Statute. See ICRC 'Issues raised regarding the Rome Statute of the ICC by national Constitutional Courts, Supreme Courts and Councils of State' (2010) *Advisory Service on International Humanitarian Law*.

145 See the case of *Akhbar Beirut S.A.L. Ibrahim Mohamed Ali Al Amin*, Case. No. STL-14-06/T/CJ, Trial Chamber Judgement, 15 July 2016 (Akhbar, Trial Chamber Judgement). For more thoughts on the case, see also N. Bernaz 'Corporate Criminal Liability under International Law: The New TV S.A.L. and Akhbar Beirut S.A.L. Cases at the Special Tribunal for Lebanon' (2015) 13 *JICJ* 2, 313–330.

146 See H.G. van der Wilt 'Corporate Criminal Responsibility for International Crimes: Exploring the Possibilities' (2013) 12 *Chinese Journal of International Law* 1, 43–77.

tion on the Prevention and Punishment of Crimes Against Humanity.[147] Article 5(7) of the text provides that '[S]ubject to the provisions of its national law, each State shall take measures, where appropriate, to establish the liability of legal persons for the offences referred to in this draft article. Subject to the legal principles of the State, such liability of legal persons may be criminal, civil or administrative.' One author argued that the caveats in this provision are a result of 'a compromise between competing views on corporate liability'.[148] The part that urges states to take measures where appropriate, also allows states without corporate liability in their domestic system, to conclude that in the specific case of crimes against humanity, corporations could be made liable.[149] Additionally, trends in Europe reveal that the Council of Europe[150] and the European Union[151] have both adopted measures that included corporate criminal responsibility (CCR). Another author had previously traced the origin of CCR to ancient Roman and Medieval eras.[152]

Flowing from this, the inclusion of CCR in the Malabo protocol reflects ongoing trends and states' growing interest in the issue. In Africa, there have been instances where corporations have fuelled or elongated conflicts. This is one of the reasons why the continental body chose to address this issue through the codification of CCR. Aside from the idea that its codification reflects problems specific to Africa, there are other advantages to codifying the CCR. One of such is the 'pressure' that this codification puts on scholars of international law to speedily clarify the roles of corporations in ICL and how they can be held accountable.[153] It is also noteworthy that 'as the bulk

---

147 See UN Doc: A/71/10, Draft Convention on the Prevention and Punishment of Crimes against Humanity. For an analysis of the provisions of the draft convention, see M. Bergsmo and S. Tianying *On the Proposed Crimes Against Humanity Convention* (Torkel Opsahl Academic EPublisher 2014).

148 Corporate War Crimes, 'Draft convention on crimes against humanity to include provision on corporate liability?' 26 March 2017 [available at https://corporatewarcrimes.com/2017/03/26/draft-convention-on-crimes-against-humanity-to-include-provision-on-corporate-liability/ – accessed on 12 January 2023].

149 *Ibid.*

150 See the text of its 'Liability of enterprises for offences: Recommendation No. R (88) 18 adopted by the Committee of Ministers of the Council of Europe on 20 October 1988 and explanatory memorandum' (1990) at https://rm.coe.int/16804c5d71.

151 For thoughts on this, see G. Vermeulen & Ors '*Liability of legal persons for offences in the EU* (Maklu Publishers 2010).

152 A. Bassi 'Corporate criminal liability: an analytical study with special reference to penal laws in India' PhD Thesis, Rajiv Gandhi National University of Law Punjab, 2016.

153 J. Kyriakakis 'Article 46C: Corporate Criminal Liability at the African Criminal Court' in C. Jalloh and Ors., (eds) The African Court of Justice and Human and Peoples' Rights in Context: Development and Challenges (CUP 2019) 784–785.

of economic activity nowadays takes place through corporations, so does economic criminality'.[154] Apart from governments and their agents, corporations are the most active actors within our societies.[155] It is therefore necessary that ICL should be extended to include norms that rein in on their actions, when necessary. Hitherto, there have been difficulties in imputing criminal liability to them in ICL.

Glanville Williams classified the difficulties in imputing CCR to corporations into substantive and procedural.[156] On the procedural point, it has been argued that in answering charges, a defendant must be physically present, and a legal person cannot be physically present nor physically punished, upon conviction, in that sense. Substantively, it has been argued that corporations can only act through humans and as such, they could only be principals or agents with vicarious liability. In common law, however, vicarious liability did not apply to crimes, and as such, no criminal responsibility could be imputed to crimes. The other substantive point was that since corporations have no mind of their own, they could technically not have a guilty mind which is a fundamental requirement in imputation of crimes.[157] Over the decades though, domestic approaches to sanctioning crimes by corporations have evolved, especially in places like the USA and Europe – with specific examples of developments in Germany, France, Italy and the UK.[158] It became obvious that 'corporate crime is, in the end, committed by individuals'.[159] Thus, the advancement in international corporate criminal responsibility regime has been driven, quite understandably, by development at the national and regional level.

Returning to Article 46C of the Malabo protocol, as with many provisions in the Malabo protocol, this provision presents both challenges and opportunities. There are challenges relating to its drafting, model of liability, complementarity with national mechanisms as well as its eventual enforcement, if

154 G. Stessens 'Corporate Criminal Liability: A Comparative Perspective' (1994) 43 *The International and Comparative Law Quarterly* 3, 493.

155 K. Balakrishnan 'Corporate criminal liability – Evolution of the concept' (1998) *Cochin University Law Review* 255.

156 Glanville William *Criminal Law – The General Part* 2ed, (Stevens and Sons 1961) 853.

157 *Ibid.*

158 E. Brunelle and ors 'Global Enforcement Outlook: Europe's Evolving Corporate Criminal Liability Laws' (2022) [available at https://riskandcompliance.freshfields.com/post/102hh57/global-enforcement-outlook-europes-evolving-corporate-criminal-liability-laws – accessed on 10 May 2023].

159 J. Arlen 'Evolution of Corporate Criminal Liability: Implications for Managers' in R. Gandossy & J. Sonnenfeld (eds) *Leadership and Governance from the Inside Out* (John Wiley & Sons Inc 2004).

the protocol comes into force. For example, the provision uses the term 'corporation' and 'legal persons' interchangeably, although the two terms are not the same. 'Legal person' connotes a wider meaning compared to corporation. There are non-corporate legal entities, and it is not clear if they can be criminally liable under this provision. Throughout Article 46C, except for paragraph 6, the use of the term 'corporation' was consistent. But with the use of the term 'legal persons' in paragraph 6, there is the tendency to think that non-corporate entities are also contemplated in the provision. This is either a case of bad drafting, or the drafters left this ambiguity for the court to pronounce upon.

Also, in terms of the mode of liability under this provision, previous research[160] has revealed that no African country – with corporate criminal liability – has the specific mode of liability such as that is contained in Article 46C. A look across countries in Africa that recognize corporate criminal capacity would reveal that the two dominant modes of corporate criminal liability are vicarious liability[161] and identification model.[162] However, the drafters of the Malabo protocol adopted the 'organizational liability mode' which is specific to Australia. This model of liability makes a corporation guilty of crime because its organizational culture and policies encourage or permit the commission of offence.[163] Since no African country adopts this model of liability, it already presents a compatibility problem between national laws and the Malabo protocol for states who may wish to ratify it. For the purposes of complementarity, the model of liability also affects the relationship between the ACC and a national mechanism that chooses to prosecute, since the issue then becomes a non-criminal matter if different models of liability are applied. However, a careful reading of Article 46H of the Malabo protocol suggests that all that is required for the ACC to find a case inadmissible is an ongoing or a concluded investigation or prosecution, irrespective of the mode of liability recognized or applied by the national mechanism. Paragraph 2C further strengthens this suggestion when it provides that a case shall be held inadmissible 'if the person concerned has already been tried for conduct, which is the subject of the complaint'. Emphasis here is on the conduct. As such, once the conduct or acts upon which a corporation is tried by the national mechanism,

160 See W. Jordash & N Bracq 'Modes of Liability and Individual Criminal Responsibility' in C. Jalloh, K. Clarke and another (eds) *The African Court of Justice and Human and Peoples' Rights in Context: Development and Challenges* (CUP 2019) 784–785.

161 For thoughts on this mode of liability, see J. Edwards 'Vicarious Liability in Criminal Law' (1951) 14 *The Modern Law Review* 3, 334–340.

162 See C. de Magalie 'Models of Corporate Criminal Liability in Comparative Law' (2005) 4 *Washington University Global Studies Law Review* 3, 547–566.

163 See J. Fanto 'Organizational Liability' (2010) 19 *Journal of Law and Policy* 45.

is the same as the one that the ACC is attempting to investigate or prosecute, irrespective of the mode of liability, the case will be inadmissible at the ACC.

Lastly, in terms of enforcing CCR, the general problems with enforcing ICL remain. However, accountability for international crimes by multinational corporations who are often registered in one country but work through subsidiaries in other countries, may prove more problematic. Previous efforts to hold multinational oil giants like Shell and Chevron accountable for human rights abuses in places like Nigeria have been unsuccessful.[164] The usual scenario is that powerful multinationals hide behind their subsidiaries to avoid accountability. This is an often-recurrent problem in the context of human rights litigation and may, with certainty, re-emerge in an attempt to hold multinationals accountable for international crimes. There have been cases in the UK, for example, where the court ruled that a parent company cannot be held accountable for the human rights violations of its subsidiary.

Considering that this scenario is rampant, it is surprising that the Malabo protocol does not address this possibility. However, lessons can be drawn from previous approaches that have been adopted by courts across Europe. In *AAA and others v Unilever PLC and Unilever Tea Kenya Limited,* the UK Appeal Court considered the nature and degree of control which the parent company exercised over the subsidiary.[165] While the decision was unfavourable to the appellants, the ACC could, in a future case, decide on a similar situation by considering the relationship between the parent company and their subsidiary, by investigating the nature and degree of control that latter has over the former. However, this becomes more complex where the parent company exists in a jurisdiction which may not have CCR included in their laws. In this circumstance, the choices before the ACC are limited. It could, however, still proceed against the subsidiary company while showing that sufficient grounds are available to prove that the subsidiary carried out the act as part of the organizational 'culture' of the parent company, in line with the model of liability under Article 46C.

164 For example, see *HRH Emere Godwin Bebe Okpabi & Ors v Royal Dutch Shell Plc & Anor* [2017] EWHC 89 (TCC) where the English High Court decided that it could not impose a duty of care on the parent company as a result of acts carried out by its subsidiary operating in the Niger Delta region of Nigeria.

165 Case No: A2/2017/0721, In the Court of Appeal (Civil Division) on Appeal from the High Court of Justice Queen's Bench Division the Honourable Mrs Justice Elisabeth Laing DBE [2017] EWHC 371 (QB).

5 Conclusion

The opportunities and challenges that the inclusion of CCR in the Malabo protocol presents are some of the focuses of this chapter. I presented a brief history of the efforts to codify CCR, while tracing its trajectory to current development. I find that the opportunity that this codification in the Malabo protocol presents is manifold, with the most obvious being the pressure it now puts on international law to clarify the roles of legal persons and how the framework for bringing them to ICL can be strengthened.

Moreover, Africa's long journey to international criminal justice has led to the proposal to establish an ICL section in its single court. It is shown that the evolution of regionalism in ICL is traceable to the need to address some of the fundamental structural critiques of international criminal justice. The Malabo Protocol contains several innovative features. I found also that these features are included, again to probably address some of those fundamental structural critiques. While the universal system has concentrated largely on civil and political rights, the protocol has also brought social and economic rights into perspective through its criminalization of offences relating to these. The analysis here suggests that the Malabo Protocol is ahead of its time and appears a little more advanced than the ICC system in certain respects. I have shown regional institutions can be a lot more modern and innovative, while they incorporate regional contexts much better than a universal mechanism. On the other hand, regional mechanisms might have certain features which stand in contradiction to certain universal norms, including the *nullum crimen sine lege* argument. There is also the tendency to over-criminalize conducts; a tendency to do too much, as though there is competition between the regional and the universal. If the African court becomes operationalized, the protocol will provide a rare opportunity for African countries to address crimes that are well known to the continent, but which are subject of very few trials and convictions at the international level. A rationale for the protocol's inclusion of them alongside 'core crimes' would be that 'many of them are capable of destabilizing a state, which in turn leads to the proliferation of core international crimes'.[166] Their prosecution may then 'have a preventative or deterrent consequence…'[167] thus helping to fulfil the overall goal of ICL which is to close the impunity gap. This ties closely to the idea of regional complementarity and

166 M. Sirleaf 'The African Justice Cascade and the Malabo Protocol' (2017) 11 *International Journal of Transitional Justice*, 71–91.

167 S. Nimigan 'The Malabo Protocol, the ICC, and the idea of 'Regional Complementarity' (2019) 0 *JICJ* 1–25 at 3.

the possibility of a regional court dispensing justice within the territory of the region. In all, the analysis on the question as to 'what lessons can be learnt from the Malabo Protocol as an example of a proposed fully independent strand of regionalism in ICL' reveals patterns and practices that may be useful for arranging the relationship between the ICC and any other future or proposed regional or hybrid international criminal tribunal.

CHAPTER 6

Regional Complementarity in Other Notions of Complementarity

1 Introduction

The concept of complementarity has long served as the cornerstone of the international criminal justice system. Initially conceived as a principle of deference between international and national jurisdictions, it has evolved into a dynamic framework that governs the allocation of authority across multiple judicial levels. Within this evolving architecture, regional complementarity introduces a distinct and increasingly relevant dimension. It extends the classical idea of complementarity by incorporating regional institutions as legitimate and functional actors in the shared pursuit of accountability for international crimes. This chapter examines how regional complementarity mirrors, refines, and interacts with the existing theories of complementarity that have developed under the International Criminal Court (ICC) system.

The discussion begins by situating regional complementarity within the broader genealogy of complementarity theories, including positive, classical (or negative), proactive, horizontal, constructive, and radical complementarity. Each of these notions captures a specific aspect of how international justice systems interact with other legal orders. While classical complementarity focuses on admissibility and restraint, positive and proactive complementarity emphasize cooperation, capacity-building and mutual reinforcement. Regional complementarity resonates most strongly with these latter forms, as it reimagines complementarity as a horizontal partnership between institutions of varying scales – international, regional, and national – rather than a strictly vertical hierarchy.

By examining these parallels, the chapter argues that regional complementarity enriches the existing theory of complementarity by addressing an institutional gap between the global and the domestic. It provides an intermediate platform for cooperation that reflects shared legal traditions, political realities, and geographical proximity. This arrangement not only enhances legitimacy and accessibility but also distributes the burdens of enforcement across a wider range of actors. The inclusion of regional institutions allows complementarity to function as a more polycentric model, in which authority is exer-

© 2026 THE AUTHOR(S) | HTTPS://DOI.ORG/10.1163/9789004761803-008

cised collaboratively across multiple levels rather than concentrated in a single global institution.

Furthermore, the chapter explores how regional complementarity engages with the organizing principles of mutual deference, monitoring, regulation, and cooperation. These principles define the operational logic of positive complementarity and are equally applicable in a regional context. Through mechanisms such as case allocation, evidence sharing, and mutual assistance, regional and international courts can coordinate their mandates without duplication or conflict. This cooperative dynamic strengthens the legitimacy of both levels of justice while expanding the reach of international criminal law.

Ultimately, this chapter demonstrates that regional complementarity is not a departure from established theories but rather their natural extension. It offers a framework through which regional institutions can reinforce, rather than undermine, the authority of the ICC and other universal mechanisms. By situating regional complementarity within the broader spectrum of complementarity theories, the analysis reveals how a pluralistic system of justice can operate effectively in a fragmented international legal order. This understanding is crucial for shaping future institutional design and ensuring that accountability efforts remain both principled and pragmatic in an increasingly regionalized world.

2 Defining Complementarity

Complementarity was not defined in the Rome Statute.[1] During the drafting, 'several delegations felt that an abstract definition of the principle would serve no useful purpose and found it preferable to have a common understanding of the practical implications of the principle for the operation of the international criminal court'.[2] As a continuously evolving concept, its exact meanings are difficult to ascertain; hence the desirability of describing, instead of defining, it. It has been variously described as a 'technical concept and a systemic feature of the ICC',[3] 'an organising principle for the regulation of concurrent jurisdiction', and 'one of the cornerstones of the architecture of the Rome

1 See UN Doc A/50/22 'Report of the Ad Hoc Committee on the Establishment of an International Criminal Court' General Assembly Official Records Fiftieth Session, Supplement No. 22 (A/50/22); para. 30.

2 *Ibid.*

3 C. Stahn, 'Taking complementarity seriously: On the sense and sensibility of "classical", "positive" and "negative" complementarity' in C. Stahn & M. El Zeidy (eds) *The International*

Statute'.[4] Politi refers to it as 'one of the key features (if not the key feature) of the Court'.[5] Kleffner calls it one of the three fundamental cornerstones of the ICC, the others being its permanent nature and its jurisdiction over the most serious crimes of international concern.[6]

The concept serves at least four different functions *to wit*:

> a) It protects sovereignty, by reaffirming the primary role of States in exercising criminal jurisdiction over international crimes; b) it promotes effective investigation and prosecution, by encouraging states to make genuine efforts to hold perpetrators accountable in line with their duty to investigate and prosecute crimes; c) it facilitates a certain division of labor between different layers of jurisdiction, i.e. by resolving conflicts of jurisdiction and limiting cases that come before the ICC; and d) it stimulates cooperation and sharing of good practices between international and domestic justice actors.[7]

The Rome Statute establishes the ICC as a judicial body complementary to national criminal jurisdictions.[8] This complementary relationship is not only based on respect for the primary jurisdiction of States, but also on practical considerations of efficiency and effectiveness since States will most likely have the best access to evidence, witnesses and resources,[9] as well as their law enforcement capacities. It is in this respect that there exists a marked difference between the jurisdiction of the ICC and that of the UN *ad hoc* tribunals (ICTY and ICTR). While the ICC can only act when there is an inaction, unwillingness or an inability of the national jurisdiction to act in the prosecution of crimes within the jurisdiction of the Court, the situation before the *ad hoc* tribunals presents a different picture: the primacy of the tribunals vis-à-vis

---

Criminal Court and Complementarity: From Theory to Practice (Cambridge University Press 2011) 234.

4 C. Stahn, 'Introduction: bridge over troubled waters: Complementarity themes and debates in context' in Stahn & El Zeidy (CUP 2011) 1.

5 M. Politi, 'Reflections on complementarity at the Rome Conference and beyond' in Stahn & El Zeidy (CUP 2011) 142.

6 J.K. Kleffner, 'Complementarity in the Rome Statute and National Jurisdictions' (Oxford University Press 2008) 4.

7 See generally C. Stahn, 'Fair and Effective Investigation and Prosecution of International Crimes, Inventory and State-of-the-Art: Context, Cluster 1 and Cluster 2' (International Nuremberg Principles Academy 2018) 5.

8 Article 1 of the Rome Statute.

9 R. Cryer & Ors, *An Introduction to International Criminal Law and Procedure* 3rd edn (CUP 2014) 154.

national courts.[10] This implies that 'at any stage of the procedure, the International Tribunal may formally request national courts to defer to the competence of the International Tribunal'.[11]

As per the Rome Statute, the circumstances that may constitute 'unwillingness' or 'inability' are outlined in article 17, which has been described as the 'centrepiece' of the principle of complementarity.[12] Such circumstances may include instances where proceedings are carried out for the purposes of shielding a person from criminal responsibility,[13] unjustified delay in the proceedings at the domestic level,[14] lack of impartiality and independence, as well as conducting proceedings in a manner not consistent with bringing the accused person to justice.[15] These circumstances suggest that the existence of proceedings at the domestic level is not in itself a bar to an ICC intervention, except if the proceedings at the domestic level fulfil certain requirements. On the other hand, inability may be established where there is a total or substantial collapse or unavailability of the domestic judicial system, which may be exemplified by the State's inability to obtain the accused or the necessary evidence and testimony or otherwise unable to carry out its proceedings.[16]

The primary duty to exercise jurisdiction over the core crimes defined under the ICC Statute lies on national institutions. The ICC only steps in to remedy the deficiencies resulting from the failure of one or more States to fulfil their duties.[17] As El Zeidy puts it, 'the ICC is intended to supplement the domestic punishment of international violations, rather than supplant domestic enforcement of international norms [by] balancing its supranational power against the sovereign right of States to prosecute their own nationals without external interference'.[18] Thus, if a State with jurisdiction possesses a functional criminal adjudicatory mechanism and also demonstrates the will to investigate and prosecute, it would be given the opportunity

---

10 See article 9(1) and (2) of the ICTY Statute and article 8 of the ICTR Statute.

11 *Ibid.*

12 D. Robinson, 'Three Theories of Complementarity: Charge, Sentence or Process?' (2012) 53 *Harvard International Law Journal Online* at 177.

13 Article 17(2)(a) of the Rome Statute.

14 Article 17(2)(b) of the Rome Statute.

15 Article 17(2)(c) of the Rome Statute.

16 Article 17(3) of the Rome Statute.

17 M. El Zeidy, *The Principle of Complementarity in International Criminal Law: Origin, Development and Practice* (Martinus Nijhoff Publishers 2008) 4.

18 *Ibid*, 158.

to act before there could be an ICC intervention.[19] In this regard, the concept has become a bridge that connects, as well as a structure that enables, the distinctive and autonomous international and domestic justice systems working together, while it also gives rise to some challenges. The challenges are partly because the concept has broader implications and continues to shape various dimensions of the ICC and domestic practice.[20]

3 Existing Theories of Complementarity and Regional Complementarity

There is no shortage of legal scholarship and significant academic publications on complementarity,[21] but there remain many grey areas in its theorization and understanding. The concept has undergone significant transformation,[22] perhaps because, like the Greek Hydra god,[23] it 'has many faces'.[24] It appears simple, but it is extremely complex, such that the ICC has been faced with pressing questions regarding its interpretation.[25] Since its formal insertion into the Rome Statute, however, different notions of complementarity have emerged. Accordingly, the following notions have been theorized in available academic literature:[26] positive complementarity,[27] classical complementarity,[28] proactive complementarity,[29] horizontal complementarity,[30] negative complementarity,[31] constructive complementarity,[32] radical complementar-

19 A. Okuta, 'Smallest Share of the Pie? Accountability for International Crimes at the Domestic Level: Case Studies of Kenya, Uganda and Cote D' Ivoire' (Unpublished PhD Thesis, University of Amsterdam 2016) 34.

20 Stahn (n. 4) 1.

21 See footnote 61 in the Introduction.

22 Stahn (n. 3) 233.

23 E.M. Berens, *The Myths and Legends of Ancient Greece and Rome* (MetaLibri 2009) 199.

24 Stahn (n. 4) 1.

25 El Zeidy (n. 17) 1.

26 Stahn (n. 7) 5.

27 ICC-OTP, 'The principle of complementarity in practice' (2003).

28 C. Stahn, 'Complementarity: A Tale of Two Notions' (2008), 19 *Criminal Law Forum*, 87–113.

29 W. Burke-White, 'Proactive Complementarity: The International Criminal Court and National Courts in the Rome System of International Justice' (2008), 49 *Harvard International Law Review* 53–108.

30 C. Ryngaert, 'Horizontal complementarity' in Stahn & El Zeidy (CUP 2011) 855–887.

31 Stahn (n. 4) 1.

32 M. Newton, 'The Quest for Constructive Complementarity' in Stahn & El Zeidy (CUP 2011) 304–340.

ity,[33] and regional complementarity.[34] The emergence of these notions remains one of the direct consequences of the heavy academic scrutiny that the concept has been subjected to. It has [generally] been 'theorized in antagonisms, such as "global" versus "local or regional" interests, "policy" versus "judicial" issues, "vertical" versus "horizontal", "negative" versus "positive" or "passive" versus "proactive" complementarity'.[35] I will focus on the negative versus positive, as well as the global versus regional theorizations of the concept. I present a short discussion on the theories underpinning each of the already identified notions. I then present regional complementarity as an example of a wider and more strategic interpretation of the concept. I distinguish classical complementarity from positive complementarity and note that this distinction remains the traditional theorization of the concept.[36]

3.1 Positive Complementarity

Positive complementarity 'foresees a coordinated approach to the prosecution of crimes by the ICC and national authorities'.[37] It implies that the ICC will not only prosecute persons who bear the most responsibility for crimes under its investigation, but also that the Court will encourage and support national trials where possible.[38] The ICC's Office of The Prosecutor (OTP) noted that the Court's approach to complementarity may be guided by principles of partnership and vigilance.[39] This partnership dimension, as different from the admissibility loop,[40] requires the ICC to maintain a constructive and positive relationship with States that are genuinely investigating and prosecuting international crimes.[41] In practice, the OTP can variously encourage States to initiate national proceedings; can help to develop cooperative anti-impunity strategies; provide advice and assistance to facilitate national efforts;

---

33 K. Heller, 'Radical Complementarity' (2016) 14 *Journal of International Criminal Justice* 637–665.

34 M. Jackson, 'Regional Complementarity: The Rome Statute and Public International Law' 14 *Journal of International Criminal Justice* 1061–1072.

35 Stahn (n. 4), 7.

36 Stahn (n. 3) 233.

37 F. Donlon, 'Positive Complementarity in Practice' in Stahn & El Zeidy (CUP 2011) 920–954.

38 *Ibid.*

39 ICC-OTP (n. 27) 3.

40 M. Hosain, 'Positive Complementarity: An Approach to Enhance Cooperation with States and End Impunity under International Criminal Court' (2013) 2 *AALCO Journal of International Law* 2 at 206.

41 ICC-OTP (n. 27) 3.

as well as agree with States that a consensual division of labour will serve the best interests of justice.[42]

General approaches towards implementing the idea of positive complementarity include partnership and dialogue with States through encouraging national actions, promoting anti-impunity measures and providing direct assistance and advice to States. Here, the OTP commits to actively reminding States of their obligation to adopt and implement effective legislation either in public statements or in private bilateral meetings; commits to exchange information and evidence to facilitate a national investigation or prosecution; commits to motivate genuine national proceedings by committing funds and resources to these activities; commits to proceed gradually on trainings for officials at the national level; commits to providing technical advice and broker other assistance that may be appropriate within the mandates of the OTP.[43]

The ICC's Assembly of State Parties (ASP) defined positive complementarity as 'all activities/actions whereby national jurisdictions are strengthened and enabled to conduct genuine national investigations and trials of crimes included in the Rome Statute'.[44] It involves legislative assistance from the ICC to national mechanisms, and these may include 'assistance with drafting appropriate legislative frameworks, assistance in overcoming domestic hurdles for passing such legislations and also, assistance in ratification of an Agreement of Privileges and Immunities and other legal instruments pertaining to investigating and prosecuting the most serious crimes'.[45] Additionally, it connotes technical assistance and capacity building with regard to domestic judicial systems. Examples of such assistance may include 'training of police, investigators and prosecutors, capacity building with regard to protection of witnesses and victims, forensic expertise, training of judges and training of defence counsel, security for and independence of officials'.[46] Lastly, the notion also entails 'assistance with construction of physical infrastructure, such as courthouses and prison facilities, and the sustainable operation of such institutions'.[47]

The notion is grounded in 'certain legal aspects, such as cooperation of the ICC with domestic jurisdictions under article 93(10), managerial duties of the

42 *Ibid,* 4.

43 *Ibid,* 5–6.

44 ICC-ASP 'Report of the Bureau on Stocktaking: Complementarity' (2010) at para. 16, ICC-ASP/8/51, 18 March 2010.

45 *Ibid,* para. 17.

46 *Ibid.*

47 *Ibid.*

OTP under article 54, as well as policy considerations'.[48] It 'implies interdependency between two fora rather than the complete independence of the ICC from domestic courts'[49] and 'introduces an element of flexibility and a managerial division of labour into the relationship between the Court and domestic jurisdictions'.[50] It has been referred to as the 'more gentle side [of complementarity], which defines the relationship between the Court and domestic jurisdictions in a positive fashion (e.g. burden-sharing on the basis of the comparative advantages and assistance from the Court to States)'.[51]

Positive complementarity began with its articulation in the 2003 OTP's expert informal paper.[52] In 2004, the Prosecutor noted in an address to the Diplomatic Corps in The Hague that one of his office's key strategic priorities would be to take a positive approach to complementarity and that, instead of competing with national systems for jurisdiction, the OTP would encourage national proceedings wherever possible.[53] In the 2006 Report on Prosecutorial Strategy, the OTP reiterated its understanding of positive complementarity to include encouragement of genuine national proceedings, reliance on national and international networks, as well as participation in a system of international cooperation.[54] In his address to the ICC-ASP in 2009, the Prosecutor summarized the focus of positive complementarity as 'the role that different stakeholders can play to ensure the achievements of the goals defined by the Rome Statute'.[55]

In paragraph 17 of the ICC-OTP Prosecutorial Strategy 2009–2012, the OTP stated that 'the positive approach to complementarity means that the Office will encourage genuine national proceedings where possible, including in situation countries, relying on its various networks of cooperation, but without involving the Office directly in capacity building or financial or technical assistance'. The Strategy outlines the OTP's approach in this regard to include: a) providing information collected by the Office to national judiciaries upon their request pursuant article 93(10), subject to the existence of a credible local system of protection for judges or witnesses and other security-related caveats; sharing databases of non-confidential materials or crime patterns; b)

48 Stahn (n. 7) 6.

49 H. Takemura, 'A Critical Analysis of Positive Complementarity' in *Max Planck Encyclopedias of International Law* (Oxford Public International Law – undated).

50 Stahn (n. 28) 88.

51 *Ibid,* 89.

52 ICC-OTP (n. 27).

53 Statement of the ICC Prosecutor to the Diplomatic Corps, 12 February 2004.

54 ICC-OTP 'Report on Prosecutorial Strategy' (2006).

55 'ICC Prosecutor's Address to the Assembly of State Parties' (18 November 2009) 9.

calling upon officials, experts and lawyers from situation countries to participate in OTP investigative and prosecutorial activities, taking into account the need for their protection; inviting them to participate in the Office's network of law enforcement agencies; sharing with them expertise and trainings on investigative techniques or questioning of vulnerable witnesses; c) providing information about the judicial work of the Office to those involved in political mediation, such as UN and other special envoys, thus allowing them to support national/regional activities which complement the Office's work; and d) acting as a catalyst with development organizations and donors' conferences to promote support for relevant accountability efforts.[56] It was, however, at the 2010 Kampala Review Conference that the most visible development of the notion of positive complementarity was enunciated and elaborated upon.[57] The 2023 Draft Policy on Complementarity and Cooperation has further built on the work done in Kampala in 2010.[58]

Like positive complementarity, my theory of regional complementarity also anticipates that a region ought to be prepared to prosecute but must also support and encourage national trials. In the Hissène Habré case, as has been shown in Chapter 4, the African Union supported the prosecution of the former ruler in the territory of Senegal. Such support is recommended as part of efforts to activate regional complementarity. Regional complementarity espouses the virtues of partnership, vigilance, assistance and burden-sharing between states and the regional tribunal. Implementing regional complementarity will require dialogue between the region and states to provide support and partnership to themselves where necessary.

3.2 Classical or Negative Complementarity

Classical complementarity is the notion that complementarity is 'an instrument to overcome sovereignty fears against the exercise of jurisdiction by the Court and a tool to remedy shortcomings or failures of domestic jurisdiction through application of the criteria listed in article 17 of the Rome Statute'.[59] It is sometimes referred to as the 'negative' notion of complementarity.[60] By this latter reference, it exists as a theoretical counterpart to the notion

56 ICC-OTP 'Prosecutorial Strategy 2009–2012' (2010) 5, para. 17(a–d).
57 Hosain (n. 40) 208. See also ICC-ASP (n. 44).
58 ICC-OTP, OTP Draft Policy on Complementarity and Cooperation (2023), para. 19.
59 Stahn (n. 28), 88.
60 G. Boffey, 'Assessing Complementarity: The ICC and Human Rights Policy in Colombia' (Unpublished Ph.D. Thesis, University of Western Australia 2015) 66.

of positive complementarity[61] and proceeds from the understanding that 'positive complementarity could not exist without negative complementarity'.[62] The notion 'does not suffice to explain the relationship between the Court and domestic jurisdictions'.[63] In theory, the notion is the '"threat-based" side of complementarity which is designed to foster compliance through a sophisticated system of carrots and sticks'.[64] It is also the 'competition' and 'dispute-settlement' based perception of the role of complementarity as a principle under international law.[65]

The origin dates to the idea of settling disputes through 'delineation of competencies'.[66] Its objectives are 'to preserve State sovereignty and to reconcile it with the judicial independence of the Court'.[67] These objectives were meant to address two concerns that arose during the negotiations that preceded the adoption of the Rome Statute. In the first place, it was believed that 'complementarity would provide solution to various dimensions of the "primacy dilemma" of the *ad hoc* tribunals, i.e., to concerns relating to the authority of international criminal tribunals, and their limited capacity'.[68] Secondly, this notion of complementarity was to address the fears about the Court's independence, particularly the *proprio motu* powers of the Prosecutor.[69]

The classical notion espouses the three ideas behind the 'backstop' role of the Court. First is the idea that the ICC is a sword, while the domestic jurisdiction is a shield. The underlying assumption here is that 'international and domestic jurisdiction operate as competing layers of jurisdiction' and the Court should intervene as a guardian where there is non-compliance from States. It is a buffer for domestic jurisdictions against ICC intervention through challenges of jurisdiction and admissibility. Secondly, it focuses on the idea that the ICC is meant to compensate for the weaknesses of domestic jurisdiction. This proceeds from the understanding that it is the failure of national mechanisms that triggers an ICC intervention. The role of the ICC would be limited to acting when the national jurisdiction, which is the first forum for investigation and prosecution, fails to act. The ICC is then called

61 Stahn (n. 3) 260.

62 See ICC Review Conference, 'Taking Stock of the Principle of Complementarity: Bridging the Impunity Gap, Informal Summary by the Focal Points', RC/ST/CM/1 (22 June 2010), para. 4.

63 *Ibid.*

64 *Ibid.*

65 *Ibid,* 93.

66 Stahn (n. 3) 251–252.

67 *Ibid.*

68 *Ibid,* 252.

69 *Ibid.*

upon to complement the weakness of the national mechanisms. Thirdly, it focuses on the idea that the ICC should enhance compliance through threat. States are not only expected to act by investigating and prosecuting where necessary, their compliance is also expected to undergo continuous monitoring and supervision or as 'checks and balances' from the ICC.[70]

3.3 Proactive Complementarity

Given the ICC's limited legal mandate, resources and capacity, and in the light of the high hopes and expectations that were invested in the Court at its inception, a policy approach that allows 'the ICC to participate more directly in efforts to encourage national governments to prosecute international crimes themselves' is what Burke-White calls 'proactive complementarity'.[71] It emphasizes the Court's ability to 'motivate and assist national judiciaries', 'cooperate with national governments' and 'use political leverage to encourage States to undertake their own prosecutions of international crimes'.[72] The Court can only fulfil its mandate where States have fulfilled their obligations to hold international crimes perpetrators accountable. While admitting that this notion is similar to the notion of positive complementarity, Burke-White argues that the current notion 'better reflects the nature of the policy and better highlights its distinction from the Court's present approach that might be termed "passive complementarity"'.[73] The notion 'recognizes that the ICC can and should encourage, and perhaps even assist, national governments to prosecute international crimes'.[74] With an understanding that the Rome Statute does not only limit the Court's power but also creates a system that allows the prosecution of crimes at both domestic and international levels, proactive complementarity seeks to put in place a system where the Court can 'catalyze national judiciaries to fulfill their own obligations to prosecute international crimes through the use of the Court's legal and political powers'.[75] The underlying idea here is that the Rome Statute envisages that national mechanisms and the ICC would be involved in various interactions for the purposes of accountability for international crimes. It provides mechanisms for regulating the allocation of authority between them.[76] This system

70 *Ibid*, 252–253.
71 Burke-White (n. 29) 54.
72 *Ibid.*
73 *Ibid* at footnote 4.
74 *Ibid*, 56.
75 *Ibid*, 57.
76 *Ibid.*

of cross-interactions is the basis for proactive complementarity, as it envisages ICC's ability and potential to encourage prosecutions at the national level, and also contribute effectively to functional domestic judiciaries thereby reducing the number of cases that the ICC would prosecute to the ones where there is no available domestic alternative.[77] Thus, ICC's efforts would be expected to spur or incentivize national governments to action in fulfilling their primary legal obligation to investigate and prosecute crimes. This notion admits that national efforts can not only be catalyzed but also supported by external assistance.[78]

Regional complementarity mirrors proactive complementarity in the sense that a region or its tribunals could participate more directly in all efforts to encourage a state to prosecute international crimes in their national courts. Given the homogeneity that often exists between states in the same region, regional complementarity may better achieve the same aims as proactive complementarity. Interventions from states within the same region may enjoy more legitimacy as it would reduce the tendency to accuse the regional tribunal of imperialism – a charge that had been levelled against the ICC.[79]

3.4 Horizontal Complementarity

The notion of horizontal complementarity takes a departure from the vertical nature of the relationship between States and the ICC, wherein compliance entails the ICC's duty to 'supervise the investigative and prosecutorial work of states, and assume its responsibilities if that work proved to be below acceptable standards'.[80] Ryngaert examines the proper legal relationship between 'bystander' states (those states that do not have a strong nexus with an international crime situation) and 'territorial' states (states on the territory of which a crime has been committed). This relationship is horizontal in the sense that it does not involve a vertical relationship between ICC – a supranational entity – and states. Rather, it is an examination of the proper relationship between two or more 'equal' states, which are at par under international law. The notion attempts to answer the question: 'are "bystander" states that have no link with those crimes but nevertheless want to prosecute them required to defer to states that have a stronger link and that are able and

77 *Ibid.*
78 *Ibid.*
79 F. Cowell, 'Inherent Imperialism: Understanding the Legal Roots of Anti-imperialist Criticism of the International Criminal Court' (2017) 15 *JICJ* 4, 667–687.
80 Ryngaert (n. 30) 855.

willing to investigate and prosecute?'[81] Put differently, should there be a principle or a notion of horizontal complementarity?

To explain this, the principle of universal jurisdiction 'is understood as the exercise of jurisdiction over a crime by… a State in the absence of a territorial, personal, or other nexus to the crime. It is jurisdiction that is based solely on the (heinous) nature of the crime'.[82] The principle allows states to prosecute a crime irrespective of the location of the crime and the nationality of the perpetrator or the victim.[83] Now, where a State attempts to exercise its obligation under this principle, likely questions that may arise would include: what will be the nature of the prosecutorial role played by such a state; which state would have precedence in a situation where a territorial state is willing and able to investigate and prosecute same crime?

In an attempt to answer some of these questions, Ryngaert turns the vertical nature of the relationship between the ICC and States into a horizontal one between States and submits that, just like the ICC is only able to step in when a State has failed in its duty to prosecute, a bystander State should only step in where a territorial state has failed. He admits that this is, however, problematic when examined under certain elements of the international legal system.[84]

First, from a sovereignty perspective, States are equals, and 'the jurisdiction of the bystander State is concurrent with, and not complementary to, the jurisdiction of the territorial or national state'.[85] Under the principle of universal jurisdiction, if a violation was in respect of 'a peremptory norm of general international law', all States could, in principle, have an interest or obligation to prosecute, irrespective of their status as bystander or territorial States. This means that horizontal complementarity negates the principle of universal jurisdiction and thus enjoys little support. In the separate opinion of some Judges of the ICJ in the *Arrest Warrant* judgment of 2002, it was noted that '[a] State contemplating bringing criminal charges based on universal jurisdiction must first offer to the national State of the prospective accused person the opportunity itself to act upon the charges concerned'.[86] Secondly, there is the

81 *Ibid.*

82 C. Ryngaert, 'The International Criminal Court and Universal Jurisdiction' (March 2010) *Working Paper* No. 46 Leuven Centre for Global Governance Studies 3.

83 X. Philippe, 'The principles of universal jurisdiction and complementarity: how do the two principles intermesh?' (2006) 88 *IRRC* 862 at 377.

84 Ryngaert (n. 30) 859.

85 *Ibid.*

86 See *Case Concerning the Arrest Warrant of 11 April 2000 (Democratic Republic of the Congo v. Belgium)*, ICJ, Separate Opinion of Judge Higgins *et al.*, Judgment, 14 February 2002, para. 59.

absence of *ne bis in idem* principle. The principle holds very strongly at the domestic level but 'there is as yet no universally accepted *ne bis in idem* rule available at the international level'.[87] In essence, at the transnational level, the principle does not seem to hold the same force of law as it does at the domestic level. The UN Human Rights Committee in *AP* v. *Italy* stated *inter alia* that '[t]he Committee observes that this provision prohibits double jeopardy only with regard to an offence adjudicated in a given State'.[88] Now, if a territorial state had indeed investigated and prosecuted a certain crime, a subsequent trial of the same defendant and crime by a bystander State would not be invalid, given this position.[89] Thirdly, there is the absence of a credible threat posed by a bystander State. The classical notion of complementarity contextualizes the threat-based side of complementarity, which is designed to foster compliance. The resultant effect cannot obviously be the same where a bystander State attempts to enforce compliance from a territorial State for the former's requests to arrest and deliver a defendant. A bystander State can probably not muster enough international support to enforce cooperation from the territorial State. Even the ICC, with all its international weight, often lacks cooperation from States for the purposes of executing an arrest warrant.[90] Fourthly, although positive complementarity implies that States and the ICC can cooperate effectively and may even share tasks, there is no evidence 'that positive complementarity is approached *in a systematic fashion* by States'. For example, bystander States would probably not (and in previous examples, did not) directly encourage territorial States to prosecute crimes, as the ICC would do to States. Asking for information on investigation and prosecution would not qualify as encouraging territorial States to prosecute.[91] Lastly, Ryngaert asks whether it is discernible from state practice that States 'generally apply the principle of horizontal complementarity and consider themselves to be bound by it as a matter of law'.[92] He found that there is 'little practice of States conducting complementarity analysis and it cannot reason-

87 See V. Bockel & W. Bastiaan, *The Ne Bis in Idem Principle in EU Law European Monograph Series* (Kluwer Law International 2010). See also COE *Extradition: European Standards: Explanatory Notes on the Council of Europe Convention and Protocols and Minimum Standards Protecting Persons Subject to Transnational Criminal Proceedings* (Council of Europe Publishing 2006) 140.

88 See Communication 204/1986, pg. 67 at para. 7.3 in CCPR/C/OP/2 International Covenant on Civil and Political Rights: Selected Decisions of The Human Rights Committee under The Optional Protocol, Volume 2, Seventeenth to Thirty-Second Sessions (October 1982–April 1988).

89 See generally Ryngaert (n. 30).

90 *Ibid.*

91 *Ibid*, 865–866.

92 Ryngaert (n. 30) 871.

ably be stated that States concerned consider a complementarity analysis to be mandated by law'.[93] He then concluded that 'there is no strong legal requirement of horizontal complementarity [but that] nevertheless, it amounts to proper criminal policy [for bystander State] to defer to "territorial" States that intend to embark in good faith on their own investigations and prosecutions'.[94]

Regional complementarity does not anticipate a horizontal relationship between regions and states, although it prescribes a horizontal relationship between a regional mechanism and the ICC, considering that each of these mechanisms is a conglomeration of states, properly constituted. However, the relationship between regions and states, as well as the relationship between the ICC and member states, is vertical. However, the vertical nature of the relationship does not suggest that regional tribunals will be in a situation to dictate to states. That would contradict the tenets underpinning the positive dimension of regional complementarity. This dimension requires that mutual respect, assistance and partnership are the guiding principle of the vertical relationship between states and regional tribunals.

3.5 Constructive Complementarity

Constructive complementarity proposes a framework of cooperative synergy that allows States to work with the Court to help end impunity.[95] This framework anticipates 'ICC working with States to enhance their domestic capacity and defer to domestic investigations or prosecutions in any feasible conditions'.[96] In practice, this implies that the Court can defer to the 'good faith reasoning' of national officials applying the local law, 'even where the form of the domestic charges varies from the prosecutorial preferences of the OTP or the Pre-Trial Chamber'.[97] It cautions against the development of the ICC's jurisprudence and practice to such an extent that domestic efforts are replaced with ICC prosecutions, thereby giving the impression that 'domestic investigation or adjudication is somehow less desirable than ICC disposition'.[98]

Through an analysis of three emerging trends, with examples from past practices of the ICC, Newton observed that a model of 'a healthy and cooper-

93 *Ibid*, 871.
94 *Ibid*, 855.
95 M. Newton, 'The Quest for Constructive Complementarity' in Stahn & El Zeidy (CUP 2011) 304–340.
96 *Ibid.*
97 *Ibid.*
98 *Ibid.*

ative synergy' between the ICC and States risked being replaced by a model of competition. He noted that while the Rome Statutes demand and expect cooperation with the Court from States, the Statute contains no requirement from the Prosecutor or the Registry to cooperate with States.[99]

In his discussion on the first of the three trends, Newton examined the ICC's extension of judicial constructs beyond those envisioned by states. He noted that the Court's early cases show a court straining to expand its own jurisprudential boundaries. He cited the example of the Court's reticence to employ the doctrine of command responsibility against non-state actors.[100] In the *Lubanga* case, for instance, he argued that the Court resorted to a theory of individual responsibility known as 'co-perpetratorship', instead of applying the principle of command responsibility, which has provisions in the Statute. This is in spite of the fact that the Court found that 'there are reasonable grounds to believe that the perpetrator founded the military organization and served as its Commander-in-Chief throughout the relevant time period'.[101] In the Darfur situation, the Court also found that Omar Al Bashir played essential roles, alongside other leaders, in the crimes against civilians, but only issued the warrant on the basis that he acted as an 'indirect perpetrator'.[102] He concluded that with these positions, 'the ICC is artificially injecting its own view of the law rather than sustaining strict fidelity to the intent of states parties'.[103] On the second trend, Newton analysed the nature of complementarity and asked whether the Court is corroding the concept. He submitted that the concept is meant to serve as a limiting principle rather than an affirmative tool for an aggressive prosecutor to target non-state parties or their nationals. Defining this concept in the context of legal mechanisms has become one of the greatest challenges of the Court. Having established that the subjective nature of the words constituting the admissibility framework may generate non-cooperation by States, he concluded that 'the appropriate power of the ICC Prosecutor will be sustained only by a relationship based on respect and an authentic partnership with sovereign authorities'.[104] In the third place, excessive politicization of charging decisions is a trend that may jeopardize a regime of cooperation between States and the ICC. The danger is that when prosecutorial charging powers of the States are brought under ICC prosecutorial discretion and subordination, it completely negates the purpose

99 *Ibid.*
100 *Ibid.*
101 *Ibid.*
102 *Ibid.*
103 *Ibid.*
104 *Ibid.*

of complementarity and turns the principle on its head.[105] He then proposed certain textual amendments to the Rome Statute to revitalize constructive complementarity.[106]

Regional complementarity also proposes a regime of cooperation between states and the regional tribunal on one hand, and the regional tribunal and the ICC on the other hand. A regional tribunal sits in a midpoint position to both the ICC and the states. It can bridge the gap between these jurisdictions. As with constructive complementarity, regional complementarity may be applied to function as a tool to enhance the domestic capacity of states to investigate and prosecute. This will also imply that, irrespective of the prosecutorial strategy that a state employs, the regional tribunal can defer to 'the good faith reasoning' of states in the application of their national laws to international crimes.

3.6 Radical Complementarity

According to Heller, '[r]adical complementarity is the idea that as long as a state is making a genuine effort to bring a suspect to justice, the ICC should find his or her case inadmissible regardless of the conduct the State investigates or the prosecutorial strategy the State pursues'.[107] Heller argues that the ICC is struggling and may never fulfil its lofty aspirations until it has fundamentally re-considered its relationship with national institutions. Based on inconsistency with complementarity, he criticized the ICC's decision that Simone Gbagbo's case remains admissible on the ground that her domestic prosecution was not for the same crimes as those charged by the OTP.

The theory criticizes the 'same person' and 'same conduct' requirements as being too restrictive and inconsistent with complementarity. Heller argued that there is a need to review the 'substantially same conduct' test, which had earlier been 'adopted in the *Kenya* cases to determine whether national and international prosecutions involve the same case, as required by article 17(1) of the Rome Statute'.[108] In that case, the Appeals Chamber had held that an admissibility challenge could not succeed unless the State is actively investigating the same suspects as the OTP is investigating. This was criticized on the basis that the Appeals Chambers invented the extraneous requirement

105 *Ibid.*

106 *Ibid.*

107 K. Heller, 'Radical Complementarity' (2016) 14 *Journal of International Criminal Justice* 637–665.

108 *Ibid.*

that investigative steps being taken by the State must be 'progressive' as well as 'concrete', whereas article 17 only requires that '[t]he case is being investigated', without more.[109] This suggests 'that *any* investigative step involving the same suspect will satisfy the investigation requirement'.[110]

The 'substantially same conduct' test is applied by the Appeals Chamber in two circumstances: one, in the context of a state's admissibility challenge on OTP's request to open investigation, and two, when a State or a suspect makes an admissibility challenge in relation to a specific case.[111] Heller argued that the effect of applying this test is that 'States are completely at the mercy of the OTP. If the OTP is sufficiently committed to prosecuting a suspect itself, it will almost always be able to do so. This is not complementarity – it is primacy.'[112] Heller argued that the application of this test may 'needlessly undermine sound national prosecutorial strategies', discourage development of national capacity, hinder state cooperation with the ICC, and may not be cost-effective for the ICC itself.[113]

This theory mirrors the idea behind constructive complementarity, in the sense that both theories anticipate the ICC deferring to national mechanisms for the overall goal of ending impunity. However, unlike the proponents of constructive complementarity, Heller identifies the notorious difficulties inherent in amending the Rome Statute and instead proposes that the ICC judges can relax the 'same conduct' test by allowing 'pyramidal (and similar) investigative strategies and eliminating the "substantially the same conduct" requirement as a matter of law'.[114]

Radical complementarity also shares similarities with regional complementarity. Jackson had earlier argued that one way through which a state can make genuine efforts to bring a suspect to justice is through a regional tribunal.[115] In that regard, the ICC ought to find such a case inadmissible. Beyond that, regional complementarity agrees with radical complementarity that when states or any competent regional tribunal are making genuine efforts to prosecute a case, the ICC must find the same case inadmissible. Radical complementarity goes further to state that it will find a case inadmissible if either the ICC or a state is making genuine efforts to investigate and prosecute

109 *Ibid.*
110 *Ibid.*
111 *Ibid.*
112 *Ibid.*
113 *Ibid.*
114 *Ibid.*
115 M. Jackson, 'Regional Complementarity: The Rome Statute and Public International Law' (2016) 14 *JICJ* 5, 1071.

such conducts. This will be based on clear rules as are contained in the regional tribunal's enabling laws.

4 Regional Complementarity and Other Supporting Notions of Complementarity

Drawing from the coinage of radical complementarity, I propose regional complementarity as the idea that 'if a regional judicial mechanism is prosecuting or investigating a particular crime within the jurisdiction of the ICC, the ICC ought to find the prosecution of the suspect's case inadmissible, *in so far* as the regional mechanism displays genuine will and ability to properly investigate and prosecute the same case'.[116] This definition anticipates that there could be instances where there is an overlap of cases of international crimes, or differences in cases where, for example, international and transnational crimes are mixed in the same case. These may necessitate the need to defer to the jurisdiction of the relevant Court, based on certain criteria as to whether the individual is a subject of investigation by the prosecutor. Such criteria might include the seriousness of the offence, the status of the accused at the time of the alleged offences, and/or the general importance of the legal questions involved in the case. This definition of regional complementarity is a narrow admissibility-related definition and represents one of the strands of a broader understanding that I propose.

On the flip side, regional complementarity also anticipates that 'as long as a state is making genuine efforts to bring a suspect to justice, the regional tribunal would find the case inadmissible regardless of the conduct the state investigates or the prosecutorial strategy the state pursues'.[117] There is already an assumption that the conduct the state is investigating falls within the jurisdiction of the regional tribunal.

These two sides of regional complementarity are proposed to ensure that there is no friction between the regional tribunal and the ICC, on the one hand, and, on the other hand, that there is no friction between states and the regional tribunal, based on the division of labour. The notion attempts to underscore the advantages of investigation and prosecution at the regional level. It also argues that regional prosecution of crimes could help close the impunity gap, thus fulfilling the overall goal of the Rome Statute. Regional complementarity agrees with other notions that allocate lesser roles to the

---

116 This is my coinage as adapted from the notion of radical complementarity.

117 My coinage as adapted from the notion of radical complementarity.

ICC while encouraging more efforts at the national and regional levels. It advocates a regime of positive and constructive relationships between the ICC and regional courts, on one hand, and a similar relationship between the regional mechanism and states, on the other hand. For the purposes of this work, a regional judicial mechanism is defined more broadly as mechanisms of supranational institutions whose memberships consist of governments or authorities from the same geopolitical region. These judicial mechanisms often include the human rights systems of specific regions.

As has been argued earlier, regional complementarity agrees with positive, proactive, constructive and radical complementarity. The principles that it espouses are found in these conceptions of complementarity. Like positive complementarity, it encourages interdependence, flexibility, burden-sharing, division of labour, partnership, vigilance, mutual assistance and interaction between regional tribunals and the ICC, on the one hand, and the regional tribunal and states, on the other hand. These are all principles that should govern the interactions between these levels of court. In its proactive connotation, regional complementarity requires a regional tribunal to be more directly involved in all measures to encourage the prosecution of international crimes by national mechanisms. As a constructive concept, regional complementarity envisages cooperation between states and the regional tribunal, as well as cooperation between regional tribunals and the ICC, to help fulfil the goal of ending impunity. Lastly, as a notion that reflects the ideas underpinning radical complementarity, regional complementarity holds that the ICC ought to find a case inadmissible if a regional judicial mechanism is investigating or prosecuting the case. It also requires a regional judicial mechanism to hold itself to the same standards by finding a case inadmissible if a state is genuinely investigating or prosecuting a case.

In summary, all the theories earlier discussed reveal certain common denominators. First is the idea of a lesser role for the ICC and a greater role for national and – in this case – regional institutions. Secondly, they variously emphasize the ICC's ability to encourage, incentivize, catalyze and assist national (or regional) efforts at crimes prosecution. Thirdly, they all favour a regime of cooperation between the states or the conglomeration of states and the ICC for the purposes of furthering the goals of the ICC.

5 Exploring the Classical and Positive Dimensions of Regional Complementarity

Regional complementarity has both positive and classical dimensions. In its classical dimension, it can be understood simply as an organizing principle for competing jurisdiction between the ICC and a regional tribunal, on the one hand, and between a regional tribunal and states, on the other hand. In its positive dimension, however, it could mean a regime of cooperation between regional courts and the ICC, as well as between the regional tribunal and states.

5.1 Classical Notion of Regional Complementarity

Classical complementarity is the original notion of complementarity as enshrined in the Rome Statute. The notion has been fully discussed in section 1.2 of this chapter. A classical notion of regional complementarity, therefore, refers to the idea that states would be forced to carry out national investigations and prosecutions of international crimes in their territories to avoid intervention by the regional tribunal. Three normative assumptions underpin the classical notion of complementarity: 'preservation of domestic jurisdiction', 'domestic failure activates the ICC's jurisdiction' and 'compliance is enhanced through threat'.[118] These assumptions could be transposed into regional complementarity.

A classic interpretation of regional complementarity views complementarity as a tool to preserve state sovereignty and jurisdiction over international crimes. This implies that states will have to continuously fend off the regional tribunal by asserting their primary responsibility to investigate and prosecute international crimes in their territory. This competition-based relationship is not proposed. Secondly, the idea that a state's failure to investigate or prosecute is what activates a regional tribunal's jurisdiction belongs in the classic notion of regional complementarity. This negative approach requires that a regional tribunal monitors the states' activities for unwillingness, inability or failure. Thirdly, regional complementarity could be interpreted to mean that a regional tribunal will step in if a state fails to perform its duty of enforcing international criminal law in its territory. State failure could be a potential source of embarrassment, hence the threat-based inducement to ensure genuine investigation or prosecution.

This notion interprets regional complementarity as an organizing principle for competing jurisdictions between a regional tribunal and states. While it preserves state's sovereignty, it also reserves roles for regional tribunals, based on the failure of states. It aims to delineate roles for each mechanism, as well as clarify limitation. The goal is to reduce the possibility of friction between these mechanisms.

118 C. Stahn, 'Complementarity: A Tale of Two Notions' (2008), 19 *Criminal Law Forum* 96–98.

5.2 Positive Dimension of Regional Complementarity

The positive dimension of complementarity requires that a global criminal justice institution like the ICC works collaboratively with states to achieve the aim of international criminal justice. As currently proposed, regional complementarity flows upwards and downwards. In its upward flow, it seeks to establish a regime of cooperation between a regional tribunal and the ICC. On the other hand, it also seeks cooperation between a regional tribunal and states. The relationship between the tribunal and the ICC is open to debate. Depending on the interpretation adopted, the relationship could be vertical or horizontal. However, the relationship between the tribunal and states is vertical in nature. The underlying assumptions in their relationship are that the regional tribunal and states are working for a common goal, comparative advantage is the basis for intervention by any of the mechanisms, and parties are willing and ready to offer help and assistance where they are needed.[119]

The core elements of positive complementarity that could be transposed to regional complementarity are burden-sharing or division of labour, support for national prosecution and capacity building.[120] Others are mutual deference, monitoring and regulation, collaboration and cooperation, among others.

5.2.1 Burden Sharing or Division of Labour

At the ICC, division of labour in relation to positive complementarity has consistently been interpreted as the strategy whereby the OTP concentrates on those who bear greater responsibility and are alleged to have committed the most serious crimes, while other defendants are left to be dealt with by the national mechanism.[121] This strategy appears to have originated from the Nuremberg tribunals, which focused largely on 'major war criminals'.[122] This concurrent jurisdiction is also proposed for regional tribunals. An approach that allows burden-sharing between a regional tribunal and states will support the positive dimension of regional complementarity.

Another approach to burden-sharing is self-referral of cases or situations. Self-referral of cases by states is one of the effects of positive complementarity.[123] It has been instrumental in creating a partnership between states and

119 *Ibid*, 101–102.
120 Takemura (n. 49).
121 *Ibid*, para. 18.
122 *Ibid.*
123 P. Hobbs, 'The Catalysing Effect of the Rome Statute in Africa: Positive Complementarity and Self-Referrals' (2020) *31 Criminal Law Forum* 345–376.

the ICC, instead of a competitive relationship.[124] Regional complementarity also encourages self-referral of cases by states to the regional tribunal where a state deems it fit to do so. On the flip side, a regional tribunal may, under certain circumstances, refer cases to either a state or the ICC. Considering that regional complementarity could flow upwards and downwards, the regional tribunal, which sits at a midpoint between states and the ICC, could also exercise its powers to refer cases upwards or downwards.

The idea of transferring cases from a tribunal to a national mechanism is not novel. It has been observed in the ICTY and ICTR.[125] At the time of writing, a total of eight cases involving thirteen persons have been transferred from the ICTY to national mechanisms in the former Yugoslavia.[126] The ICTR referred four cases to the national mechanism in Rwanda.[127] A region that proposes to establish a regional criminal tribunal may include provisions in the tribunal's statute and rules of procedure and evidence that would allow transfer of cases between the tribunal and other mechanisms like states and the ICC. Where the relevant state is not a party to the Rome Statute, the regional tribunal would not be able to refer such cases to the ICC unless the state has made an article 12.3 declaration. Secondly, as there is no provision in the Rome Statute that stipulates a transfer of cases from the ICC to a regional tribunal, and in the absence of a textual amendment to the Rome Statute, it may be that a state itself, or other member states of the regional tribunal, would be the entity that refers the situation or case to the ICC.

5.2.2 Support for National Prosecution

It is the idea that the ICC should employ various methods to ensure that states are encouraged to prosecute international crimes domestically. This dimension aims to strengthen national capacities to achieve the ultimate goal of deterring the future commission of international crimes.[128] The support and encouragement that the ICC gives is to ensure that states can undertake genuine investigations and prosecutions of international crimes in their territo-

124 K. Marshall, 'Prevention and Complementarity in the International Criminal Court: A Positive Approach' [available at https://tinyurl.com/hykda478 – accessed 21 February 2024].

125 Relevant provisions in the Rules of Procedure and Evidence of both ICTY and ICTR are found in Rule 11*bis*.

126 ICTY 'Transfer of cases' at https://www.icty.org/en/cases/transfer-cases.

127 UNICTR 'cases referred to national jurisdictions' at https://unictr.irmct.org/en/cases/key-figures-cases.

128 Marshall (n. 124).

ries. The support given by the ICC could include information sharing, knowledge sharing and training, as well as partnership that encourages states to act and own the process of international crimes investigation and prosecution. The support given by the ICC may vary between states that are willing but unable, those unable but willing, those unwilling and unable, and finally, those willing and able. For those states that are able but unwilling, ICC's intervention may take the form of pressure that leaves the state with no choice but to act on a particular case. For those who are willing but unable, support may involve measures to enhance the national mechanism's ability.

A broad-based positive interpretation of regional complementarity requires a regional tribunal to work in collaboration with states and the ICC to achieve the aim of ending impunity. As it is possible for the ICC to employ different measures to encourage states, so it is for regional tribunals. Instances abound where regional organizations have helped states in their region to establish and activate the jurisdiction of a criminal tribunal. For instance, the role played by the AU in the Hissène Habré trial is well-documented.[129] The positive dimension of regional complementarity also foresees a situation where evidence gathered by a regional tribunal can be used before a national mechanism, or indeed the ICC. Article 93(10)(b)(i)(1) of the Rome Statute already provides this in the ICC context. A regional tribunal may include similar provisions in its statute.

5.2.3 Capacity-Building

Positive complementarity also anticipates that global bodies institute measures to develop the capacity of national mechanisms to investigate and prosecute international crimes in their territories.[130] Capacity-building could entail legal assistance, legislative assistance, training for judges and judicial officers in the states, exchange of officers, etc. The ICC itself has committed to 'enhance the capacity of national jurisdictions to prosecute the perpetrators of the most serious crimes of international concern'.[131] It has promised finan-

129 R. Brody, 'Bringing a Dictator to Justice: The Case of Hissène Habré' (2005) 13 *JICJ* 2, 209–217.

130 O. Bekou, 'The ICC and Capacity Building at the National Level' in C. Stahn (ed) *The Law and Practice of the International Criminal Court* (OUP 2015) 1245–58.

131 See generally ICC ASP Doc: ICC-ASP/16/33 'Report of the Bureau on Complementarity' (2017).

cial contributions,[132] technical assistance,[133] and various other capacity-building activities for states.[134]

In the same manner, capacity building as a core element of the positive dimension of regional complementarity suggests that the regional tribunal may be able to support national mechanisms with legal assistance, training and other capacity-building activities. Dialogue is proposed as one approach towards understanding the state's capacity needs. A regional tribunal must be ready to engage states in dialogues to offer the necessary support in capacity building.

6 Other Organizing Principles for Positive Regional Complementarity

6.1 Mutual Deference

To reiterate, my notion of regional complementarity prescribes that 'if a regional judicial mechanism is prosecuting or investigating a particular crime within the jurisdiction of the ICC, the ICC ought to find the prosecution of the suspect's case inadmissible, *in so far* as the regional mechanism displays genuine will and ability to properly investigate and prosecute the same case'. This immediately raises questions as to what organizational concepts do we use to arrange such relationships? Am I, for instance, suggesting the application of 'deference', thereby requiring that the ICC automatically defers to the jurisdiction of the regional court where there is genuine will and ability to investigate and prosecute? Also, what are my indicators for genuine will and ability, and what criteria will we use to assess those?

In response, it is now clear that the positive notion of regional complementarity will better serve the purpose of a cooperative regime between a regional tribunal and the ICC on the one hand, as well as the relationship between a regional tribunal and states on the other hand. On the face of it, it appears that my concept of regional complementarity mirrors the classical notion of complementarity, where the ICC is expected to automatically defer to states in respect of primacy in the exercise of jurisdiction. However, a closer analysis suggests that a positive-based conception of regional complementarity does not envisage an automatic withdrawal from exercising jurisdiction by the ICC.

132 *Ibid*, para 6.
133 *Ibid*, para 13.
134 *Ibid*, para 41.

The conditions that must be met before a regional tribunal can exercise jurisdiction at the expense of the ICC are included in my coinage. As such, thorough analysis that considers the unwillingness and/or inability of the regional tribunal must be ascertained. Even more so, the idea of deference of the ICC to domestic prosecution has been criticized.[135] If the same deference were to automatically apply between regional mechanisms and the ICC, such approach will open itself to the same criticisms that have attended the classical notion of complementarity.

In a different scenario, the idea that a forum that has a comparative advantage over the other, in a specific situation, should be the appropriate forum for prosecution is also embedded in the notion of positive regional complementarity. For example, if the case is more complex or comprehensive at the regional level, where, for instance, we have transnational crimes charges in addition to atrocity crimes charges, it would probably make more policy sense for such case to be prosecuted at the regional tribunal. Additionally, it could also be that the regional tribunal is better placed to handle a case given its proximity to the crime scenes, among other factors.

There are many other instances where the regional mechanism might be better placed to prosecute a case, but this should be guided by 'the opportunity principle'. This implies that, for example, either a regional mechanism or the ICC who is seized of a matter, can give notice to the other mechanism, where it perceives that the other mechanism is better placed. It will operate as a provision of notice, cooperation and an opportunity for that other mechanism to act. But there is always a cut-off point where the mechanism that provides the opportunity for the other to act, steps in, where no action has emanated from the mechanism. It operates more like a right of refusal. The converse, where the ICC gives a national mechanism 'a fair opportunity to exercise jurisdiction', has been earlier proposed, in the Yekatom Defence Appeal Brief on Admissibility.[136]

My idea of regional complementarity should, therefore, not be based only on the unwillingness and inability tests. This could be the beginning of the analysis, but it goes beyond the ICC text and takes into consideration the broader structural principles of mutual deference where necessary, capacity building and collaboration, cooperation, consultation and division of labour, rather than the strict ICC-text test of unwillingness and inability.

135 C. Stahn, 'Complementarity: A Tale of Two Notions' (2008), 19 *Criminal Law Forum* 109.

136 ICC Doc: ICC-01/14-01/18-523 'Yekatom Defence Appeal Brief – Admissibility' in *The Prosecutor v. Alfred Yekatom and Patrice-Edouard Ngaissona*, para. 59.

Mutual deference mirrors the idea behind 'qualified deference' that Mark Drumbl's work promotes,[137] and that has been supported by Professor Stahn.[138] In an admissibility assessment before the ICC, for instance, Stahn argued that judges should be prepared to 'award the state reasonable time to investigate and build the case after the notice of an admissibility challenge and prior to a final decision on admissibility'.[139] The concept is also different from subsidiarity and cannot be applied in the same way as subsidiarity is applied between the EU and states.

On the second question as to the indicators for assessing unwillingness and inability to prosecute, I will again take the ICC text and the Court practice as a starting point. The OTP informal expert paper on the principle of complementarity already identifies 'unjustified delay', 'lack of independence of the judiciary', 'lack of impartiality' and several other indicators as 'background context issues that may be gathered in order to inform an admissibility assessment'.[140] Inability may be established through lack of judges and other personnel, lack of judicial infrastructure, among other factors.[141] However, as with my earlier proposition on how to implement regional complementarity, any assessment on admissibility should go beyond these factors. Such assessments must also contextualize the level of support, cooperation and capacity building that have been provided to the regional mechanism, where the ICC, for example, moves to assess admissibility. This same approach applies if, for instance, the assessment is being made in respect of an interaction between a regional mechanism and the state. What this requires, therefore, is that an assessment based on these factors alone should not result in establishing unwillingness and/or inability against a mechanism if adequate support had not been given to that mechanism. The advantage of this approach lies in the catalysing effect that such approach will have on a mechanism's capacity to investigate and prosecute.

137 See M. Drumbl, *Atrocity, Punishment and International Law* (CUP 2007). See also M. Drumbl, 'Policy Through Complementarity: The Atrocity Trial as Justice' in Stahn C. and El Zeidy M. (eds) *The International Criminal Court and Complementarity: From Theory to Practice* (Cambridge University Press 2011) 222–224.

138 C. Stahn, 'Admissibility Challenges before the ICC: From Quasi-Primacy to Qualified Deference?' in C. Stahn (ed) *The Law and Practice of the International Criminal Court* (OUP 2015) 228.

139 *Ibid.*

140 OTP 'Informal expert paper: The principle of complementarity in practice' (2003) 28–29.

141 *Ibid.*

6.2 Monitoring and Regulation

The idea of monitoring and regulation in the application of complementarity flows from the classical understanding of complementarity and prescribes that a mechanism is subservient to the other and would need to be monitored and regulated so that they could deliver effectively on their mandate. Monitoring and regulation are closely tied to the idea of compliance through threat.[142] However, monitoring and regulation, as envisaged within the context of regional complementarity, suggest that a regional mechanism may require regular and periodic reports on the status of activities in relation to cases before domestic mechanisms from states. This is not altogether novel. It had been proposed in earlier years of the court and continues to be utilized by the Assembly of State Parties to the ICC.[143] The periodic reports to be submitted were to identify gaps and needs in the domestic system that could form the basis for support from the ICC. In this regard, if such approach were transposed to regional complementarity, monitoring and regulation will operate to provide what Stahn has termed 'an incentive for implementation'.[144] Also, the important point to note is that the motivation for regulation and monitoring remains an effort to support and incentivize prosecution at the domestic level, and not necessarily to take over investigation and prosecution. If monitoring and regulation operate within that context, there will be less acrimony in the way regional complementarity is operationalized.

6.3 Collaboration and Cooperation

The other organizing principle is collaboration and cooperation. There already exists an understanding of the prime place of other stakeholders, especially regional organizations, in the work that the ICC does. In a 2016 report of the court on cooperation, the ASP stated that 'the Court continued to develop its interaction and cooperation with international and regional organizations in order to maintain and foster further support for its activities'.[145] It specifically noted cooperation between the court and a number of other regional organizations, including the Inter-American Court of Human Rights and the EU, among others.[146] This is already a template for cooperation and collabo-

142 C. Stahn, 'Complementarity: A tale of two notions' (2008) 19 *Criminal Law Forum* 97.
143 See Report of the Bureau on cooperation, ICC-ASP/8/44, 15 November 2009.
144 C. Stahn, 'Complementarity: A tale of two notions' (2008) 19 *Criminal Law Forum* 87–113 at 97.
145 ICC-ASP/15/9 'Report of the court on cooperation' (2016) para. 2.
146 *Ibid*, para. 5.

ration between states and regional mechanisms on one hand, and also between regional mechanisms and the ICC on the other hand. The ICC has already perfected the art of entering into cooperation and collaboration Memorandum of Understanding (MOUs) with states in order to avoid jurisdictional friction and to enhance cooperation. Recent examples include the OTP's MOU with the state of Guinea.[147] Article 1 of the MOU binds the parties to 'work actively and collaboratively to further the principle of complementarity'.[148] Other older examples include the MOU regarding administrative arrangements between the ICC and the SCSL;[149] the Cooperation Agreement between the Office of the Prosecutor of the International Criminal Court and the Government of Colombia;[150] the MOU with Sudan on the trial of Ali Kushayb; and the MOU with the Government of Venezuela,[151] among others. The use of MOUs and cooperation agreements as tools to enhance collaboration between levels of courts, to clarify the relationship, and to avoid jurisdictional friction appears to have become an acceptable practice that can be transposed into the cooperative regime of regional complementarity.

One other approach to collaboration and cooperation that has emerged in practice is the use of joint investigative teams between two or more states for conducting criminal investigations.[152] In this regard, in the field of ICL, a JIT consisting of the OTP and relevant organs within the domestic system or the relevant tribunal have been proposed and utilized, albeit with attendant challenges. While neither the ICC nor the regional tribunal has police officials with enforcement powers at their disposal, such joint investigative teams will increasingly depend on enforcement officials from states, especially where the terms of such engagement are clearly spelt out in such MOUs or other enabling instruments of the tribunal. The Special Criminal Court of the Central African Republic (SCCCAR) offers a good example in this regard.[153]

---

147 'Memorandum of Understanding between the Republic of Guinea and the OTP' 28 September 2022.

148 *Ibid.*

149 ICC-PRES/03/01/06, MOU between ICC and SCSL.

150 Cooperation Agreement between the Office of the Prosecutor of the International Criminal Court and the Government of Colombia, 28 October 2021.

151 Press Release, ICC Prosecutor, Mr. Karim A.A. Khan QC, opens an investigation into the situation in Venezuela and concludes Memorandum of Understanding with the Government, 5 November 2021.

152 On the use of JITS in ICL, see A. Furger, 'Can they deliver? The practice of Joint Investigation Teams (JITS) in core international crimes investigations' (2024) 22 *JICJ* 3, 43–58.

153 See Article 37 of the Organic Law of the SCCCAR.

Recall also that a JIT under the EU framework, consisting of domestic organs of several EU states and the OTP, has existed since March 2022.[154]

It is part 9 of the Rome Statute that contains provisions on cooperation between the court and states. However, cooperation between international tribunals and states has been traditionally construed as one-sided.[155] Stahn had theorized on 'reverse cooperation' and 'mutual cooperation'.[156] In operationalizing regional complementarity, mutual cooperation is proposed. Its application ensures that a regional tribunal supports states while a state does the same where the case is before a regional mechanism or the ICC. This cooperative regime puts the regional mechanism at a midpoint to be able to offer assistance, help and support to either the ICC or the state, wherever the need arises. It forestalls competition and friction, as all parties engage with a sense of shared responsibility. The idea of shared responsibility proposes that each mechanism sees itself as part of a whole ecosystem of international criminal justice, with the same goal as the other constituent parts of the ecosystem. Mutual cooperation will require a regional mechanism to be able to expect, demand and rely on cooperation from states and the ICC in the same manner as the ICC expects from states and a regional organization.

7 Conclusion

In this chapter, I have delved into the meaning, function and existing theories of complementarity. I have also argued that while regional complementarity is the newest notion of complementarity, it shares some features with many of the existing notions of complementarity – positive, proactive, constructive and radical complementarity. It advocates more restricted roles for the ICC in international crimes investigation and prosecution. I argued that regional complementarity also has both classical and positive dimensions. In its classical dimension, it can be understood simply as an organizing principle for competing jurisdiction between a regional tribunal and states, as well as between regional tribunals and the ICC. In its positive dimension, however, it facilitates a regime of cooperation between regional courts and the ICC, as

154 Furger (n. 152).

155 C. Stahn, 'Taking complementarity seriously: On the sense and sensibility of 'classical', 'positive' and 'negative' complementarity' 249.

156 *Ibid.*

well as regional courts and states. I have shown that a regional tribunal must be ready to support national prosecutions, build capacities and work collaboratively with states in an atmosphere of partnership, mutual assistance and comparative advantage. The proposal, therefore, is to interpret regional complementarity from its positive dimension.

CHAPTER 7

Regional Complementarity and the Rules of Interpretation

1 Introduction

Interpretation lies at the heart of international criminal law and determines how its norms adapt to an evolving global justice system. The development of regional complementarity, as an emerging principle within that system, depends not only on institutional design but also on interpretive creativity. The rules of interpretation under international law, particularly those reflected in the Vienna Convention on the Law of Treaties (VCLT), provide the legal and conceptual framework through which regional complementarity can be reconciled with the Rome Statute of the International Criminal Court. This chapter explores how interpretive techniques can be used to support a reading of complementarity that accommodates regional judicial mechanisms as genuine partners in the enforcement of international criminal law.

The discussion begins by analysing the interpretive foundations of complementarity in the Rome Statute, especially Article 17, which regulates admissibility. Through an examination of the VCLT's interpretive methods – textual, contextual and teleological – the chapter demonstrates that a purposive reading of Article 17 can sustain an inclusive understanding of complementarity that recognizes legitimate prosecutions before regional courts. Such an interpretation would not depart from the Statute's object and purpose but would rather advance them by promoting accountability through a wider range of competent forums. A teleological or functional interpretation, informed by the principles of effective implementation and systemic integration, thus supports a broader conception of complementarity in which regional courts can contribute meaningfully to global justice without undermining the ICC's authority.

In addition, the chapter explores the notion of international delegation and the principle of 'overriding benefit', both of which provide interpretive justification for recognizing regional mechanisms within the complementarity framework. International delegation theory allows for the diffusion of jurisdictional competence to entities that share the international community's goals, while the overriding benefits approach supports a reading of international law that privileges practical justice outcomes over formal institutional hierarchies.

© 2026 THE AUTHOR(S) | HTTPS://DOI.ORG/10.1163/9789004761803-009

Together, these interpretive tools demonstrate that complementarity should be understood as a cooperative rather than exclusionary principle.

The chapter further examines the practical dimensions of regional complementarity by analysing how interpretive principles could govern interactions among different judicial levels. It considers the potential relationships between regional courts and national jurisdictions, between one regional court and another, between regional and sub-regional bodies, between regional courts and hybrid tribunals and, finally, between regional courts and the ICC. In each scenario, interpretation plays a vital role in determining jurisdictional boundaries, resolving overlaps and fostering a coherent system of mutual deference.

Ultimately, this chapter argues that the interpretation of complementarity through the lens of the VCLT and related doctrines can transform how international criminal law conceptualizes the division of labour among judicial actors. Rather than viewing regional mechanisms as exceptions to the Rome Statute system, interpretation grounded in the Convention and in general international law offers a path to their integration within the global accountability architecture. Regional complementarity thus emerges not as a challenge to the ICC, but as a logical extension of its mandate to ensure that the most serious crimes of concern to the international community do not go unpunished.

2 Regional Complementarity: A Description

While the term 'regional complementarity' is somewhat new to ICL,[1] many of the underlying strands of the notion are already quite familiar. The idea that the ICC is a court of last resort, which should have a limited role in international crimes prosecution, is one of such strands.[2] The understanding that states bear the primary duty to punish crimes and that this could be done

1 Du Plessis was one of the first scholars to use the coinage. He had used the term in his 2012 blog post titled 'A case of negative regional complementarity? Giving the African Court of Justice and Human Rights Jurisdiction over International Crimes' (2012) *EJILTalk* at https://www.ejiltalk.org/a-case-of-negative-regional-complementarity-giving-the-african-court-of-justice-and-human-rights-jurisdiction-over-international-crimes/. Miles Jackson also used the term in his article titled 'Regional Complementarity: The Rome Statute and Public International Law' (2016) 14 *Journal of International Criminal Justice* 1061–1072.

2 ICC as a court of last resort, see M. C. Bassiouni 'The ICC – *Quo Vadis?* (2006) 4 *Journal of International Criminal Justice* 3, 421–427.

through international cooperation, even at a regional level, is another.[3] Again, the view that regional efforts towards the maintenance of international peace and security is a welcome development[4] is yet another strand. More specifically, the idea that regional courts could serve as intermediary between national and international courts has received some scholarly attention.[5] This attention is partly because there is a debate among scholars on different rules of interpretation that applies to the Rome Statute. In international law, there are two major schools of interpretation – the literal and pragmatist/purposive schools of interpretations.[6] This is in line with the Vienna Convention on the Law of Treaties (VCLT). However, opinions are divided on the applicability of the VCLT to the Rome Statute. Dov Jacobs argues that ICL's principle of legality makes it inappropriate to apply VCLT to the Rome Statute.[7] Akande proposes that the VCLT applies to the Rome Statute, but not in its entirety.[8] I hold the view, just as the ICC does, that the VCLT applies to the Rome Statute.[9] I aim to clarify the point that regional complementarity could be construed within the ambit of the relevant provisions of the ICC Statute. The role that interpretation plays and the extent to which conflict can be resolved through interpretation of the existing statutes is my focus. In answering the

---

3 Paragraph 6 of the preamble to the Rome Statute provides that '[R]ecalling that it is the duty of every State to exercise its criminal jurisdiction over those responsible for international crimes.' Paragraph 4 also requires that effective prosecution of 'the most serious crimes of concern to the international community' must be 'ensured by taking measures at the national level and by enhancing international cooperation'. The joint reading of the two paragraphs suggests then that the Rome Statute also envisages that states are expected to take joint action in order to punish international crimes.

4 An example of this can be found in UN Doc: S/PRST/2016/8, 'Statement by the President of the Security Council' where the President of the UNSC states in paragraph 3 that '[T]he Security Council reiterates its primary responsibility under the Charter for the maintenance of international peace and security, and recalls that cooperation with regional and subregional organizations in matters relating to the maintenance of international peace and security and consistent with chapter VIII of the Charter of the United Nations can improve collective security.'

5 Sarah P. Nimigan 'Exceptional or Exceptionalism? The Malabo Protocol and 'Regional Complementarity' (2019) 17 *Journal of International Criminal Justice* 5, 1005–1029.

6 T. Lonnquist 'The Trend Towards Purposive Statutory Interpretation: Human Rights at Stake' (2003) *Revenue Law Journal* 19.

7 D. Jacobs 'International Criminal Law' in Kammerhofer J and D'Aspremont J, *International Legal Positivism in a Post-Modern World* (Cambridge University Press 2014) 473.

8 D. Akande 'Treaty Interpretation, the VCLT and the ICC Statute: A Response to Kevin Jon Heller & Dov Jacobs' *EJIL: Talk* 25 August 2013.

9 ICC-01/04-01/07 OA 6 Situation in the Democratic Republic of the Congo the Prosecutor V. Germain Katanga and Mathieu Ngudjolo Chui, Judgment on the Appeal Against the Decision on Joinder rendered on 10 March 2008 by the PreTrial Chamber, para. 5.

question as to how the rules of interpretation support the theory of regional complementarity, I establish the claim that the VCLT also envisages an interpretation that favours regional complementarity.

3 Interpretation of Statutes: The VCLT and the Rome Statute

Article 31 of the VCLT embodies the general approach to treaty interpretation.[10] It provides that '[a] treaty shall be interpreted in good faith in accordance with the ordinary meaning to be given to the terms of the treaty in their context and in the light of its object and purpose'. This provision refers to three aspects of interpretation. They are literal, systematic or contextual and teleological interpretation that concentrates on the object and purpose of a treaty.[11] None of these approaches takes precedence over the others as they are meant to be used in a 'single combined operation'.[12] Thus, interpreting a treaty provision has to take into account these three steps enquiry in order to achieve the right interpretative outcome. However, the literal analysis or an identification of the ordinary or plain meaning of the text is often the point to begin.[13]

In this regard, an analysis of Article 17(1) of the ICC statute to ascertain if the word 'states' as contained in the provision refers only to a state is necessary. There is no doubt as to the meaning of the term states in Article 17. What is, however, a subject of debate is whether the literal interpretation also precludes an interpretation that favours collective actions of states under a regional arrangement. To answer this, let me begin by borrowing the words of Field J. in *Williams v Evans* (1849) 6 Notes of Cases 695. 1 Ex D 277 at 284 offers some guidance:

> No doubt it is a maxim to be followed in the interpretation of statutes, that the ordinary grammatical construction is to be adopted; but when this leads to a manifest absurdity, a construction not strictly grammatical is allowed, if this will lead to a reasonable conclusion as to the intention of the legislature.[14]

An interpretation that precludes joint efforts by states, on an action for which they individually have a right to act upon may amount to manifest absurdity.

10 P. Viebig, *Illicitly obtained evidence at the International Criminal Court* (TMC Asser 2006) 17.

11 *Ibid.*

12 *Ibid.*

13 R. Gardiner, *Treaty Interpretation* (OUP 2017) 2.

14 F.A.R. Bennion *Bennion on Statute Law* (Longman 1990) 168.

However, in this case, a textual interpretation of the Rome Statute may be flawed but does not necessarily lead to manifest absurdity. The use of expressions such as 'a State' and 'the State' in Article 17(1)(a) suggests that the drafters intended for the provision to refer to a single state that has jurisdiction over the alleged crimes. My thesis is that it may well be that drafters simply did not envisage the possibility of regional courts being engaged for international crimes prosecution. That it was not envisaged at that time does not make its emergence illegal or inappropriate. The text reflects this idea, without necessarily showing manifest absurdity.

Moreover, the VCLT also proposes a teleological interpretation. This places equal importance on the object and purpose of the statute, as it does on the literal meaning. An application of teleological interpretation helps to arrive at a proper meaning of 'State' that agrees with the entirety of the Rome Statute. In that regard, an interpretation that favours an analysis of the object and purpose of the Rome Statute would not be out of place and will be firmly within the contemplation of the VCLT, and thus valid. A teleological approach to interpretation is not without its faults. One example in international criminal law is when it yields odd results as to make the outcome of the purposive interpretation erode the meanings to be derived from text and other purposes of the treaty.[15] The interpretation of 'State' to also mean 'a group of States' that I propose here does not yield an odd result that negates the text, context and purpose of the Rome Statute.

3.1 Literalists vs Pragmatists

Jackson explored how criminal prosecutions before regional (or sub-regional) tribunals would fit into the provisions of Article 17(1)(a) of the Rome Statute. He concluded that 'a genuine criminal prosecution by a lawfully constituted regional tribunal means that 'the case is being... prosecuted by a State which has jurisdiction over it' for the purposes of Article 17(1)(a). He argued that regional complementarity agrees with a proper understanding of the nature of the relationship between states and regional tribunals; with the provisions of Article 31 of the VCLT; is consistent with the values underlying the principle of complementarity and makes sense as a matter of policy.[16] With this view, Jackson belongs in the pragmatist school of thought: those who favour a stra-

15 D. Robinson 'The Identity Crisis of International Criminal Law' (2008) 21 *Leiden Journal of International Law* 935.

16 M. Jackson 'Regional Complementarity: The Rome Statute and Public International Law' (2016) 14 *Journal of International Criminal Justice* 1, 1061–1072.

tegic and creative interpretation of the Rome Statute. In this school, scholars like Scharf hold that the Rome Statute was deliberately drafted to preserve what they termed a 'creative ambiguity'. This ambiguity leaves room for ICC Prosecutor and judges to improve on the Rome Statute by deferring to truth commissions or other restorative justice mechanisms.[17] Others argue that certain provisions in the Rome Statute can be creatively interpreted to allow the ICC to defer to regional courts. According to one such author, 'if the ICC is to fulfill its promise, its role in ending impunity should not be limited solely to pursuing cases. Instead, the ICC should defer to regional courts…'[18] They argue that the Rome Statute, like the UN Charter,[19] is a 'living document that is capable of adapting to changing circumstances and needs'.[20] They also favour a 'purposive interpretation' of the complementarity provisions of the Rome Statute.[21]

However, scholars in the literalist school of thought hold otherwise. Vaid notes that '[B]ased on the *plain text* of the complementarity provisions of Article 17, this action must begin with *a domestic investigation* before the state either prosecutes or decides not to prosecute a particular case.'[22] Du Plessis argued that '…the prosecution of a case by the African Court [cannot] bar the ICC from prosecuting the very same case under the principle of complementarity, as Article 17 of the Rome Statute refers to 'states' and not to other courts'.[23] This approach favours a strict textual interpretation of the

17 See A. Seibert-Fohr 'The Relevance of the Rome Statute of the International Criminal Court for Amnesties and Truth Commissions' (2003) *Max Planck Yearbook of United Nations Law* 553–590. See also M. P. Scharf, 'The Amnesty Exception to the Jurisdiction of the International Criminal Court', 32 *Cornell Int'l L.J.* 526–527.

18 T. E. Sainati 'Divided We Fall: How the International Criminal Court Can Promote Compliance with International Law by Working with Regional Courts' (2016) 49 *Vanderbilt Journal of Transnational Law* 191–243.

19 D. Kastrup 'From Nuremberg to Rome and Beyond: The Fight against Genocide, War Crimes, and Crimes Against Humanity' (1999) 23 *Fordham International Law Journal* 2, 414.

20 M. Crowley, *Chemical Control: Regulation of Incapacitating Chemical Agent Weapons, Riot Control Agents and their Means of Delivery* (Palgrave Macmillan 2016) 194.

21 G. Werle, L. Fernandez and M. Vormbaum (eds.), *Africa and the International Criminal Court* (Asser Press 2014) 231.

22 K. Vaid 'What Counts as "State Action" under Article 17 of the Rome Statute? Applying the ICC's Complementarity Test to Non-Criminal Investigations by the United States into War Crimes in Afghanistan' (2012) 44 *Journal of International Law and Politics* 573–628, at 535.

23 M. Du Plessis 'Implications of the AU Decision to Give the African Court Jurisdiction Over International Crimes' (2012) 235 *Institute for Security Studies Paper* 11.

ICC Statute,[24] and reflects the view that Article 17(1) of the Rome Statute would need to be amended to reflect an action by a group of states acting under a regional arrangement, since it currently speaks of states and not 'group of states'. Some other scholars have also drawn from Article 22(2) to argue that the Rome Statute itself, or at least its provisions on the definition of crimes, should be 'strictly construed and not be extended by analogy'.[25] They generally urge judges not to usurp the authority and role of the legislature or drafters of the law. Many reasons have been advanced for a preference for strict interpretation of statutes. They include the need to give notice on the consequences of criminal actions; upholding the principle of separation of power as well as limiting arbitrary enforcement of criminal law.[26] While these reasons are valid, they do not apply to the issue under discussion. My argument relates to an interpretation that expands the forum of prosecution, and not about giving notice on consequences of criminal actions. My interpretation does not erode the principle of separation of power. And lastly, it does not promote arbitrary enforcement of criminal law. If anything, a regional court is also expected to uphold these values.

With an understanding of the tension between these schools, this chapter makes a case for the pragmatist school of thought. It argues that to the extent that the drafters of the Rome Statute contemplated the possibility of other prosecution avenues and strategies beyond strict prosecutions before formal judicial mechanisms of a state, prosecution of crimes before regional entities is permissible, even if not expressly stated in the Rome Statute. Additionally, this view is reflected in the OTP's recent policy on complementarity and cooperation where it argued that '[A]lthough article 17 of the Statute directs its attention to whether a case is being investigating or prosecuted by a State, this does not limit the potential application and operability of the admissibility provisions to other criminal accountability mechanisms capable of satisfying the admissibility requirements set out in the Statute.'[27]

---

24 For reflections on different approaches to interpreting the ICC statute, see L. Sadat & J. Jolly 'Seven Canons of ICC Treaty Interpretation: Making Sense of Article 25's Rorschach Blot' (2014) 27 *Leiden Journal of International Law* 3, 755–788.

25 C. Davidson 'How to Read International Criminal Law: Strict Construction and the Rome Statute of the International Criminal Court' (2017) 91 *St. John's Law Review* 1, Article 3 at 37.

26 *Ibid*, 56–68.

27 ICC-OTP 'DRAFT Policy on Complementarity and Cooperation' September 2023, para. 80.

In the next sub-section, I will examine different principles under international law to argue that prosecution of international crimes in a regional court that is properly constituted is not incompatible with the Rome Statute.

3.2 The Functionalist or Teleological Interpretation of Statutes

Regional complementarity agrees with the overarching function and purpose of the Rome Statute, which is 'to end impunity for mass atrocity crimes'.[28] This teleological approach to interpretation considers the overall function of the law to be interpreted. Assessing the procedural features of an institution cannot be done unless there is some understanding of its goals.[29] In essence, adopting an interpretation that accommodates international crimes prosecution before a regional court may help further the goals of the Rome Statute. After all, accountability for international crimes should not be a matter of exclusive concern to the ICC alone. As Nmehielle puts it, '[no] treaty has an exclusionary character in terms of having totally occupied the field for purposes of treaty-making in an area of human endeavor or international regulation'.[30]

In practical terms, there are ample instances where the ICC may not even be the appropriate or choice forum for prosecuting crimes, especially since many key states are not members.[31] As an example, key members of the UNSC have refused to join the Court. A regional court might be able to fill the gap. A study which does not specifically focus on a regional criminal court found that 'powerful states' are more eager to join regional organizations, than they would a universal one.[32] Another study found that joining judicial regional organizations can promote economic integration.[33] States are likely to be more willing to join a regional criminal court than a universal one. Reasons may include the ability to set the agenda and influence negotiations of

---

28 Mr. James Stewart Deputy Prosecutor of the International Criminal Court 'Transitional Justice in Colombia and the role of the International Criminal Court' 13 May 2015.

29 P. Viebig *Illicitly obtained evidence at the International Criminal Court* (T.M.C Asser Press 2006) 17.

30 V. O. Nmehielle "Saddling' the New African Regional Human Rights Court with International Criminal Jurisdiction: Innovative, Obstructive, Expedient?' (2014) 7 *African Journal of Legal Studies* 7–42 at 24–35.

31 F.K. Tiba 'Regional International Criminal Courts: An Idea Whose Time Has Come?' (2016) 17 *Cardozo Journal of Conflict Resolution* 52, 523.

32 D. Panke & S. Stapel 'Architects of regional regime complexity: states and regional organizations' (2021) *Journal of Contemporary European Studies* 1–18.

33 E. Voeten 'Regional Judicial Institutions and Economic Cooperation: Lessons for Asia?' (2010) *ADB Working Paper Series on Regional Economic Integration*, 2–4.

such organizations.[34] Note, however, that a state's refusal to join the ICC does not preclude the UNSC's power to make a referral as it did in the Darfur situation in 2005 and the Libya situation in 2011,[35] although UNSC members with veto powers may frustrate any attempt by the UNSC to refer a situation that may affect them or their allies to the ICC. In 2014, for example, Russia and China vetoed a UNSC resolution to refer Syria to the ICC.[36] Also, the ICC's jurisdiction is limited to the most serious crimes of genocide, war crimes and crimes against humanity. While these are indeed serious crimes, they are not the only crimes of concern to the international community. Thus, the ICC may not be well-placed to prosecute such other crimes that are of particular concern to different regions of the globe.[37]

Turning to the preamble of the Statute, paragraph 4 provides that 'affirming that the most serious crimes of concern to the international community as a whole must not go unpunished and that their effective prosecution must be ensured by taking measures at the national level and by enhancing international cooperation'. The involvement of regional bodies in crimes prosecution is an example of attempts at 'enhancing international cooperation'. To this end, where cooperative international efforts are geared towards effective prosecution of crimes, such activities not only promote international justice, but also further the goals of the Rome Statute. The sixth recital of the preamble further provides 'that it is the duty of every state to exercise its criminal jurisdiction over those responsible for international crimes'. If a state chooses to exercise such jurisdiction in a case, through 'internationalized trials' at the regional court, it will defeat the purposes of the Statute, as established in the preamble, to argue that such trials do not fit within Article 17 of the Rome Statute.

In a similar sense, if the crimes punishable by the ICC are indeed of concern to the international community as whole, the specific usage of the term 'international community' connotes the inclusion of 'regional communities' within the wider meaning of the term 'international community'. International community implies the aggregate sum of national entities. In the same way, regional communities can be subsumed under that larger term and thus owe a duty to punish international crimes and close the impunity gaps as national entities would, under the principle of complementarity. To

34 Panke & Stapel, (n. 32) 8.

35 Tiba (n. 30) 523.

36 UN Press Release 'Russia, China block Security Council referral of Syria to International Criminal Court' 22 May 2014.

37 Tiba (n. 31) 523.

the extent that such crimes are of concern to the international community (and by extension, regional communities), the duty to prosecute rests with regional communities with the same degree to which it rests with national entities.

Moreover, the purposive or contextual approach to interpretation of legal texts deals with the mischief that the law to be interpreted was meant to cure. If the same question is asked in the context of the Rome Statute, the answer will be found in the preamble, especially paragraph 4 and 6. Thus, if the goal of the Rome Statute is to end impunity by taking measures at the national level, which may involve or include the delegation of such duties by national actors to regional bodies, the purpose of the Statute would have been fulfilled and the world would be edging closer to ending impunity.

Overall therefore, it is necessary to underscore complementarity's potential to create a broader culture of accountability and prevention of mass atrocity crimes.[38] In this regard, this work promotes regional complementarity's broad capacity to hasten the realization of this goal by bringing justice to the victims of international crimes, thus closing the impunity gap.

3.3 The Expanded Interpretation of Statute

In finding further support for regional complementarity, I attempt an expanded and comparative analysis of Articles 17(1)(a) & (c) and 20(3) of the Rome Statute. The analysis here is speculative. The ICC is yet to interpret certain unresolved ambiguities regarding the application of the principle of *ne bis in idem*.[39] The analysis relates to forum and timing of investigation and prosecution. It considers the difference in the formulation of Articles 17(1)(a) and (c) and 20(3).

First, Article 17(1)(a) partly reads that 'the Court shall determine that a case is inadmissible where: (a) The case is being investigated or prosecuted by a State which has jurisdiction over it…'. Article 17(1)(c), however, reads as follows: '[T]he person concerned has already been tried for conduct which is the subject of the complaint, and a trial by the Court is not permitted under Arti-

38 C. Stahn "Taking complementarity seriously: On the sense and sensibility of 'classical', 'positive' and 'negative' complementarity" in C. Stahn & M. El Zeidy (eds) *The International Criminal Court and Complementarity: From Theory to Practice* (Cambridge University Press 2011) 234.

39 For an analysis on the ambiguities around *ne bis in idem* and gravity at the ICC, see M. M deGuzman 'Complementarity at the Africa Court' in C. Jalloh and Ors. (eds) The African Court of Justice and Human and Peoples' Rights in Context: Development and Challenges (CUP 2019) 18–22.

cle 20, paragraph 3.' The first observation as to timing is that while sub (a) refers to a situation where a state is investigating or prosecuting, the operative word is 'being', a present continuous action. Sub (c), however, refers to a situation where a person has already been tried. This implies that perhaps, in the minds of the drafters of the Rome Statute, if the other factors in Article 20 are met, the provisions herein could be interpreted to accommodate a likely situation where ICC jurisdiction may not be barred before a verdict is reached by a court, but may be barred after such court has concluded its proceedings and reached a verdict. This distinction between the investigation and prosecution stage as per sub (a) and the verdict or completion stage as per sub (c) presents the possibility for prosecution before other entities outside of a domestic court (e.g. regional court). What is not in doubt, however, is that Article 17(1) distinguishes between sub (a) and sub (c) to the effect that an ICC jurisdiction can be activated when investigation and prosecution is ongoing as per sub (a) but may be impermissible after a verdict has been reached, as per sub (c). Taking this further, a thorough analysis of Article 17(1)(a) and (c) cannot be done without due reference to Article 20(3) as has been mentioned in sub (c).

Article 20(3) provides that '[N]o person who has been tried by another court for conduct also proscribed under article 6, 7, 8 or 8bis shall be tried by the ICC with respect to the same conduct….' It should be noted here that the Rome Statute employs the use of the term 'another court', without necessarily using the specific term 'National or States', as it did in Article 17(1)(a). This blanket reference to 'another court' may have opened the possibility for wide and plausible creative interpretations that can accommodate the likelihood of a regional court that has been properly constituted.

As such, the Rome Statute itself envisages the likelihood of another court – possibly, a regional court – prosecuting international crimes, which will then render inadmissible the prosecution of the same conduct before the ICC. As per rules of interpretation, the express mention of one thing excludes the other (the principle of *expressio unius exclusio alterius*). The converse is also true. The non-express mention of one thing may not exclude another, not expressly excluded. In this regard, a look at Article 20(3) of the Rome Statute reveals that the Statute here refers to 'another court', without necessarily limiting it to national courts, as found in 17(1)(a). Therefore, it can be argued that the drafters of the Rome Statute might have contemplated an interpretation of the complementarity provisions of the Statute that takes into consideration courts other than national courts, and in this case, a regional court. This creative interpretation notwithstanding, this research places much emphasis on seeing regional courts as projects emerging from the cooperation of states, rather than mechanisms that derive their legitimacy or justification from any expanded interpretation of the Rome Statute.

To conclude, the words of De Sloovere are apt, particularly in relation to interpreting Article 17 to accommodate collective efforts of states to jointly punish international crimes at a regional level. De Sloovere argued that:

> Truly, there may be an obvious meaning, and no other may be apparent even after a careful reading of the statute; but to stop there is only to solve the problem of interpretation by avoiding it… A statute, then, is not fully interpreted until it is shown that the meaning chosen accords with the subject-matter, the statutory purpose and the remaining portions of all statutory texts involved.[40]

A careful contextual interpretation of the word 'states' in Article 17 of the Rome Statute will also accommodate all efforts that are collectively undertaken by states at a regional level to punish international crimes, including through a regional tribunal.

3.4 The Principle of International Delegation

One of the consequences of the proliferation of international organizations is 'the shift in the locus of decision-making on a whole range of governance issues from national governments to international organizations'.[41] This is referred to as the principle of international delegation.[42] The principle is defined as a grant of authority by a state to an entity to make decisions or take actions that bind the state or commit its resources.[43] This grant of authority traditionally empowers the latter to act on behalf of the former; in this instance, the regional organization acting on behalf of the states in question. The principle is not a novelty in international relations,[44] and there is no question that states

40 F. J. De Sloovere 'Contextual Interpretation of Statutes' (1936) 5 *Fordham Law Review* 2, 219.

41 D. Sarooshi 'Some Preliminary Remarks on the Conferral by States of Powers on International Organizations' (2003) *Jean Monnet Working Paper 4/03* at 3.

42 For a general discussion on the principle, see the following: C. Bradley & G. Kelley 'The Concept of International Delegation' (2008) 71 *The law and Politics of International Delegation* 1, 1–36; O.A. Hathaway 'International Delegation and State Sovereignty' (2008) 71 *Law and Contemporary Problems* 115–149 and J. Erne 'Conferral of Powers by States as a Basis of Obligations of International Organizations' (2009) *Nordic Journal of International Law* 1.

43 Bradley & Kelley (n. 42).

44 P. Jessup *A Modern Law of Nations* (Macmillan Publishers 1948).

with primary jurisdiction can indeed delegate jurisdiction to an international organization. What has, however, been a question of debate is the legal effect and limits of such delegation. It is a trite principle which has become common state practice.[45] This delegation is often done through ratification of treaties, as every state possesses the capacity to conclude treaties.[46] The effect of treaty ratification, according to the VCLT, is that states, by virtue of the principle of *pacta sunt servanda*, are bound by their obligations under that treaty.[47]

What is the legal effect of a state's delegation of its criminal jurisdiction to an international tribunal? The legality of states delegating their criminal jurisdiction to one another has been fully established and is not in doubt.[48] Indeed, as stated by Akande, 'the fact that overwhelming majority of states have been prepared to delegate and to accept delegations of jurisdiction…is evidence that states generally take the view that such delegations of jurisdiction are lawful'.[49] In fact, there is almost no state that is not a party to at least one treaty that delegates criminal jurisdiction to another state.[50]

The pertinent question therefore is whether delegating such authority to a regional tribunal would amount to nullity under international law. This is important because once the legal effect of such conferral of powers is shown, then the idea of regional complementarity makes sense as a legal theory. Akande answers this question in the affirmative. Although his focus was on the effect of such delegation of powers to the ICC, especially the jurisdiction over nationals of non-party states, his reasoning is equally applicable to regional tribunals. He noted Morris' divergent view. Morris had argued that 'there are very significant differences in the consequences and implications of ICC jurisdiction as distinct from state jurisdictions [and] that it cannot be said that the option of delegating state's jurisdiction to an international court is an already established feature of customary law of universal or territorial jurisdiction'.[51] Akande disagrees and states that there are reasons to suggest that delegation of national jurisdictions to the ICC is lawful. First, majority of the

45 S. Wallerstein 'Delegation of Powers and Authority in International Criminal Law' (2015) 9 *Criminal Law and Philos* 123–140.

46 Art. 6 of the VCLT.

47 Art. 26 of the VCLT.

48 D. Akande 'The Jurisdiction of International Criminal Court over Nationals of Non-Parties: Legal Basis and Limits' (2003) 1 *Journal of International Criminal Justice* 618–650 at 625–626.

49 *Ibid* at 624.

50 *Ibid.*

51 M. Morris 'The Jurisdiction of the International Criminal Court over Nationals of Non-Party States: Conference Remarks' (2000) 6 *ILSA Journal of International and Comparative Law* 366.

crimes in the ICC statute are offences over which states can exercise universal jurisdiction if the accused is present in their territory. Second, all states are permitted or required to exercise jurisdiction over certain crimes because 'those crimes are deemed to be prejudicial to the interest of the international community as a whole'.[52] Thus, when a state acts in this manner, such state is acting on behalf of the international community. Akande rightly concludes that it will be incoherent to argue that a rule that permits states to act individually will disqualify them from acting collectively in respect of the same crimes, in the absence of a specific rule that disqualifies collective action.[53]

Wallerstein had maintained a position similar to Akande, when he submitted that 'in principle, delegation of power may ground the jurisdictional authority of any international criminal tribunal'.[54] The former was reacting to Luban's argument that the authority of international criminal courts cannot be based on delegated authority.[55] While admitting that it is not in all cases that the principle of delegated powers can be the basis for the jurisdiction of a criminal tribunal, he suggests that two questions must be asked in order to arrive at a proper answer: 'were powers, in fact, delegated to the tribunal? If so, were the delegating states right in delegating their power to punish in the specific case?'[56] He submitted that it is only when the two questions have been affirmatively answered that we can safely base the jurisdiction of a tribunal on delegated powers.[57]

Flowing from this principle of international delegation because of treaty ratification, parties to a treaty establishing a regional mechanism could be said to have delegated their national criminal jurisdiction to such a regional mechanism.

There are, however, other alternative approaches to understanding the principle of international delegation, in relation to the jurisdiction of international criminal mechanisms. Some authors have expressed views that fundamentally challenge the idea that the jurisdiction of an international criminal mechanism flows from the principle of international delegation. One of such is the view as championed by Sadat that 'States "confer upon" or "accept" the jurisdiction of international courts and tribunals like the ICC not to transfer a

52 Akande (2003) 626.
53 *Ibid.*
54 S. Wallerstein (n. 45) 124.
55 See D. Luban Authority and responsibility in international criminal law' in J. Tasioulas & S. Besson (eds) *The Philosophy of International Law* (Oxford University Press 2009).
56 Wallerstein (n. 45) 139.
57 *Ibid.*

subset of their own power to those entities, but because they often want and need those courts and tribunals to do things that they cannot do in their national systems'.[58] The other view, as championed by Frédéric Mégret is the understanding that the two broad views of the ICC as either a court of the world, or one for only the state parties, is insufficient in capturing the court's jurisdictional foundation.[59]

3.5 The Overriding Benefits Approach

There are many benefits of regional prosecution over international or centralized prosecution. Placed side by side with prosecutions at the ICC, prosecution before a regional court has many advantages. These advantages make the theory and practice of regional complementarity a necessity. For one, the ICC's justice is symbolic and often far removed from the victims as it is ensconced in faraway city of the Hague in the Netherlands, while regional efforts figuratively bring justice home.[60] The idea of bringing justice home does not only imply proximity to the geographical location where the crimes occurred. For example, a regional tribunal based, say, in Addis Ababa may not necessarily 'bring justice home' in Lagos or in Bamako. Regional tribunals are not necessarily based in the country most affected. However, the fact that a regional court will most likely be officiated by people of the same region with the defendants and victims may improve the perception of credibility and legitimacy. Also, regional efforts may in themselves enhance positive perception of prosecution of international crimes. This is because justice is seen as being dispensed within the continent, by people of the continent, and may be deemed as a practical local solution to local problems. This echoes the idea behind the call for 'African solutions to African problems'.[61] Again, regional courts are sited in the same continent where the crimes occurred. They are therefore closer to the scenes and perpetrators of crimes and as such may be more suitable for evidence gathering, procuring witnesses, victims and indeed defendants. Lastly, there are less chaos and uncertainties around the applica-

58 L. Sadat 'The Conferred Jurisdiction of the International Criminal Court' (2023) *Washington University in St. Louis Legal Studies Research* Paper No. 23-03-01, 1–63.

59 See F. Mégret 'The International Criminal Court: Between International Ius puniendi and State Delegation' (2020) 23 *Max Planck Yearbook of United Nations Law*, 1–47.

60 O.A. Maunganidze & A. du Plessis 'The ICC and the AU' in C. Stahn (ed) *The Law and Practice of the International Criminal Court* (Oxford Univ. Press 2015) 82.

61 N.C. Ani 'Three Schools of Thought on "African Solutions to African Problems"' (2019) 50 *Journal of Black Studies* 2 135–155.

ble legal systems for crimes prosecution at the regional level, thus enhancing the credibility perception of the entire process.

With support for the theory of regional complementarity, disputes over the application of regional complementarity can be resolved through a contextual interpretation of the Rome Statute and other international law instruments. This is a way to make Rome Statute less strict and to accommodate the prosecution of international crimes in a properly constituted regional tribunal.

In the next section, I will explore five relationship dimensions that are anticipated in the operationalization of regional complementarity.

4 Relationship Dimensions of Regional Complementarity

Complementarity is a tool for organizing the relationship between the ICC and national criminal mechanisms.[62] However, there are other variations in which the concept has been contextualized.[63] Accordingly, complementarity has been observed in the context of the relationship between the *ad hoc* tribunals and their national mechanisms; between hybrid courts and national courts; between regional and/or sub-regional courts and national courts, on the one hand, and also between regional courts and global courts like the ICC, on the other hand; and lastly, complementarity variation in state to state cooperation.[64] My focus is on regional complementarity and the multi-layered dimensions of the relationships that a regional court could have with other courts. A regional court may interact with national mechanisms, sub-regional mechanisms, a hybrid court, other regional mechanisms and universal criminal jurisdiction like the ICC. These levels of interactions reveal either horizontal or vertical hierarchy. For instance, the relationship between a regional court and other regional courts is horizontal in nature. This is without any debate. Also, the relationship between national mechanisms and a regional court is vertical. But the hierarchical nature of the relationship

62 There are several academic works detailing this understanding. For example, see C. Stahn & M. El Zeidy (eds) *The International Criminal Court and Complementarity: From Theory to Practice* (Cambridge University Press 2011). See also J.K. Kleffner 'Complementarity in the Rome Statute and National Jurisdictions' (2008) *Oxford University Press;* ICJ Kenya 'International Criminal Justice: The ICC and Complementarity' (2014) ICJ Kenya ISBN No. 9966-958-70-3.

63 C. Stahn *Fair and Effective Investigation and Prosecution of International Crimes, Inventory and State-of-the-Art: Context, Cluster 1 and Cluster 2* (International Nuremberg Principles Academy 2018).

64 *Ibid.*

between a regional court and the ICC, as well as a regional court and sub-regional courts in a region, is open to debates. In the next sub-section, I will analyse each of these relationships to explore how jurisdictional clashes that arise from competing obligations could be resolved if they were to arise.

4.1 Regional Court and National Courts

The first dimension that regional complementarity entails is the relationship between a regional court and state criminal jurisdictions. This is similar to the relationship envisaged by the classical notion of complementarity in the Rome Statute. To that end, the ICC will only intervene when a state is either unable or unwilling to carry out investigation or prosecution. In the same manner, this dimension implies that the relationship between a regional court and its member states will be governed by complementarity. I am, however, only able to attempt a speculative analysis of this dimension. The reasons are obvious. There is only one region that has made a move towards full regionalism in ICL. Even at that, the regional court is not yet operational. Hence, all analysis relating to complementarity practice can only be futuristic. This is why the Malabo Protocol becomes my reference point in this section.

The actual provisions on complementarity in the protocol are contained in Article 46H. It provides partly that '[T]he jurisdiction of the Court shall be complementary to that of the National Courts….' This hierarchical relationship is vertical in nature. It is like the vertical relationship between the ICC and national courts. The regional court is an 'international' entity in relation to national mechanisms. In this regard, the regional court enjoys 'superiority and a sense of authority' over national mechanisms.[65] This contrasts with the horizontality of the inter-state relationship dimension.[66] The provision of Article 46H of the Malabo Protocol largely replicates Article 17 in the Rome Statute, with minor differences.

4.2 Regional Court and a Similar Regional Court

If another region decides to establish a regional criminal court as the African Union has attempted, what will be the nature of the relationship between these regional courts? Secondly, if these two courts have jurisdiction over a

---

65 F. Mégret 'In Search of the 'Vertical' An Exploration of What Makes International Criminal Tribunals Different (and why)' in Larissa van den Herik & Carsten Stahn (eds.), *Future Perspectives on International Criminal Justice*, (T.M.C. Asser 2010) 5.

66 *Ibid.*

situation, which court will have primacy? The answer to the first question appears straightforward. The hierarchical relationship will be horizontal. It is similar to the relationship that exists between courts of coordinate jurisdictions within a state. Regional practices in the EU offer certain perspectives on which national court will have jurisdiction where more than one national mechanism has competence to prosecute a crime. Certain factors must be assessed to determine which jurisdiction is better placed to prosecute. These factors include territoriality, location of suspects, interest of victims, among others.[67]

4.3 Regional Court and the ICC

The third relationship dimension of regional complementarity is the idea of complementarity between global institutions like the ICC, on the one hand, and regional criminal tribunals, on the other hand. The relationship between these levels of courts presents two possible scenarios. One is a vertical relationship where the ICC is hierarchically superior to the regional court. The second is a horizontal relationship where they relate as equals.[68] These two scenarios have different implications. In a horizontal dimension, it could be argued that the two courts are supranational entities, whose memberships consist of a conglomeration of states.[69] Since there is only one region that has made a move to full regionalism, the AU remains the example for reference. As identified by Du Plessis, one of the limitations inherent in Article 46H of the Malabo Protocol is its complete silence on any possible future relationship between the African Court and the ICC specifically. In his words, 'It is unfathomable that the draft protocol nowhere mentions the ICC'.[70] This lacuna shows that the jurisdictional relationship between the African Court and the ICC is not entirely clear.[71] Unless the Rome Statute or the treaty establishing a regional criminal tribunal specifically provides for a relationship between these two levels of courts, the debate about the nature of their relationship will continue. The underlying assumptions in their relationship should be that the regional tribunal and states are working for a common goal and as such, comparative

67 Eurojust 'Guidelines for Deciding 'Which Jurisdiction Should Prosecute?' (2016).

68 M. du Plessis 'Implications of the AU Decision to Give the African Court Jurisdiction Over International Crimes' (2012) *Institute for Security Studies Paper* 235: 1–14.

69 *Ibid.*

70 *Ibid.*

71 H.G. Van der Wilt 'Complementary Jurisdiction (Article 46H)' in G. Werle & M. Vormbaum (eds) *The African Criminal Court: A Commentary on the Malabo Protocol* (TMC Asser Press 2017).

advantage should be the basis for intervention by any of the mechanisms. Either party should also be willing and ready to offer help and assistance where it is needed.

One practical approach towards resolving a likely conflict in this regard is a textual amendment to the Rome Statute or the instrument establishing the regional mechanism. At this point that the Malabo Protocol has not come into effect, it is not out of place to undertake a review that specifically mentions the ICC and clarifies many aspects of the possible future relationship between the two courts. Additionally, while it is admittedly a herculean task, an amendment of the Rome Statute that adds the phrase 'groups of states acting under a regional arrangement', to the provisions of Article 17 will readily address the challenges posed by a strict interpretation of the text. In that regard, if Article 17(1)(a) is amended to read as follows: 'The case is being investigated or prosecuted by a State (or a group of states acting under a regional arrangement) which has jurisdiction over it…', this would address the challenge of jurisdictional conflict between the ICC and any regional tribunal with an ICL mandate. Also, as noted in chapter 6, the use of MOU on cooperation and to clarify roles between the ICC and states has become a common practice. The use of such soft instruments between a regional mechanism and states, as well as between the ICC and a regional court, could be adopted for similar purposes.

4.4 Regional Courts and Sub-regional Courts

The fourth relationship dimension that regional complementarity connotes is complementarity between a regional court and sub-regional courts within the same region. For the reasons stated earlier, the Malabo Protocol will be the basis for this analysis. The Protocol specifically provides for a relationship between a regional court and sub-regional courts. It says the court will be complementary to national courts and 'the courts of the Regional Economic Communities where specifically provided for by the Communities'. The AU, through the African Economic Community (AEC), officially recognizes eight Regional Economic Communities (RECs).[72] These regional groupings of African states were established 'as the basis for wider African integration, with a

72 These are the Arab Maghreb Union (AMU); the Common Market for Eastern and Southern Africa (COMESA); the Community of Sahel-Saharan States (CEN-SAD); the East African Community (EAC); the Economic Community of Central African States (ECCAS); the Economic Community of West African States (ECOWAS); the Intergovernmental Authority on Development (IGAD); and the Southern African Development Community (SADC). See African Union, 'Regional Economic Communities (RECs)' at https://au.int/en/organs/recs.

view to regional and eventual continental integration'.[73] Some of these RECs possess active judicial organs known as courts or tribunals. ECOWAS has a court, while SADC has a tribunal. The challenge that these judicial organs of the RECs pose is that they not only interpret the African Charter, as the African court, they also 'constitute the overlapping regimes that contend and contest with the African Court for authority in the field of human rights'.[74] This then explains why the Malabo Protocol specifically created a complementary relationship between them and the African court. In fact, as noted by Ebobrah, the RECs judicial organs 'represent some of the greatest danger to the unity and coherence of Africa's international human rights law'.[75] Importantly, they could serve as transitional justice mechanisms.[76] As of today, none of the judicial organs of the RECs has explicit provision on complementarity between them and the African court. More importantly, none has a criminal jurisdiction. But that may also happen, seeing that the African court, which hitherto had no such jurisdiction, now has same. If that were to happen, it would add to the existing confusion on what the relationship should look like. But then, the same arguments that have been advanced for operationalizing the relationship between the ICC and the African court may be applied in the case of the African court and RECs.

Article 46H of the Protocol strongly suggests that 'the African Court can accept a case, not only after the national court of an indicted person has proved "unwilling" or "unable" to prosecute, but also after a REC court that has jurisdiction has also failed to prosecute that person'.[77] This twin-layered complementarity provision is innovative but also presents multiple challenges. The complexities that are involved in an analysis on whether a state is unable and/or unwilling become double where the regional court must conduct the same analysis for a state as well as a sub-regional court. Also, as Kamari Clarke and others have noted,[78] many states in Africa belong to multiple RECs, so it implies that the 'unwilling' and 'unable' analysis would need to

73 S. Ebobrah 'Complementarity between the African Court and the judicial organs of Regional Economic Communities in Africa' in *PALU Guide to Complementarity within the African Human Rights System* (PALU 2014) 52.

74 *Ibid.*

75 *Ibid.*

76 A. Heinrich 'Sub-Regional Courts as Transitional Justice Mechanisms: The Case of the East African Court of Justice in Burundi' in J. T. Gathi (ed) *The Performance of Africa's International Courts: Using Litigation for Political, Legal, and Social Change* (Oxford University Press 2021) 88–105.

77 K. Clarke & ors 'Introduction' in C. Jalloh & ors 'The African Court of Justice and Human and Peoples' Rights in Context: Development and Challenges' (CUP 2019) 47.

78 *Ibid.*

be done in respect of many RECs that a defendant's state belongs to. This, undoubtedly, is a herculean task and its operationalization remains in the realm of imagination.

As I have earlier argued while discussing the relationship between regional courts and the ICC, the relationship between a regional and sub-regional court also presents two possible scenarios. One is a vertical relationship where the regional court is hierarchically superior to the sub-regional court. The second is a horizontal relationship where they relate as equals. Again, the two scenarios have different implications. In a horizontal dimension, it could be argued that the two courts are supranational entities, whose memberships consist of a conglomeration of states.

4.5 Regional Courts and Hybrid Tribunals: The Case of the SCCCAR

The fifth relationship dimension that regional complementarity connotes is complementarity between a regional court and a hybrid tribunal. Current practices suggest that despite the existence of the ICC, and the move towards regionalism in ICL, the establishment of hybrid tribunals to try atrocities associated with specific conflicts continues. In fact, regions that are moving towards full ICL regionalization are also involved in the project of establishing hybrid tribunals to address specific contexts. It is therefore not impossible that a hybrid tribunal could exist alongside the national mechanism, in a country that is a state party to both the ICC and a regional criminal court. We could even add a state's membership of a sub-regional court to the mix. The relationship between such hybrid tribunal and the regional court will depend on a proper analysis of the enabling instrument of both courts. The current example of a situation like this is the hybrid court in the Central African Republic – The Special Criminal Court in the Central African Republic (SCCCAR).

The SCCCAR is the first hybrid tribunal to have been established in a country where the ICC is also investigating international crimes. The tribunal was established to try crimes that were committed in the context of the political violence that engulfed the CAR from 2011 to 2014. Like the ECCC that was earlier discussed, it was established by domestic legislation (organic law) and embedded into the domestic system of CAR. It applies national and international laws. It will prosecute national and international crimes. It has a mixture of local and international staff and judges. It held its inaugural session in 2018. Stahn submits that its establishment shows that an ICC involvement in a situation cannot sufficiently deal with accountability dilemmas.[79] Its

79 C. Stahn *A Critical Introduction to International Criminal Law* (OUP 2019) 208.

establishment also grounds the argument that the ICC cannot sufficiently respond to all the justice needs arising in the world. Hence, the need for other accountability measures like regional criminal courts.

In May 2014, the CAR government made a self-referral to the ICC. In September 2014, the OTP opened an investigation. The ICC has made three arrests since investigation was opened.[80] The organic law establishing the SCCCAR provides for a relationship between the ICC and the tribunal. While the SCCCAR enjoys primacy over national courts, the ICC enjoys primacy over the SCCCAR.[81] Authors like Labuda have criticized this provision as contradicting ICC's complementarity regime and incompatible with international law.[82] I agree with this submission. Article 41 of the SCCCAR's rules of procedure and evidence requires that the SCCCAR Prosecutor should, 'in the interests of efficiency and judicial economy, consult, as much as possible, [with] the Prosecutor of the ICC regarding the implementation of his investigation and prosecution strategy'.

The nature of the relationship between a hybrid tribunal and a regional court will depend largely on the hybrid or regional court's enabling laws. Where there is a specific provision in that regard, the law would be interpreted accordingly. Where the law is silent, a creative interpretation would be made. The picture is clearer for hybrids which form part of the domestic system. Their relationship to a regional court would be vertical, in the same manner that the domestic system interacts with the regional court. However, in the case of the SCCCAR, the relationship between the ICC and the tribunal is also vertical. Verticality should not always imply superiority. The superior may defer to the other party. For instance, the OTP had envisaged a future relationship with hybrids when it stated that it would defer to investigations and prosecutions if carried out genuinely by a hybrid tribunal, in the same way it defers to states.[83] How this plays out in practice is a different matter altogether.

80 J. Elderfield 'The Rise and Rise of the Special Criminal Court (Part II)', *Opinio Juris*, 4 July 2021 [available at, https://opiniojuris.org/2021/04/07/the-rise-and-rise-of-the-special-criminal-court-part-ii/ – accessed on 10 May 2023].

81 Section 37 of the Organic Law.

82 P. Labuda 'The Special Criminal Court in the Central African Republic: Failure or Vindication of Complementarity?' (2017) 15 *Journal of International Criminal Justice*, 175–206, 192.

83 ICC-OTP 'Informal expert paper: The principle of complementarity in practice' (2003) 5.

4.6 Concurrent Jurisdictions

If three or more of the courts I have discussed have concurrent jurisdiction over a situation, how will such jurisdictional clash be resolved? One possible example is SCCCAR. Imagine that the ICC, the national court, the SCCCAR and a regional court all have jurisdiction over a particular situation, the question as to who should prosecute does not lend itself to an easy answer. This analysis is futuristic, but it is nonetheless important as its likelihood cannot be overlooked. In the case of the ICC, the national court, and the hybrid, the analysis in the sub-section above suggests that the ICC will have primacy because of Section 37 of the Organic Law. Even though this position is flawed under international law, it remains the position of the law insofar as the relationship between the ICC, SSSCR and the national court in CAR is concerned. In a situation where a regional court is added to the mix, a creative interpretation suggests that the national court will still have primacy. This is because complementarity, properly interpreted, places an obligation on the international court – or a regional court – to defer to a national jurisdiction that is genuinely investigating or prosecuting. This, however, depends on the mechanism that is entertaining a challenge to jurisdiction. If the ICC is entertaining the case, it will be bound by the Rome Statute and not the laws establishing the regional court or the tribunal. The same is true for any of these courts. The submission here is therefore that a proper interpretation of the complementarity regime – as we have it both in the ICC statute and Malabo Protocol (our regional reference document) – invests in national mechanisms the primary duty to prosecute international crimes in their domain. Unless, of course, there is unwillingness or inability on the part of a national mechanism. A fuller discussion on resolving jurisdictional clashes has been made in Chapter 8 of this book.

5 Conclusion

This chapter has argued that a more strategic interpretation of Article 17 of the Rome Statute will accommodate regional complementarity. This view contrasts with the position of scholars who argued that prosecution of a case before a regional court [the African Court] would not bar the ICC from prosecuting, simply because Article 17 specifically refers to 'states' *strictu sensu*. From an analysis of a few provisions in the Rome Statute as well as other international treaties like the VCLT, I propose and find support for the theory of regional complementarity. In explaining the need for theories, Wright notes that understanding a phenomenon requires the construction of a theory.[84] She argues that theories are the basis for 'predicting, manipulating, controlling and counteracting the phenomenon', as well as 'relating the phenomenon to other phenomena'.[85] Theories are used to make sense of certain complexities in knowledge.[86] They also help scholars to climb the 'ladder of abstraction'.[87] In this chapter, I related the notion of regional complementarity with other existing notions of complementarity, in order to simplify the strands of that notion. I looked through existing theories on complementarity and I conclude that a golden thread runs through them. This golden thread is the idea that the intention of the drafters of the Rome Statute is for a limited role for the ICC in international crimes prosecution. This has been expressed as the ICC's place as a court of last resort. The notion of regional complementarity also lends credence to this golden thread. It promotes the idea that states have the primary duty to prosecute crimes, whether international or otherwise. It goes a step further to assert that if states choose to do this through international cooperation at a regional level, the ICC should consider a genuine action before such a regional tribunal sufficient to preclude admissibility of cases before the ICC. The argument is that this promotes the overall goals of the Statute. In this chapter, I assume that the regional tribunal in question is validly established and properly constituted. Also, that the crimes and conduct being investigated or prosecuted are those that are seen to be 'international crimes' in line with the statutes or the enabling acts of the tribunal and lastly, that a prima facie case has been established against the defendants such that the preliminary question of whether the accused persons ought to be tried or

84 The term 'constructivism' was coined by Emeritus Professor Nicholas Greenwood Onuf in his 1989 book titled World of Our Making. Constructivism is a system of concepts and proposition and '[it] makes it feasible to theorize about matters that seem to be unrelated…' See N.G. Onuf *Making Sense, Making Worlds: Constructivism in social theory and international relations* (Routledge 2013) 3.

85 B.D. Wright 'Theory construction from empirical observations' (1994) 8 *Rasch Measurement Transactions* 2.

86 J.N. Rosenau & M. Durfee *Thinking theory thoroughly: coherent approaches to an incoherent world* (Boulder, CO, Oxford: Westview 1995) 1–218.

87 The Ladder of Abstraction is itself a theory that was created by S.I Hayakawa in his 1941 book titled 'Language in Action'. As explained by Paul Achar, '[A] ladder presents the perfect imagery for this concept. Like the ladder rests on solid ground, the bottom of the ladder of abstraction represents concrete things or ideas. The Middle of the ladder represents things or an idea that not entirely concrete, and yet not completely abstract, while the top of the ladder represents abstract ideas or concepts.' See P. Achar 'Understanding the Ladder of Abstraction and its Application in Communication' (15 June 2016) [available at https://paulachar.wordpress.com/2016/06/15/understanding-the-ladder-of-abstraction-and-its-application-in-communication/ – accessed on 12 January 2023].

not does not arise. My notion of regional complementarity implies that if a regional judicial mechanism is prosecuting or investigating a particular crime within the jurisdiction of the ICC, the ICC ought to find the prosecution of the suspect's case inadmissible, *in so far* as the regional mechanism displays genuine will and ability to properly investigate and prosecute the same case.

In the second part of the chapter, I have analysed five relationship dimensions that regional complementarity entails. I show that a future regional criminal mechanism will probably need to interact with domestic courts, subregional courts, other regional courts, hybrid tribunals and, lastly, the ICC. The hierarchical nature of the interaction between these multiple layers of courts reveals both horizontal and vertical relationships. I show that in an instance where all the levels of court have competent jurisdiction over the same situation, an analysis of the enabling acts of the competing institutions will offer guidance. In the case of the SCCCAR, I establish that a proper interpretation of complementarity of both the ICC and the Malabo Protocol invests primary jurisdiction on the national mechanism.

CHAPTER 8

Resolving Challenges to the Application of Regional Complementarity: The ICC and the African Criminal Chamber

1 Introduction

This chapter provides cross-cutting analysis by synthesizing normative insights from previous chapters, especially with information on specific institutions. It analyses normative and procedural challenges in the practical application of regional complementarity. The goal is to meet specific objectives of each case study by discussing real or perceived legal challenges that have arisen or may arise in the attempt to operationalize regional complementarity. It examines the institutions discussed in chapters 4 and 5 to draw lessons that may be learnt from institutions that have completed their assignments, like the Habré court, and offer lessons to 'future' institutions like the Criminal Chamber of the African Court. While chapter 8 focuses exclusively on the ICC and the Criminal Chamber of the African court, the proposals for resolving conflicts are applicable between the ICC and any regional tribunal with an ICL mandate.

2 Jurisdictional Overlap and Competing Obligations between the ICC and the ACC

Soon after the Malabo Protocol was adopted, one of the issues that attracted wide criticism was the complete silence of the protocol on any possible relationship between the African Criminal Chamber that the Malabo Protocol seeks to establish and the ICC which had pre-existed the former. The silence was shocking, considering that the earlier draft of the protocol mentioned the ICC but was later deleted.[1] The following section creates hypothetical but possible challenges that may be encountered in the attempt to activate and operationalize regional complementarity.

1 See K. Clarke and ors., 'Introduction' in C. Jalloh & ors (eds) *The African Court of Justice and Human and Peoples' Rights in Context: Development and Challenges* (OUP 2019) 46.

© 2026 THE AUTHOR(S) | HTTPS://DOI.ORG/10.1163/9789004761803-010

In the introduction to this work, I had established that membership of multiple international organizations may birth a situation of conflicting obligations and jurisdictional overlap.[2] This has been seen in the context of the AU-ICC relationship when the AU instructed its members not to cooperate with the ICC in the execution of the arrest warrant against Omar Bashir, the former President of Sudan. The AU decision was in clear violation of ICC member states obligation in Article 87 of the Rome Statute. The PTC of the ICC emphasized this point when it ruled against South Africa for its failure to arrest Al-Bashir, in violation of its obligation under the Rome Statute. The court found 'that South Africa failed to comply with its obligations by not arresting and surrendering Omar Al-Bashir to the Court while he was on South African territory between 13 and 15 June 2015'.[3] This is irrespective of the fact that the AU decision was also binding on member states.[4]

Thus, one of the most contentious issues that may yet emerge from the mutual existence of both the ICC and the international criminal chamber of the ACJHPR is jurisdictional overlap and competing obligations. Jackson stated it more concisely when he opined that '[I]n the (probable) long-life of the ICC, the rise of overlapping regional tribunals should be expected.'[5] Philippa Webb also argued that the possibility of jurisdictional overlap between international courts is no longer hypothetical and deserves critical examination.[6] According to Huneeus:

> ...from six international courts in 1985, today there are roughly two dozen international courts adjudicating disputes between states... As these courts proliferate and their memberships grow, their work increasingly overlaps with greater frequency they find themselves interacting with the same actors and institutions over the same policy areas.[7]

2 *Ibid.*

3 ICC 'Al-Bashir case: ICC Pre-Trial Chamber II decides not to refer South Africa's non-cooperation to the ASP or the UNSC', 6 July 2017.

4 On the binding nature of the AU decision, see M. Du Plessis & C. Gevers 'Balancing Competing Obligations: The Rome Statute and AU Decisions' (2011) *ISS Paper* 225 where the authors argued that judging by Article 23 of the AU Constitutive Act and the contextual reading of the entire act, in addition to the doctrine of implied powers, it is clear that the AU decision to its members not to cooperate with the ICC was a binding obligation.

5 M. Jackson 'Regional Complementarity: The Rome Statute and Public International Law' (2016) 14 *Journal of International Criminal Justice* 1061–1072 at 1062.

6 P. Webb 'Scenarios of jurisdictional overlap among international courts' (2006) 19 *Revue quebecoise de droit international* 2, 277.

7 A. Huneeus 'Legitimacy and Jurisdictional Overlap: The ICC and the Inter-American Court in Colombia' in N. Grossman & Ors (eds) *Legitimacy and International Courts* (Cambridge University Press 2018) 114.

One of the major reasons for this is because international tribunals operate independently of themselves. As Webb puts it, 'there are no rules on what should happen when more than one court has jurisdiction over the same conflict…or how one court should treat the decisions of another court'.[8] In the case of the ACC and the ICC, the likelihood is real considering that many African member states of the ICC are also potential parties to the Malabo Protocol. The converse is also possible in theory. Some state parties to the ACC will also be state parties to the Rome Statute. There is therefore a higher likelihood that both the ICC and the ACC may deal with issues involving the same persons or conducts.

However, the likelihood of overlapping jurisdiction is reduced since the ICC and the ACC only have similar jurisdictions on the core crimes, while the latter has other crimes within the Malabo Protocol over which the ICC does not have jurisdiction. Secondly, the possibility of jurisdictional overlap is reduced in relation to the category of perpetrators that both courts can try. The ICC is interested in perpetrators of the most serious crimes. An OTP policy paper[9] further clarified that 'the office of the Prosecutor should focus its investigative and prosecutorial efforts and resources on those who *bear the greatest responsibility*, such as the leaders of the state or organization allegedly responsible for those crimes'.[10] Further, Article 27 of the Rome Statute specifically provides that official capacity of a suspect or defendant shall not bar the court from exercising its jurisdiction. This is perhaps why the jurisprudence of the ICC has shown a consistent pattern of focusing on the 'most senior leaders suspected of being the most responsible for the crimes within the jurisdiction of the court'.[11] Conversely, the Malabo Protocol confers immunity on heads of states and governments in Article 46Abis and withdraws immunity for all crimes in the protocol from defendants who are not heads of states or governments, as per Article 46B (2). This is in addition to the fact that the ICC confers jurisdiction on the court to pursue only natural persons, while the Malabo Protocol empowers the court to proceed against natural and legal persons, as per Article 46C. Thus, it appears that the two instruments are focused on different classes of perpetrators, thus further reducing the possibility of juris-

8 Webb (n. 6) 278.

9 ICC OTP 'Paper on Some Policy Issues before the Office of the Prosecutor' (2003).

10 *Ibid.*

11 Prosecutor v. Dyilo, Case No. ICC-01/04-01/06, Decision Concerning Pre-Trial Chamber I's Decision of 10 February 2006 and the Incorporation of Documents into the Record of the Case against Mr. Thomas Lubanga Dyilo (24 February 2006), para. 50.

dictional clash.[12] As I had noted earlier, 'the mode of responsibility in the Malabo Protocol clearly catches in its net all sorts of low-level defendants who may have incited, instigated, organized, directed, facilitated, financed, counselled or participated as a principal, co-principal, agent or accomplice…, [who] aid or abet the commission of any of the offences in the protocol'.[13]

Despite this, there remain several possible scenarios where jurisdictional clashes may occur. The first is if the Peace and Security Council (PSC) of the AU and the UNSC refer same issues to both the ACC and the ICC simultaneously. The second scenario is where the two courts indict the same person and perhaps, order his or her arrest and surrender. These possibilities are further enhanced given that the drafters of the Rome Statute did not mention or contemplate regional criminal courts in the statute's provisions. I have also earlier noted the silence of the Malabo Protocol, in relation to the ICC.

In a general sense, jurisdictional overlap may give rise to different types of conflicts. One, where more than one court has jurisdiction over the same matter, a conflict that may lead to inaction from one or both courts may arise in the circumstance. An example was the theatrics that attended the attempt to prosecute Hissène Habré by both Senegal and Belgium. This led to more than a decade stalemate before his eventual prosecution in Senegal, through the AU established Extraordinary Chamber.[14] This is therefore a classic example of harms that international criminal justice may suffer if issues of jurisdictional overlap are not promptly attended to.

Another conflict that may engender jurisdictional overlap is what Higgins called 'competition of norms'.[15] This is when the body of substantive laws of two international courts differ in material terms. In this regard, the ICC and the ACC do not codify the same crimes; the ACC has an extensive catalogue of crimes, compared to the ICC. One common example of this competition of norms is instances where a country's criminal code may be different from the international criminal law that it is bound to enforce as a result of ratifying a treaty.

Where there is no competition of norms, a third kind of conflict could arise where international courts interpret same normative provisions differently.

12 See Z.B Abebe 'The African Court with a Criminal Jurisdiction and the ICC: A Case for Overlapping Jurisdiction?' (2017) 25 *African Journal of International and Comparative Law* 3, 418–429.

13 Article 28N of the Malabo Protocol.

14 See 'Concurrent Jurisdiction' at https://www.brandeis.edu/ethics/pdfs/internationaljustice/biij/Con_Juris_2012.pdf.

15 R. Higgins 'A Babel of Judicial Voices? Ruminations from the Bench' (2003) 55 *International and Comparative Law Quarterly* 4, 791–804.

Higgins had pointed out the example of the ICJ and the ICTY where the former in the Nicaragua vs. USA case had adopted the 'effective control' test, as against the latter's adoption of the 'overall control' test in the Tadić case.[16] In analysing similar normative provisions, the two courts had different interpretations.[17]

2.1 Addressing Jurisdictional Overlap and Competing Obligations

Many suggestions have been made on how to reduce the likelihood of jurisdictional overlap between the ICC and the ACC. Some authors[18] have suggested that it is better for the ACC to focus on cases bordering on the novel crimes contained in its protocol while referring any cases concerning the core crimes to the ICC. This is, however, not as simple as it sounds. Many of the situations before international criminal tribunals will contain a basket-mix of subject matter jurisdictional issues. As such, a case of genocide may have the crimes of corruption and unconstitutional change of government as undergirding crimes, in a manner that becomes difficult to separate them as one crime leads to the commission of another. Where this happens and these crimes are committed as part of the same chain of events, how possible is it that some crimes be prosecuted at the ICC while the others be tried at the ACC, for example?

Thus, from the totality of previous submissions by scholars, a few approaches could be adopted to resolve or reduce the likelihood of jurisdictional clash or overlap between the ICC and the ACC.

For cases that border on the novel crimes contained in the Malabo Protocol, I hold that it is indeed practicable to ensure that such cases are handled only by the ACC while the ICC focuses on the core crimes. This can be achieved through an agreement between the two courts that recognizes the possibility of transfer of cases between them. Similar relationship already exists between the ICTY and ICTR, on the one hand, and national mecha-

16 On the control tests, see A. Cassese 'The Nicaragua and Tadić Tests Revisited in Light of the ICJ Judgment on Genocide in Bosnia' (2007) 18 *European Journal of International Law* 4, 649–668; see also S. Talmon 'The Various Control Tests in the Law of State Responsibility and the Responsibility of Outside Powers for Acts of Secessionist Entities' (2009) 58 *International and Comparative Law Quarterly*.

17 R. Higgins (n. 15).

18 For example, see N. Boister 'Transnational Crimes Jurisdiction of the Criminal Chamber of the African Court of Justice and Human and Peoples' Rights' in C. Jalloh & ors (eds) *The African Court of Justice and Human and Peoples' Rights in Context: Development and Challenges* (OUP 2019) 336–361.

nisms, on the other hand. Except amendment is made to either the Malabo Protocol or the Rome Statute, there is currently no legal basis for transfer of cases between the ICC and the ACC. This could, however, be achieved through other means – either by MOU or the conclusion of other procedural agreements.

On the practical side, the analysis on whether a case revolves around any of the novel crimes in the Malabo Protocol is a determination that the pre-trial chamber of the ACC can make at the preliminary stages of any proceeding. This, however, implies that a regime of partnership must exist between these two courts to achieve positive cooperation that allows for case transfer and knowledge sharing. A regime of partnership and cooperation will not preclude any of the two courts from trying a case, where they both have jurisdictions, but one is more suitable than the other for the purposes of prosecution. Many factors could guide suitability: proximity to the location of crimes for the purpose of investigation and evidence-gathering; availability of resources; richness of the jurisprudence as well as legitimacy that the tribunal enjoys with victims, witnesses and, indeed, the defendants. Both tribunals must understand that in most instances, they are working towards complementary ('improved human rights on the ground') and same ('fostering domestic investigation and punishment of atrocity crimes') goals and that oftentimes, they could work as one court – where the ACC's goals are enforced through ICC means and vice versa.[19]

In other ways, Higgins had argued that 'creating an institutional hierarchy'; 'establishing a hierarchy of international norms'; and 'developing a respect for and use of other courts' judgments to promote consistency' are means through which international courts can avoid jurisdictional overlap.[20] How these measures will be operationalized in the context of the relationship between the ACC and the ICC is yet to be seen. But it is necessary to point out that the emerging relationship between the ICC and the ACC needs to be well thought out, to avoid this anticipated jurisdictional overlap. In previous chapters, I had argued for more subtle and pragmatic concepts that emphasize cooperation, as against hierarchical competition.

The bulk of the duty lies with state parties to the Malabo Protocol, especially those who are also parties to the Rome Statute. For them, avoiding conflict in substantive laws needs to happen on many levels. First, they must avoid conflict between their domestic criminal law, and both the ICC statute as well as the Malabo Protocol. It then implies that meticulous comparison

19 See A. Huneeus (n. 7).
20 R. Higgins (n. 15).

between their domestic laws and these international statutes, to avoid inconsistencies, is an exercise that needs to precede ratifying any international statute. The other approach is to amend local laws to come in conformity with international standards. This is what Senegal did, when it was preparing to try Hissène Habré. A third approach, which has been seen across many nations, is making international treaties a part of the domestic laws, through for example, domestication acts by the law-making organ of each state. There is nothing novel about this, but it is also one approach through which many states have been able to reduce inconsistency that could birth jurisdiction overlap and competing obligations.

However, in a hypothetical situation in which the ACC must take a decision on an issue that is 'settled law' as per previous ICC decision, what would be the proper approach? In other words, if the ICC had previously rendered a decision on a similar issue that now confronts the ACC, how much of reliance can the ACC put on the previous ICC decision, or put more clearly, will the ACC be bound to follow a previous decision of the ICC, if the former finds itself in a similar situation. As simple as this seems, it is slightly more difficult because, the ICC, has in the past, maintained different positions on the same issue.[21]

In responding to a similar situation, Webb had developed a two-question test where she asked the following: 'has international criminal law evolved between the moment when the ICTY began to render decisions and the establishment of the ICC'; and secondly, 'should the ICC be given a priority position, considering the fact that it is the general jurisdictional body in international criminal law'.[22] While her analysis was focused on the ICTY and the ICC, mine will be focused on the ACC and the ICC. The proper starting point would be the applicable law of the ACC. Thus, Article 31 of the Protocol on the Statute of the African Court of Justice and Human Rights, which is the substantive instrument that the Malabo Protocol purports to amend and complement, provides as follows:

> In carrying out its functions, the Court shall have regard to: a) The Constitutive Act; b) International treaties, whether general or particular, ratified by the contesting states; c) International custom, as evidence of a general practice

21 See, for example, ICC's reference to the decision of ICTY and ICTR in many cases, while on at least one occasion, the PTC reprimanded the OTP for relying on case law of ICTR and ICTY in its submission on the Uganda redaction issue. See ICC Doc: ICC-02/04-01/05, Decision on the Prosecutor's Position on the Decision of Pretrial Chamber II to Redact Factual Descriptions of Crimes from the Warrants of Arrest, Motion for Reconsideration, and Motion for Clarification, para. 19.

22 P. Webb (n. 6) 282.

> accepted by law; d) The general principles of law recognised universally or by Africa States; e)…Judicial decisions; writings of publicists…; f) Any other law relevant to the determination of the case.

While this provision lists a few sources, it does not provide a hierarchy which the court must follow in their application. Unlike the Rome Statute, where a similar provision on 'applicable law' provides the order in which the court may consider the sources of law. For example, the Rome Statute says the ICC can apply, 'in the first place…'. Also, this provision, unlike the Rome Statute, empowers the court to consider the decisions of other 'courts', albeit 'as subsidiary means for determining the rules of law'. This mirrors a similar provision in Article 38(1)(d) of the Statute of the ICJ. This provision of the protocol therefore suggests that the ACC can adopt a previous decision by the ICC. For the ICC, seeing that the Rome Statute is silent on whether the court can consider the decision of other international courts, it is unlikely that the ICC will consider a decision by the ACC. Although, it must be noted that the ICC jurisprudence has shown reference to decisions of other international tribunals, while at other times, it refused to do so.[23]

In conclusion, it is fair to assume that once the ACC becomes functional, it will increasingly look to the jurisprudence of the ICC to draw inspiration, given the provisions relating to its applicable laws. Also, given ICC's place as 'the general jurisdictional body in international criminal law', it will not be out of place for the ACC to treat its jurisprudence with some measure of respect and I conclude that the ACC will be careful to depart from the well-settled positions of law that had earlier been arrived at by the ICC. If a regime of partnership and cooperation that I had earlier advocated is adhered to, exchange of information and regular inter-court dialogue could also reduce the likelihood of departure from well laid down principles of law.

2.2 Complementarity: The ACC and the ICC

Like the Rome Statute, the protocol provides that the relationship between the African court and its member states will be governed by complementarity. But this section can only attempt a speculative analysis of the complementarity provisions in the protocol. The reasons are obvious: The African court is not yet operational. Hence, all analysis relating to complementarity practice can only be futuristic. Theoretically, however, complementarity in the protocol is generally aimed at strengthening cooperation between various organi-

23 *Ibid.*

zations, for the purpose of furthering the goals of human rights promotion and protection on the African continent.[24] In this regard, the protocol mentions complementarity or related terms in a few provisions beginning with the preamble. It alludes to the complementary nature of the relationship between the African Commission on Human and Peoples' Rights and the African Court on Human and Peoples' Rights, which will, by virtue of this protocol, translate to the African Court of Justice, Human and Peoples' Rights. Also, the protocol reveals the intention of African countries to ensure a complementary regime between 'national, regional and continental bodies and institutions in preventing serious and massive violations of human and peoples' rights…'. Further, the protocol provides in Article 4 that the African court will complement the protective mandate of the African Commission. This mandate is as set out in Article 45 of the African Charter on Human and Peoples' Rights.

The actual provisions on complementarity in the protocol are contained in Article 46H. It provides partly that '[T]he jurisdiction of the Court shall be complementary to that of the National Courts, and to the Courts of the Regional Economic Communities where specifically provided for by the Communities.' The provision largely replicates Article 17 in the Rome Statute. The similarities between the complementarity provisions in the two instruments have necessitated a question on whether the African court will observe the same threshold of admissibility, in its relationship with state parties to the Malabo Protocol, as the ICC.[25] To answer that question, I wish to stress that there are several differences between the complementarity provisions in the two instruments. These differences therefore suggest that the admissibility threshold and probable interpretation of the complementarity provisions in the two instruments may not be the same.

2.2.1 Differences between the Complementarity Provisions of the Malabo Protocol and the Rome Statute

One major difference between the two instruments is that the African court as per 46H (1) is complementary to national courts as well as courts of the Regional Economic Communities (RECs) while the ICC is *only* complementary to national courts.[26] In practical terms, however, it does not appear that

24 M. deGuzman 'Complementarity at the African Court' in K. Clarke & C. Jalloh (eds) *The African Court of Justice and Human and Peoples' Rights* (CUP 2019).

25 H.G. Van der Wilt 'Complementary Jurisdiction (Article 46H)' in G. Werle and M. Vormbaum (eds.) *The African Criminal Court: A Commentary on the Malabo Protocol* (TMC Asser 2017) at 191.

26 *Ibid.*

there is any significant disagreement between the Rome Statute and this protocol, on this issue. This is because, while Article 46H (1) provides that the African Court shall be complementary to both national courts and the courts of the RECs, the rest of the Article only provides that the African court will defer to investigations and prosecutions by 'a State which has jurisdiction over it', similar to the complementarity nature of the relationship between the ICC and national courts. There is no mention of investigation or prosecution by RECs. There could be many explanations for this omission.

The first is that the drafters probably envisaged that an investigation or prosecution by the REC is already an action of a state done through the REC, by virtue of the principle of delegated authority.[27] Secondly, it could be the result of a 'careless replication' of the Rome Statute that fails to tie all the loose ends. A third explanation is that paragraphs 2 and 3 may have intentionally excluded RECs and the provision may only apply to situations where states and states alone are investigating or prosecuting a case that is before the African court. The import of this is that the judges of the African court will need identify and apply other rules of complementarity where a case before the court is being investigated or prosecuted by the RECs.[28]

Irrespective of what the explanation is, this complementarity provision in the protocol gives due recognition to the progressive roles that some of the courts of the RECs in Africa have played. For instance, the ECOWAS court has been hailed as the most progressive sub-regional human rights court in Africa.[29] It has recognized continuing violations and also held that no time limits can bar human rights complaints.[30] It has also done away with the requirement for exhausting local remedies before complaints of rights violations can be brought before the court.[31] These are in sharp contrasts with the

---

27 See Chapter 6 of this book for a full discussion of the principle of delegated authority, as it relates to prosecution of international crimes by supranational bodies.

28 M. deGuzman (n. 24).

29 For a general understanding of its role as a human rights promoter in the sub-region, see S. H. Adjolohoun 'The ECOWAS Court as a Human Rights Promoter? Assessing Five Years Impact of the Koraou Slavery Judgment' (2013) 31 *Netherlands Quarterly of Human Rights* 3, 342–371.

30 In *The Federation of African Journalists (FAJ) and others Vs. The Gambia*, Suit No: ECW/CCJ/AP/36/15, the Court maintained a most progressive position by holding that a claim for enforcement of human rights by nationals of Member States cannot be barred by the three-year limitation stated in the Court's Supplementary Protocol.

31 The ECOWAS Court held in *Ocean King Nigeria Ltd v. Republic of Senegal*, Suit No: ECW/CCJ/AP/05/08 that 'the exhaustion of local remedies is not a condition precedent for the institution of an action for the relief of violation of human rights before [this Court]'. In the case of *Hadijatou Mani Koraou v. Niger*, Suit No: ECW/CCJ/APP/08/08,

jurisprudence of the African Commission on Human and People's Rights, which has upheld that time limits can bar human rights complaints, and strictly requires the exhaustion of local remedies.[32]

Another notable difference between the complementarity provisions of the two instruments is that while the Rome Statute provides that the ICC would have no jurisdiction in a case that is being investigated or prosecuted by a state with jurisdiction, unless the state is unwilling or unable to 'genuinely' investigate or prosecute, the AU's protocol omits the word 'genuinely'. It has been suggested that the omission was because African leaders were 'reluctant to grant the African court the power to evaluate the genuineness of their states' criminal proceedings'.[33] The opposition of African leaders to the ICC on the issues of immunity of heads of states and the application of universal jurisdiction may have lent credence to this suggestion of reluctance.

Whatever the rationale, this omission renders it difficult if not impossible, for any proceeding to be taken over by the African court, irrespective of the genuineness or otherwise, of the proceeding at the state level. It leaves a lot of room for shielding suspects and defeating the ends of justice through shoddy and non-genuine investigation and prosecution at the national level. This was the mischief that the drafters of the Rome Statute had intended to cure by the inclusion of the requirement for genuine investigation or prosecution in the statute. Thus, to operationalize this provision, the judges of the African court will have to 'invent' innovative approaches towards analysing the genuineness of a proceeding or an investigation before a national mechanism. It is easier to assume, however, that the African court will necessarily read the word 'genuinely' back into that provision to assess whether such investigation or prosecution before a national court would satisfy the threshold of the admissibility provisions of the protocol.

A third difference between the complementarity provisions of the AU Protocol and the Rome Statute relates to the inclusion of Articles 18 and 19 of the Rome Statute which are titled 'Preliminary Rulings Regarding Admissibility' and 'Challenges to the Jurisdiction of the Court or the Admissibility of a Case', respectively. The Protocol does not contain similar provisions. While there is no explanation for these omissions too, it is important to note that the proto-

the Court further confirmed that the existence of concurrent domestic proceedings was no bar to an otherwise admissible application to the Court.

32 For a general understanding of the exhaustion of local remedies rule in the jurisprudence of the African Commission, see N. J. Udombana 'So far, so fair: the local remedies rule in the jurisprudence of the African Commission on Human and Peoples' Rights (2003) 97 *American Journal of International Law* 1, 1–37.

33 M. deGuzman (n. 24).

col does not contain as many procedural details as are included in the Rome Statute. This may suggest that the drafters of the protocol intend that the judges of the African court will have wide interpretative powers in their attempts at applying the provisions of the protocol. The Rome Statute also contains such constructive ambiguities.[34]

There is also a difference in titular nomenclature. While Article 17 of the statute is titled 'Admissibility', Article 46H of the Protocol is titled 'Complementary Jurisdiction'. There is no explanation for this difference either. But, Article 46H only deals with issues of admissibility, which is one of the aspects of the principle of complementarity. *Ne bis in idem* is another aspect.[35] The OTP had earlier noted that *ne bis in idem* and the concepts of admissibility jointly serve to implement the principle of complementarity.[36] Thus, Article 46H may have been wrongly titled, considering that it only covers one of the aspects of complementarity. But as noted by deGuzman, this difference in nomenclature is likely to 'have little practical effect'.[37]

It is Article 46I of the protocol that deals with *ne bis in idem*. The corresponding provision is Article 20 of the Rome Statute. Again, there are differences between these two provisions. Most of the differences relate to omissions and additions that operate to allow for more flexibilities on adhering to the decisions of the African courts by member states.[38]

Overall, what has emerged from the analysis on the differences between the provisions of these two instruments, in respect of admissibility and *ne bis in idem*, is that the protocol leaves room for more flexibility, thus accommodating national or regional specificities. This may not be surprising, since the protocol was adopted many years after the Rome Statute and may have learnt from some of the inherent pitfalls of the statute.

These differences notwithstanding, the Rome Statute and the Malabo Protocol have both shown that the place of complementarity cannot be overemphasized in international criminal justice. How and with whom complementarity is exercised may differ, but the underlining principle remains the same: where another mechanism (whether national or (sub)regional) is already investigating or prosecuting a conduct, the ICC or the African Court must find same inadmissible. This horizontal relationship that is

34 On constructive ambiguity, see chapter 4 of this book.

35 On the principle of ne bis in idem, see chapter 2 of this book.

36 OTP, ICC Doc: ICC-01/11-01/11 'Corrigendum to Prosecution Response to the "Document in Support of the Government of Libya's Appeal against the Decision on the admissibility of the case against Saif Al-Islam Gaddafi"' dated 23 July 2013, 26 at para. 55.

37 M. deGuzman (n. 24).

38 *Ibid.*

being proposed between the ICC and the African court is more desirable in order to engender a regime of mutual cooperation and respect between the two courts.[39] It has been suggested that such a model be based on the understanding that states have primary duty to prosecute but where there is a failure, the two courts 'must confer as to who should intervene'.[40] Such delineation of jurisdiction may be based on certain factors like the nature of the crime and their geographical scope.[41] This model of division of labour holds promises of promoting mutual respect between the ICC and the African court. But outside of theory, what does the inter-relationship between the African court and the ICC mean in practical terms? What is to be expected in operationalizing this relationship? How will the complementarity provisions play out in a more practical scenario? These questions and the answers they generate will be the focus of the next section.

2.2.2 Complementarity in Practice at the African Court

This chapter assumes that at some point in the future, the African court will be operational, alongside the ICC, which is already functional. It also assumes that when this happens, there may arise a need to address the relationship between the latter and the former. These assumptions create a few questions that must be addressed in order to ensure that probable frictions between these two courts are properly managed. Accordingly, likely questions relate to how the relationship between the two courts will be arranged, where both courts seek to exercise jurisdiction over the same conducts and same defendants. This is a real possibility, for obvious reasons: The two courts have similar or overlapping roles, and more importantly, there are member states who belong to the two organizations, with the resultant effect of a likely clash in obligations. The possibility of a clash is even more likely because the Malabo Protocol does not make any reference, either direct or veiled, to the ICC. In the same manner, the Rome Statute did not make a direct reference to 'regional courts', for the purposes of international crimes' prosecution. As such, the relationship between the two is not clear, thus adding to the likelihood of a clash in jurisdiction.

---

39 On the horizontal and vertical relationships between judicial mechanisms, see W. Schabas & M. El Zeidy, 'Article 17: Issues of Admissibility' in K. Ambos and O. Triffterer (eds) *The Rome Statute of the International Criminal Court: A Commentary* (2015) at 781.

40 H.G. Van der Wilt 'Complementary Jurisdiction (Article 46H)' in G. Werle and M. Vormbaum (eds.) (2017), *The African Criminal Court: A Commentary on the Malabo Protocol* at 191.

41 *Ibid.*

With this likelihood, the question that arises is which court will defer to the jurisdiction of the other, if there is a jurisdictional clash or in a situation of concurrent referrals that necessitate the exercise of concurrent jurisdictions by both the ICC and African chamber?

To begin, there are two situations in which there could be the concurrent jurisdiction between the two courts. The first is in the case of self-referral by the state; where a state refers a matter to both the ACC and the ICC. This is a highly unlikely but probable situation. Instances could be when a state refers a matter and feels obliged to refer to another entity, perhaps because of slow response from the earlier entity the matter had been referred to or as a result of any other supervening factor. The second is where the UNSC and the AUPSC or any other relevant organ of the AU took independent decisions to refer same matter to the ICC and the ACC, in accordance with their independent powers under Articles 24(2), 25 and 103 of the UN Charter on the one hand, and Article 16 of the African Union Protocol Relating to the Establishment of the Peace and Security Council (AUPREPSC), in giving effect to Article 46(F) of the Malabo Protocol itself. Apart from self-referral as provided in Article 3 and 46(f)(1) of the Malabo Protocol, Article 46(F)(2) lists the AUPSC and the Assembly of Heads of State and Government as the other two organs of the AU who may refer a matter to the Prosecutor of the Criminal Chambers. But in specific relation to the AUPSC, its powers under the Malabo Protocol and Article 16 of the AUPREPSC are like the powers of the UNSC to maintain global peace and order, albeit, on a continental level.

In both scenarios painted above, the question as to what should happen remains valid. This question, though complex, has already received significant attention in the case of national courts and the ICC. For regional courts, however, there has not been an operational regional court with overlapping jurisdictions with the ICC; hence, the absence of any jurisprudence in this regard. But if this situation occurs, what will be the proper approach?

The answer to this question is not straightforward. For one, judges of the ICC and the African court would have to ascertain whether there is any provision that permits deference of one court to another, thus triggering a complementarity analysis. The direction of such an analysis will take root from the relationship between national courts and the ICC. This is the most similar scenario from which guidance can be sought. If that happens, a likely interpretation is as proposed in chapter 4 of this book: the understanding that when a regional court acts, it is doing so in line with the delegated powers that states have given to it in that instant case.[42] The import of that interpre-

42 See arguments advanced on 'delegated authority' in chapter 7 of this work.

tation is that the ICC may, for example, defer to the investigative or prosecutorial actions of the African court, on the understanding that it is doing so for a state, since the African court indeed derived its powers from the authority delegated to it by states. This analysis is not as simple as that, for it will also require that the ICC assesses, for example, the genuineness of the procedure before the African court. This will certainly amount to an unwanted assessment, capable of occasioning frictions between the two courts. Hence, there must be a way to avoid this possibility.

A number of authors have proposed that a more positive approach towards complementarity, especially between the ICC and regional bodies is the idea of 'burden sharing' or 'division of labour', as against, a hierarchical or vertical relationship that the ICC currently maintains with states.[43] According to professor H. van der Wilt, a number of considerations ought to guide the selection of cases and which forum will be best placed to investigate or prosecute a crime. He proposes that such considerations will include division of cases based on gravity. Drawing from the words of Article 17(1)(d) of the Statute that provides that a case is inadmissible if it is not of sufficient gravity, he proposes that while the ICC concentrates on prosecuting the gravest crimes, the African court could be useful in prosecuting less serious crimes.[44] Additionally, he suggests that the nature of crimes could be a basis for delimiting jurisdiction. In this regard, while the Malabo Protocol criminalizes many transnational crimes, which are outside the jurisdiction of the ICC, the African court could focus on these.[45]

However, I disagree with the position of professor van der Wilt, even though I fully understand that the purport of these suggestions is to chart out a way for managing the likely contentious relationship between the ICC and the African court. However, an approach that robs a court or tribunal of the powers to exercise its full mandate will be counterproductive. In this regard, any approach that encourages a tribunal to use less and less of its powers risks the tendency of reducing the overall effectiveness of a tribunal,

43 Van der Wilt calls it 'a cooperative model'. See H.G. Van der Wilt 'Complementary Jurisdiction (Article 46H)' in G. Werle and M. Vormbaum (eds.) (2017) *The African Criminal Court: A Commentary on the Malabo Protocol* at 198. DeGuzman calls it the burden sharing approach. See M. deGuzman 'Complementarity at the African Court' in K. Clarke & C. Jalloh (eds) The African Court of Justice and Human and Peoples' Rights (CUP 2019).

44 H.G. Van der Wilt 'Complementary Jurisdiction (Article 46H)' in G. Werle and M. Vormbaum (eds.) (2017) *The African Criminal Court: A Commentary on the Malabo Protocol* at 199.

45 *Ibid.*

thus defeating its purpose. In a situation where the African court is better placed to investigate and prosecute a crime, it will be ingenious and injurious to the ends of justice, to suggest that the African court should desist from exercising jurisdiction simply because the crime is of a grave nature.

Instead, I propose a more nuanced approach that considers the relevant overriding benefits or perceived advantages that prosecution before one court enjoys over the other. In common law, this approach I propose, is like the well-known doctrine of *forum non conveniens*[46] which was proposed and applied in civil actions. In the literal sense, the doctrine is translated to mean 'non convenient forum'. What it implies is that 'trial courts could refuse to hear cases when the ends of justice would best be served by trial in another (more convenient) forum'.[47] While the origin of the doctrine is not well known, some of its earliest practices date back to decisions from Scottish courts.[48] The doctrine largely operates to allow 'courts that have jurisdiction over a case to stay or dismiss the case upon a determination that the case may be heard more appropriately in another court. The trial court is given substantial discretion in determining whether a more appropriate forum exists and if so, whether to stay or dismiss in favour of that other court'.[49] The criteria developed by US Supreme Court under this doctrine are, first, a determination by a trial court that a more convenient forum that exists is an adequate forum and, secondly, a combination of other public and private interest factors.[50]

While not much of the doctrine has been seen in international criminal law, – although it is codified in some countries, including in the USA's Federal Rule of Criminal Procedure 21(b)[51] –, there have been debates about applying it in the context of international human rights.[52] I propose that international criminal law, especially as it relates to international tribunals, could benefit greatly from the application of this doctrine, to resolve jurisdictional clashes in the most pragmatic way, on a case-by-case basis.

46 See E. L. Barrett Jr. 'The Doctrine of Forum Non Conveniens' (1947) 35 *California Law Review* 3 380–422.

47 *Ibid*, 387.

48 For thoughts on this, see A. Arzandeh 'The origins of the Scottish forum non conveniens doctrine' (2017) 13 *Journal of Private International Law* 1, 130–151.

49 R. A. Brand 'Forum non conveniens' *OUP Encyclopaedia entries* (2013).

50 R.A Brand 'Challenges to Forum Non Conveniens' (2013) 45 *New York University Journal of International Law and Politics* 4, 1005–1006.

51 See Stephen H. Weiner 'Forum Non Conveniens' (1995) 64 *Fordham Law Review* 3, 848.

52 F.F. Martin 'The International Human Rights and Ethical Aspects of the Forum Non-conveniens Doctrine' (2003) 35 *The University of Miami Inter-American Law Review* 1,101–1121.

This proposition does not assume that an analysis to determine a forum that is more convenient is an easy task. In fact, it has been admitted that '*forum non conveniens* is an imperfect doctrine... and subject to easy criticism'.[53] However, in order to put this doctrine to practice, the starting point is to admit that there are many factors that may enhance the effectiveness of investigating or prosecuting at the African court, in comparison to the ICC and vice versa. Such factors may include proximity to the scenes of crimes, difficulty with procuring defendant and witnesses, expertise of relevant authorities within the court, etc. In so doing, there is an assumption that both courts understand that the relationship between them is that of partners in the goal of international criminal justice. Thus, as partners, there is a perception of equality, which does not relegate one of the partners to performing lesser functions than the other. This position supports the notion of burden sharing, as proposed by van der Wilt and deGuzman. However, it is a cooperative model that does not reduce a partner to lesser roles but allows for each partner to understand the limits of its abilities, within a healthy partnership. It allows for an assessment of strengths and weaknesses – as all tribunals possess these – and then suggests arriving at a decision that is mutually beneficial.

How to operationalize this kind of relationship that is based on the perceived benefits that an institution has over the other, is yet to be seen in practice. This proposal, however, provides templates for a workable agreement between different levels of tribunals. A case in point is the Memorandum of Understanding that the ICC entered with the Inter-American Court. Accordingly, such agreements are capable of 'defining the terms of mutual cooperation...in affording each other assistance...subject to observance of their respective applicable legal regimes'.[54] The agreement also enjoins the parties to 'cooperate closely with each other and consult each other on matters of mutual interest'.[55] Parties are expected to maintain contacts, hold meetings, exchange visits and establish appropriate liaison arrangements.[56] These arrangements afford both institutions opportunities to collaborate in different ways. Thus, a similar arrangement between the ICC and the African court may provide a basis for cooperation that allows both courts to jointly

53 R.A Brand 'Challenges to Forum Non Conveniens' (2013) 45 *New York University Journal of International Law and Politics* 4, 1003.

54 ICC-PRES/17-01-16. Memorandum of Understanding between the International Criminal Court and the Inter-American Court of Human Rights, 15 February 2016, Article 1.

55 *Ibid*, art. 3(a).

56 *Ibid*, art 3(b).

assess, in each situation, the tribunal that is best placed to investigate or prosecute a particular conduct or defendant.

One of the factors that may determine the form and nature of complementarity between institutions is the probable or anticipated challenges that complementarity was introduced to address. In the case of the African Court and the ICC, the likely challenges are numerous. The most probable of them are issues relating to who acts first in situations where the two courts are interested and have jurisdiction over a particular crime; probable fight for cases and competition for the same evidence; issues of *ne bis in idem*; possibilities of witnesses being interviewed multiple times; jurisdictional overlap; *res judicata* and judicial notice of adjudicated facts; and, perhaps, decisions on who is best equipped to try specific crimes. My proposition in this regard is that if a horizontal relationship is cultivated, as against a vertical relationship between the two courts, many of these likely challenges would have been sufficiently navigated before they arise at all. For this reason, I submit that a more positive complementarity approach between these courts should be based on the principles of amity, partnership, 'sustainable and continuous dialogue', *res judicata* and referral, instead of review.

Authors like Carsten Stahn have promoted an understanding that suggests that what I am proposing mirrors a 'polycentric justice model'. In his view, this idea that prosecution of international crimes could have many centres that run independently within a larger whole, augurs well for the pluralist system that international criminal justice has become.[57] As such, while this may suggest that my argument points more to polycentricity, as against complementarity, I will hasten to add that polycentricity does not negate my idea of regional complementarity, rather it mirrors the strands of regional complementarity in so far as it prescribes that regional and international centres of justice relate as equals. This is like the counterview that complementarity as a concept is too heavily shaped by ICC practice and semantics and thus should not be the proper concept for arranging the relationship between the ICC and regional entities. In response, however, it must be stressed that the idea behind regional complementarity promotes different frames of interaction that are based on cooperation and partnership among equals – a framing that the hierarchical nature of the ICC complementarity regime negates.

57 C. Stahn 'Re-imagining the ICC in a Multipolar World' in C. Stahn (ed) *The International Criminal Court in its Third Decade: Reflecting on Law and Practices* (Brill Nijhoff 2024) 569.

2.3 African Court: Promoting Regional Complementarity?

The previous section's analysis on the establishment, jurisdiction and crimes of the African Court helps to situate the discussion on the Court within the ambit of the wider discussion on complementarity, especially the notion of regional complementarity. As noted earlier, the creation of the ICL section generated both optimistic and pessimistic reactions. While some argued that it helps to advance international criminal justice at the regional level, others argue that it is an attempt to shield suspects of international crimes and thus defeat the goals of international criminal justice.[58] Whatever the view is, the establishment of the ICL section, in spite of all the shortcomings inherent in the Malabo Protocol, marks an important milestone in international criminal justice. This optimistic view is in tandem with the idea that all efforts at closing the impunity gap, at the national, regional and international levels must be encouraged. This chapter further aligns with the position that if properly operationalized, the African Court may yet justify and promote the ideas behind the notion of regional complementarity in several ways.

First, the idea that the African court purports to respond to specific African problems mirrors the 'overriding benefits approach' earlier discussed. It is the contention of scholars that regional-specific challenges require regional solutions.[59] Thus, to advance international criminal justice at the regional level, employing the use of regional specific mechanisms, especially one that responds to the specific challenges at that regional level may be an acceptable best practice.

Secondly, the Malabo Protocol does not make any reference, either direct or veiled, to the ICC. This awkward silence has been referred to as a case of 'negative complementarity' which raises pertinent question as to the real motivation for establishing the ICL section of the African Court.[60] Irrespective of the motivation, however, it is my contention that it does not detract from the advantages inherent in criminal justice at the regional level, especially if the court functions in strict adherence with its enabling acts and

58 Kenyans for Peace With Truth and Justice, 'Seeking Justice or Shielding Suspects: An Analysis of the Malabo Protocol' [available at http://kptj.africog.org/wp-content/uploads/2016/11/Malabo-Report.pdf – accessed on 12 February 2024].

59 C. Jalloh 'Regionalizing International Criminal Law?' (2009) 9 *ICLR* 3 445–499.

60 M. du Plessis 'A case of negative complementarity? Giving the African Court of Justice and Human Rights Jurisdiction over International Crimes' *EJIL: Talk!* available https://www.ejiltalk.org/a-case-of-negative-regional-complementarity-giving-the-african-court-of-justice-and-human-rights-jurisdiction-over-international-crimes/ (accessed on 21 May 2023).

other rules as may be developed from time to time. The underlining principle behind regional prosecution still avails itself in the African court.

Lastly, justifying and advocating regional complementarity through the lens of the African court is not an attempt to downplay the inherent challenges that operationalizing the African Court may face. Additionally, this chapter notes the many challenges inherent in the Malabo Protocol itself. Issues around *ne bis in idem* and what constitutes the same crimes, who acts first between the two courts in a given situation, fight for evidence and cases, *etc.*, are some of the practical issues that need to be resolved at some point. But again, these likelihoods do not detract from the many advantages of prosecution at the regional level. Overall, the establishment and operationalization of the African court are in the wider interest of justice and may serve more to advance the wider goal of ICL, which is to bridge impunity gaps and punish perpetrators of international crimes.

3 Conclusion

The principle of complementarity continues to widen in scope and application. Its latest offspring is the notion of regional complementarity. The notion, as espoused in this and previous chapters, implies that 'if a regional judicial mechanism is prosecuting or investigating a particular crime within the jurisdiction of the ICC, the ICC ought to find the prosecution of the suspect's case inadmissible, *in so far* as the regional mechanism displays genuine will and ability to properly investigate and prosecute the same case'. But this depends on the relationship between such regional body and the ICC. For instance, if there is a relationship of equals between the ICC and such regional body, it would be possible to read the present idea of regional complementarity into their interaction. Now, considering that the Malabo Protocol is completely silent on any form of cooperation or relationship with the ICC, the question that arises is whether we can glean the possibility of such relationship between the two organizations. This is what this chapter has attempted to investigate.

One of my theses has been that though the jurisdictional relationship between the African court and the ICC is not entirely clear, a horizontal relationship of equals is preferable. This understanding is premised on the idea that both institutions are conglomerations of states with vertical relationships with their member states. As such, a horizontal relationship, between them, based on division of labour, will better serve the ends of international criminal justice. The proposed establishment of the ICL section of the African court might signal an important development in ICL. Its proposed establishment will be a story of many firsts: it will be the first regional human rights mechanism to be invested with international criminal law jurisdiction as well as corporate criminal jurisdiction, and it combines the already-known three core international crimes with nine new crimes that have hitherto been unknown to be part of any international criminal justice mechanism.[61] As stated by Chile Eboe-Osuji, former president of the ICC, '[T]here is immense value in conferring criminal jurisdiction to the AC – both as regards crimes within the Rome Statute and more so as regards crimes over which the ICC has no jurisdiction.'[62] Its operationalization, however, remains to be seen.

---

61 K. Clarke & ors 'Introduction' in C. Jalloh & ors *The African Court of Justice and Human and Peoples' Rights in Context: Development and Challenges* (CUP 2019).

62 C. Eboe-Osuji 'Administering International Criminal Justice through the African Court: Opportunities and Challenges in International Law' in C. Jalloh & Ors (eds) The *African Court of Justice and Human and Peoples' Rights in Context: Development and Challenges* (CUP 2019) 849.

CHAPTER 9

Conclusion

This book has explored the need to organize legal pluralism occasioned by the emerging four-tiered justice paradigm. In shifting attention away from universalism, it interrogates specific organizing principles for legal pluralism. It also introduces the idea of system of justice which seeks to organize the relationships between different levels of courts and tribunals that exist as different parts of an ecosystem of criminal justice. Beyond the ICC, this system of justice approach presents a normative framework for analysis of principles to navigate the chaos that would attend the interaction between domestic, hybrid, regional and international courts with similar and overlapping jurisdictions. As there is now a maturation of the justice system which should involve encouraging and clarifying the role of regional mechanisms in international criminal justice, the study shows that regionalism is not a challenge to international criminal justice. While some aspects are challenging, it is a progress to have this four-tiered model that encourages different levels of courts dispensing justice in the spirit of cooperation and mutual deference. It shows that regionalism is not a challenge to international law; rather, it is an asset. It argues that regionalism should therefore not be seen as opposition to the universal conception of international criminal justice, but as a concept that promotes the latter in a different language and in a more contextualized way. It submits that a polycentric idea of international criminal justice bodes well for regional complementarity, instead of a monocentric or an ICC-centric approach.

Also, there is a need to regulate regional complementarity itself. Many of the challenges that the application and practice of other notions of complementarity have presented between states and the ICC related to the proper approach towards regulating the relationship between these levels of court. This goes beyond the initial question of whether regional complementarity should be regulated or not. There is no doubt that the answer to that question is in the affirmative. Regulating regional complementarity is also important, if its application will not be subjected to the same criticisms that other notions of complementarity have been subjected to. As has been shown, in theory, we now have this four-tiered model of justice. International tribunals like the ICC; regional tribunals like the ACC; hybrid tribunals that continue to be established to deal with specific atrocity situations; and domestic systems, whose primary duty is to prosecute international crimes in their territory, are all

© 2026 THE AUTHOR(S) | HTTPS://DOI.ORG/10.1163/9789004761803-011

existing side by side. The overarching question that I have tried to answer in this research is: to what extent is regionalism a challenge to the universality or coherence of international criminal law? I focused on how different levels of court can work together in a harmonious and complementary fashion, instead of working as competitors. How to make sense of this four-tiered justice paradigm is the theoretical macro-point of this book. As I have shown, the identification of regional complementarity may involve at least three elements, namely complementarity through division of labour, deference in prosecutorial strategies and cooperation on many levels.

The idea of legal pluralism occasioned by the fragmentation of international law and the notion of regional complementarity as a tool to make sense of the four-tiered justice paradigm are the two broad themes of the study. While regionalism contributes to the fragmentation of international law, regional complementarity can be employed as a tool of relational coordination. Recent development is not the first time that regionalism is interacting with international law. Since this had happened in the context of international human rights law, ICL could draw certain lessons from how human rights addressed the issue. There are no doubts that there are already scattered efforts at regionalizing ICL, in at least four regions. These efforts have now brought us to the point where there are now attempts to upscale the involvement of regions in international criminal justice, through the establishment of independent ICL mechanisms.

A historical venture to inquire why regionalism came so late in the development of ICL and complementarity reveals that there are at least four factors that could explain why the continuous reshaping of complementarity as a concept did not accommodate the notion of regional complementarity. The failure of ICL to embrace regionalism earlier in its development ties to some of the narratives on why the drafters of the Rome Statute ignored regionalism during the negotiations at Rome. ICL's obsession with universality and cosmopolitanism; the liberal foundation of ICL; the understanding that ICL is an enemy of sovereignty; and the fact that ICL had developed more slowly and less dynamically are some of the factors responsible for the neglect of regionalism and regional complementarity in the history of ICL. At the discussion in Rome, there was a general belief that the Security Council could still establish tribunals like the ICTY and the ICTR; hence, there was no need for a regional tribunal. Recent development relating to regional *jus cogens* at the ILC appears to suggest some openness to the idea of regional complementarity.

Moreover, whether the ICC opens or closes itself to the idea of regional complementarity through its jurisprudence, practice and policy direction deserves some attention. While our understanding and perhaps the practice of complementarity has now moved from a very strict and restrictive conception as a legal device to a broader conception as a structural principle, the ICC continues to be trapped in an 'ICC-centric' approach of the concept. Secondly, in the operation of the ICC, the existing practices are not so open towards the idea of regional complementarity. An exploration of complementarity as currently applied by the ICC shows a court that always wants to take priority and whose approach has not been inclusive of national mechanisms. The analysis shows a court that wants more power for itself, even though its first Chief Prosecutor expressed hopes that the Court's success will be assessed by the fewer number of cases it deals with. This view is tempered with the discovery that there is a difference in approach between the OTP and the chambers. As the court continues to be driven by the ideals of cosmopolitanism and universality, it has negative implications for regional complementarity. The ICC needs to open itself more to the ideals that underpin regional complementarity. It is in this regard that polycentricity is proposed as an alternative approach to the current monocentric ideals that underpin the ICC's approach to international criminal justice.

Hybrid and regional tribunals previously emerged as new accountability models in ICL. Hybridity appeared to have been a necessary precursor to regionalism. There are two strands of regionalism and two models of hybridity. The models of hybridity are the purely international hybrid tribunals that owe their establishment to the UN, and the second are those that owe their establishment to the activities of a regional organization. The latter is what is termed regional hybridity. There are also two observable strands of regional involvement in ICL. The first is the assistance-driven strand where the hybrid is embedded in the domestic system of a state, or where it applies domestic law, in addition to international law. The EAC and the KSCSPO are examples of this. The second strand relates to the fully independent model, where a region purports to establish a stand-alone criminal chamber within its regional court. Unlike the previous strand where the hybrid is created for a specific past atrocity or conflict situation, this strand sees the establishment of a tribunal to deal with future crimes, and its jurisdiction is activated by accession and ratification of member states. Hybridity points to the fact that the future of international criminal justice is in its past, where hybrid tribunals are created to address specific atrocity situation, despite the existence of the ICC. This development has now led us to the possibility of the existence of a full-fledged regional criminal tribunal. Regionalism in ICL is inevitable. One reason for this is that the turn to regionalism in ICL is not novel. It is rooted in the UN Charter's provisions on states responsibility to take joint actions within a regional arrangement to ensure global peace and security. Development in different regions also suggests that there is a progressive move towards the second strand of regionalism: the establishment of regional courts to deal with transnational and international crimes. Other regions might be encouraged by the steps taken by the African Union in the adoption of the Malabo Protocol. As states continue to face common transnational crimes in their region, their joint responses may continue to deepen regional interaction with international criminal justice.

Regional hybridity or the assistance-driven strand of hybridity is what the EAC and the KSCSPO signify. The EAC and the KSCSPO were both silent on any possible relationship between them and the ICC. These regionally backed tribunals had convicted and indicted past heads of state. This symbolically demonstrates the capacity of regional tribunals to dispense justice quicker than perhaps, a universal institution like the ICC could do.

With the Malabo Protocol comes the probable practice of regional complementarity in the full and independent strand of regionalism. As an instrument, the Malabo Protocol contains several innovative features. These features are included, probably to address some of the fundamental structural critiques of international criminal justice. While the universal system has concentrated largely on civil and political rights, the protocol has also brought social and economic rights into perspective through its criminalization of offences relating to these. The Protocol is ahead of its time and appears a little more advanced than the ICC system in certain respects. It shows that regional institutions can be a lot more modern and innovative, while they incorporate regional contexts much better than a universal mechanism. There are also a few dangers, including the tendency to over-criminalize conduct and outperform, in a bid to justify the regional mechanism's existence. New mechanisms often appear as though they are in competition with existing mechanisms. If the African court becomes operationalized, the protocol provides a rare opportunity for African countries to address crimes that are well known to the continent, but which are subjects of very few trials and convictions at the international level. A rationale for the protocol's inclusion of them alongside 'core crimes' would be that 'many of them are capable of destabilizing a state, which in turn leads to the proliferation of core crimes'. Criminalizing and prosecuting these conducts may 'have a preventative or deterrent consequence…', thus helping to fulfil the overall goal of ICL which is to close the impunity gap. This ties closely to the idea of regional complementarity and the possibility of a regional court dispensing justice within its territory.

Additionally, regional complementarity mirrors other existing notions of complementarity. Some of these notions of complementarity already support the theories underpinning regional complementarity. Regional complementarity, like other notions, has both classical and positive dimensions. The positive dimension is a more functional model. That dimension has the capacity to facilitate a regime of cooperation between regional courts and the ICC, as well as regional courts and states, especially when certain organizing principles that are useful for arranging these relationships are employed.

Interpretation of statutes also helps to find support for the notion of regional complementarity. In addition to interpretation, there are other means of solving disputes which include the formation of new organizing principles like mutual deference, division of labour, monitoring, regulation, collaboration and cooperation. The ICC indeed ought to develop a different complementarity reading that agrees with the Vienna Convention. Article 17(1) of the Rome Statute could be interpreted to support the view that the ICC should consider genuine action before a regional tribunal as sufficient to preclude the admissibility of a case before the ICC. We can also apply the VCLT to the Rome Statute to provide some support for the theory of regional complementarity. With five possible relationship dimensions in the operationalization of regional complementarity come proposals on addressing conflicts that may arise in the relationship dimensions.

1 Making Sense of the Four-Tiered Justice Paradigm: Looking Behind

The analysis in this book already shows that we have moved towards a four-tiered model of justice system in international criminal law. We must now think of relationships in terms of cooperation and in terms of admissibility, as against a relationship based on competition. I have examined the extent to which we can have division of labour and some of the principles on which such divisions can be organized. I have also analysed, for instance, whether we should focus on the gravity of the crime or on the most responsible perpetrators. I have shown that both approaches have their downsides. As we have seen in the SCCCAR, I have argued more about consultations between prosecutors, including joint investigative teams between the ICC and domestic systems.

Moreover, we need to have monitoring structures to ensure that if one level of court does not perform, another level can step in, while ensuring that we keep track of cases and progress made in an atmosphere of self-reporting.[1] The

1 Chapter 6.

principles that should inform further debates are mutual deference, division of labour, burden sharing, cooperation and collaboration, monitoring and regulation, among others.[2] To further make sense of the four-tired justice paradigm that has emerged, I have shown that we clearly have bits and pieces of this system in place. For instance, the Special Criminal Court in CAR offers an example of what is in place, and that could fit into the framework that I have attempted to develop. Article 37 of the Organic Law of the SCCCAR makes provision for coordination between the prosecutor of the ICC and the SCCCAR prosecutor. This provision has been criticized for its potential to prevent the tribunal's prosecutor from exercising prosecutorial discretion, without first asking for permission from ICC's prosecutor.[3] In spite of this criticism, this provision, if properly operationalized, has the capacity to reduce jurisdictional conflicts between those courts. In another interesting example from SCCCAR, it has been reported that the early investigations by the tribunal were made possible because prosecutors of the ordinary courts in CAR handed files over to the SCCCAR prosecutor.[4] This regime of cooperation between institutions given to similar or overlapping jurisdictions is what I advocate in this book. Additionally, the use of MoUs and similar tools between the ICC and domestic systems on one hand, and between the ICC and regional judicial mechanisms, on the other hand, are examples of existing practices that can be enhanced and transposed into arranging regional complementarity. Of course, MOUs are soft laws that do not have the same force as treaties. If there is therefore a conflict between such MOUs and treaties, the treaty shall prevail. It is, however, the exact reason why such MOUs are crafted carefully to avoid ambiguity and to clarify roles.

In the discussion on the Criminal Chamber of the African Court, I have highlighted some of the problems that emerge in the interplay between the ICC and regional institutions. The book has differentiated between these different relationship dimensions and has made recommendations in relation to each of those relationships. It has, for instance, advocated for the African court to apply positive complementarity in its relationship with domestic courts. It made the provisions of the Rome Statute the starting point and recommended that admissibility challenges be resolved by going beyond the textual provi-

---

2 Chapter 6.

3 P. Labuda 'The Special Criminal Court in the Central African Republic: Failure or Vindication of Complementarity' (2017) 15 *JICJ* 193.

4 P. Labuda 'Institutional design and Non-Complementarity: Regulating Regulations between Hybrid Tribunals and other Judicial and Non-Judicial Institutions in K. Ainley and M. Kersten (eds), *Hybrid Justice: Innovation and Impact in the Prosecution of Atrocity Crimes* (Oxford University Press 2020) 3.

sions to accommodate other organizing principles. Moreover, it has proposed a textual amendment to Article 17 to provide for Rome Statute's accommodation of prosecution before a regional tribunal, in order for the ICC to find such case inadmissible.[5] In another breath, it identified that in the case of the Malabo Protocol and indeed, any future regional tribunal's instrument, provisions that spell out a clear relationship between the ICC and such mechanism would be useful to address the possibility of jurisdictional clash. This three-pronged approach of textual amendment to the Rome Statute, use of MOUs and an inclusion of relevant provisions in the instruments of the regional court will provide a holistic approach to resolving jurisdictional clashes while enhancing cooperation between levels of courts in this four-tiered justice paradigm.

2 Making Sense of the Four-Tiered System: Looking Ahead

There is no doubt that hybrid tribunals will continue to be established. In the last decade alone, many examples exist of proposals to create such institutions.[6] More recently, especially in the context of the Russian Ukrainian conflict, there are already debates about the merits and demerits of establishing a Special Hybrid Tribunal to prosecute the crime of aggression, for which the ICC lacks jurisdiction. Different proposals and opinions exist on this.[7] There are scholars who argue for[8] and against[9] the establishment of such tribunal for Ukraine. In the latter part of this chapter, I have discussed the establishment of the Tribunal and its import for regional complementarity.

---

5 Chapter 7.

6 See different examples in the introductory chapter of this study.

7 T. Dannenbaum 'Mechanisms for Criminal Prosecution of Russia's Aggression Against Ukraine' *Just Security*, 10 March 2022 [available at https://www.justsecurity.org/80626/mechanisms-for-criminal-prosecution-of-russias-aggression-against-ukraine/ – accessed on 12 January 2023].

8 'Statement calling for the creation of a special tribunal for the punishment of the crime of aggression against Ukraine' [available at https://gordonandsarahbrown.com/wp-content/uploads/2022/03/Combined-Statement-and-Declaration.pdf – accessed on 12 March 2023].

9 S. Vasiliev, 'Aggression against Ukraine: Avenues for Accountability for Core crimes', *EJIL: Talk*, 3 March 2022 [available at https://www.ejiltalk.org/aggression-against-ukraine-avenues-for-accountability-for-core-crimes/ – accessed on 12 March 2024]; Heller J, 'Creating a Special Tribunal for Aggression Against Ukraine is a Bad Idea' *OpinioJuris*, 7 March 2022 [available at https://opiniojuris.org/2022/03/07/creating-a-special-tribunal-for-aggression-against-ukraine-is-a-bad-idea/ – accessed on 12 March 2024].

For the avoidance of doubt, there is nothing wrong with this approach of establishing a hybrid tribunal to address specific atrocity situations, even in cases where the proposed tribunal is to be established by a regional body. While some may have questioned the legality or the motive of establishing regional mechanisms, especially since the ICC exists for the same purpose, there are a few grounds upon which to justify the latter's establishment.

First, there is nothing wrong with any region seeking to establish regional mechanisms to prosecute international crimes within that region.[10] In fact, it is consistent with the principles of the UN Charter as enshrined in Article 52(1) of the UN Charter.[11] Experiences from Africa and other regions have shown that violent conflicts often threaten international peace and security. These conflicts sometime overwhelm national mechanisms and may make it impossible for justice to be served to the perpetrators of international crimes in the context of those conflicts. One way to ensure peace and security in that context is to hold perpetrators accountable through a regional arrangement. One of such arrangements could be the establishment of a hybrid or full regional criminal court to ensure justice for victims of crimes. Further, in relation to the International Court of Justice, Article 95 of the UN Charter provides that 'Nothing in the present Charter shall prevent Members of the United Nations from entrusting the solution of their differences to other tribunals by virtue of agreements already in existence or which may be concluded in the future'. While regional criminal courts may not fall under this formula, this Charter provision suggests that regional efforts at resolving challenges, including those that are of an international criminal nature, are not incompatible with the UN Charter. A broad interpretation of Article 95 suggests that regional tribunals – whether of a civil or criminal nature – may be established by UN member states. The interpretation suggests that the UN Charter does not foreclose the possibility of states establishing future tribunals to address future problems, including those relating to a resolution of their differences as the ICJ does.

If a case is made about possible conflict between Article 52(1) of the UN Charter and any other rule which may otherwise make the establishment of a regional criminal court illegal, Article 103 of the UN Charter becomes appropriate. It provides as follows '[I]n the event of a conflict between the obligations of the Members of the United Nations under the present Charter and

---

10 A. Abass 'The Proposed International Criminal Jurisdiction for the African Court: Some problematic aspects' (2013b) *Netherlands International Law Review* 27–50.

11 F.K. Tiba 'Regional International Criminal Courts: An Idea Whose Time Has Come?' (2016) 17 *Cardozo Journal of Conflict Resolution* 52, 535.

their obligations under any other international agreement, their obligations under the present Charter shall prevail.' Thus, the effect of the combined reading of Articles 52(1) and 103 of the UN Charter is that it is not impermissible for states within a region to organize themselves together with a view to prosecuting international crimes within their region.[12] This appears a self-evident thesis – it is legal to establish regional institutions to combat crimes.

Furthermore, there is no provision in the Rome Statute that forbids, precludes or forecloses the existence of a regional mechanism for the purposes of international crimes prosecution. The ICC has also not made any pronouncement on this issue. However, it is already a matter of settled practice in international law that states, acting under the umbrella of a regional or sub-regional entity can establish a regional court – be it the more common regional human rights entities, or even an international criminal prosecution mechanism. As far back as during the trials at the Nuremberg Tribunal, the judges had declared that the Allies, through the creation of the IMT had 'done together what anyone of them might have done singly; for it is not to be doubted that any nation has the right thus to set up special courts to administer law'.[13]

Seeing then that we might continue to witness the establishment of hybrid and regional tribunals, the enduring question remains: how do we arrange the relationship between these levels of courts to reduce the likelihood of jurisdictional clashes? Finding answers to this is what this book has attempted. This task invites us to rethink the entire debate around legal pluralism and the fragmentation of international law. As shown, regionalism and fragmentation are not curses to international law. If anything, they promote international criminal law in a different language and in a more contextualized way. Van den Herik and Stahn previously argued that 'fragmentation is an inherent part of international criminal law in part because it reconciles 'the "universalist" aspirations of public international law, the "humanist" dimensions of human rights law and the legality and fairness-oriented foundations of criminal law'.[14] They concluded their thoughts by inviting us not to view fragmentation of international criminal law as a challenge, but 'as an opportunity in that it offers a lens to view developments in the discipline… from a pluralist perspec-

12 *Ibid.*

13 *France & ors v. Goring & ors* (1948) 22 IMT 411, 461.

14 L. van den Herik and C. Stahn "'Fragmentation', Diversification and '3D' Legal Pluralism: International Criminal Law as the Jack-in-the-Box?" in L. van den Herik and others (eds) *The Diversification and Fragmentation of International Criminal Law* (Martinus Nijhoff 2012), 23.

tive'.[15] In this era of multiplicity of hybrid and regional tribunals, the ICC must see itself as one of many options to dispense international criminal justice. The court's practices and jurisprudence must therefore reflect this understanding.

3 Regional Complementarity and the Prospects of an Aggression Tribunal for Ukraine

The renewed attention to the crime of aggression following Russia's full-scale invasion of Ukraine in 2022 has reopened one of the most enduring gaps in the structure of international criminal law: the inability of the International Criminal Court (ICC) to reach the crime that lies at the origin of the conflict. The ICC has moved quickly in investigating war crimes, crimes against humanity, and genocide committed during the war.[16] Yet, it remains legally unable to prosecute the decision to wage the war itself. The jurisdictional framework adopted in Kampala, particularly Articles 8 *bis*, 15 *bis*, and 15 *ter* of the Rome Statute, restricts the Court from exercising jurisdiction over aggression committed by nationals of or on the territory of a non-State Party without a Security Council referral. Russia's status as a non-party and its veto power within the Council have made such a referral impossible. The result is a jurisdictional vacuum that leaves the most fundamental crime of the conflict, the unlawful use of force, beyond the reach of the universal court. The proposal for a Special Tribunal for the Crime of Aggression against Ukraine (STCoA) therefore goes to the heart of the four-tiered justice paradigm explored in this book. It illustrates the potential of regional institutions to act where global mechanisms are structurally blocked.

3.1 The Institutional Landscape and the Question of Complementarity

There are now at least four possible fora for prosecuting atrocities arising from the Russian Ukrainian conflict: the ICC, an ad hoc international tribunal (whether established through a General Assembly resolution or multilateral treaty), domestic courts exercising territorial jurisdiction (in Ukraine, Russia,

15 F. Lattanzi 'Introduction' in L. van den Herik and others (eds) *The Diversification and Fragmentation of International Criminal Law* (Martinus Nijhoff 2012) 4.

16 ICC 'Statement of ICC Prosecutor, Karim A.A. Khan QC, on the Situation in Ukraine: Receipt of Referrals from 39 States Parties and the Opening of an Investigation', 2 March 2022.

or Belarus) and national courts exercising universal jurisdiction.[17] The ICC's involvement is limited by its lack of jurisdiction over aggression. After Ukraine accepted the Court's jurisdiction under Article 12(3) of the Rome Statute,[18] the ICC opened investigations into the three core crimes upon referrals from more than forty States.[19] Aggression, however, can only be prosecuted by a competent tribunal with jurisdiction over that crime. Various options have been proposed,[20] including a General Assembly-backed international tribunal,[21] or a hybrid model grounded in Ukraine's domestic jurisdiction, which already criminalizes aggression under national law.[22]

If a special tribunal on aggression is established, it would exist alongside the ICC and Ukrainian courts, each with distinct but related mandates. This arrangement raises intricate questions about complementarity, cooperation, and potential overlap. Unlike traditional complementarity between the ICC and national jurisdictions, this scenario involves what may be called *horizontal complementarity* between two international or internationalized institutions.[23] The central question is how these courts will interact in terms of case selection, admissibility, evidence sharing, and transfer of suspects, while also coordinating with domestic proceedings. The challenge is not simply legal but also structural, as the aggression tribunal may be regionally anchored within the Council of Europe (CoE) or another regional body, bringing an additional layer of institutional complexity.

The starting point is that these courts must act as partners, not competitors. Their relationship should be founded on mutual deference, information sharing and cooperation. The Office of the Prosecutor (OTP) of the ICC has, in its Draft Policy on Complementarity and Cooperation, recognized the importance of engaging with what it terms 'specialised accountability mechanisms',

17 Dannenbaum (n. 7).

18 Ukraine accepts ICC jurisdiction over alleged crimes committed since 20 February 2014, 8 September 2015.

19 ICC 'Statement of ICC Prosecutor, Karim A.A. Khan QC, on the Situation in Ukraine: Receipt of Referrals from 39 States Parties and the Opening of an Investigation', 2 March 2022.

20 K Jon Heller 'The Best Option: An Extraordinary Ukrainian Chamber for Aggression' *Opinio Juris*, 16 March 2022 [available at http://opiniojuris.org/2022/03/16/the-best-option-an-extraordinary-ukrainian-chamber-for-aggression/ – accessed on 12 May 2023].

21 On powers of UNGA to create, see C. Stahn 'From 'United for Peace' to 'United for Justice?': Reflections on the Power of the United Nations General Assembly to Create Criminal Tribunals or Make Referrals to the ICC' (2023) 55 *Case Western Reserve Journal of International Law* 1, 251.

22 Dannenbaum (n. 7).

23 For thoughts on Horizontal Complementarity, see Chapter 6 of this book.

which include regional and hybrid tribunals.[24] This represents a progressive development compared with its earlier Informal Expert Paper on Complementarity,[25] which made no reference to cooperation with such institutions. The Draft Policy commits the ICC to deferring to genuine proceedings before *any competent accountability mechanism*.[26] This commitment provides a conceptual framework for cooperation between the ICC and any future aggression tribunal.

3.2 Normative, Structural and Jurisdictional Foundations of a Special Tribunal

At the core of the proposal lies the legal proposition that States may, through a multilateral treaty, establish an international tribunal to prosecute aggression when the ICC is unable to do so.[27] The Council of Europe has taken the lead in transforming this idea into an institutional reality. Building upon the creation of the Register of Damage Caused by the Aggression of the Russian Federation against Ukraine,[28] an Enlarged Partial Agreement established in 2023 and hosted in The Hague, the CoE has advanced plans for a complementary criminal mechanism.[29] In May 2025, the Committee of Ministers endorsed the initiative, and in June 2025 Ukraine and the Council of Europe signed the Agreement on the Special Tribunal for the Crime of Aggression, comprising both the constitutive treaty and the draft Statute.[30]

This treaty-based tribunal is grounded in Ukraine's consent, and the collective will of participating States, consistent with Article 52 of the UN Charter, which recognizes regional arrangements for maintaining international peace and security. Rather than undermining the UN system, the CoE initiative dem-

24 ICC-OTP 'Draft policy on Complementarity and Cooperation' September 2023.

25 ICC-OTP 'Informal expert paper: The principle of complementarity in practice' (2003).

26 ICC-OTP Draft Policy on Complementarity and Cooperation, September 2023, para. 80.

27 J.G Kestenbaum 'Closing Impunity Gaps for the Crime of Aggression' (2016) 17 *Chicago Journal of International Law* 1.

28 https://www.rd4u.coe.int/en/ [accessed on 24 October 2025].

29 Ukraine and the Council of Europe Sign Agreement on Establishing a Special Tribunal on the crime of Agression against Ukraine' at https://www.coe.int/en/web/portal/-/ukraine-and-the-council-of-europe-sign-agreement-on-establishing-a-special-tribunal-for-the-crime-of-aggression-against-ukraine [accessed on 24 October 2025].

30 For more information on this, see B. Bowring 'Introductory Note to Documents on the Consequences of the Aggression of the Russian Federation against Ukraine, namely The Enlarged Partial Agreement on The Register of Damage Caused' (2024) Published by Cambridge University Press on behalf of The American Society of International Law, DOI:10.1017/ilm.2024.3.

onstrates that regional institutions can lawfully complement universal ones when the latter are immobilized. The prohibition of aggression, firmly established in customary international law since the Kellogg–Briand Pact,[31] Nuremberg and General Assembly Resolution 3314, predates the 2022 invasion and satisfies the principle of legality (*nullum crimen sine lege*).[32]

Additionally, the proposal to establish the *Special Tribunal* raises other important structural, jurisdictional, and procedural considerations that speak directly to questions of legitimacy, legality, and the evolving architecture of international criminal justice. In particular, three dimensions merit emphasis: (1) the issue of *immunity* for the so-called *Troika*; (2) the requirement that the *initiative for prosecution* must emanate from Ukraine itself; and (3) the *leadership scope* of the tribunal's jurisdiction.

First, the question of immunity remains central to the tribunal's normative coherence and international legality. The so-called *Troika* – namely the President, Prime Minister and Foreign Minister of the Russian Federation – are ordinarily entitled to immunity *ratione personae* under customary international law while in office.[33] These immunities protect sitting heads of state and senior officials from the jurisdiction of foreign national courts, reflecting principles of sovereign equality and the stability of international relations. However, the draft statute of the proposed tribunal (Article 4(2)) explicitly provides that official capacity shall not constitute a defence or ground for mitigation of punishment, echoing Article 27 of the Rome Statute and Article 6(2) of the Charter of the Nuremberg Tribunal.[34] This approach situates the Special Tribunal within a line of international jurisprudence rejecting immunity before international courts and tribunals.[35] In *Prosecutor v. Charles Taylor*, the Special Court for Sierra Leone affirmed that a sitting head of state enjoys no immunity before an internationalized tribunal with a mandate grounded in international law.[36] Likewise, the International Law Commission's Draft Articles on Immunity of State Officials (2022) acknowledge exceptions to immunity for international crimes, further supporting the tribunal's

31 See M. Limberg 'In Relation to the Pact: Radical Pacifists and the Kellogg-Briand Pact, 1928–1939' (2014) 39 *Peace & Change* 3, 289–437.

32 Nuremberg Judgment (1946), paras. 41–43.

33 Hannah Lobel & Nema Milaninia, Building a Special Tribunal for the Crime of Aggression against Ukraine, EJIL: Talk!, 25 July 2025.

34 Draft Statute of the Special Tribunal for the Crime of Aggression against Ukraine, Art. 4(2); see also Rome Statute of the International Criminal Court, Art. 27; Charter of the International Military Tribunal (1945), Art. 6(2).

35 For recent debates on immunity for heads of states, see C. Eboe-Osuji 'International Law Rejects Immunity for International Crimes – Full Stop' (2023) 21 *JICJ* 461–485.

36 *Prosecutor v. Charles Taylor*, SCSL-2003-01-I, Decision on Immunity (31 May 2004).

position. While such a stance will undoubtedly attract contestation, particularly from non-State Parties to the Rome Statute, it aligns with the tribunal's hybrid international character and its aim of ensuring individual criminal responsibility for aggression.

Secondly, the proposed tribunal's establishment rests on the principle that the initiative for prosecution must originate from Ukraine. The tribunal's constitutive framework envisages its creation through a bilateral agreement between Ukraine and the Council of Europe, endorsed by the United Nations General Assembly.[37] This ensures that the tribunal derives its legitimacy from Ukraine's sovereign consent, which is a crucial element distinguishing it from tribunals created under Chapter VII of the UN Charter. Accordingly, the tribunal's prosecutorial mandate would only be activated upon Ukraine's referral or cooperation request, maintaining respect for its territorial sovereignty. The mechanism envisages close coordination with Ukraine's Office of the Prosecutor General, which would transmit evidence and case files to the tribunal for review and potential indictment.[38] This Ukrainian initiative model ensures coherence between domestic and international processes and avoids the perception of an externally imposed justice mechanism. It also reflects a principle of procedural complementarity, whereby the tribunal functions not as a substitute for Ukraine's courts but as an auxiliary structure capable of addressing crimes of aggression beyond Ukraine's jurisdictional or practical reach.

Third, the tribunal's leadership scope will be restricted to those who 'effectively exercise control over, or direct the political or military action of a State',[39] drawing upon Article 8 bis (1) of the Kampala Amendments to the Rome Statute.[40] This leadership clause confines criminal liability to those occupying positions of decision-making authority in the planning, preparation, initiation, or execution of the act of aggression. By limiting jurisdiction to senior political and military figures, the tribunal preserves the *Nuremberg principle* that aggression is fundamentally a *leadership crime*.[41] It is thus not intended to prosecute low-level operatives or field commanders but rather

37 Council of Europe, *Information Note on the Proposed Special Tribunal for the Crime of Aggression against Ukraine* (2024).

38 Asser Institute, The Special Tribunal for the Crime of Aggression against Ukraine: Legal Assessment and Policy Recommendations (2025), 11–15.

39 Article 4 of the Statute – CM (2025)103-final – [1532/2.3] Consequences of the aggression of the Russian Federation against Ukraine – Statute of the Special Tribunal for the Crime of Aggression against Ukraine.

40 Rome Statute, Amendments on the Crime of Aggression (Kampala, 2010, Art. 8 bis (1).

41 *Judgment of the International Military Tribunal for the Trial of German Major War Criminals*, Nuremberg (1946), at 435.

those responsible for the deliberate use of state power in violation of the UN Charter. This focus also ensures a functional division of labour with the International Criminal Court. While the ICC may investigate and prosecute war crimes, crimes against humanity and genocide in the context of Ukraine, the STCoA's jurisdiction over aggression will concentrate exclusively on leadership accountability, thereby reinforcing rather than duplicating the ICC's mandate.

In sum, the STCoA reflects a carefully calibrated model of legitimacy and legality. By addressing the issue of immunities, grounding prosecutions in Ukraine's sovereign initiative and confining liability to the highest leadership, the tribunal seeks to bridge the gap between international and national justice. As recent analyses have underscored, this approach not only fills the jurisdictional lacuna left by the ICC's limited aggression mandate but also demonstrates how hybrid and regionalized mechanisms can adapt to emerging geopolitical realities while upholding the principles of accountability and complementarity.[42]

3.3 How Complementarity Might Function in Practice

Complementarity between the ICC and an aggression tribunal will need to rest on a functional division of labour. The ICC will continue to prosecute individuals suspected of committing genocide, crimes against humanity and war crimes, while the aggression tribunal focuses exclusively on leadership-level decisions to wage war. Article 8 *bis* (1) of the Rome Statute defines aggression as a leadership crime, attaching liability to those who exercise control over state policy. Consequently, the aggression tribunal would deal with senior political and military figures, whereas the ICC would handle those directly responsible for atrocity crimes. This much is clear from the wordings of Article 4(1).

Nevertheless, overlaps will occur. Some defendants may be implicated in both aggression and other core crimes. In such cases, the ICC could use its prosecutorial discretion to defer to the aggression tribunal on charges relating to aggression, while continuing to pursue charges for atrocities. This would amount to a form of reverse complementarity, where the ICC defers upwards to a specialized tribunal, recognizing that the latter may be better placed to prosecute crimes beyond the ICC's jurisdiction.

---

42 See Hannah Lobel & Nema Milaninia, 'Building a Special Tribunal for the Crime of Aggression against Ukraine', *EJIL: Talk!* (2025).

A remaining question concerns overlap in leadership-level prosecutions. Should the ICC defer to an aggression tribunal even where its own investigation is broader? For example, if both courts have jurisdiction over a senior leader such as Vladimir Putin, but on different charges, deference might depend on which forum is more likely to secure accountability in practice. The principle of *ne bis in idem* would not bar both prosecutions, provided that each addresses distinct conduct and legal interests.[43]

Beyond case allocation, complementarity should extend to evidence sharing. Both courts will gather overlapping material evidence and witness testimony from the same conflict. To avoid duplication and ensure consistency, evidence collected by one court should be admissible in the other, subject to confidentiality and chain-of-custody rules. The Rules of Procedure and Evidence of the ICTY and ICTR offer useful precedents, having allowed for cooperation and transfer of materials between courts.[44] A similar arrangement would govern the ICC and STCoA.

Procedurally, admissibility questions should be raised early. When one court begins investigating a suspect, it should notify the other and coordinate its activities. Either court could challenge admissibility if the other is already pursuing the same case. This would prevent parallel investigations and reinforce efficient sequencing.

3.4 Cooperation with the International Criminal Court in the Context of Regional Complementarity

Article 46 of the Statute of the Special Tribunal for the Crime of Aggression against Ukraine[45] stands out as one of the most forward-looking provisions in the architecture of contemporary international criminal justice. It explicitly

---

43 Rome Statute, Article 20; ICC jurisprudence on *ne bis in idem*.

44 ICTY/ICTR Rules of Procedure and Evidence, Rules 9 and 11 bis.

45 The exact wordings of the provision are:

Article 46 – Co-operation with the International Criminal Court

(1) The Special Tribunal shall co-operate with the International Criminal Court on all matters of mutual concern. The Special Tribunal may conclude agreements or practical arrangements with the International Criminal Court with a view to ensuring the effective exercise of their respective jurisdictions.

(2) Nothing in this Statute shall negate the existing obligations of States Parties to the Rome Statute of the International Criminal Court to co-operate fully with the International Criminal Court in its investigation and prosecution of crimes within its jurisdiction. Whenever a person subject to an arrest warrant by the International Criminal Court is detained in the detention facilities of the International Criminal Court, the Special Tribunal shall give priority to the proceedings before the International Criminal Court.

mandates cooperation with the International Criminal Court (ICC), thereby formalizing a horizontal relationship between two international institutions that will likely operate within the same factual and legal terrain. Paragraph 1 establishes a clear obligation for the tribunal to cooperate with the ICC 'on all matters of mutual concern' and authorizes the conclusion of agreements or practical arrangements to ensure the effective exercise of their respective jurisdictions. This clause embodies the principle of regional complementarity developed throughout this book – the idea that regional or specialized mechanisms do not compete with universal institutions but instead work in partnership to fill jurisdictional and functional gaps. In practice, this provision enables direct cooperation on information exchange, mutual legal assistance, witness protection and coordination of investigative activities. It provides the legal foundation for joint working arrangements between the two institutions, similar in spirit to the cooperation once established between the ICTY, ICTR and national courts, but now extended to inter-institutional collaboration at the international level.

Equally significant is paragraph 2, which preserves the existing obligations of States Parties to the Rome Statute to cooperate fully with the ICC in the investigation and prosecution of crimes within its jurisdiction. By reaffirming this duty, the Statute ensures that participation in the regional mechanism does not diminish or conflict with States' obligations under the Rome Statute. The final sentence of paragraph 2 introduces an important sequencing principle, providing that where a person subject to an ICC arrest warrant is detained in ICC custody, the Special Tribunal must give priority to the ICC's proceedings. This clause is not merely procedural; it functions as a built-in mechanism for conflict avoidance and jurisdictional harmony. It ensures that the relationship between the two institutions is managed through coordination rather than competition, and that the ICC's pre-existing authority in its areas of jurisdiction is fully respected. At the same time, it reflects a pragmatic understanding of complementarity: while the ICC retains primacy over the three core crimes, the regional tribunal complements its work by addressing the one crime the ICC cannot currently prosecute – aggression.

The inclusion of such a cooperation clause is especially noteworthy when considered in light of earlier practice. Several post-ICC tribunals including the Kosovo Specialist Chambers were surprisingly silent about any formal relationship with the ICC, despite having been established after the Rome Statute entered into force. The Special Tribunal for Aggression therefore marks a clear doctrinal and institutional advance. By expressly mandating cooperation with the ICC, it transforms complementarity from a largely theoretical organizing principle into an operational framework for partnership. The provision symbolizes the maturation of the international justice system into a genuinely pluralist architecture, in which regional institutions expand the reach of accountability while reinforcing, rather than rivalling, the authority of the ICC. Through Article 46, regional complementarity is not simply affirmed in principle but implemented in practice – ensuring that the two institutions can work in concert to deliver comprehensive justice for the crimes arising from the war in Ukraine.

3.5 The Council of Europe's Role and Regional Complementarity

The decision to situate the aggression tribunal within the CoE framework is both symbolic and practical. Since 1949 the CoE has represented Europe's commitment to the rule of law and human rights. By anchoring the tribunal within this framework, States ensure independence, procedural legitimacy and compliance with the European Convention on Human Rights.[46] The CoE's 2025 documentation confirms that judges will be selected through transparent procedures and that the tribunal will cooperate closely with the ICC.

The CoE's leadership also reflects the resurgence of regional multilateralism as a force for legality. While the Security Council remains paralysed, regional organizations are stepping forward to reinforce international norms. The Register of Damage and the Special Tribunal together constitute a twin-track accountability architecture: the former handling reparations and the latter criminal responsibility. Both are headquartered in The Hague and supported by a coalition of European and non-European States. This configuration transforms The Hague into a genuine ecosystem of international justice rather than a single institutional site.[47]

3.6 Broader Significance and Future Challenges

If realized, the Special Tribunal would mark a decisive step in the evolution of international criminal law. It would be the first international court since Nuremberg dedicated solely to the crime of aggression, and the first to emerge under a regional organization. It would also affirm the *jus cogens* status of the prohibition of aggression and demonstrate that regional and universal systems can coexist harmoniously. The ICC's jurisdiction would continue to

46 Council of Europe FAQ on the Special Tribunal (2025) at https://www.coe.int/en/web/portal/frequently-asked-questions [accessed on 24 October 2025].

47 *Ibid.*

cover the three core crimes, while the tribunal would fill the remaining gap. Together, they would finally establish comprehensive accountability across all four core crimes of international concern.

Nonetheless, challenges persist. Enforcement remains the Achilles heel of international criminal justice. Arresting senior officials of a major power depends less on law than on political will. The tribunal must therefore be designed for endurance, using sealed indictments, travel bans, and asset freezes to maintain pressure even without immediate custody. Cooperation with Eurojust, Interpol and domestic agencies will be critical. Funding sustainability will also matter: a combination of assessed contributions, voluntary pledges and secondments, subject to independent audit, can ensure transparency.

Finally, legitimacy will depend on inclusivity and independence. The tribunal must avoid perceptions of bias by maintaining open membership to non-European States and insulating judicial appointments from political interference. Outreach in multiple languages and transparent communication will be essential. Over time, the tribunal's jurisprudence and archives should feed into the ICC and other courts, ensuring a lasting legacy.

In sum, complementarity between the ICC and a Special Tribunal on Aggression must be based on partnership and division of labour. Rather than a hierarchical relationship, it would reflect horizontal complementarity rooted in cooperation, sequencing and shared commitment to justice. In the wider sense, this approach embodies the idea of regional complementarity advocated in this book: that international, regional and national courts can work together to close jurisdictional gaps and reinforce accountability for the gravest crimes.

4 Regional Complementarity and the Proposed Special Tribunal for the Gambia

The proposed Special Tribunal for The Gambia (STG) represents one of the most ambitious recent developments in the evolution of regional approaches to international criminal accountability in Africa. Following the recommendations of the Truth, Reconciliation and Reparations Commission (TRRC), which concluded its work in 2021, the Government of The Gambia committed to establishing a hybrid tribunal to prosecute serious crimes committed under the regime of former President Yahya Jammeh between 1994 and 2017.[48] The

48 TRRC (The Gambia), Final Report, 2021.

TRRC's final report documented systematic acts of torture, enforced disappearances, extrajudicial executions and sexual and gender-based violence, concluding that such acts amounted to crimes against humanity.[49]

4.1 Background and Context

The Gambia's transitional justice process has been a regional and international undertaking from its inception. The TRRC's establishment, design and implementation benefited from substantial technical and financial support from the Economic Community of West African States (ECOWAS), the African Union (AU) and the United Nations (UN).[50] ECOWAS, in particular, emerged as a crucial political and institutional partner – first in facilitating the post-2016 transition that ended Jammeh's two-decade rule, and later in sustaining pressure for accountability. In 2017, ECOWAS deployed the ECOWAS Mission in The Gambia (ECOMIG), which remains in the country to stabilize the democratic transition.[51] This background is significant because it underlines ECOWAS's role not merely as a peace-keeping actor but increasingly as a normative force in West Africa's justice architecture. ECOWAS's longstanding commitment to democratic governance, reflected in its 2001 Protocol on Democracy and Good Governance, provides the legal and political foundations for its involvement in accountability processes.[52] The same normative framework that underpins ECOWAS's democracy agenda now informs its support for The Gambia's transitional justice and the establishment of the STG.

4.2 Institutional Design and Jurisdiction

The draft statute of the proposed tribunal, developed jointly by ECOWAS and The Gambia's Ministry of Justice in 2023, envisages a hybrid judicial structure combining national and international elements.[53] The tribunal would have jurisdiction over crimes against humanity, torture, enforced disappearance and other serious violations of international law committed

49 *Ibid.*

50 Information derived from ECOWAS/UN/AU reports on The Gambia Transitional Justice Framework, 2022.

51 ECOWAS, ECOMIG Deployment Report, 2017.

52 ECOWAS Protocol on Democracy and Good Governance, 2001.

53 Draft Statute for the Special Tribunal for The Gambia, 2023 (ECOWAS-Gambia Joint Working Group).

between July 1994 and January 2017.[54] The hybrid design follows the model of earlier regional experiments, notably the Extraordinary African Chambers (EAC) in Senegal, which prosecuted Hissène Habré, but it diverges in two key respects. First, it is formally grounded in a sub-regional treaty-based framework between ECOWAS and a member state, rather than an AU decision.[55] Second, it is envisioned as seated in Banjul, operating within The Gambia's legal system but drawing its legitimacy and operational support from ECOWAS. The statute provides for a mixed bench comprising Gambian and international judges and a similarly composed prosecution office. International personnel are to be seconded by ECOWAS in consultation with the AU and the UN.[56] This arrangement ensures that the tribunal reflects both domestic ownership and international oversight, a balance intended to secure legitimacy and adherence to fair-trial standards. In addition, the tribunal's legal framework provides for a distinct appellate chamber and a Victims and Witnesses Unit, mirroring best practices from hybrid courts such as the Special Court for Sierra Leone (SCSL) and the EAC. Jurisdictionally, the tribunal adopts both temporal and subject-matter limitations: its temporal jurisdiction covers the duration of the Jammeh regime, while its subject-matter jurisdiction is restricted to international crimes and serious human rights violations as defined under Gambian and international law.[57]

4.3 ECOWAS's Normative and Institutional Role

The involvement of ECOWAS in the creation of the Special Tribunal for The Gambia is a ground-breaking development in the sub-region's legal landscape. It marks the first instance where a sub-regional organization takes a lead role in establishing a criminal-accountability mechanism for international crimes committed within a member state.[58]

From a normative perspective, ECOWAS's participation signifies an expansion of its established peace and security mandate into the realm of transitional justice and accountability. The organization's Revised Treaty (1993) and its supplementary protocols empower it to intervene in the internal affairs of member states in cases of grave human rights violations, unconstitutional

54 *Ibid.*
55 *Ibid.*
56 *Ibid.*
57 *Ibid.*
58 Di Donato, Marco, 'The Special Tribunal for The Gambia: A Regional Experiment in Transitional Justice and Its Challenges', EJIL: Talk! (8 Sept 2025).

changes of government and serious breaches of democratic governance.[59] These powers, previously exercised through mediation and peacekeeping are now being extended into the domain of criminal accountability.

Institutionally, ECOWAS's role can be conceptualized along three dimensions. First, as a political sponsor, it provides diplomatic legitimacy and ensures regional endorsement of the tribunal's activities. Second, as a normative guarantor, it embeds the tribunal within the framework of regional human rights standards, thereby enhancing its legal foundation and shielding it from accusations of victor's justice. Third, as a logistical facilitator, ECOWAS contributes expertise, personnel, and resource-mobilization capacity to ensure operational sustainability.[60]

As I have argued elsewhere, 'ECOWAS as a regional organisation is well-placed to understand the socio-political dynamics of The Gambia and its neighbours, fostering a sense of ownership and legitimacy'. [61] I also note that 'regional mechanisms often operate at a fraction of the cost of international tribunals… making them more sustainable and accessible', which underscores the STG's potential in delivering efficient justice.[62] In this sense, ECOWAS's involvement goes beyond the precedent set by the AU in the establishment of the EAC, where the AU acted largely as an intermediary. Here, ECOWAS becomes an active co-creator of a judicial mechanism, reflecting a deeper institutionalization of regional complementarity in practice.

4.4 The Tribunal and Regional Complementarity

The creation of the STG offers critical insights into the evolving notion of regional complementarity as articulated in this book. It demonstrates how a sub-regional organization can operationalize complementarity between national and regional levels in three main ways.

First, by anchoring the tribunal within The Gambia's domestic legal system, ECOWAS ensures that the principle of subsidiarity is respected – national institutions retain primacy, while regional structures provide reinforcement where national capacity or political will is lacking. Second, the tribunal illustrates horizontal complementarity among regional institutions: ECOWAS collaborates with the AU and potentially the African Court of Justice and Human

59 ECOWAS Revised Treaty, 1993.

60 *Ibid.*

61 Seun Solomon Bakare, 'Analysis: How ECOWAS-backed Special Criminal Court in The Gambia can be successful', Premium Times (26 January 2025). Premium Times Nigeria.

62 *Ibid.*

Rights, creating a network of mutually reinforcing regional mechanisms. Third, the tribunal could serve as a model of functional complementarity with the ICC, as it addresses crimes of international concern that are unlikely to be prosecuted by the ICC due to jurisdictional or resource constraints.[63]

My commentary reinforces this point by arguing that the STG 'could serve as a model for other regional initiatives seeking to address impunity in contexts where national systems are weak and international interventions are limited'.[64] The STG thus exemplifies the four-tiered justice paradigm advanced in this book, where regional and sub-regional mechanisms fill the gaps between national and international criminal jurisdictions. It reaffirms the argument that regional complementarity can strengthen the coherence of international criminal law rather than fragment it, provided that regional bodies adhere to international procedural and substantive norms.

4.5 Challenges and Prospects

Despite its promise, the proposed tribunal faces significant challenges. Financing remains a major obstacle. ECOWAS's capacity to fund long-term judicial operations is limited, and donor dependence may threaten the tribunal's independence.[65] The experience of the SCSL, which struggled with sustainability despite UN support, underscores this concern.A second challenge concerns the tribunal's jurisdictional reach. The possibility that former President Jammeh may never be extradited from Equatorial Guinea raises questions about the tribunal's ability to deliver justice for high-level perpetrators. Without Jammeh, the tribunal risks being perceived as symbolic rather than transformative.[66] Third, institutional complexity could impede efficiency. The multiplicity of actors – The Gambia, ECOWAS, the AU and potential UN partners – may complicate decision-making and delay proceedings. Balancing domestic and international participation will require careful management to avoid conflicts of competence.

Nevertheless, the tribunal presents an unprecedented opportunity to consolidate regional accountability in West Africa. It could strengthen ECOWAS's institutional legitimacy, foster jurisprudential development in the field of hybrid justice and contribute to a growing body of regional practice underpinned by principles of complementarity and subsidiarity. In my conclusion

63 *Ibid.*
64 *Ibid.*
65 JusticeInfo.net, 'Gambia: a special court in search of funds', 18 March 2025.
66 Bakare (n. 61 above).

elsewhere, 'while significant challenges remain, this initiative has the potential to be a landmark achievement in regional complementarity, reaffirming the critical role of regional bodies in promoting human rights and the rule of law in Africa'. [67] If successfully implemented, the STG would extend the normative trajectory inaugurated by the EAC and the Malabo Protocol, affirming that African regional and sub-regional bodies can take ownership of accountability processes without external imposition.

67 Seun Bakare, 'The ECOWAS-backed Special Criminal Court in The Gambia: A Triumph for Regional Complementarity?' The Cable, available at https://www.thecable.ng/the-ecowas-backed-special-criminal-court-in-the-gambia-a-triumph-for-regional-complementarity/.

Bibliography

Table of Cases

International Criminal Court

Prosecutor v. Dyilo, ICC-01/04-01/06, Decision Concerning Pre-trial Chamber I's Decision of 10 February 2006 and the Incorporation of Documents into the Record of the Case against Mr. Thomas Lubanga Dyilo, 24 February 2006.

Prosecutor v. Katanga & Chui, ICC-01/04-01/07OA 8, Judgment on the Appeal of Mr. Germain Katanga against the Oral Decision of Trial Chamber II of 12 June 2009 on the Admissibility of the Case, 25 September 2009.

Prosecutor v. Katanga and Ngudjolo, ICC-01/04–01/07–949, of 11 March 2009 (Katanga Admissibility Challenge), 30 September 2008.

Prosecutor v. Katanga and Ngudjolo, ICC-01/04–01/07-T-67-ENG ET, 12 June 2009.

Prosecutor v. Ntaganda, ICC-01/04–02/06–20-Annex 2, 21 July 2008.

Prosecutor v. Kony et al., ICC-02/04–01/05–1-US-Exp, 12 July 2005, 2 (unsealed pursuant to ICC-02/04–01/05–52, 13 October 2005).

Prosecutor v. Lubanga, ICC-01/04–01/06–8-Corr (reclassified as public pursuant to ICC01/04–01/06–37), 9 March 2006, para. 33 (Lubanga Arrest Warrant Decision).

Prosecutor v. Mathieu Ngudjolo Chui (ICC-01/04-02/12-4), Judgment Pursuant to Article 74 of the Statute, 18 December 2012.

Prosecutor v Katanga and Ngudjolo, ICC-01/04–01/07–1497, 25 September 2009.

Prosecutor v. Omar Hassan Ahmad Al Bashir, ICC Second Warrant of Arrest for Omar Hassan Ahmad Al Bashir, ICC-02/05-01/09-95, 12 July 2010.

Prosecutor v. Lubanga, ICC-01/04-01/06-803-tEN), Decision on the Confirmation of Charges, 29 January 2007.

Prosecutor v+. Saif Al-Islam Gaddafi and Abdullah Al-Senussi, ICC-01/11-01/11, Decision on the admissibility of the case against Saif Al-Islam Gaddafi.

Prosecutor v. Saif Al-Islam Gaddafi and Abdullah Al-Senussi. ICC-OI/II-OI/IIOA6, ICC, Judgment on the appeal of Mr. Abdullah Al-Senussi against the decision of Pre-trial Chamber I of 11 October 2013 entitled Decision on the admissibility of the case against Abdullah Al-Senussi, 24 July 2014.

Prosecutor v. Simone Gbagbo: Judgment on the appeal of Côte d' Ivoire against the decision of Pre-trial Chamber I of 11 December 2014 entitled Decision on Côte d' Ivoire's challenge to the admissibility of the case against Simone Gbagbo, 27 May 2015.

Prosecutor v. Uhuru Muigai Kenyatta, ICC-01/09-02/11-1005, ICC, Decision on the withdrawal of charges against Mr. Kenyatta, 13 March 2015.

Prosecutor v. Alfred Yekatom and Patrice-Edouard Ngaissona, ICC Doc: ICC-01/14-01/18-523, Yekatom Defence Appeal Brief on Admissibility.

Prosecutor v. Jean-Pierre Bemba Gombo: Decision on the Admissibility and Abuse of Process Challenges 24 June 2010.

Prosecutor v. Germain Katanga and Mathieu Ngudjolo Chui, ICC-01/04-01/07, Judgment on the Appeal of Mr. Germain Katanga against the Oral Decision of Trial Chamber II of 12 June 2009 on the Admissibility of the Case.

Prosecutor v. Germain Katanga and Mathieu Ngudjolo Chui, ICC-01/04-01/07 Judgment on the Appeal against the Decision on Joinder rendered on 10 March 2008 by the PreTrial Chamber.

Prosecutor v. William Ruto and others; ICC Doc: ICC-01/09-01/11, Judgment on the appeal of the Republic of Kenya against the decision of Pre-trial Chamber II of 30 May 2011 entitled Decision on the Application by the Government of Kenya Challenging the Admissibility of the Case Pursuant to Article 19(2)(b) of the Statute, Dissenting Opinion of Judge Anita Ušacka.

International Court of Justice

Case Concerning the Arrest Warrant of 11 April 2000 (*Democratic Republic of the Congo v. Belgium*), Judgement of 14 February 2002.

Case Concerning the Arrest Warrant of 11 April 2000 (*Democratic Republic of the Congo v. Belgium*), ICJ, Separate Opinion of Judge Higgins *et al.*, Judgment, 14 February 2002.

International Criminal Tribunal for the Former Yugoslavia (ICTY)

Prosecutor v. Milomir Stakic, Case No. IT-97–24-A, Judgment, 22 March 2006.

Prosecutor v. Milan Kovacevic, Decision on Prosecutor's Request to File an Amended Indictment, 5 March 1998.

Special Tribunal for Lebanon

Akhbar Beirut S.A.L. Ibrahim Mohamed Ali Al Amin, Case. No. STL-14-06/T/CJ, Trial Chamber Judgement, 15 July 2016 (Akhbar, Trial Chamber Judgement).

Other Cases

France & ors v. Goring & ors (1948) 22 IMT 411.

Case No: A2/2017/0721, In the Court of Appeal (Civil Division) on Appeal from the High Court of Justice Queen's Bench Division the Honourable Mrs. Justice Elisabeth Laing DBE [2017] EWHC 371 (QB).

The Federation of African Journalists (FAJ) and others Vs. The Gambia, Suit No: ECW/CCJ/AP/36/15.
Hadijatou Mani Koraou v. Niger, Suit No: ECW/CCJ/APP/08/08.
Hissène Habré v. Republic of Senegal ECW/CCJ/JUD/06/10).
HRH Emere Godwin Bebe Okpabi & Ors v Royal Dutch Shell Plc & Anor [2017] EWHC 89 (TCC).
Michael Domingues v. United States, Case No. 12.285.
Ocean King Nigeria Ltd v. Republic of Senegal, Suit No: ECW/CCJ/AP/05/08.
Roach and Pinkerton v. United States, Inter-American Commission on Human Rights Petition 12-439, No. 3/87.

International Instruments

Treaties and Conventions

International Criminal Tribunal for the former Yugoslavia Statute, 25 May 1993.
The International Criminal Tribunal for Rwanda Statute, 8 November 1994.
Tunisian Organic Law No. 2013-53 on Establishing and Organizing Transitional Justice, 15 December 2013.
Protocol on Amendments to the Protocol on the Statute of the African Court of Justice and Human Rights otherwise known as the Malabo Protocol, June 2014.
Rome Statute of the International Criminal Court, 17 July 1998.
Slave Trade Act, 25 March 1807.
Slave Trade Felony Act 1811.
Slavery Abolition Act 1833.
Statute of the Extraordinary African Chambers within the courts of Senegal created to prosecute international crimes committed in Chad between 7 June 1982 and 1 December 1990.
The Convention on the Prevention and Punishment of the Crime of Genocide, 9 December 1948.
Convention against Torture and Other Cruel, Inhuman or Degrading Treatment or Punishment, 10 December 1984.
Protocol to the African Charter on Human and Peoples' Rights on the Establishment of an African Court on Human and Peoples' Rights, 10 June 1998.
Rules of Procedure of the African Commission on Human and Peoples' Rights (6 October 1995).
Treaty on Functioning of the EU, 1 January 1958.
Treaty of Neuilly, 5 November 1919.

Treaty of St. Germain, 10 September 1919.
Treaty of Sèvres, 10 August 1920.
Vienna Convention on the Law of Treaties (1969).
The Versailles Treaty, 28 June 1919.
UN Convention on Corruption 14 December 2005.
UN Convention on Laundering, Search, Seizure and Confiscation of the Proceeds from Crime (1990).
Constitutive Act of the African Union (2000).
African Union Convention on preventing and combatting corruption (2003).
African Charter on Democracy, Election and Governance, 30 January 2007.
Protocol to the OAU Convention on the Prevention and Combating of Terrorism (July 1999).
ASEAN Convention on Counter Terrorism, 13 January 2007.
Arab Convention for the Suppression of Terrorism, April 1998.

Reports

ICC Reports

ICC-OTP, OTP Report on the activities performed during the first three years (June 2003-June 2006), 12 September 2006.
ICC-ASP, Report of the Bureau on cooperation, ICC-ASP/8/44, 15 November 2009.
ICC-ASP, Report of the Bureau on the Plan of action of the Assembly of States Parties for achieving universality and full implementation of the Rome Statute of the International Criminal Court, 18 March 2010.
ICC-ASP, Report of the Bureau on complementarity, ICC-ASP/16/33, 22 November 2017.
ICC-ASP, Report of the Bureau on Stocktaking: Complementarity, ICC-ASP/8/51, 18 March 2010.
ICC-ASP, Report of the court on cooperation, ICC-ASP/15/9, 11 October 2016.
ICC-OTP, Report on Prosecutorial Strategy, 14 September 2006.
ICC-ASP, Report of the Bureau on the Plan of action of the Assembly of States Parties for achieving universality and full implementation of the Rome Statute of the International Criminal Court, ICC-ASP/18/24, 20 November 2019.
ICC Doc: ICC Second Assembly of States Parties to the Rome Statute of the International Criminal Court Report of the Prosecutor of the ICC, Mr. Luis Moreno-Ocampo, 8 September 2003.

United Nations Reports

Report of the Assessment Mission on the Establishment of an International Judicial Commission of Inquiry for Burundi, UN Doc S/2005/158, 17 December 2005.

UNMISS, Conflict in South Sudan: A Human Rights Report, 8 May 2014.

UNGA, General Assembly Official Records Volume III, Reports and other documents (2002) UN Doc A/CONF. 183/13 (Vol. III).

UN, Fourth Report on Peremptory Norms of General International Law (jus cogens) by Dire Tladi, Special Rapporteur, A/CN. 4/727 (2018).

UN, Fourth Report on the Law of Treaties by Mr. G. G. Fitzmaurice, Special Rapporteur extracted from the Yearbook of the International Law Commission, A/CN.4/120 (1959).

UNGA, Report of the Ad Hoc Committee on the Establishment of an International Criminal Court, UN Doc A/50/22 (1995).

Report of the International Law Commission on Jus Cogens, Sixty-Sixth Session (2014).

Reports from other International Bodies

Council of Europe, Council of Europe Parliamentary Assembly Report on Inhuman treatment of people and illicit trafficking in human organs in Kosovo, Document 12462 of 7 January 2011.

AU, Report of the Committee of Eminent African Jurists on the Case of Hissène Habré (Undated).

ICJ, Reports of Judgments, Advisory Opinions and Orders on Questions Relating to the Obligation to Prosecute or Extradite (Belgium v. Senegal) Judgment of 20 July 2012.

International Bar Association, Legal Representation, Fairness and Access to Justice in Hybrid Tribunals and Specialised Chambers, International Criminal Court and International Criminal Law Programme Report (2018).

Miscellaneous Documents of the International Criminal Court

ICC Appeals Chambers in Judgment on the appeal of Mr. Abdullah Al-Senussi against the decision of Pre-trial Chamber I of 11 October 2013.

ICC Doc: ICC-02/05-01/09 OA2, The African Union's Submission in the Hashemite Kingdom of Jordan's Appeal against the Decision under Article 87(7) of the Rome Statute on the Non-compliance by Jordan with the Request by the Court for the Arrest and Surrender of Omar Al-Bashir

Cooperation Agreement between the Office of the Prosecutor of the International Criminal Court and the Government of Colombia.

ICC-OTP, ICC-01/11-01/11 Corrigendum to Prosecution Response to the Document in Support of the Government of Libya's Appeal against the Decision on the Admissibility of the Case against Saif Al-Islam Gaddafi

Draft Statute for an International Criminal Court with Commentaries 1994: Text Adopted by the International Law Commission at Its Forty-Sixth Session, in 1994, and Submitted to the General Assembly as a Part of the Commission's Report Covering the Work of that Session.

ICC-OTP, Draft Policy on Complementarity and Cooperation (2023).

ICC-01/09, Decision Pursuant to Article 15 on the Authorization of an Investigation into the Situation in the Republic of Kenya (31 March 2010).

ICC-01/09, Decision Pursuant to Article 15 on the Authorization of an Investigation into the Situation in the Republic of Kenya, Dissenting Opinion of Judge Hans-Peter Kaul, (31 March 2010).

ICC Doc: ICC-02/04-01/05, Decision on the Prosecutor's Position on the Decision of Pretrial Chamber II to Redact Factual Descriptions of Crimes from the Warrants of Arrest, Motion for Reconsideration, and Motion for Clarification.

ICC-OTP, Informal Expert Paper: The principle of complementarity in practice (2003).

ICC-OTP, Paper on some policy issues before the Office of the Prosecutor (2003).

ICC-OTP, Situation in the Islamic Republic of Afghanistan: Prosecution Appeal Brief, 30 September 2019.

ICC-OTP, Prosecutorial Strategy 2009-2012, 1 February 2012.

Prosecutor v Saif Al-Islam Gaddafi, ICC Doc: ICC-01/11-01/11 Public Redacted version of Request for Disclosure of Memorandum on Burden Sharing between the ICC Office of the Prosecutor and the Government of Libya, 28 March 2014.

ICC Review Conference, Taking Stock of the Principle of Complementarity: Bridging the Impunity Gap, Informal Summary by the Focal Points, RC/ST/CM/1, 22 June 2010.

Judicial Seminar: Complementarity and Cooperation of Courts in an Interconnected Global Justice System. International Criminal Court (ICC), The Hague, Netherlands. Summary of seminar proceedings, Welcoming remarks by Judge Silvia Fernández de Gurmendi, ICC President, 18 January 2018.

ICC-OTP, Memorandum of Understanding between the Republic of Guinea and the OTP, 28 September 2022.

ICC-PRES, Memorandum of Understanding between The International Criminal Court and The Inter-American Court of Human Rights, 15 February 2016.

ICC-PRES, Memorandum of Understanding regarding Administrative Arrangements between the International Criminal Court and the Special Court for Sierra Leone, 13 April 2006.

ICC-OTP, Transitional Justice in Colombia and the role of the International Criminal Court: Text of a conference paper by the Deputy Prosecutor of the ICC, 13 May 2015.

Financial statements of the International Criminal Court for the year ended 31 December 2018.
ICC-PRES/01-01-06 Agreement between the International Criminal Court and the European Union on Cooperation and Assistance, 10 April 2006.

ICC Press Releases and Public Information

ICC Press Release: ICC and Inter American Court Sign Memorandum of Understanding on cooperation, 16 February 2016.
High-Level ICC Regional Seminar on Cooperation opens in Romania, 21 March 2016.
Press Release, ICC Prosecutor, Mr. Karim A.A Khan QC, opens an investigation into the Situation in Venezuela and concludes Memorandum of Understanding with the Government, 5 November 2021.
Statement of the ICC Prosecutor to the Diplomatic Corps, 12 February 2004).
Statement of ICC Prosecutor, Karim A.A Khan QC, on the Situation in Ukraine: Receipt of Referrals from 39 States Parties and the Opening of an Investigation, 2 March 2022.
ICC judges reject opening of an investigation regarding Afghanistan situation, 12 April 2019.
Ukraine accepts ICC jurisdiction over alleged crimes committed since 20 February 2014, 8 September 2015.
Statement by Mr. Luis Moreno-Ocampo, at the Ceremony for the Solemn Undertaking of the Chief Prosecutor, 16 June 2003.

Miscellaneous Documents of the United Nations

UN Doc CAT/C/36/D/181/2001, decision on Communication No. 181/2001 Suleymane Guengueng *et al.* (represented by counsel) v Senegal.
UN Doc A/AC.249/1997/L.8/Rev.1 (14 August 1997) Decisions Taken by the Preparatory Committee at its Session held from 4 to 15 August 1997, para. 1.
UN Doc A/CN.4/L.702 (2006), Fragmentation of International Law: Difficulties Arising from the Diversification and Expansion of International Law.
CCPR/C/OP/2 International Covenant on Civil and Political Rights Selected Decisions of The Human Rights Committee under The Optional Protocol Volume 2 Seventeenth to Thirty-Second, October 1982 to April 1988.
S/RES/1595 (2005) Resolution 1595 (2005) Adopted by the Security Council at its 5160th meeting, on 7 April 2005.

UN Doc S/RES/1315 (2000) Resolution 1315 (2000) Adopted by the Security Council at its 4186th meeting, on 14 August 2000.

S/RES/1757 (2007), Resolution 1757 Adopted by the Security Council at its 5685th meeting, on 30 May 2007.

United Nations Security Council resolution 1272 (25 October 1999).

UN Doc A/CN.4/SER.A/1985/Add.l (Part 2) (1985) *Yearbook of the International Law Commission.*

UN Doc A/CN.4/SER.A/1994/Add. l (Part 2) 27 *Yearbook of the International Law Commission* (1994)Catalogue of Regulations relating to the UN Administration in East Timor.

Historical Survey of the Question of International Criminal Jurisdiction, UN Doc A/CN.4/7/Rev.1, 18.

UN Doc A/CONF.183/C.1/L.25 (29 June 1998), in *United Nations Diplomatic Conference of Plenipotentiaries on the Establishment of an International Court* (*Rome 15 June-17 July 1998*).

United Nations Transitional Administration in East Timor Regulation 2000/15.

UN Doc A/50/22 General Assembly Official Records, Fiftieth Session Supplement No. 22.

UN Doc A/CONF. 183. C. 1/SR. 11, Summary Records of the 1998 Diplomatic Conference (22 June 1998), in '*The UN United Nations Diplomatic Conference of Plenipotentiaries on the Establishment of an International Criminal Court' Rome, 15 June – 17 July 1998 Official Records Volume II.*

Regulation No. 2000/11 on the Organization of Courts in East Timor UN Doc: S/2005/762, Letter dated 5 December 2005 from the Chargé d' affaires of the Permanent Mission of Lebanon to the United Nations addressed to the Secretary-General.

S/2005/783 Letter dated 13 December 2005 from the Chargé d' affaire of the Permanent Mission of Lebanon to the United Nations addressed to the Secretary-General.

UN Press Release: Russia, China block Security Council referral of Syria to International Criminal Court, 22 May 2014.

War Crimes Denial, Failure to Cooperate with National Authorities Hampering Progress of Former Yugoslavia Tribunal, Security Council Told, 7 June 2017.

Miscellaneous Documents of Other International Bodies

African Union

Decision on the Hissene Habre case and the African Union Doc Assembly/AU/Dec.127 (VII) (2007).

Decision at the 30th Ordinary Session of the Assembly, 28-29 January 2018, Addis Ababa Ethiopia. AU Doc: Assembly/AU/Draft/Doc.8(XXX) Draft Decision on the International Criminal Court Doc EX.CL/1008(XXXII).

African Union Press Release: AU expresses grave concern over State of Emergency, insists President Yahya Jammeh must hand-over power to President-elect Adama Barrow, 18 January 2017.

Regional Economic Communities (RECs) [available at https://au.int/en/organs/recs – accessed 9th February 2024].

Association of Southeast Asian Nations

The 1997 ASEAN Declaration on Transnational Crimes, 20 December 1997.

Council of Europe

Liability of enterprises for offences: Recommendation No. R (88) 18 adopted by the Committee of Ministers of the Council of Europe on 20 October 1988 and explanatory memorandum (1990).

Convention on on Laundering, Search, Seizure and Confiscation of the Proceeds from Crime (1990).

Council of Europe, 'Extradition: European Standards: explanatory notes on the Council of Europe convention and protocols and minimum standards protecting persons subject to transnational criminal proceedings' (Council of Europe Publishing 2006) 140.

European Union

Council Decision 2011/168/CFSP of 21 March 2011 on the International Criminal Court and repealing Common Position 2003/444/CFSP.

Directive 2014/41/EU of The European Parliament and of The Council of 3 April 2014regarding the European Investigation Order in criminal matters.

The European Union Counter-Terrorism Strategy (2005).

European Commission, Helping international justice to thrive: support to Kosovo Specialist Chambers and EUAM Ukraine, 17 July 2023.

Eurojust, Guidelines for Deciding 'Which Jurisdiction Should Prosecute?' (Revised 2016).

European Public Prosecutor's Office, Missions and Tasks [available at https://www.eppo.europa.eu/en/mission-and-tasks – accessed 12 January 2024].

Europol 'Working Arrangement establishing cooperative relations between the KSCSPO and the European Union Agency for law Enforcement Cooperation (EUROPOL)' (2020).

Extraordinary Chambers in the Courts of Cambodia

Agreement between the United Nations and the Royal Government of Cambodia concerning the prosecution under Cambodian law of crimes committed during the period of Democratic Kampuchea, 6 June 2003.

Global Organization of Parliamentarians against Corruption

GOPAC, Prosecuting Grand Corruption as an International Crime (2013).

International Committee of the Red Cross (ICRC)

ICRC, Issues raised regarding the Rome Statute of the ICC by national Constitutional Courts, Supreme Courts and Councils of State, Advisory Service on International Humanitarian Law (2010).

International Court of Justice

Case concerning Questions Relating to the Obligation to Prosecute or Extradite (Belgium v. Senegal), Memorial of the Kingdom of Belgium, 1 July 2010.
Case concerning Questions Relating to the Obligation to Prosecute or Extradite (Belgium v. Senegal), Senegal's Counter-Memorial, 23 August 2011.

Caribbean Court of Justice

Agreement Establishing the Caribbean Court of Justice, 14 February 2001.

Miscellaneous

Counter-terrorism in Central Asia [available at https://www.un.org/counterterrorism/cct/counter-terrorism-in-central-asia – accessed 9th February 2024].
Latin American Criminal Court against Transnational Organised Crime [available at http://www.europarl.europa.eu/meetdocs/2014_2019/documents/dlat/dv/07_copla_abstractnov2016/07_copla_abstractnov2016en.pdf – accessed 8 February 2024].

International Law Commission, 'Draft conclusions on identification of customary international law, with commentaries (2018).

International and Hybrid Criminal Tribunals [available at; https://www.un.org/ruleoflaw/thematic-areas/international-law-courts-tribunals/international-hybrid-criminal-courts-tribunals/ – accessed 15 June 2023].

Opinion by Legal Advisory Committee to the Minister of Foreign Affairs of the Republic of Poland on immunities of State officials from foreign criminal jurisdiction, 27 April 2015.

United Nations International Residual Mechanism for Criminal Tribunals Cases referred to national jurisdictions [available at https://unictr.irmct.org/en/cases/key-figures-cases – accessed 23 May 2023].

OAS, IACHR Signs Cooperation Agreement with International Criminal Court [available at https://www.oas.org/en/iachr/media_center/PReleases/2012/039.asp – accessed 21 May 2022].

Accord de coopération judiciaire entre la République du Senegal et la République du Tchad pour la poursuite des crimes internationaux commis au Tchad durant la période du 7 juin 1982 au 1 décembre 1990', 3 May 2013.

Kosovo Specialist Chambers & Specialist Prosecutor's Office, 'Cases' available at https://www.scp-ks.org/en/cases. (accessed 12 February 2024).

Kosovo Specialist Chambers & Specialist Prosecutor's Office, 'Law on Specialist Chambers and Specialist Prosecutors Office' available at https://www.scp-ks.org/en/documents/law-specialist-chambers-and-specialist-prosecutors-office (accessed 12 February 2024).

Kosovo Specialist Chambers & Specialist Prosecutor's Office, Republic of Kosovo, Amendment of the Constitution of the Republic of Kosovo [available at https://www.scp-ks.org/sites/default/files/public/amendment_of_the_constitution_-no_24.pdf – accessed 12 February 2024].

Law No.05/L-053 on Specialist Chambers and Specialist Prosecutor's Office. Official Gazette of the Republic of Kosova / No. 27 / 31 August 2015, Pristina available at https://gzk.rks-gov.net/ActDocumentDetail.aspx?ActID=11036.

Report of the Working Group on the Hissène Habré Affair, Ministry of Justice, referenced in Human Rights Watch 'Hissène Habré and the Senegalese Courts: A Memo for International Donors', March 2007.

UK Fraud Advisory Panel, Hidden in plain sight: domestic corruption, fraud and the integrity deficit, 27 October 2023.

United States Institute of Peace, Chad: Report of the Commission of Inquiry into the Crimes and Misappropriations Committed by Ex-President Habré, his Accomplices and/or Accessories: Investigation of Crimes against the Physical and Mental Integrity of Persons and their Possessions, 7 May 1992.

United States Institute of Peace, Truth Commission: Chad [available at https://www.usip.org/publications/1990/12/truth-commission-chad – accessed 8 February 2024].

US Department of State, First Trial Judgment by the Special Criminal Court in the Central African Republic (CAR) (2022) [available at https://www.state.gov/first-trial-judgment-by-the-special-criminal-court-in-the-central-african-republic-car/ – accessed 5 February 2024].

US Department of State (archived), 2015 International Narcotics Control Strategy Report (INCSR) [available at https://shorturl.at/lKNTX- accessed 5 February 2024].

Secondary Sources

Academic Journal Articles

Abass A, 'The Proposed International Criminal Jurisdiction for the African Court: Some Problematic Aspects' (2013) *Netherlands International Law Review* 27–50.

Abass A, 'Prosecuting International Crimes in Africa: Rationales, Prospects and Challenges' (2013) 24 *European Journal of International Law* 933.

Abdollahi M and Behzadi K, 'Regional Jus Cogens: Conceptual Difficulties and Practical Challenges' (2020) 3 *The Iranian Review for UN Studies* (*IRUNS*), 33–74.

Abebe Z, 'The African Court with a Criminal Jurisdiction and the ICC: A Case for Overlapping Jurisdiction?' (2017) 25 *African Journal of International and Comparative Law* 3, 418–429.

Acevedo J, 'Victims at the Central Africa's Republic Special Criminal Court' (2020) 39 *Nordic Journal of Human Rights* 1, 1–17.

Adjolohoun H, 'The ECOWAS Court as a Human Rights Promoter? Assessing Five Years Impact of the Koraou Slavery Judgment' (2013) 31 *Netherlands Quarterly of Human Rights* 3, 342–371.

Akande D, 'The Jurisdiction of International Criminal Court over Nationals of Non-parties: Legal Basis and Limits' (2003) 1 *Journal of International Criminal Justice* 618–650 at 625–626.

Akande D, 'International Law Immunities and the International Criminal Court' (2004) 98 *American Journal of International Law* 3, 407–433 at 410.

Akande D, 'The Legal Nature of Security Council Referrals to the ICC and its Impact on Al Bashir's Immunities' (2009) 7 *Journal of International Criminal Justice* 333.

Akande D and Shah S, 'Immunities of State Officials, International Crimes and Foreign Domestic Courts: A Rejoinder to Alexander Orakhelashvili' (2011) 22 *European Journal of International Law* 3, 857–858.

Anderson M, 'International Money Laundering: The Need for ICC Investigative and Adjudicative Jurisdiction' (2013) 53 *Virginia Journal of International Law* 1.

Anghie A, 'The evolution of international law: colonial and postcolonial realities' (2006) 27 *Third World Quarterly* 5, 751.

Ani N, 'Three Schools of Thought on "African Solutions to African Problems"' (2019) 50 *Journal of Black Studies* 2, 135–155.

Arzandeh A, 'The origins of the Scottish forum non conveniens doctrine' (2017) 13 *Journal of Private International Law* 1, 130–151.

Asongu S and Kodila-Tedika O, 'Crime and Conflicts in Africa: Consequences of Corruption?' (2013) 2 *European Economic Letters* 2, 50–55.

Aston W, 'Problems of Roman Criminal Law' (1913) 2 *Journal of the Society of Comparative Legislation* 213–231.

Balakrishnan K, 'Corporate criminal liability – Evolution of the concept' (1998) *Cochin University Law Review* 255.

Bantekas I, 'Corruption as an International Crime and Crime against Humanity: An Outline of Supplementary Criminal Justice Policies' (2006) 4 *Journal of International Criminal Justice* 3, 466–484.

Barrett Jr E, 'The Doctrine of Forum Non Conveniens' (1947) 35 *California Law Review* 3, 380–422.

Bassiouni M, 'The ICC-Quo Vadis?' (2006) 4 *Journal of International Criminal Justice* 3, 421–427.

Benzing M, 'The Complementarity Regime of the International Criminal Court: International Criminal Justice between State Sovereignty and the Fight against Impunity' (2003) 7 *Max Planck Yearbook of United Nations Law* 1.

Berg B, 'The 1994 I.L.C. Draft Statute for an International Criminal Court: A Principled Appraisal of Jurisdictional Structure' (1996) 28 Case Western Reserve Journal of International Law 2, 223.

Bernaz N, 'Corporate Criminal Liability under International Law: The New TV S.A.L. and Akhbar Beirut S.A.L. Cases at the Special Tribunal for Lebanon' (2015) 13 *Journal of International Criminal Justice* 2, 313–330.

Betts P, 'Germany, International Justice and the Twentieth Century' (2005) 17 *History & Memory* 1/2 45–86.

Bianchi A, 'Immunity vs Human Rights: The Pinochet Case' (1999) 10 *European Journal of International Law* 2, 237–277.

Binder G, 'The Dialectic of Duplicity: Treaty Conflict and Political Contradiction' (1985) 34 *Buffalo Law Review* 1.

Bhuta N, 'Conflicting International Obligations and the Risk of Torture and Unfair Trial: Critical Comments on *R (Al-Saadoon and Mufdhi) v Secretary of State for Defence; Al-Sadoon and Mufdhi v United Kingdom*'(2009) 5 *Journal of International Criminal Justice* 7, 1133.

Bjork C and Goebertus J, 'Complementarity in Action: The Role of Civil Society and the ICC in Rule of Law Strengthening in Kenya' (2014) 14 *Yale Human Rights and Development Journal* 5.

Boister N, 'Transnational Criminal Law?' 14 (2003) *European Journal of International Law* 953–976.

Bodansky D, 'The Concept of Customary International Law' (1995) 16 *Michigan Journal of International Law* 3, 667.

Bohrer Z, 'International Criminal Law's Millennium of Forgotten History' (2016) 34 *Law and History Review* 2, 393–485.

Bouhabib M, 'Power and Perception: The Special Tribunal for Lebanon' (2010) 3 *Berkeley Journal of Middle Eastern & Islamic Law* 1, 174.

Bouwknegt T, "Beyond 'African Solutions to African Problems' at the Extraordinary African Chambers and 'Distant Justice' at the International Criminal Court" (2019) 0 *Journal of International Criminal Justice*, 1–24 at 1.

Brand R, 'Challenges to Forum Non Conveniens' (2013) 45 *New York University Journal of International Law and Politics* 4, 1005–1006.

Brand R, 'Forum non conveniens' (2013) *Oxford University Press Encyclopedia entries* 1.

Brody R, 'The Prosecution of Hissène Habré: An African Pinochet' (2001) 35 *New England Law Review* 321–345.

Brody R, Bringing a Dictator to Justice: The Case of Hissène Habré' (2015) 13 *Journal of International Criminal Justice*, 209–217.

Bruch E, 'Hybrid Courts: Examining hybridity through a post-colonial lens' (2010) 28 *Boston University International Law Journal* 1.

Burchill R, 'International Criminal Tribunals at the Regional Level: Lessons from International Human Rights Law' (2007) 4 *New Zealand Yearbook of International Law* 25.

Burke-White W, 'Regionalization of International Criminal Law Enforcement: A Preliminary Exploration' (2003) 38 *Texas International Law Journal* 732.

Burke-White W, 'Complementarity in Practice: The International Criminal Court as Part of a System of Multi-level Global Governance in the Democratic Republic of Congo' (2005) 18 *Leiden Journal of International Law* 557.

Burke-White W, 'Implementing a Policy of Positive Complementarity in the Rome System of Justice' (2008) 19 *Criminal Law Forum* 59–85.

Burke-White W, 'Proactive Complementarity: The International Criminal Court and National Courts in the Rome System of International Justice' (2008) 49 *Harvard International Law Journal* 1.

Borgen C.J, 'Resolving Treaty Conflicts', (2005) 37 *George Washington International Law Review*, 574.

Carozza P, 'Subsidiarity as a Structural Principle of International Human Rights Law' (2003) 97 *American Journal of International Law* 38–79.

Carroll C, 'Hybrid Tribunals Are the Most Effective Structure for Adjudicating International Crimes Occurring within a Domestic State' (2013) 90 *Seton Hall University Law School Student Scholarship Paper* 1.

Cassese A, 'The Nicaragua and Tadić Tests Revisited in Light of the ICJ Judgment on Genocide in Bosnia' (2007) 18 *European Journal of International Law* 4, 649–668.

Cayley A, 'The Prosecutor's Strategy in Seeking the Arrest of Sudanese President Al Bashir on Charges of Genocide' (2008) 6 *Journal of International Criminal Justice* 829.

Ceia E, 'The Contributions of the Inter-American Court of Human Rights to the Development of Transitional Justice' (2015) 14 *The Law and Practice of International Courts and Tribunals* 3.

Chadwick M, 'Piracy and the Origins of Universal Jurisdiction: On Stranger Tides?' (2018) 34 *Queen Mary Studies in International Law* 1.

Charney J, 'International Criminal Law and the Role of Domestic Courts' (2001) 95 *The American Journal of International Law* 120.

Charney J, 'Is international law threatened by multiple international tribunals' (1998) 271 *Collected Courses of the Hague Academy of International Law* 101.

Chehtman A, 'The Extraterritorial Scope of the Right to Punish' (2010) 29 *Law and Philosophy* 127–157.

Chimni B, 'International Institutions Today: An Imperial Global State in the Making' (2004) 15 *European Journal of International Law* 1.

Chimni B, 'Third World Approaches to International Law: A Manifesto' (2006) 8 *International Community Law Review* 3, 11.

Christensen M and Kjeldgaard-Pedersen A, 'Competing Perceptions of Hybrid Justice: International v. National in the Extraordinary Chambers of the Courts of Cambodia' (2018) 18 *International Criminal Law Review* 127.

Cimiotta E, 'The First Steps of the Extraordinary African Chambers: A New Mixed Criminal Tribunal?' (2015) 13 *Journal of International Criminal Justice* 185.

Cimiotta E, 'The Specialist Chambers and the Specialist Prosecutor's Office in Kosovo: The Regionalization' of International Criminal Justice in Context' (2016) 14 *Journal of International Criminal Justice* 1, 53–72.

Ciorciari J and Heindel A, 'Experiments in International Criminal Justice: Lessons from the Khmer Rouge Tribunal' (2014) 35 *Michigan Journal of International Law*, 369.

Clapham A, 'On Complementarity: Human Rights in the European Legal Orders' (2000) 21 *Human Rights Law Journal* 313.

Clarke L, 'Complementarity as Politics' (2016) 2 *Journal of International and Comparative Law* 2.

Clarke K, 'New frontiers in international human rights: Actionable non-actionables and the (non)performance of perpetual becoming' (2021) *Journal of Human Rights* 2, 141–157, at 152.

Cohen D, 'Seeking Justice on the Cheap: Is the East Timor Tribunal Really a Model for the Future?' (2002) 61 *Analysis from the East-West Center* 1.

Cohen D, 'Intended to Fail: The Trials Before the Ad Hoc Human Rights Court in Jakarta' (2003) *International Center for Transitional Justice Occasional Paper Series* 12.

Cook S and Ors. 'Corruption and the Arab Spring' (2012) 18 *The Brown Journal of World Affairs* 2, 21–28.

Conway G, 'Ne Bis in Idem in International Law' (2003) 3 *International Criminal Law Review* 217–244.

Cowell F, 'Inherent Imperialism: Understanding the Legal Roots of Anti-imperialist Criticism of the International Criminal Court' (2017) 15 *Journal of International Criminal Justice* 4, 667–687.

Currie R and Leon J, 'COPLA: A Transnational Criminal Court for Latin America and the Caribbean' (2019) 88 *Nordic Journal of International Law* 592.

Cryer R, 'International Criminal Law vs State Sovereignty: Another Round?' (2006) 16 *The European Journal of International Law* 5.

Dadhich R, Understanding SAARC: Regional Cooperation in neo-colonial context' (2005) 18 *Indian Journal of Asian Affairs* 1, 49–64.

Davidson C, 'How to Read International Criminal Law: Strict Construction and the Rome Statute of the International Criminal Court' (2017) 91 *St. John's Law Review* 1, article 3, 37.

De Hert P, Weis K and Cloosen N, 'The Framework Decision of 18 December 2008 – A Critical Assessment' (2009) 1 *New Journal of European Criminal Law* 55–78.

Delbruck J, 'A More Effective International Law or a New "World Law?" – Some Aspects of the Changing Development of International Law in a Changing International System' (1993) 8 *Indiana Law Journal* 705.

Delmas-Marty M, 'Ambiguities and Lacunae: The International Criminal Court Ten Years on' (2013) 11 *Journal of International Criminal Justice* 1.

Dickinson L, 'The Relationship between Hybrid Courts and International Courts: The Case of Kosovo' (2003) *New England Law Review* 1071.

Donnelly J, 'State Sovereignty and International Human Rights' (2014) 28 *Ethics & International Affairs* 2, 225.

Du Plessis M, 'Complementarity and Africa: The promises and problems of international criminal justice' 17 *African Security Review* 4.

Du Plessis M, 'The International Criminal Court and its work in Africa; Confronting the myths' (2008) 173 *Institute for Security Studies* 1.

Du Plessis M, 'The International Criminal Court that Africa wants' (2010) *Institute for Security Studies* 1.

Du Plessis M and Gevers C, 'Balancing competing obligations: The Rome Statute and AU decisions' (2011) *Institute for Security Studies*.

Du Plessis M, 'Implications of the AU decision to give the African Court jurisdiction over international crimes' (2012) 235 *Institute for Security Studies Paper* 1.

Du Plessis M & Ors, 'Africa and the International Criminal Court' (2013) *Chatham House International Law*.

Dursun-Özkanca O, 'The European Union Rule of Law Mission in Kosovo: An Analysis from the Local Perspective' (2018) 17 *Ethnopolitics* 1.

Edwards J, 'Vicarious Liability in Criminal Law' (1951) 14 *The Modern Law Review* 3, 334–340.

El Zeidy M, 'The Principle of Complementarity: A New Machinery to Implement International Criminal Law' (2002) 23 *Michigan Journal of International Law* 869.

Eboibi F, 'Jurisdiction of the International Criminal Court: Analysis, Loopholes and Challenges' (2012) *Nnamdi Azikiwe University Journal of International Law and Jurisprudence* 28–46.

Ebobrah S, 'Towards a positive application of complementarity in the African human rights system: issues of functions and relations' (2011) 22 *European Journal of International Law* 1.

Ebobrah S, 'Towards a Positive Application of Complementarity in the African Human Rights System: Issues of Functions and Relations' (2011) 22 *European Journal of International Law* 3.

Erne J, 'Conferral of Powers by States as a Basis of Obligations of International Organizations' (2009) *Nordic Journal of International Law* 1.

Fanto J, 'Organizational Liability' (2010) 19 *Journal of Law and Policy* 45, 45–54.

Fawcett L, 'Exploring Regional Domains: A Comparative History of Regionalism' (2004) 80 *International Affairs* 429, 435.

Fichtelberg A, 'Liberal Values in International Criminal Law: A Critique of Erdemović' (2008) 6 *Journal of International Criminal Justice* 1, 12.

Finch G, 'The Peace Conference of Paris, 1919' (1919) 13 *The American Journal of International Law* 2, 159–186.

Findlay M, 'The Challenges for Asian Jurisdictions in the Development of International Criminal Justice' (2010) 32 *Sydney Law Review* 2 205–219.

Fombad C and Nwauche E, 'Africa's Imperial Presidents: Immunity, Impunity and Accountability' (2012) 5 *African Journal of Legal Studies* 91–118.

Freeland S, 'International Criminal Justice in the Asia-Pacific Region: The Role of the International Criminal Court Treaty Regime' (2013) 11 *Journal of International Criminal Justice* 5.

Furger A, 'Can they deliver? The practice of Joint Investigation Teams (JITS) in core international crimes investigations' (2024) 22 *JICJ* 3, 43–58.

Gaeta P, '*Ratione Materiae* Immunities of Former Heads of State and International Crimes: The Hissène Habré Case' (2003) 1 *Journal of International Criminal Justice* 1 186–196.

Gaeta P, 'Is the Practice of "Self-Referral" a Sound Start for the ICC' (2004) 2 *Journal of International Criminal Justice* 312.

Gaeta P, 'Does President Al Bashir Enjoy Immunity from Arrest?' (2009) 7 *Journal of International Criminal Justice* 312.

Gaja G, 'Jus Cogens Beyond the Vienna Convention' (1981) 172 *Collected Courses of the Hague Academy of International Law*, 284.

Geib R and Bulinckx N, 'International and internationalised criminal tribunals: a synopsis' (2006) 88 *International Review of the Red Cross* 861.

Goredema C, 'Money laundering in Southern Africa Incidence, magnitude and prospects for its control' (2004) 92 *Institute for Security Studies Paper* 1–12.

Gordon G, 'The Trial of Peter Von Hagenbach: Reconciling History, Historiography, and International Criminal Law in K Heller & G Simpson *The Hidden Histories of War Crimes Trials* (Oxford Scholarship Online 2013).

Galbraith J and Ors 'The Pace of International Criminal Justice' (2009) 31 *Michigan Journal of International Law* 1.

Garcia-Casas M, 'The Crime of Unconstitutional Change of Government: Concept and Main Hurdles in Its Implementation' (2021) 19 *Journal of International Criminal Justice* 3, 565–581.

Garrod M, 'The Protective Principle of Jurisdiction over War Crimes and the Hollow Concept of Universality' (2012) 12 *International Criminal Law Review* 12.

Gegout C, 'The International Criminal Court: limits, potential and conditions for the promotion of justice and peace' (2013) 34 *Third World Quarterly* 5, 800–818.

Gioia F, 'State Sovereignty, Jurisdiction and Modern International Law: The Principle of Complementarity in the International Criminal Court' (2006) 19 *Leiden Journal of International Law* 1095.

Gross A, 'Introduction: "A Crime against Humanity": Slavery and The Boundaries of Legality, Past and Present' (2017) 35 *Law and History Review* 1, 1–8.

Hall C.K, 'The First Two Sessions of the UN Preparatory Committee on the Establishment of an International Criminal Court' in "Current Developments" (1997) 91 *American Journal of International Law* 177–181.

Hall C.K, 'The Third and Fourth Sessions of the UN Preparatory Committee on the Establishment of an International Criminal Court' in "Current Developments" (1998) 92 *American Journal of International Law* 124.

Hall C.K, 'The Fifth Session of the UN Preparatory Committee on the Establishment of an International Criminal Court' in "Current Developments" (1998) 92 *American Journal of International Law* 331.

Hall C.K, 'The Sixth Session of the UN Preparatory Committee on the Establishment of an International Criminal Court' in "Current Developments" (1998) 92 *American Journal of International Law* 548.

Hall J, 'Nulla Poena Sine Lege' (1937) 47 *The Yale Law Journal* 2, 165.

Hamilton T, 'Case Admissibility at the International Criminal Court' in (2015) 14 *The Law & Practice of International Courts and Tribunals* 2, 305–317.

Hamilton T and Ramsden M, 'The Politicisation of Hybrid Courts: Observations from the Extraordinary Chambers in the Courts of Cambodia' (2014) *International Criminal Law Review* 115–147.

Hansen T, 'A Critical Review of the ICC's Recent Practice Concerning Admissibility Challenges and Complementarity' (2013) 13 *Melbourne Journal of International Law*, 16.

Haskell J, 'TRAIL-ing TWAIL: Arguments and Blind Spots in Third World Approaches to International Law' (2014) 27 *Canadian Journal of Law & Jurisprudence* 2, 389.

Hathaway O, 'International Delegation and State Sovereignty' (2008) 71 *Law and Contemporary Problems* 115–149.

Hayden P, 'Cosmopolitanism and the Need for Transnational Criminal Justice: The Case of the International Criminal Court' (2004) 104 *Theoria* 69–70.

Heerten L and Moses A, 'The Nigeria-Biafra war: postcolonial conflict and the question of genocide' (2014) 16 *Journal of Genocide Research* 169–203.

Heller K, 'The Shadow Side of Complementarity: The Effect of Article 17 of the Rome Statute on National Due Process' (2006) 17 *Criminal Law Forum* 255.

Heller K, 'A Sentenced-Based Theory of Complementarity' (2012) 53 *Harvard International Law Journal* 1.

Heller K, 'Radical Complementarity' (2016) 14 *Journal of International Criminal Justice* 637–665.

Higgins R, 'A Babel of Judicial Voices? Ruminations from the Bench, (2003) 55 *International and Comparative Law Quarterly* 4.

Higonnet E, 'Restructuring Hybrid Courts: Local Employment and National Criminal Justice Reforms' (2006) 23 *Arizona Journal of International and Comparative Law* 347.

Hill D, 'Why Governments Cede Sovereignty: Evidence from Regional Human Rights Courts' (2016) 14 *Foreign Policy Analysis* 3, 299–325.

Hobbs H, 'Victim Participation in International Criminal Proceedings: Problems and Potential Solutions in Implementing an Effective and Vital Component of Justice' (2014) 49 *Texas International Law Journal* 9–12.

Hobbs H, 'Hybrid Tribunals and the Composition of the Court: In Search of Sociological Legitimacy' (2016) 16 *Chicago Journal of International Law* 2.

Hobbs P, 'The Catalysing Effect of the Rome Statute in Africa: Positive Complementarity and Self-Referrals' (2020) 31 *Criminal Law Forum* 1.

Høgestøl S, 'The Habré Judgment at the Extraordinary African Chambers: A Singular Victory in the Fight against Impunity' (2016) 34 *Nordic Journal of Human Rights* 3, 147–156.

Holmes Jr O, 'The Path of the Law' (1987) 10 *Harvard Law review*. 57, 460–461.

Holvoet M, 'Introducing the Special Issue 'Critical Perspectives on the Law and Politics of the Kosovo Specialist Chambers and the Specialist Prosecutor's Office' (2020) 20 *International Criminal Law Review* 3.

Holvoet M and de Hert P, 'International Criminal Law as Global Law: An Assessment of the Hybrid Tribunals' (2012) 17 *Tilburg Law Review* 228–240.

Hosain M, 'Positive Complementarity: An Approach to Enhance Cooperation with States and end Impunity under International Criminal Court' (2013) 2 *AALCO Journal of International Law* 2, 206.

Huneeus A, 'International Criminal Law by Other Means: The Quasi-Criminal Jurisdiction of the Human Rights Courts' (2013) 107 *American Journal of International Law* 1.

Huneeus A and M R. Madsen 'Between Universalism and Regional Law and Politics: A Comparative History of the American, European, and African Human Rights Systems' (2018) 16 *International Journal of Constitutional Law* 1, 136–160.

Huong P, 'A Changing Notion of Complementarity under the Rome Statute of the International Criminal Court' (2002) [available at https://nagoya.repo.nii.ac.jp/record/15001/files/nujlp_245_18.pdf – accessed 12 May 2023].

Imoedemhe O, 'Unpacking the tension between the African Union and the International Criminal Court: the way forward' (2015) 23 *African Journal of International and Comparative Law* 1, 74–105.

Jackson M, 'Regional Complementarity: The Rome Statute and Public International Law' (2016) *Journal of International Criminal Justice* 1070.

Jalloh C, 'Regionalizing International Criminal Law?' (2009) 9 *International Criminal Law Review* 3, 445–499.

Jalloh C, 'Universal Jurisdiction, Universal Prescription? A Preliminary Assessment of the African Union Perspective on Universal Jurisdiction' (2010) 21 *Criminal Law Forum* 29.

Jalloh C, 'Kenya vs. The ICC Prosecutor' (2009) 53 *Harvard International Law Journal Online* 269.

Jalloh C, 'The Nature of the Crimes in the African Criminal Court' (2017) 15 *Journal of International Criminal Justice* 799–826.

Johnson D, 'The Draft Code of Offences against the Peace and Security of Mankind' (1945) 4 *International and Comparative Law Quarterly* 445.

Jones A, 'Insights into an Emerging Relationship: Use of Human Rights Jurisprudence at the International Criminal Court (2016) 16 *Human Rights Law Review* 4.

Jurdi N, 'The Subject-Matter Jurisdiction of the Special Tribunal for Lebanon' (2007) 5 *Journal of International Criminal Justice* 5, 1125–1138.

Katzenstein S, 'Hybrid Tribunals: Searching for Justice in East Timor' (2003) 16 *Harvard Human Rights Journal* 245.

Kampmark B, 'Sacred Sovereigns and Punishable War Crimes: The Ambivalence of the Wilson Administration towards a Trial of Kaiser Wilhelm II' (2007) 53 *Australian Journal of Politics and History* 4, 519–537.

Kastrup D, 'From Nuremberg to Rome and Beyond: The Fight against Genocide, War Crimes, and Crimes against Humanity' (1999) 23 *Fordham International Law Journal* 2, 414.

Kaunert C, 'Without the Power of Purse or Sword: The European Arrest Warrant and the Role of the Commission' (2007) 29 *European Integration* 4, 388.

Keen M, 'Treason Trials under the Law of Arms' (1962) 12 *Transactions of the Royal Historical Society* 85–103 at 98.

Kelsen H, 'Collective and Individual Responsibility in International Law with Particular Regard to the Punishment of War Criminals' (1943) 31 *California Law Review* 5 at 533.

Kemp Gerhard & Nortje Windell, 'Prosecuting the Crime against Humanity of Apartheid: The Historic First Indictment in South Africa and the Application of Customary International Law' (2023) 21 *Journal of International Criminal Justice* 430.

Keppler E, 'Managing setbacks for the International Criminal Court in Africa' (2012) 56 *Journal of African Law* 1, 1–14.

Keijser J and Ors 'Wrongful convictions and the Blackstone ratio: An empirical analysis of public attitudes' (2014) 16 *Punishment and Society* 1, 32–49.

Kirsch P and Valerie Oosterveld 'Negotiating an Institution for the Twenty-First Century: Multilateral Diplomacy and the International Criminal Court (2001) 46 *McGill Law Journal* 1141–1160.

Kirsch P and Oosterveld V, 'The Preparatory Commission for the International Criminal Court' (2001) 25 *Fordham International Law Journal* 3, 563–588.

Klabbers J, 'On Epistemic Universalism and the melancholy of International Law' (2019) 29 *European Journal of International Law* 4, 1057–1069.

Kleffner J, 'The Impact of Complementarity on National Implementation of Substantive International Criminal Law' (2003) 1 *Journal of International Criminal Justice* 86.

Kleinlein T, 'Jus Cogens Re-examined: Value Formalism in International Law' (2017) 28 *The European Journal of International Law* 1.

Kontorovich E, 'The Constitutionality of International Courts: The Forgotten Precedent of Slave Trade Tribunals' (2009) 158 *University of Pennsylvania Law Review* 1, 58–59.

Korsgaard C, 'Kant's formula of universal law' (1985) 66 *Pacific Philosophical Quarterly* 1–2.

Konfort M and Vajda M, 'The Principle of Complementarity in the Jurisprudence of the ICC' (2014) 3 *ZPR* 1, 9–27 at 10.

Kreß C, 'The Crime of Genocide and Contextual Elements: A Comment on the ICC Pre-trial Chamber's Decision in the Al Bashir Case' (2009) 7 *Journal of International Criminal Justice* 1.

Krings B, 'The Principles of 'Complementarity' and Universal Jurisdiction in International Criminal Law: Antagonists or Perfect Match?' (2012) 4 *Goettingen Journal of International Law* 3 737–763.

Labuda P, 'The Special Criminal Court in the Central African Republic: Failure or Vindication of Complementarity?' (2017) 15 *Journal of International Criminal Justice*, 192.

Landauer C, 'Regionalism, Geography, and the International Legal Imagination' (2011) 11 *Chicago Journal of International Law* 2, 539.

Lima L and Marotti L, 'An unlikely duo? Regionalism and jus cogens in international law' (2022) 12 *Goettingen Journal of International Law* 1, 219–239.

Linton S, 'Rising from the ashes: The creation of a viable criminal justice system in East Timor' (2001) 25 *Melbourne University Law Review* 122, 178.

Linton S, 'Completing the Circle: Accountability for the Crimes of the 1971 Bangladesh War of Liberation' (2010) 21 *Criminal Law Forum* 2, 191–311.

Ljuboja L, 'Justice in an uncooperative world: ICTY and ICTR foreshadow ICC ineffectiveness' (2010) 32 *Houston Journal of International Law* 780.

Londras F and Kingston S, 'Rights, Security and Conflicting International Obligations: Exploring Inter-Jurisdictional Judicial Dialogues in Europe' (2010) American Journal of Comparative Law 1.

Lonnquist T, 'The Trend Towards Purposive Statutory Interpretation: Human Rights at Stake' (2003) *Revenue Law Journal* 19.

Luban D, 'After the Honeymoon: Reflections on the Current State of International Criminal Justice' (2013) 11 *Journal of International Criminal Justice* 505 at 509.

Luckau A, 'Unconditional Acceptance of the Treaty of Versailles by the German Government, June 22–28, 1919' (1945) 17 *Journal of Modern History* 3, 215–220.

de Magalie C, 'Models of Corporate Criminal Liability in Comparative Law' (2005) 4 *Washington University Global Studies Law Review* 3, 547–566.

Magliveras K, 'Substituting International Criminal Justice for an African Criminal Justice?' (2017) 14 *International Organizations Law Review* 291–320.

Maharajh A, 'The Caribbean Court of Justice: A Horizontally and Vertically Comparative Study of the Caribbean's First Independent and Interdependent Court' (2014) 47 *Cornell International Law Journal* pg. 747.

Mansfield E and Milner H, 'The New Wave of Regionalism' (1999) 53 *International Organization* 3, 589–6272.

Martin F, 'The International Human Rights & Ethical Aspects of the Forum Non Conveniens Doctrine' (2003) 35 *The University of Miami Inter-American Law Review* 1,101–1121.

Martinez J, 'Antislavery Courts and the Dawn of International Human Rights Law' (2008) 117 *Yale Law Journal* 4.

Marshall K, 'Prevention and Complementarity in the International Criminal Court: A Positive Approach' [available at https://tinyurl.com/hykda478 – accessed 21 February 2024].

Maučec G, 'The International Criminal Court and the Issue of Intersectionality – A Conceptual and Legal Framework for Analysis' (2021) *International Criminal Law Review* 1.

McAuliffe P, 'Hybrid Tribunals at Ten: How International Criminal Justice's Golden Child Became an Orphan' (2011) 7 *Journal of International Law and International Relations* 1 at 1.

McAuliffe P, 'From Watchdog to Workhorse: Explaining the Emergence of the ICC's Burden-sharing Policy as an Example of Creeping Cosmopolitanism' (2014) 13 *Chinese Journal of International Law* 266–267.

McConville M, 'A global war on drugs: Why the United States should support the prosecution of drug traffickers in the International Criminal Court' (2000) 37 *American Criminal Law Review* 75, 92–93.

McDonald G, 'Problems, Obstacles and Achievements of the ICTY' (2004) 2 *Journal of International Criminal Justice* 558–571.

McGowan P, 'Coups and Conflict in West Africa, 1955–2004 Part I, Theoretical Perspectives' (2005) 32 *Armed Forces and Society* 1, 5–23.

Mendez K, 'The new wave of hybrid tribunals: A sophisticated approach to enforcing international humanitarian law or an idealistic solution with empty promises?' (2009) 20 *Criminal Law Forum* 53, 95.

Mégret F, 'In Defense of Hybridity: Towards a Representational Theory of International Criminal Justice' (2005) 38 *Cornell International Law Journal* 3, 725.

Mégret F, 'The International Criminal Court: Between International *Ius puniendi* and State Delegation' (2020) 23 *Max Planck Yearbook of United Nations Law* 1–47.

Mégret F, 'What Sort of Global Justice Is International Criminal Justice' (2015) 13 *Journal of International Criminal Justice* 77–96.

Milanovic M, 'The Oddity that Is the Hariri Tribunal' [available at https://papers.ssrn.com/sol3/papers.cfm?abstract_id=1014906 – accessed 12 March 2023].

Mitsilegas V, 'European prosecution between cooperation and integration: The European Public Prosecutor's Office and the rule of law' (2021) 22 *Maastricht Journal of European and Comparative Law* 1.

Mnawar A, 'Corruption and the "Arab spring" as one of the main elements leading to revolutions' (2015) 1 *Polish Journal of Political Science* 3, 36–49.

Moghadam T, 'Revitalizing Universal Jurisdiction: Lessons from Hybrid Tribunals Applied to the Case of Hissene Habre' (2008) 39 *Columbia Human Rights Law Review* 471.

Morris M, 'The Jurisdiction of the International Criminal Court over Nationals of Non-party States: Conference Remarks' (2000) 6 *ILSA Journal of International and Comparative Law* 366.

Mucaj A, 'The Kosovo Specialist Chambers and Specialist Prosecutor's Office Paradox' (2021) 21 *International Criminal Law Review* 380.

Mueller A and Stegmiller I, 'Self-Referrals on Trial: From Panacea to Patient' (2010) 8 *Journal of International Criminal Justice*, 1293.

Mudukuti A, 'South Africa abandoning the International Criminal Court? The build-up and potential consequences' (2016) 1 *European Human Rights Law Review* 1–10.

Muharremi R, 'The Concept of Hybrid Courts Revisited: The Case of the Kosovo Specialist Chambers' (2018) 18 *International Criminal Law Review* 4.

Muharremi R, 'The Kosovo Specialist Chambers and Specialist Prosecutor's Office' (2016) 76 *ZaöRV* 967.

Murphy S, 'Immunity Ratione Personae of Foreign Government Officials and other Topics: The Sixty-Fifth Session of the International Law Commission' (2014) 108 *American Journal of International Law* 1–30.

Murithi T, 'The African Union and the International Criminal Court: An embattled relationship' (2013) 8 *The Institute for Justice and Reconciliation Policy Brief* 1.

Murphy S, 'New Mechanisms for Punishing Atrocities in Non-international Armed Conflicts' (2015) 16 *Melbourne Journal of International Law* 1.

Murungu C, 'Towards a Criminal Chamber in the African Court of Justice and Human Rights' (2011) 9 *Journal of International Criminal Justice* 5, 1.

Mustakimur R 'Has the International Crimes Tribunal Bangladesh (ICT-BD) assisted to Reconcile Society?' (2023) 19 *AUDJ* 2, 115–149.

Mutua M, 'What Is TWAIL' (2000) 94 *American Society of International Law Proceedings* 31.

Mutua M, 'The African Human Rights System: A Critical Evaluation' (2000) *UNDP Human Development Report* 1.

Niang M, 'The Senegalese Legal Framework for the Prosecution of International Crimes' (2009) 7 *Journal of International Criminal Justice* 5, 1047.

Nielsen E, 'Hybrid International Criminal Tribunals: Political Interference and Judicial Independence' (2010) 15 *UCLA Journal of International Law and Foreign Affairs* 289.

Nimigan S, 'Exceptional or Exceptionalism? The Malabo Protocol and Regional Complementarity' (2019) 17 *Journal of International Criminal Justice* 5, 1005–1029.

Nimigan S, 'The Malabo Protocol, the ICC, and the idea of 'Regional Complementarity' (2019) o *Journal of International Criminal Justice* 1–25 at 3 .

Nouwen S, 'Hybrid Courts': The hybrid category of a new type of international crimes courts' (2010) 2 *Utrecht Law Review* 213.

Nouwen S & Werner W, 'Doing Justice to the Political: The International Criminal Court in Uganda and Sudan' (2011) 21 *European Journal of International Law* 4, 941–965.

Nmehielle V, "Saddling' the New African Regional Human Rights Court with International Criminal Jurisdiction: Innovative, Obstructive, Expedient?' (2014) 7 *African Journal of Legal Studies* 24–35.

O'Connell M, 'The UN, NATO, and International Law after Kosovo' (2000) 22 *Human Rights Quarterly* 1, 57–89.

Okafor O and Ngwaba U, 'The International Criminal Court as a 'Transitional Justice' Mechanism in Africa: Some Critical Reflections' (2014) 9 *International Journal of Transitional Justice*, 1–19.

Okafor O, 'Is There a Legitimacy Deficit in International Legal Scholarship and Practice?' 1997 *International Insights* 13, 91–120.

O'Keefe R, 'Universal Jurisdiction: Clarifying the Basic Concept' (2004) 2 *Journal of International Criminal Justice* 3 735–760.

O'Keefe R, 'Immunity Ratione Materiae from Foreign Criminal Jurisdiction and the Concept of "Acts Performed in an Official Capacity"'[available at https://rm.coe.int/1680097836 – accessed 12 January 2023].

Panke D & Stapel S, 'Architects of regional regime complexity: states and regional organizations' (2021) *Journal of Contemporary European Studies* 1–18.

Partan D & Rogic P, 'Sovereignty and International Criminal Justice' (2003) *International Law: Revista Colombiana de Derecho Internacional* 1, 53–82.

Parrish A, 'Domestic Responses to Transnational Crime: The Limits of National Law' (2012) 23 *Criminal Law Forum* 4, 275–293.

Pati R, 'The ICC and the Case of Sudan's Omar Al Bashir: Is Plea-Bargaining a Valid Option?' (2009) 15 *University of California at Davis Journal of International Law and Policy* 265.

Pellet A, 'Comments in Response to Christine Chinkin and in Defense of Jus Cogens as the Best Bastion against the Excesses of Fragmentation' (2006) *Finnish Yearbook of International Law* 89.

Philippe X, 'The principles of universal jurisdiction and complementarity: how do the two principles intermesh?' (2006) 88 *International Committee of the Red Cross* 862, 375–398.

Pinto M, 'Awakening the Leviathan through Human Rights Law – How Human Rights Bodies Trigger the Application of Criminal Law' (2018) 34 *Utrecht Journal of International and European Law* 2, 161–184.

Powell S and Pirez C, 'Global Laws, Local Lives: Impact of the New Regionalism on Human Rights Compliance' (2011) 17 *Buffallo Human Rights Law Review* 117–154.

Rastan R, 'What Is 'Substantially the Same Conduct'?: Unpacking the ICC's 'First Limb' Complementarity Jurisprudence' (2017)15 *Journal of International Criminal Justice* 1, 1–29.

Reiger C and Wierda M, 'The Serious Crimes Process in Timor-Leste: In Retrospect' (2006) *International Center for Transitional Justice, Prosecutions Case Studies Series* 1.

Rauxloh R, 'Regionalisation of the International Criminal Court' (2007) 4 *New Zealand Yearbook of International Law* 67.

Reisman W.M, 'International Law after the Cold War' (1990) 84 *American Journal of International Law* 1.

Robinson D, 'Identity Crisis of International Criminal Law' (2008) *21 Leiden Journal of International Law* 928.

Robinson D, 'Three Theories of Complementarity: Charge, Sentence or Process?' (2012) 53 *Harvard International Law Journal Online* 1.

Robinson D, 'A Sentenced-Based Theory of Complementarity' (2012) 53 *Harvard International Law Journal* 1.

Robinson D, 'International Criminal Law as Justice' (2013) 11 *Journal of International Criminal Justice* 3, 699–711.

Robinson D, 'The Mysterious Mysteriousness of Complementarity' (2010) 21 *Criminal Law Forum* 1.

Paul D Aligica & Vlad Tarko 'Polycentricity: From Polanyi to Ostrom, and Beyond' (2012) 25 *Governance* 167–361.

Perkins R, 'The Territorial Principle in Criminal Law' (1971) 22 *Hastings Law Journal* 5.

Renzo M, 'Crimes against humanity and the limits of international criminal law' (2012) 31 *Law and Philosophy* 4, 443–476.

Roessler P, 'The enemy within: Personal rule, coups and civil war in Africa' (2011) 63 *World Politics* 2, 300–346.

Rossetti L, 'The Pre-trial Chamber's Afghanistan Decision: A Step Too Far in the Judicial Review of Prosecutorial Discretion?' (2019) 17 *Journal of International Criminal Justice* 1.

Rutman D, 'The War Crimes and Trial of Henry Wirz' (1960) 6 *Civil War History* 2, 117–133.

Sadat L, 'The Conferred Jurisdiction of the International Criminal Court' (2023) *Washington University in St. Louis Legal Studies Research* Paper No. 23-03-01, 1–63.
Scharf M, 'The Amnesty Exception to the Jurisdiction of the International Criminal Court' (1999) 32 *Cornell International Law Journal* 526–527.
SáCouto S and Cleary K, 'The Gravity Threshold of the International Criminal Court' (2008) 23 *American Journal of International Law* 5, 807–854 at 820.
Sadat L and Jolly J, 'Seven Canons of ICC Treaty Interpretation: Making Sense of Article 25's Rorschach Blot' (2014) 27 *Leiden Journal of International Law* 3, 755–788.
Sainati T, 'Divided We Fall: How the International Criminal Court Can Promote Compliance with International Law by Working with Regional Courts' (2016) 49 *Vanderbilt Journal of Transnational Law* 191–243.
Sansani I, 'The Pinochet Precedence in Africa: Prosecution of Hissène Habré' (2001) 8 *Human Rights Brief* 1.
Sagalyn A, 'Preservation of Law and Order: A Fundamental Function of Government' (1965) 40 *Notre Dame Law Review* 549–551.
Schabas W, 'Prosecutorial Discretion v. Judicial Activism at the International Criminal Court' (2009) 6 *JICJ* 751.
Schabas W, 'Regions, Regionalism and International Criminal Law' (2007) *New Zealand Yearbook of International Law* 2.
Schabas W, 'The Contribution of the Eichmann Trial to International Law' (2013) 26 *Leiden Journal of International Law* 2.
Schabas W, 'The United Nations War Crimes Commission Proposal for an International Criminal Court' (2014) 25 *Criminal Law Forum* 171–189.
Schaack van B, 'Crimen Sine Lege: Judicial Lawmaking at the Intersection of Law and Morals' (2008) 97 *The Georgetown Law Journal* 121.
Schaack B and Slye R, 'A Concise History of International Criminal Law' (2007) *Santa Clara Law Digital Commons* 7.
Scharf M, 'Special Court for Sierra Leone' (2000) 6 *Int'l Peacekeeping* 156.
Scharf M and Taylor M, 'A Contemporary Approach to the Oldest International Crime' (2017) 33 *Utrecht Journal of International and European Law* 84, 77–89.
Schreuer C, 'Regionalism v. Universalism' (1995) 6 *European Journal of International Law* 477–499.
Schuldt L, 'Southeast Asian Hesitation: ASEAN Countries and the International Criminal Court' (2015) 16 *German Law Journal* 1, 77.
Seibert-Fohr A, 'The Relevance of the Rome Statute of the International Criminal Court for Amnesties and Truth Commissions' (2003) *Max Planck Yearbook of United Nations Law* 553–590.
Serio J, 'Fueling global crime: the mechanics of money laundering' (2007) 18 *International Review of Law, Computers and Technology* 3, 435–444.

Sinclair G, 'State formation, liberal reform and the growth of international organizations' (2015) 26 *European Journal of International Law* 1.

Singh S, 'The impact of clawback clauses on human and peoples' rights in Africa' (2009) 18 *African Security Studies* 4, 95–104 at 100.

Sirleaf M, 'Regionalism, Regime Complexes, and the Crisis in International Criminal Justice' (2016) 54 *Columbia Journal of Transnational Law* 699–778.

Sirleaf M, 'The African Justice Cascade and the Malabo Protocol' (2017) 11 *International Journal of Transitional Justice* 1.

Sirleaf M, 'Not Your Dumping Ground: Criminalization of Trafficking in Hazardous Waste in Africa' (2018) 35 *Wisconsin Journal of International Law* 348.

Slaughter A, 'The Future of International Law Is Domestic' (2006) 47 *Harvard International Law Journal* 2.

Solera O, 'Complementary jurisdiction and international criminal justice' (2002) 84 *International Review of the Red Cross* 845.

de Sloovere F, 'Contextual Interpretation of Statutes' (1936) 5 *Fordham Law Review* 2, 219.

Sperfeldt C, 'From the Margins of Internationalized Criminal Justice: Lessons Learned at the Extraordinary Chambers in the Courts of Cambodia' (2013) *11 Journal of International Criminal Justice* 1113.

Sperfeldt C, 'The trial against Hissène Habré: networked justice and reparations at the Extraordinary African Chambers' (2017) 21 *The International Journal of Human Rights* 9, 1243–1260 at 1247.

Spiga V, 'Non-retroactivity of Criminal Law: A New Chapter in the Hissene Habre Saga' (2011) 9 *Journal of International Criminal Justice* 5–23 at 17.

Smith R, 'Book Reviews: Legal Responses to Transnational and International Crimes: Toward an Integrative Approach' (2018) 46 *International Journal of Legal Information* 3, 200–201.

Sriram C and Brown S, 'Kenya in the Shadow of the ICC: Complementarity, Gravity and Impact' (2012) 12 *International Criminal Law Review* 2, 219–244.

Stahn C, 'The Geometry of Transitional Justice: Choices of Institutional Design' (2005) 18 *Leiden Journal of International Law* 425–466.

Stahn C, 'Complementarity: A Tale of Two Notions' (2008) 19 *Criminal Law Forum* 1.

Stahn C, 'Perspectives on Katanga: An Introduction' (2010) 23 *Leiden Journal of International Law* 1.

Stahn C, 'One Step Forward, Two Steps Back? Second Thoughts on a 'Sentence-Based' Theory of Complementarity' (2012) *Harvard International Law Journal* 85.

Stahn C, 'Complementarity and cooperative justice ahead of their time? The United Nations War Crimes Commission, fact-finding and evidence' (2014) 25 *Criminal Law Forum* 1, 223–260 at 223.

Stahn C, 'From 'United for Peace' to 'United for Justice?': Reflections on the Power of the United Nations General Assembly to Create Criminal Tribunals or Make Referrals to the ICC' (2023) 55 *Case Western Reserve Journal of International Law* 1, 251.

Stephen C, 'International Criminal Law: Wielding the Sword of International Criminal Justice' (2012) 61 *International & Comparative Law Quarterly* 55.

Stessens G, 'Corporate Criminal Liability: A Comparative Perspective' (1994) 43 *The International and Comparative Law Quarterly* 3, 493.

Tallgren I, 'Completing the "International Criminal Order": The Rhetoric of International Repression and the Notion of Complementarity in the Draft Statute for an International Criminal Court' (1998) 67 *Nordic Journal of International Law* 107, 120.

Talmon S, 'The Various Control Tests in the Law of State Responsibility and the Responsibility of Outside Powers for Acts of Secessionist Entities' (2009) 58 *International and Comparative Law Quarterly* 1.

Tedeschini M, 'Complementarity in Practice: the ICC's Inconsistent Approach in the Gaddafi and Al-Senussi Admissibility Decisions' (2015) 7 *Amsterdam Law Forum* 1.

Teitelbaum A, 'Statute of the International Criminal Court: A Critique' (1999) 26 *Social Justice* 107–114.

Tiba F, 'Regional International Criminal Courts: An Idea Whose Time Has Come?' (2016) 17 *Cardozo Journal of Conflict Resolution* 52, 523.

Tladi D, 'Complementarity and cooperation in international criminal justice: Assessing initiatives to fill the impunity gap' (2014) 235 *Institute for Security Studies Paper* 1.

Tladi D, 'The African Union and the International Criminal Court: The battle for the soul of international law' (2009) 34 *SAYIL* 1.

Udombana N, 'So far, so fair: the local remedies rule in the jurisprudence of the African Commission on Human and Peoples' Rights (2003) 97 *American Journal of International Law* 1, 1–37.

Vaid K, 'What Counts as "State Action" under Article 17 of the Rome Statute? Applying the ICC's Complementarity Test to Non-criminal Investigations by the United States into War Crimes in Afghanistan' (2012) 44 *Journal of International Law and Politics* 573–628, at 535.

Vierucci L, 'The European Arrest Warrant: An Additional Tool for Prosecuting ICC Crimes' (2004) 2 *Journal of International Criminal Justice* 27–285.

Vilmer J, 'The African Union and the International Criminal Court: counteracting the crisis' (2016) 92 *International Affairs* 6, 1341.

Wald P, 'Accountability for War Crimes: What Role for National, International and Hybrid Tribunals?' (2004) *American Society of International Law: Proceeding of Annual Meeting* 192.

Wallerstein S, 'Delegation of Powers and Authority in International Criminal Law' (2015) 9 *Criminal Law and Philos* 123–140.

Webb P, 'Scenarios of jurisdictional overlap among international courts' (2006) 19 *Revue quebecoise de droit international* 2, 277–285 at 277.

Weldehaimanot S, 'Arresting Al-Bashir: the African Union's opposition and the legalities' (2011) 19 *African Journal of International and Comparative Law* 2, 208–235.

Weiner S, 'Forum Non Conveniens' (1995) 64 *Fordham Law Review* 3, 848.

Westbury S, 'Analysing a regional slave trade: The West Indies and Virginia, 1698–1775' (1986) 7 *Slavery and Abolition* 3, 241–256.

Wierda M and Ors 'Early Reflections on Local Perceptions, Legitimacy and Legacy of the Special Tribunal for Lebanon' (2007) 5 *Journal of International Criminal Justice* 1065.

Williams S, 'The Rome Statute on the International Criminal Court: From 1947–2000 and beyond' (2000) 38 *Osgoode Hall Law Journal* 2, 302.

Williams S, 'The Extraordinary African Chambers in the Senegalese Courts: An African Solution to an African Problem?' (2013) 11 *Journal of International Criminal Justice* 1139–1160.

Williams S, 'The Specialist Chambers of Kosovo: The Limits of Internationalization?' (2016) 14 *Journal of International Criminal Justice* 27.

Williams S, 'Hybrid Tribunals: A Time for Reflection' (2016) 10 *International Journal of Transitional Justice* 539.

de Wet E, 'The Prohibition of Torture as an International Norm of *jus cogens* and Its Implications for National and Customary Law' (2004) 15 *European Journal of International Law* 97–121.

van der Wilt H, 'Unconstitutional Change of Government: A New Crime within the Jurisdiction of the African Criminal Court' (2017b) 30 *Leiden Journal of International Law* 4.

van der Wilt H, 'Corporate Criminal Responsibility for International Crimes: Exploring the Possibilities' (2013) 12 *Chinese Journal of International Law* 1, 43–77.

Wright B, 'Theory construction from empirical observations' (1994) 8 *Rasch Measurement Transactions* 2, 362 [available at https://www.rasch.org/rmt/rmt82h.htm – accessed 17 January 2023].

Author Unnamed 'Commission on the Responsibility of the Authors of the War and on Enforcement of Penalties: Report presented to the Preliminary Peace Conference' (1920) 14 *The American Journal of International Law*, No. 1/2, 95–154.

Texts and Book Chapters

Abass A, 'Historical and Political Background to the Malabo Protocol' in G Werle & M, Vormbaum (eds) *The African Criminal Court: A Commentary on the Malabo Protocol* (Asser Press 2017) 15.

Abegunrin O, 'From Organization of African Unity to African Union' in *Africa in Global Politics in the Twenty First Century* (Palmgrave Macmillan 2009) 141–172.

Adibe C, 'The Liberian Conflict and the ECOWAS-UN Partnership' in Weiss T.G (eds) *Beyond UN Subcontracting: International Political Economy Series* (Palmgrave Macmillan 1998).

Alter K and Hooghe L, 'Regional Dispute Settlement' in T Börzel and T Risse (eds) *The Oxford Handbook of Comparative Regionalism* (Oxford University Press 2018) 1.

Ambos K, 'International Criminal Law at the Crossroads: From Ad Hoc Imposition to a Treaty Based Universal System' in C Stahn & L van den Herik (eds) *Future Perspectives on International Criminal Justice* (TMC Asser Press 2010) 161–177.

Ambos K, *Treatise on International Criminal Law – Volume III: International Criminal Procedure* (Oxford University Press 2016) 257.

Arlen J, 'Evolution of Corporate Criminal Liability: Implications for Managers' in R Gandossy & J Sonnenfeld (eds) *Leadership and Governance from the Inside Out* (John Wiley &Sons 2004).

Ba O, *States of Justice: The Politics of the International Criminal Court* (Cambridge University Press 2020).

Bassiouni M, *Introduction to International Criminal Law* (Martinus Nijhoff 2013), 1047.

Batros B, 'The Evolution of the ICC jurisprudence on admissibility' in C Stahn & M El Zeidy (eds) *The International Criminal Court and Complementarity: From Theory to Practice* (Cambridge University Press 2011).

Beigbeder Y, 'Special Panels for Serious Crimes in East Timor – Now Timor-Leste' in *International Criminal Tribunals: Justice and Politics* (Palmgrave Macmillan 2011).

Bekou O, 'The ICC and Capacity Building at the National Level' in C Stahn (ed), *The Law and Practice of the International Criminal Court* (Oxford University Press 2015) 1245.

Bennion F, *Bennion on Statute Law* (Longman 1990) 168.

Berens E, *The Myths and Legends of Ancient Greece and Rome* (MetaLibri 2009) 199.

Bergsmo M, Ling C and Ping Y, (eds) *Historical Origins of International Criminal Law: Volume 1* (Torkel Opsahl Academic EPublisher 2004) 398.

Bergsmo M and Tianying S *On the Proposed Crimes against Humanity Convention* (Torkel Opsahl Academic EPublisher 2014).

Blackstone W, *Commentaries on the Laws of England* (Clarendon Press 1765) 358.

Bockel V and Bastiaan W, *The Ne Bis in Idem Principle in EU Law: European Monograph Series* (Kluwer Law International 2010).

Boister N, 'Responding to Transnational Crime: The Distinguishing Features of Transnational Criminal Law' in H Van der Wilt & C Paulussen (eds) *Legal Responses to Transnational and International Crimes: Towards an Integrative Approach* (EE Publishing 2017) 48.

Boister N, 'Transnational Crimes Jurisdiction of the Criminal Chamber of the African Court of Justice and Human and Peoples' Rights' in C Jalloh & Ors (eds) *The African Court of Justice and Human and Peoples' Rights in Context: Development and Challenges* (Oxford University Press 2019) 336–361.

Bower A, *The History of the Popes: From the Foundation of the See of Rome, To the Present Time, Vol VI* (Kessinger Publishing 2005) 14.

Brody R, Updated Edition after the Final April 2017 Verdict, *Victims Bring a Dictator to Justice: The Case of Hissène Habré* (Bread for the World 2017) 33.

Broude T, *Fragmentation(s) of International Law: On Normative Integration as Authority Allocation* (Hart Publishing 2008).

Broomhall B, *International Justice and the International Criminal Court: Between Sovereignty and the Rule of Law* (Oxford University Press 2003).

Brown C, *Sovereignty, Rights and Justice* (Polity Press 2002) 33.

Bradley C and Kelley G, 'The Concept of International Delegation' (2008) 71 *The law and Politics of International Delegation* 1, 1–36.

Butchard P and Walker N *Potential merits of a Special Tribunal on Ukraine* (House of Common's Library Debate Pack 2023).

Clarke K and Ors, 'Introduction' in C Jalloh & Ors (eds) *The African Court of Justice and Human and Peoples' Rights in Context: Development and Challenges* (Cambridge University Press 2019) 47.

Cassese A, Gaeta P and Jones J, 'The Path to Rome and Beyond, Drafting History and Further Developments' in Cassese, Gaeta & Jones (eds) *The Rome Statute of the International Criminal Court: A Commentary* (Oxford University Press 2002) 15.

Carlson K, 'Trying Hissène Habré 'On Behalf of Africa: Remaking Hybrid International Criminal Justice at the Chambres Africaines Exraordinaires' in J Nicholson (ed) *Strengthening the Validity of International Criminal Tribunals* (BRILL 2018).

Carter L, Ellis M and Jalloh C *The International Criminal Court in an Effective Global Justice System* (Edward Elgar Publishing 2016) 39–40.

Chesterman S *You, The People: The United Nations, Transitional Administration, and State-Building* (Oxford Scholarship Online 2004).

Clarke K and Ors, 'Africa and the ICC: An Introduction' in K.M Clarke and Ors (eds) *Africa and the ICC: perceptions of justice* (Cambridge University Press 2016).

Clarke K and Ors. 'Introduction' in C Jalloh and Ors, (eds) *The African Court of Justice and Human and Peoples' Rights in Context: Development and Challenges* (Cambridge University Press 2019) 33.

Clark P, *Distant Justice: The Impact of the International Criminal Court on African Politics* (Cambridge University Press 2018).

Crowley M, *Chemical Control: Regulation of Incapacitating Chemical Agent Weapons, Riot Control Agents and their Means of Delivery* (Palgrave Macmillan 2016) 194.

Cryer R and Ors *An Introduction to International Criminal Law and Procedure* (Cambridge University Press 2014) 154.

Darcy S and Powderly J *Judicial Creativity at the International Criminal Tribunals* (Oxford University Press 2009).

De Hert P and Ors (eds) *Convergences and Divergences between International Human Rights, International Humanitarian and International Criminal Law* (Intersentia 2018).

Dicker R and Keppler E, 'Beyond the Hague: The Challenges of International Justice' [available at https://www.hrw.org/legacy/wr2k4/download/10.pdf – accessed 12 January 2024].

Donlon F, 'Positive Complementarity in Practice: ICTY Rule 11bis and the use of the tribunal's evidence in the Srebrenica Trials before the Bosnian War Crimes Chamber' in Stahn & El Zeidy (eds) *The International Criminal Court and Complementarity: From Theory to Practice* (Cambridge University Press 2011) 920–954.

Drumbl M, *Atrocity, Punishment and International Law* (Cambridge University Press 2007).

Drumbl M Policy through Complementarity: The Atrocity Trial as Justice in Stahn C and El Zeidy M, (eds) *The International Criminal Court and Complementarity: From Theory to Practice* (Cambridge University Press 2011) 222–224.

Dupuy P, 'Formation of Customary International Law and General Principles' in D Bodansky and Ors, (eds) *The Oxford Handbook of International Environmental Law* (Oxford University Press 2008).

Du Plessis A, 'A snapshot of international criminal justice cooperation against terrorism since 9/11' in L van den Herik & N Schrijver (eds) *Counter-Terrorism Strategies in a Fragmented International Legal Order: Meeting the Challenges* (Cambridge University Press 2013) 29–67.

Du Plessis M, (ed) *African Guide to International Criminal Justice* (Institute for Security Studies 2008).

Ebobrah S 'Complementarity between the African Court and the Judicial Organs of Regional Economic Communities in Africa' in *PALU Guide to Complementarity within the African Human Rights System* (PALU 2014) 52.

Eboe-Osuji C, 'Administering International Criminal Justice through the African Court: Opportunities and Challenges in International Law' in C Jalloh & Ors (eds) The *African Court of Justice and Human and Peoples' Rights in Context: Development and Challenges* (Cambridge University Press at 2019) 849.

Ellis M, *Sovereignty and Justice: Balancing the Principle of Complementarity between International and Domestic War Crimes Tribunals* (Cambridge Scholars Publishing 2014) 13.

van Ellis R, *Transnational Organized Crime in Latin America and the Caribbean: From Evolving Threats and Responses to Integrated, Adaptive Solutions* (Lexington Books 2018).

El Zeidy *The Principle of Complementarity in International Criminal Law: Origin, Development and Practice* (Martinus Nijhoff Publishers 2008).

Fabbricotti A, Universalism and Regionalism in International Trade Law: Is the WTO a Truly Universal International Organization? in *Scritti in memoria di Maria Rita Saulle* (Editoriale Scientifica 2014) 559–574.

Fantaye D, *Regional Approaches to Maritime Security in the Horn of Africa* (Friedrich-Ebert-Stiftung 2014).

Fernandez L, Corruption (Article 28I) and Money Laundering (Article 28Ibis) in G Werle & M Vorbaum (eds) *The African Criminal Court International Criminal Justice Series* (TMC Asser Press 2017).

Fitchtelberg A, *Hybrid Tribunals: A Comparative Examination of Their Origins, Structure, Legitimacy and Effectiveness* (Springer Press 2015).

Gardiner R, *Treaty Interpretation* (Oxford University Press 2017).

Gawanas B, 'The African Union: Concepts and Implementation Mechanisms Relating to Human Rights', [available at https://www.kas.de/c/document_library/get_file?uuid=6e7446b1-0662-d706-50c6-53879e22f65f&groupId=252038 – accessed 5 February 2024)].

Giffard-Lindsay, *Post-conflict Peacebuilding: Lessons from Transitional Administrations in Cambodia and East Timor* (Lambert Academic Publishing 2012).

Grant, A.J and Söderbaum, F, *The New Regionalism in Africa* (Oxford Routledge 2003).

de Guzman M, Complementarity at the Africa Court in C Jalloh and Ors (eds) *The African Court of Justice and Human and Peoples' Rights in Context: Development and Challenges* (Cambridge University Press 2019) 18–22.

Hankel G, *The Leipzig Trials. German War Crimes and Their Legal Consequences after World War I* (Republic of Letters Publishing 2014).

Harwood C, 'The UN International Independent Investigation Commission in Lebanon' in Jens Meierhenrich (ed) *The Law and Practice of International Commissions of Inquiry* (Oxford University Press 2018).

Haslam E, *The Slave Trade, Abolition and the Long History of International Criminal Law: The Recaptive and the Victim* (Routledge 2020).

Haslam E, Redemption, Colonialism and International Criminal Law: The Nineteenth Century Slave Trading Trials of Samo and Peters in Kirkby D, (ed) *Past Law Present Histories* (ANU press 2012).

Heinrich A, Sub-regional Courts as Transitional Justice Mechanisms: The Case of the East African Court of Justice in Burundi' in J.T Gathi (ed) *The Performance of Africa's International Courts: Using Litigation for Political, Legal, and Social Change* (Oxford University Press 2021) 88–105.

van den Herik L and Carsten Stahn "Fragmentation', Diversification and '3D' Legal Pluralism: International Criminal Law as the Jack-in-the-Box?' in Larissa van den Herik and others (eds) *The Diversification and Fragmentation of International Criminal Law* (Martinus Nijhoff 2012) 23.

Hicks C, *The Trial of Hissène Habré: How the People of Chad Brought a Tyrant to Justice (ZED books 2018)*.

Holmes J T, Complementarity: National Courts versus the ICC in Cassese A and Ors (eds) in *The Rome Statute of the International Criminal Court: A Commentary*, Vol. I, (Oxford University Press 2002) 667–685.

Holmes J.T, 'The Principle of Complementarity' in R.S Lee (ed.) *The International Criminal Court, the Making of the Rome Statute, Issues, Negotiations, Results* (Kluwer Law International 1999) 52.

Howell T.B and Howell T.J, *Cobbett's Complete Collection of State Trials and Proceedings for High Treason and Other Crimes and Misdemeanor from the Earliest Period to the Present Time* (R Bagshaw 1809) Vol 13, 455.

Huneeus A, 'Legitimacy and Jurisdictional Overlap: The ICC and the Inter-American Court in Colombia' in N Grossman & Ors (eds) *Legitimacy and International Courts* (Cambridge University Press 2018) 114.

Jacobs D, 'International Criminal Law' in Kammerhofer J and D'Aspremont J, *International Legal Positivism in a Post-modern World* (Cambridge University Press 2014) 473.

Jalloh C, 'The Place of the African Criminal Court in the Prosecution of Serious Crimes in Africa' in Jalloh C and Ors (eds) *The African Court of Justice and Human and Peoples' Rights in Context: Developments and Challenges* (Cambridge University Press 2019) 295.

Jalloh C and others 'The Place of the African Criminal Court in the Prosecution of Serious Crimes in Africa' in C Jalloh & I Bantekas (eds) *The International Criminal Court and Africa* (Oxford University Press 2017) 304.

Jalloh C and others (eds) *The African Court of Justice and Human and Peoples' Rights in Context: Development and Challenges* (Cambridge University Press 2019).

Jessup P, *A Modern Law of Nations* (Macmillan Publishers 1948).

Jordash W and Bracq N, 'Modes of Liability and Individual Criminal Responsibility' in C Jalloh, K Clarke and another (eds) *The African Court of Justice and Human and Peoples' Rights in Context: Development and Challenges* (Cambridge University Press 2019) 784–785.

Kendal D, *The ICC and the Principle of Complementarity: How Denmark Can Help Strike a Balance between International and Domestic Justice Mechanisms* (Kendal Human Rights Consulting 2013).

Kersten M and Ainley K, 'Hybridization: A Spectrum of Creative Possibilities' in *The Habré Trial and Beyond: New Models of Prosecuting International Crime?* (Oxford University Press 2020).

Kirsch P and Robinson D, 'Initiation of Proceedings by the Prosecutor' in Cassese A, Gaeta P and J.R.W.D Jones (eds) *The Rome Statute of the International Criminal Court: A Commentary* (OUP 2002) 622–623.

Klabbers J, *An Introduction to International Organizations Law* (Cambridge University Press 2015).

Kleffner J, *Complementarity in the Rome Statute and National Jurisdictions* (Oxford University Press 2008) 60.

Kleffner and Kor G, (eds) *Complementary Views on Complementarity: Proceedings of the International Roundtable on the Complementary Nature of the International Criminal Court* (TMC 2006).

Klučka, J, Elbert L, *Regionalism and Its Contribution to General International Law* (Košice 2015).

Knottnerus A and de Volder E, 'International Criminal Justice and the Early Formation of an African Criminal Court' in K.M Clarke and Ors (eds) *Africa and the ICC: perceptions of justice* (Cambridge University Press 2016).

Kolb R, *Peremptory International Law (Jus Cogens): A General Inventory* (Oxford, Hart 2015).

Korieh C, *The Nigeria-Biafra War: Genocide and the Politics of Memory* (Cambria Press 2012).

Krisch N, 'Ch.VII Action with Respect to Threats to the Peace, Breaches of the Peace, and Acts of Aggression, Introduction to Chapter VII: The General Framework' in B Simma & Ors (eds) *The Charter of the United Nations: A Commentary, Volume II* (Oxford University Press 2012).

Kyriakakis J, 'Article 46C: Corporate Criminal Liability at the African Criminal Court' in K Clarke & C Jalloh (eds) The *African Court of Justice and Human and Peoples' Rights* (Cambridge University Press 2019).

Labuda P, 'Institutional design and Non-complementarity: Regulating Regulations between Hybrid Tribunals and other Judicial and Non-judicial Institutions in K Ainley and M Kersten (eds), *Hybrid Justice: Innovation and Impact in the Prosecution of Atrocity Crimes* (Oxford University Press 2020).

Lattanzi F, 'Introduction' in Larissa van den Herik and others (eds) *The Diversification and Fragmentation of International Criminal Law* (Martinus Nijhoff 2012) 4.

Lewis M, *The Birth of the New Justice: The Internationalization of Crime and Punishment, 1919–1950* (Oxford University Press, 2014) 79.

Luban D, 'Authority and responsibility in international criminal law' in J Tasioulas & S Besson (eds) *The Philosophy of International Law* (Oxford University Press 2009).

Maogoto J, 'The 1919 Paris Peace Conference and the Allied Commission: Challenging Sovereignty through Supranational Criminal Jurisdiction' in M Bergsmo & Ors (eds) *Historical Origins of International Criminal Law* (Torkel Opsahl Academic E-Publisher 2014) 171–193.

Martinez J, *The Slave Trade and the Origins of International Human Rights Law* (Oxford University Press 2011).

Maunganidze O and A du Plessis 'The ICC and the AU' in C Stahn (ed) *The Law and Practice of the International Criminal Court* (Oxford University Press 2015) 82.

McCormack T, 'From Sun Tzu to the Sixth Committee: The Evolution of an International Criminal Law Regime' in McCormack T and Wheatley S, *The Law of War Crimes* (BRILL 1996).

McDermott Y, *Fairness in International Criminal Trials* (Oxford University Press 2016).

Mégret F, 'In Search of the 'Vertical': An Exploration of What Makes International Criminal Tribunals Different (and why)' in van den Herik L & Stahn C (eds) *Future Perspectives on International Criminal Justice* (T.M.C. Asser 2010).

Mullins C, *The Leipzig Trials: An Account of the War Criminals' Trials and a Study of German Mentality* (H.F. & G. Witherby 1921).

Neldjingaye K, 'The Trial of Hissène Habré in Senegal and its Contribution to International Criminal Law' in Murungu C and Biegon J (eds) *Prosecuting International Crimes in Africa* (Pretoria University Law Press 2011) 193.

Newton M, 'The Quest for Constructive Complementarity' in Stahn & El Zeidy *International Criminal Court and Complementarity: From Theory to Practice* (Cambridge University Press 2011) 304.

Nouwen S *Complementarity in the Line of Fire: The Catalysing Effect of the International Court in Uganda and Sudan* (Cambridge University Press 2013).

O'Keefe R, *International Criminal Law* (Oxford University Press 2014).

Onuf N, *Making Sense, Making Worlds: Constructivism in Social Theory and International Relations* (Routledge 2013).

Orentlicher D, 'Striking a Balance: Mixed Law tribunals and Conflicts of Jurisdiction' in L Mark & S Philippe (eds) *Justice for Crimes against Humanity* (Hart Publishing 2003) 212.

Pevehouse J, 'Democratisation, Credible Commitments, and Joining International Organizations' [available at http://www.press.umich.edu/pdf/0472112899-ch1.pdf (– accessed 5 February 2024)].

Politi M, 'Reflections on Complementarity at the Rome Conference and Beyond' in Stahn C & El Zeidy M *The International Criminal Court and Complementarity: From Theory to Practice* (Cambridge University Press 2011) 142.

Robinson D, 'The Rome Statute and Its Impact on National Law' in Cassese A & others (eds.) *The Rome Statute of the International Criminal Court: A Commentary* (Oxford University Press 2002) 5.

Rose C, 'Money Laundering and the African Court of Justice and Human and Peoples' Rights' in C Jalloh and Ors (eds) *The African Court of Justice and Human and Peoples' Rights in Context: Development and Challenges* (Cambridge University Press 2019).

Rosenau J and Durfee M, *Thinking Theory Thoroughly: Coherent Approaches to an Incoherent World* (Boulder, CO, Oxford: Westview 1995) 1–218.

Ruffert M and Walter C, *Institutionalised International Law* (CH. Beck, Hart & Nomos 2014).

Ryngaert C, 'Horizontal Complementarity' in Stahn & El Zeidy (Cambridge University Press 2011) 855–887.

Schabas W, *The International Criminal Court: A Commentary on the Rome Statute* (Oxford University Press 2010) 309.

Schabas W and El Zeidy M, 'Article 17: Issues of Admissibility' in K Ambos and O Triffterer (eds) *The Rome Statute of the International Criminal Court: A Commentary* (CH. Beck, Hart & Nomos 2015) 781.

Schabas W, *The Trial of the Kaiser* (Oxford University Press 2018).

Schabas W, 'International Criminal Courts' in Cesare P.R Romano, K.J Alter and Y Shany (eds) *The Oxford Handbook of International Adjudication* (Oxford University Press 2013).

Schermers H and Blokker N, *International Institutional Law* (BRILL Fifth Revised Edition 2011) Preface.

Schwöbel-Patel C, 'The Core Crimes of International Criminal Law' in K.J Heller and others (eds), *The Oxford Handbook of International Criminal Law* (Oxford University Press 2020).

Scott J.B, 'The Trial of the Kaiser' in House E and Seymour C (eds), *What Really Happened at Paris: The Story of the Peace Conference 1918–1919* (C. Scribner's Sons) 231–258.

Simpson G, (ed) *The Law of War Crimes: National and International Approaches* (Kluwer Law International 1997) 31–63 at 37.

van Sliedregt E and Vasiliev S (eds), *Pluralism in International Criminal Law* (Oxford University Press, 2014).

Vasiliev S, 'Trial Process at the ECCC: The Rise and fall of the Inquisitorial Paradigm in International Criminal Law' in Meisenberg S & Stegmiller I (eds) *The Extraordinary Chambers in the Courts of Cambodia: Assessing Their Contribution to International Criminal Law* (Asser Press 2016).

Sterio M and Scharf M (eds) *The Legacy of Ad Hoc Tribunals in International Criminal Law: Assessing the ICTY's and the ICTR's Most Significant Legal Accomplishments* (Cambridge University Press 2019) 1–10.

Stahn C, 'Introduction: Bridge over Troubled Waters: Complementarity Themes and Debates in Context' in Stahn C & El Zeidy M *The International Criminal Court and Complementarity: From Theory to Practice* (Cambridge University Press 2011) 1.

Stahn C, 'Admissibility Challenges before the ICC: From Quasi-primacy to Qualified Deference' in Stahn C (ed) *The Law and Practice of the International Criminal Court* (Oxford University Press 2015) 228.

Stahn C, *A critical Introduction to International Crimina*l Law (Cambridge University Press 2019) 9.

Stahn C, 'Taking Complementarity Seriously: On the Sense and Sensibility of 'Classical', 'Positive' and 'Negative' Complementarity' in Stahn C & El Zeidy M (eds) *The International Criminal Court and Complementarity: From Theory to Practice* (Cambridge University Press 2011) at 234.

Stahn C, *Fair and Effective Investigation and Prosecution of International Crimes Inventory and State-of-the-Art: Context, Cluster 1 and Cluster 2* (International Nuremberg Principles Academy 2018) 3–4.

Stahn C and Sluiter G, *The Emerging Practice of the International Criminal Court* (BRILL 2009).

Stahn C and van Den Herik L.J (eds), *The Diversification and Fragmentation of International Criminal Law* (Martinus Nijhoff Publishers 2012).

Stahn C and El Zeidy M, (eds) *The International Criminal Court and Complementarity: From Theory to Practice* Vols 1&2 (Cambridge University Press 2011).

Stahn C, "Re-imagining the ICC in a Multipolar World" in Stahn C (ed) *The International Criminal Court in its Third Decade: Reflecting on Law and Practices* (Brill Nijhoff 2024).

Stegmiller I, 'Positive Complementarity and Legitimacy: Is the International Criminal Court Shifting from Judicial Restraint towards Interventionism?' in N Hayashi & C Bailliet (eds) *The Legitimacy of International Criminal Tribunals* (Cambridge University Press 2017).

Stigen J, *The Relationship between the International Criminal Court and National Jurisdictions: The Principle of Complementarity* (Martinus Nijhoff 2008).

Suzuki H, *The Suppression of the Transoceanic Slave Trade* (Oxford University Press 2022).

Swart M, 'The Prospects for Regional and Sub Regional Complementarity in Africa' in R Slye (ed) *The Nuremberg Principles in Non-Western Societies: A Reflection on their Universality, Legitimacy and Application* (International Nuremberg Principles Academy Press 2017) 217.

Takemura H, 'A Critical Analysis of Positive Complementarity' in *Max Planck Encyclopedias of International Law* (Oxford Public International Law – undated).

Takemura H, 'The Asian Region and the International Criminal Court' in Nakanishi Y (ed) *Contemporary Issues in Human Rights Law* (Springer 2018) 107–125.

Triffterer O and Ambos K, *The Rome Statute of the International Criminal Court: A Commentary* (CH. Beck, Hart & Nomos 2015) 791.

Trakman L and Ranieri N, *Regionalism in International Investment Law* (Oxford Scholarship Online 2013).

Ubeda-Saillard M, 'Foreign Officials Entitled to (Absolute) Personal Immunity during Their Time in Office' in T Ruys & Ors (eds) *The Cambridge Handbook of Immunities and International Law* (Cambridge University Press 2019) 481–495.

Vermeulen G and Ors, *Liability of Legal Persons for Offences in the EU* (Maklu Publishers 2010).

Viebig P, *Illicitly Obtained Evidence at the International Criminal Court* (TMC Asser 2006).

Visoka G, *Assessing the Potential Impact of the Kosovo* Specialist Court (PAX 2017) PAX 1–48.

Waddell N and Clark P, 'Courting Conflict? Justice, Peace and the ICC in Africa' *Royal African Society* (2008) 8.

Werle G, Fernandez L and Vormbaum M (eds) *Africa and the International Criminal Court* (Asser Press 2014) 231.

William S, *Hybrid and Internationalised Criminal Tribunals: Selected Jurisdictional Issues* (HART Publishing 2012).

van der Wilt H, 'Complementary Jurisdiction (Article 46H)' in G Werle and M Vormbaum (eds) *The African Criminal Court: A Commentary on the Malabo Protocol* (T.M.C Asser Press 2017) 626.

van der Wilt H, 'Complementary Jurisdiction (Article 46H)' in G Werle and M Vormbaum (eds.) (2017), *The African Criminal Court: A Commentary on the Malabo Protocol* (T.M.C Asser Press 2017) 190.

van der Wilt H, 'On Regional Criminal Courts as Representatives of Political Communities: The Special Case of the African Criminal Court' in K.J Heller and others (eds) *The Oxford Handbook of International Criminal Law* (Oxford University Press 2020) 194–212.

Weill S and others (eds) *The President on Trial: Prosecuting Hissène Habré* (Oxford University Press, 2020) 267–281.

William G, *Criminal Law: The General Part* (Stevens and Sons 1961) 853.

Wouters J and Basu S, 'The Creation of a Global Criminal Justice System: The European Union and the International Criminal Court' in C Ryngaert (ed) *The Effectiveness of International Criminal Justice* (Intersentia 2009) 117–140.

Zappalà S, *Judicial Activism v. Judicial Restraint in International Criminal Justice* (The Oxford Companion to International Criminal Justice 2009).

Working Papers

Andvig J, 'Corruption and Armed Conflicts: Some Stirring around in the Governance Soup' (2007) *Norwegian Institute of International Affairs Working Paper 720.*

Appazov A, 'Judicial Activism and the International Criminal Court' (2015) 17 *iCourts Working Paper Series.*

van den Herik L and van Sliedregt E 'International Criminal Law and the Malabo Protocol About Scholarly Reception, Rebellion and Role Models' (2017) *Grotius Center Working Paper Series* 2017/066-ICL.

Ryngaert C, 'The International Criminal Court and Universal Jurisdiction' (March 2010) *Working Paper* No. 46 Leuven Centre for Global Governance Studies 3.

Sarooshi D, 'Some Preliminary Remarks on the Conferral by States of Powers on International Organizations' (2003) *Jean Monnet Working Paper 4/03*, 3.

Voeten E, 'Regional Judicial Institutions and Economic Cooperation: Lessons for Asia?' (2010) *ADB Working Paper Series on Regional Economic Integration*, 2–4.

Blogposts

Fabricius P, 'Now to Make This Extraordinary Court, Ordinary' *Institute for Security Studies Today*, 11 February 2016 [available at https://issafrica.org/iss-today/now-to-make-this-extraordinary-court-ordinary – accessed 11 February 2024].

Akande D, 'The Genocide Convention and the Arrest Warrant Issued by the ICC', *EJIL: Talk*, 31 January 2011 [available at http://www.ejiltalk.org/the-genocide-convention-and-the-arrest-warrants-issued-by-the-icc/ – accessed 5 February 2024].

Akande D, 'Treaty Interpretation, the VCLT and the ICC Statute: A Response to Kevin Jon Heller & Dov Jacobs' *EJIL: Talk*, 25 August 2013 [available at https://www.ejiltalk.org/treaty-interpretation-the-vclt-and-the-icc-statute-a-response-to-kevin-jon-heller-dov-jacobs/ – accessed 23 May 2022].

Bluen K.J 'Justice, But Only for Some: The Trial of Hissene Habre' *Justice in Conflict*, 30 July 2015 [available at https://justiceinconflict.org/2015/07/30/justice-but-only-for-some-the-trial-of-hissene-habre/ – accessed 9 February 2024].

Brunelle E and Ors 'Global Enforcement Outlook: Europe's Evolving Corporate Criminal Liability Laws' (2022) [available at https://riskandcompliance.freshfields.com/post/102hh57/global-enforcement-outlook-europes-evolving-corporate-criminal-liability-laws – accessed 10 May 2023].

Clarke Kimari 'Distant Justice Symposium: How Colonial Inscriptions Continue to Matter in ICC and Africa Dynamics' (2019) [available at https://opiniojuris.org/2019/10/01/distant-justice-symposium-how-colonial-inscriptions-continue-to-matter-in-icc-and-africa-dynamics/ – accessed 6 February 2024)].

Dannenbaum T, 'Mechanisms for Criminal Prosecution of Russia's Aggression against Ukraine' *Just Security*, 10 March 2022 [available at https://www.justsecurity.org/80626/mechanisms-for-criminal-prosecution-of-russias-aggression-against-ukraine/ – accessed 12 January 2023].

Du Plessis M, 'The Obligation of African Union States to Implement ICC Arrest Warrants' *EJIL: Talk*, 4 February 2011 [available at, http://www.ejiltalk.org/the-obligation-of-african-union-states-to-implement-icc-arrest-warrants/ – accessed 5 February 2024].

Du Plessis M, 'A Case of Negative Regional Complementarity? Giving the African Court of Justice and Human Rights Jurisdiction over International Crimes' (2012) *EJIL: Talk*, 27 August 2012, [available at https://www.ejiltalk.org/a-case-of-negative-regional-complementarity-giving-the-african-court-of-justice-and-human-rights-jurisdiction-over-international-crimes/ – accessed 17 June 2022].

Du Plessis M, 'The Future of International Criminal Justice Is Domestic' *iLawyer Blog*, 17 September 2014, [available at http://ilawyerblog.com/future-international-criminal-justice-domestic/. – accessed 5 February 2024].

Du Plessis M and Gevers C, 'The Sum of Four Fears: African States and the International Criminal Court in Retrospect – Part I' *Opinio Juris*, 8 July 2019, [available at https://opiniojuris.org/2019/07/08/the-sum-of-four-fears-african-states-and-the-international-criminal-court-in-retrospect-part-i/ – accessed 23 May 2021].

Elderfield J, 'The Rise and Rise of the Special Criminal Court (Part II)', *Opinio Juris*, 4 July 2021, [available at, https://opiniojuris.org/2021/04/07/the-rise-and-rise-of-the-special-criminal-court-part-ii/ – accessed 10 may 2023].

Eskauriatza J, 'The "Cienfuegos Affair" and the Proposal for a New Regional Transnational Criminal Court in Latin America (COPLA)', *Opinio Juris*, 16 July 2021 [available at http://opiniojuris.org/2021/07/16/the-cienfuegos-affair-and-the-proposal-for-a-new-regional-transnational-criminal-court-in-latin-america-copla/ – accessed 7 February 2024].

Heller J, 'Creating a Special Tribunal for Aggression against Ukraine Is a Bad Idea' *OpinioJuris*, 7 March 2022 [available at https://opiniojuris.org/2022/03/07/creating-a-special-tribunal-for-aggression-against-ukraine-is-a-bad-idea/ – accessed 12 March 2024].

Heller J, 'The Best Option: An Extraordinary Ukrainian Chamber for Aggression' *OpinioJuris*, 16 March 2022 [available at http://opiniojuris.org/2022/03/16/the-best-option-an-extraordinary-ukrainian-chamber-for-aggression/ – accessed 12 May 2023].

Kersten M, 'The Africa-ICC Relationship – More and Less than Meets the Eye (Part 1)', *Justice in Conflict*, 17 July 2015 [available at http://justiceinconflict.org/2015/07/17/the-africa-icc-relationship-more-and-less-than-meets-the-eye-part-1/ – accessed 5 February 2024].

Kersten M, 'International Criminal Justice Redux: A New Wave of Hybrid Courts' *Justice in Conflict*, 13 March 2018 [available at https://justiceinconflict.org/2018/03/13/international-criminal-justice-redux-a-new-wave-of-hybrid-courts/ – accessed 6 February 2024].

Kersten M, 'The Trial of Hissène Habré and What It Could Mean for Justice in Africa [available at https://justiceinconflict.org/2018/03/27/the-trial-of-hissene-habre-and-what-it-could-mean-for-justice-in-africa/ – accessed 4 March 2023].

Labuda P, 'The Special Criminal Court in the Central African Republic', *ASIL Insights*, 22 January 2018 [available at https://www.asil.org/insights/volume/22/issue/2/special-criminal-court-central-african-republic – accessed 5 February 2024].

Melly P, 'Niger Coup Underlies Challenge to Democracy across West Africa' (2023) [available at https://www.chathamhouse.org/2023/08/niger-coup-underlines-challenge-democracy-across-west-africa – accessed 12 January 2024].

Muharremi R, 'The Kosovo Specialist Chambers and Specialist Prosecutor's Office' (2016) *ASIL Online Post*, [available at https://www.asil.org/insights/volume/20/issue/11/kosovo-specialist-chambers-and-specialist-prosecutors-office – accessed 6 February 2024].

Orina N, 'Should the ICJ Render an Advisory Opinion on the Immunity Question on Articles 27 & 98 of the Rome Statute?' *ICJ Africa Blog* (2018) [available at https://www.academia.edu/44290443/Should_the_ICJ_render_an_advisory_opinion_on_the_immunity_question_re_Articles_27_and_98_of_the_Rome_Statute – accessed 21 March 2024] .

Rees Y, 'Towards Positive Complementarity', *PhD Studies in Human Rights Blogpost*, 26 July 2014 [available at https://humanrightsdoctorate.blogspot.com/2014/07/towards-positive-complementarity.html – accessed 6 February 2024].

Schabas W, 'Senegal's Chambres Africaines Extraordinaires to Judge Habré', *PhD Studies in Human Rights Blogpost*, 5 February 2013 [available at https://humanrightsdoctorate.blogspot.com/2013/02/senegals-chambres-africaines.html- accessed 12 May 2023].

Stahn C, 'Tribunals Are Dead, Long Live Tribunals: MICT, the Kosovo Specialist Chambers and the Turn to New Hybridity', 23 September 2016 *EJIL: Talk Blog of the European Journal of International Law*, [available at https://www.ejiltalk.org/tribunals-are-dead-long-live-tribunals-mict-the-kosovo-specialist-chambers-and-the-turn-to-new-hybridity/ – accessed 6 February 2024].

Trigoso A, 'The Kosovo Specialist Chambers: In Need of Local Legitimacy', *Opinio Juris*, 8 July 2020 [available at https://opiniojuris.org/2020/06/08/the-kosovo-specialist-chambers-in-need-of-local-legitimacy/ – accessed 12 February 2024)].

Vasiliev S, 'Aggression against Ukraine: Avenues for Accountability for Core crimes', *EJIL:Talk*, 3 March 2022 [available at https://www.ejiltalk.org/aggression-against-ukraine-avenues-for-accountability-for-core-crimes/ – accessed 12 March 2024].

Viljoen F, 'AU Assembly Should Consider Human Rights Implications before Adopting the Amending Merged African Court Protocol', *AfricLaw*, 23 May 2012, [available at https://africlaw.com/2012/05/23/au-assembly-should-consider-human-rights-implications-before-adopting-the-amending-merged-african-court-protoco l/ – accessed 6 February 2024].

South African Institute of International Affairs, 'The Hissène Habré trial: A Triumph for Victims and Civil Society' [available at https://saiia.org.za/research/the-hissene -habre-trial-triumph-over-opposition-oblivion-and-distance-for-the-victims-and -civil-society/ – accessed 12 February 2024].

Doctoral Theses

Bassi A, 'Corporate Criminal Liability: An Analytical Study with Special Reference to Penal Laws in India' PhD Thesis, Rajiv Gandhi National University of Law Punjab, 2016.

Boffey G, 'Assessing Complementarity: The ICC and Human Rights Policy in Colombia' (Unpublished Ph.D. Thesis, University of Western Australia 2015) 66.

De Vos C, 'A Catalyst for Justice? The International Criminal Court in Uganda, Kenya, and the Democratic Republic of Congo' (2016) PhD Thesis, Leiden University, 33.

Okuta A 'Smallest Share of the Pie? Accountability for International Crimes at the Domestic Level: Case Studies of Kenya, Uganda and Cote D'Ivoire' (Unpublished PhD Thesis, University of Amsterdam 2016) 34.

Tan and Heng A, 'Advancing international criminal justice in southeast Asia through the regionalisation of international criminal law' (2014) PhD Thesis, University of Nottingham.

Vasiliev S, 'International Criminal Trials: A Normative Theory' (2014) University of Amsterdam Ph.D. Thesis, Volume I.

Miscellaneous Internet-Based Resources

Achar P, 'Understanding the Ladder of Abstraction and Its Application in Communication' (15 June 2016) [available at https://paulachar.wordpress.com/2016/06/15/understanding-the-ladder-of-abstraction-and-its-application-in-communication/ – accessed 12 January 2023].

Corporación Andina de Fomento (CAF) 'Towards a Safer Latin America: A New Perspective to Prevent and Control Crime' (2014) 137-165 [available at http://scioteca .caf.com/bitstream/handle/123456789/708/RED2014-english-towards-a-safer-latin -america.pdf?sequence=3&isAllowed=y – accessed 8 February 2024].

Corporate War Crimes, 'Draft Convention on Crimes against Humanity to Include Provision on Corporate Liability?' 26 March 2017, [available at https://corporatewarcrimes.com/2017/03/26/draft-convention-on-crimes-against-humanity-to-include-provision-on-corporate-liability/ – accessed 12 January 2023].

Extraordinary Chambers in the Courts of Cambodia, 'Why Was This Model Chosen for the ECCC?' [available at https://www.eccc.gov.kh/en/faq/why-was-model-chosen-eccc – accessed 7 February 2024].

GIABA 'About GIABA'[available at https://www.giaba.org/about-giaba/index_656.html – accessed 12 June 2024].

The Federalist Debate, Fernando A. Iglesias 'A Regional Criminal Court against Transnational Organized Crime' (2014) 1 [available at https://www.federalist-debate.org/archive/year-xxxiv-number-3-november-2021/borderless-debate/the-latin-american-criminal-court-an-approach-for-regional-integration-against-transnational-organized-crime – accessed 8 February 2024].

Statement Calling for the Creation of a Special Tribunal for the Punishment of the Crime of Aggression against Ukraine [available at https://gordonandsarahbrown.com/wp-content/uploads/2022/03/Combined-Statement-and-Declaration.pdf – accessed 12 March 2023].

The Graduate Institute Geneva 'International tribunals: Hybrid Courts' [available at http://libguides.graduateinstitute.ch/icl/hybrid – accessed 5 February 2024].

Library of Congress 'African Union: Resolution Urges States to Leave ICC' [available at https://www.loc.gov/item/global-legal-monitor/2017-02-10/african-union-resolution-urges-states-to-leave-icc/ – accessed 5 February 2024].

Nel M, 'Can A Regional Court Be a Viable Alternative to the ICC in Africa?' *The Conversation* (6 August 2018), [available at https://theconversation.com/can-a-regional-court-be-a-viable-alternative-to-the-icc-in-africa-100788 – accessed 12 February 2024].

Open Society Initiative for Southern Africa, Deya D, 'Worth the Wait: Pushing for the African Court to Exercise Jurisdiction for International Crimes' [available at http://www.osisa.org/sites/default/files/is_the_african_court_worth_the_wait_-don_deya.pdf – accessed 5 February 2024].

World Federalist Movement, COPLA Campaign, [available at https://www.wfm-igp.org/campaign/copla-campaign/ – accessed 7 February 2024].

ICC 'Situation in the Republic of Philippines' [available at, https://www.icc-cpi.int/philippines – accessed 7 February 2024].

ICC 'Situation in Ukraine' [available at https://www.icc-cpi.int/situations/ukraine – accessed 7 February 2024].

ICC 'Situation in the Bolivarian Republic of Venezuela' [available at https://www.icc-cpi.int/venezuela-i – accessed 7 May 2022].

'The opinion of the Dakar Court of Appeal on the Extradition Request for Hissène Habré' [available at http://www.asser.nl/upload/documents/20120419T034141-Habr%C3%A9_Cour_Appel_Avis_Extradition_25-11-2005(Extraits).pdf – accessed 5 February 2024].

'Corporate criminal Liability: Historic Perspective' [available at https://shodhganga.inflibnet.ac.in/bitstream/10603/200004/8/08_chapter%202.pdf – accessed 12 May 2022].

News Articles

BBC News, 'Sudan Crisis: Cash Hoard Found at al-Bashir's Home' 20 April 2019, [available at https://www.bbc.com/news/world-africa-47997729 – accessed 13 February 2024].

Chimp Reports, 'East African Courts to Hear Crimes against Humanity' 29 April 2013 [available at https://chimpreports.com/9681-east-african-court-to-hear-crimes-against-humanity/ – accessed 6 February 2024].

Citizen Digital, 'AU Adopts Uhuru's Proposal for Withdrawal from the ICC' 31 January 2016, [available at https://citizentv.co.ke/news/au-adopts-uhurus-proposal-for-withdrawal-from-icc-113241/ – accessed 5 February 2024].

Deutsche Welle, 'ICC: What Next for Africa and the Tribunal in Quest for Justice?' 02 February 2016, [available at http://www.dw.com/en/icc-what-next-for-africa-and-the-tribunal-in-quest-for-justice/a-19020659 – accessed 6 February 2024].

The Guardian 'Ex-Sudan Leader Omar al-Bashir Sentenced to Two Years for Corruption' 14 December 2019 [available at https://www.theguardian.com/world/2019/dec/14/sudanese-court-sentences-omar-al-bashir-to-2-years-in-prison – accessed 13 February 2024].

Non-governmental Organisations Reports

Amnesty International, 'Chad: Hissène Habré Appeal Ruling Closes Dark Chapter for Victims', 27 April 2017.

Amnesty International, 'Central African Republic: First-Ever SCC trials ensures alleged war criminals face justice', April 19 2022.

Amnesty International, 'Malabo Protocol: Legal and Institutional Implications of the Merged and Expanded African Court', 22 January 2016.

CAF, Development Bank of Latin America 'Towards a Safer Latin America: A New Perspective to Prevent and Control Crime' (2014) 137–165.

Coalition for the International Criminal Court, 'Africa and the ICC: Setting the Facts Straight' [available at https://coalitionfortheicc.org/explore-international-criminal-court-africa-icc – accessed 5 February 2024].

Coalition for the International Criminal Court, 'Malaysia Backtracks on Accession to the Rome Statute' 12 April 2019.

Human Rights Data Analysis Group, Silva R, Klingner J and Weikart S, 'State Coordinated Violence in Chad under Hissène Habré: A Statistical Analysis of Reported Prison Mortality in Chad's DDS Prisons and Command Responsibility of Hissène Habré, 1982–1990, 3 February 2010.

Human Rights Watch, 'Justice Denied for East Timor: Indonesia's Sham Prosecutions, the Need to Strengthen the Trial Process in East Timor, and the Imperative of U.N. Action' (2002) [available at https://www.hrw.org/legacy/backgrounder/asia/timor/etimor1202bg.htm – accessed 6 February 2024].

Human Rights Watch, 'Chad: The Victims of Hissène Habré Still Awaiting Justice', 12 July 2005.

Human Rights Watch 'Ex-Chad Dictator Indicted in Belgium: Hissène Habré to Face Extradition to Belgium for Human Rights Atrocities' 29 September 2005.

Human Rights Watch 'Hissène Habré and the Senegalese Courts A Memo for International Donors' December 2007.

Human Rights Watch, 'Briefing Paper on Recent Setbacks in Africa Regarding the International Criminal Court' (2010).

Human Rights Watch, 'Joint Civil Society Letter on the Draft Protocol on Amendments to the Protocol on the Statute of the African Court on Justice and Human Rights', 12 May 2014.

Human Rights Watch, 'Q&A: The Case of Hissène Habré before the Extraordinary African Chambers in Senegal', 3 May 2016.

Human Rights Watch, Coalition of African NGOs 'Joint Civil Society Letter on the Draft Protocol on Amendments to the Statute of the African Court of Justice and Human Rights' 12 May 2014.

Jeiranashvili N, 'The Georgian Experience: A Story of How the ICC Is Failing Victims in Its First Case Outside Africa', International Justice Monitor, 10 May 2018.

Kenyans for Peace with Truth and Justice, 'Seeking Justice or Shielding Suspects: An Analysis of the Malabo Protocol', [available at http://kptj.africog.org/wp-content/uploads/2016/11/Malabo-Report.pdf – accessed 12 February 2024].

Public International Law and Policy Group, Meinicke C, 'Domestic Prosecution of International Crimes – Africa' 15 May 2019.

Transparency International, '25 Corruption Scandals that Shook the World' 5 July 2019.

World Federalist Movement Canada, 'The Proposal for a Latin American and Caribbean Criminal Court against Transnational Organized Crime Reaches the United Nations General Assembly', December 2017.

World Federalist Movement Canada, 'COPLA Update Regional governments agree to study proposed criminal court', 23 July 2018.

Index

www.ingramcontent.com/pod-product-compliance
Ingram Content Group UK Ltd.
Pitfield, Milton Keynes, MK11 3LW, UK
UKHW020822290926
15470UKWH00003B/1315

9 789004 736795